The Torreon Cabin Murders

To Robert Sobel

Best wishes

The Torreon Cabin Murders

A False Confession and False Statement

Maurice Moya

SUNSTONE
PRESS

SANTA FE

Sunstone books may be purchased for educational, business, or sales promotional use. For information please write: Special Markets Department, Sunstone Press, P.O. Box 2321, Santa Fe, New Mexico 87504-2321.

Book and Cover design › Vicki Ahl
Body typeface › Chaparral Pro
Printed on acid-free paper

Library of Congress Cataloging-in-Publication Data

Moya, Maurice, 1946-
The Torreon cabin murders : a false confession and false statement / by Maurice Moya.
    pages cm
Includes bibliographical references.
ISBN 978-0-86534-890-5 (softcover : alk. paper)
    1. Murder--New Mexico. 2. Murder--Investigation--New Mexico. 3. Criminal investigation--New Mexico. 4. Trials (Murder)--New Mexico. I. Title.
HV6533.N4M69 2013
364.152'3092--dc23
                    2013008504

WWW.SUNSTONEPRESS.COM
SUNSTONE PRESS / POST OFFICE BOX 2321 / SANTA FE, NM 87504-2321 /USA
(505) 988-4418 / ORDERS ONLY (800) 243-5644 / FAX (505) 988-1025

THIS BOOK IS DEDICATED FIRST TO THE THREE YOUNG MEN, all falsely accused, whose lives were changed forever and their youth taken from them by a false confession and a false statement. It is also dedicated to the falsely accused who are still incarcerated by false confessions or false statements.

Contents

Foreword

MY MIND HAS ALWAYS NEEDED PROBLEMS TO SOLVE. I HAVE always enjoyed perplexing cryptograms, which by design, need the trickiest analysis. I am not a big fan of vacations but I am always looking for a mental adrenalin rush. That is why I have chosen my life style. I know I am the best of the best.

I grew up wanting to be a Sherlock Holmes or a Sir Arthur Conan Doyle. I was fascinated by the manner in which he examined the data to a crime. Like Holmes, I enjoyed the pleasure of the work itself. Holmes and his analytical reasoning fascinated me. Holmes did not have the benefit of fingerprints or DNA, just a keen and logical mind.

His simple philosophy was "In solving a problem of this sort, the grand thing is to be able to reason backward. That is a very useful accomplishment, and a very easy one, but people do not practice it much. In the everyday affairs of life it is more useful to reason forward, and so the other comes to be neglected. There are fifty who can reason synthetically for one who can reason analytically."

Growing up I knew I had the power of observation, deduction, and knowledge. Being attached to a Marine Recon unit helped me in learning how to read signs and take notes on history.

One of the greatest teaching tools provided to me was working traffic investigations. To be a true investigator, one must go through a learning process of how to discover the facts. In accident reconstruction you have all the physical facts necessary to reconstruct. You rely on those facts to create your theory, to deal with the facts, and then to apply your theory. Too often investigators create their theory and then apply the facts to them. That is a fatal mistake. When a good investigator is solving a problem, he must have the ability to reason backwards in order to reconstruct the events. Once you have gathered all the facts, it becomes very easy to do. It is a most useful way of thinking. Then and only then can you reason forward.

The other truth I grew up with was that my hero was the father of the truth seekers, Sherlock Holmes. Growing up, I loved reading the lines given to Detective Holmes by the very talented Scottish author and physician Sir Arthur Conan Doyle. The character created by Doyle so impressed me that I learned to live by his beliefs.

"You will not apply my precept, he said, shaking his head. How often have I said to you that <u>when you have eliminated the impossible, whatever remains,</u> *however improbable,* <u>must be the truth</u>? We know that he did not come through the door, the window, or the chimney. We also know that he could not have been concealed in the room, as there is no concealment possible. When, then, did he come?"

In his book *A Study in Scarlet,* Sir Arthur Conan Doyle noted, "It is a capital mistake to theorize before one has data. Insensibly one begins to twist facts to suit theories, instead of theories to suit facts."

Doyle was right when he had Holmes explain, "Eliminate all other factors, and the one which remains must be the truth." Now, I would get my chance to play Holmes. Now I would be able to apply all my powers of observation and deduction to the worst crime in the state's history, the Torreon Cabin Murders. This would be done without the use of forensic evidence or scientific evidence. The three officers, along with the Assistant District Attorney Madeline (Mady) Malka, created twisted words, twisted facts and concealed evidence. In the most heinous crime of the century in New Mexico's history, Ben Anaya Jr. and Cassandra Sedillo were shot in the back of the head execution style. Her two boys age three and five were left alive in the cabin to die of starvation and dehydration. It would be six months after their homicide that the bodies would be found. The summer cabin where the murders was located in the dense forest of Torreon, New Mexico. The decision not to send a crime team to study the evidence to eliminate the impossible twisted the facts. A false confession and a false statement took the place of real evidence.

Two days after the bodies of Ben Anaya Jr., Cassandra Sedillo, Matthew Garcia and Johnny Garcia were found, the officers had created their theory without knowing the facts. The bodies were found April 14, 1996. On April 16, 1996, the officers were conducting interviews and came up with the theory that "There was a party at the cabin, there were drugs and alcohol at the party, and the crime was gang related." They would shake hands with the devil to seal their theory. To hell with the facts, to hell with memory... just tell us what we want to hear. "There was a party at the cabin with drugs, alcohol and gang members."

This was not James Patterson's *Alex Cross* or an Agatha Christie mystery. This was real life murder with innocent lives at stake. I grew up Catholic. I knew and studied the Ten Commandments. I recall the Ninth Commandment: "Thou shall not bear false witness against thy neighbor." The Ninth Commandment is pretty simple. Offenses against the truth expressed by word or deeds are a refusal to commit oneself to moral decency.

To the three officers and the assistant district attorney, this commandment meant nothing, in my opinion. They only added to the fuel in the fires of hell. After you tell us what we want to hear we will destroy or hide the evidence of the *false statement* and *false confession*. The three officers and Assistant District Attorney Malka were out to murder the truth...with ADA Malka as the engineer of the train making sure that a false conviction and possibly death by lethal injection would be waiting at the station.

The following is from my experience and documents the conclusions I reached.

—Maurice Moya

Cast of Characters

Ben Anaya Jr.:

Ben Jr. was a young man who grew up in Albuquerque on the west side of town. He enjoyed sports growing up as well as fishing and camping. Ben Jr. while incarcerated at Springer, New Mexico had met Shawn ("Popcorn") Popeleski, Lawrence Woodrow ("Woody") Nieto, and Shaun Wilkins. They became friends and would meet up after they were released.

The last time anyone would see Ben Jr. would be on December 10th, 1995 when Ben Sr. took Ben Jr. Popcorn, Cassandra and the kids food and pizza along with a brand new dead bolt for the front door of the Torreon cabin. Ben Sr. had loaned his son his Jeep Wagoner with direct orders that he was the only one to drive it, nobody else.

Ben Anaya Sr.:

Ben Sr. a former Marine, was a strong disciplinarian, a very security conscious individual, and a very a hard workingman. Ben Sr. had built the Torreon cabin as a weekend getaway for his family. He picked a beautiful place up in the mountains of Torreon in Sherwood Forest. It was airtight for the cold winters and had no running water. There was only a 50-gallon drum that would have to be filled for cabin water.

Ben Sr. has taken strong measures to secure the cabin. He had wire mesh on the windows with pad locks and there was a chain link fence around the property.

Ben Sr. was very close to his son Ben Jr. and they had a great mutual respect for each other.

The last time Ben Sr. saw his son was December 10th, 1995. Then on December 12th Ben Sr.'s house was broken into. Popcorn was seen out in front of Ben Sr.'s house. The officers never questioned Popcorn about this incident.

Shaun Wilkins:

Shaun Wilkins grew up in Albuquerque and dropped out of school while in the 9th grade. Shaun participated in football and wrestling while in school. In March of 1993 Shaun was sentenced to the Youth Diagnostic Center in Springer New Mexico where Shaun became a member of the 18th Street Gang. While in Springer Shaun met Ben Jr. and became friends with him. Shaun met Roy Buchner at a water park in the summer of 1995. Roy, Ben Jr. and Shaun became good friends.

Roy Buchner:

Roy Buchner had strong support from his father, Ralph, and his mother, Denise, as well as from his grandfather, Dan, and grandmother, Syria Burrola. Ralph Buchner had adopted Roy when he married Denise, Roy's mother. Roy grew up in the South Valley of Albuquerque and in the Corrales area. Dan made sure Roy had found a job and took him and picked him up from work. Roy went to night school and got his GED. Roy worked every day in December, the month of the homicide. His alibi was never checked.

Roy met Ben Jr. at a shopping center when they were fifteen and they became good friends. They would hang around with each other on a daily basis. Ben Jr. had gotten Roy involved with 18th Street gang.

Shawn ("Popcorn") Popeleski:

Shawn Popeleski was born in Korea. His mother was Korean and his father was from Mississippi. His family moved to the U.S. when Shawn was eight years old. Shawn's first language was Korean and Shawn had trouble in school and with the English language. Shawn was placed into special Ed. in school because of his language skills.

Lawrence Woodrow ("Woody") Nieto:

Woody Nieto went to school until the 9th grade and was in Special Ed classes. He had been diagnosed with ADD while in custody at the Youth Diagnostic Center at the New Mexico Boy's School at Springer, New Mexico. Woody had been in Springer off and on from ages of 14 through 18. Woody did not do very well in reading or in understanding what he had read.

Cassandra Sedillo:

Cassandra was the daughter of Porfidia Sedillo; Cassandra had two sons Johnny Ray Garcia and Matthew Garcia. Cassandra lived with her mother along with her two sons. Porfidia would describe Johnny as full of life, the man in charge. He would take care of his little brother. They would often play hide and seek and read books, watch movies together, go to the zoo and the park.
Cassandra was the only one with any means of support. She was receiving help from the government for food and was the one supporting Ben Jr., Popcorn and her two kids.

Agent Michael Fenner:

Michael Fenner had been on NMSP for 11 years prior to the murders. He had never investigated a homicide before. Agent Fenner's police reports started a month before the bodies were found.

Before the trial of Roy Buchner, Agent Fenner and DA investigator Levi

Lovato entered an agreement with the District Attorney to become Popcorn's probation officers. Popcorn was to report to Fenner and Lopez once a week but never did. In trial Fenner was shown the agreement and Fenner stated, "This is the first time I have ever seen this."

During this probation period Popcorn committed aggravated burglaries, stole guns and cars and was rearrested in Pecos, Texas. Popcorn often referred to Agent Michael Fenner as "Mike."

Agent Fenner had completed polygraph school in July of 1995. Agent Fenner never did a polygraph examiner report on any of the tests he gave to Popcorn. Under New Mexico Rule 11 of 707 a polygraph examiner must have five years of experience. Agent Fenner had never testified as an expert in polygraph before. With all of Agent Fenner's involvement he never testified in Nieto's case or Wilkins's case and none of the preliminary hearings.

Agent Frank Jacoby:

Frank Jacoby had been a patrol officer for three years. He was then assigned to narcotics in June of 1995. He had never investigated a confirmed homicide before.

Officer Juan DeReyes:

Juan DeReyes had never investigated a homicide, but claimed that he had assisted in the investigation of violent crimes in locating suspects. DeReyes testified that he could not recall one homicide investigation in which he had assisted.

Madeline Malka:

Madeline Malka spearheaded the case for the DA in the beginning and was present for most of the interviews of Popcorn and Woody.

Gary Mitchell:

Gary Mitchell, one of New Mexico's top criminal defense attorneys, started in the New Mexico Public Defenders office. After that he went into private practice where he fights for the underdog, the downtrodden and the poor. Gary Mitchell is one of the best trial lawyers in the Southwest.

Steven Aarons, Kari Converse and Troy Garrity:

Attorney Steven Aarons and Investigator Troy Garrity were the defense team for Shaun Wilkins, along with Kari Converse, a defense attorney assigned to work with Steven Aarons. In the trial of Shaun Wilkins, Steve Aarons and Troy Garrity created enough doubt among the jury that the jury was hung.

We Have A Case

"THANK YOU, YOUR HONOR. THE STATE WILL CALL LAWRENCE NIETO."

This was the first time I saw Lawrence "Woody" Nieto. He walked in like an injured puppy. His head was down and he never looked up to make contact with Roy Buchner or anyone else in the courtroom. He was handcuffed to his waist and shackled around the ankles. Woody was forced to do the penguin walk, dressed in an orange jump suit with the initials Santa Fe CC on the back (Correction Center). The only noise in the courtroom was the clanging of chains from Woody's feet. Woody tried to scratch his nose but his handcuffs were attached to the chain around his waist and wouldn't allow him to seek any relief.

The court clerk stood up and looked at Woody, "Excuse me, Mr. Nieto, would you stand and raise your right hand. Do you swear or affirm that the testimony you are about to give is the truth, the whole truth, nothing but the truth, under penalty of perjury?"

All Woody could do to raise his right hand was to bend it at the wrist. He looked at the judge and asked, "Can I take the Fifth?"

Assistant District Attorney Mady Malka wouldn't even look at Woody or wait for an answer from the judge. "Thank you, your honor. If Mr. Nieto, after he is sworn in, is pleading the Fifth Amendment, then I would ask that this court, under State vs. Cuesta and State vs. South and also under, Rules of Evidence 11-1, I think it's 804, that I gave the court, to make a finding of unavailability on this witness. If the Court knows that Mr. Nieto is a defendant charged in a different case number and therefore he does, of course, have the privilege against self-incrimination. I would ask this Court pursuant to 11-804A-A1 to make a ruling that he is in a sense unavailable. The court knows that counsel was appointed for Mr. Nieto. Yesterday. Counsel is Gary Mitchell. When we came back to the office yesterday, I was preparing Mr. Nieto's subpoena, which was sent out yesterday and served upon him today. I contacted Gary Mitchell personally. I told Gary Mitchell that there was going to be a hearing today. That his client had been subpoenaed. He asked me if I would set up a telephone conversation, telephone call between himself and Mr. Nieto at the Torrance County Detention Center, which I did. Mr. Mitchell then contacted his client and I think if the court asks his client, asks Mr. Nieto, Mr. Nieto will tell you that he spoke to Mr. Mitchell."

The clerk addressed Woody, "Would you please raise your right hand?"

Again Woody just turned his right hand upward as far as the restraints would allow him to. "I do."

"Mr. Nieto, did you visit with your legal counsel yesterday?"

"No."

"You did not? Then what was your explanation that your counsel had advised you to plead the Fifth?"

Woody looked over at the judge and I noticed that he appeared to be very slow witted, as if he could have been one of my special education students when I was teaching high school. Woody had thought the judge's words had meant that he had met with Mr. Mitchell in person. Puzzled, Woody addressed the judge, "I talked to him on the phone yesterday."

"And he advised you, to plead the Fifth Amendment?" noted the judge. Woody just nodded.

"Very good. The court will rule that Mr. Nieto is unavailable." The judge didn't wait for Woody's answer. It was as if Woody wasn't in the same room.

Malka didn't waste a breath. "Thank you, your honor. Obviously, the State has no questions."

"You may step down, Mr. Nieto."

Malka had planted the seed that she and the officers had used and abused Woody. We would never get a chance to interview Woody. By charging Woody with the same crimes he was provided an attorney. We would have to work with his attorney. So much for the right to confront your accuser.

"The State may call its next witness."

Once Woody got an attorney he began taking the Fifth. Mady had to know that would happen but it didn't matter to her that the false confession was coming in by way of a duped state policeman that had nothing to do with the case except to interview Woody after his false confession. The train had left the station and was gaining speed. It would be our job to step in front of the train to try to slow it down or stop it.

On May 24, 1996, I got a call from defense attorney Ray Twohig. I had worked with Ray on other cases, including a death penalty case out of California that we were currently involved in called the Sureno 13. Ray asked me, "What's your schedule like tomorrow?"

"I have a few things I have to get done, but it's flexible."

"Good, can you meet me at Carlisle and Interstate 40? There's a preliminary hearing in Moriarty, at ten am and I would like you to go up there with me. It's an hour or so away so we can talk about the case as we drive."

I don't watch the news, nor do I read the newspapers, so I had no idea as to what was going on in Moriarty, New Mexico. I had done fifty-one homicide cases since my retirement from the police department. Little did I realize I was just about to get my fifty-second, third, fourth and fifth homicide deaths.

I had no idea what I was getting into and the type of case it was going to turn out to be. That is what was so fascinating about being involved in investigations. Twenty-one years with the police department, and you could never predict what you were going to do on any given day or the following day, unless you were a supervisor and all you had to do was push paper work around all day. When you were on call you would be assigned to carry an electronic baby sitter with you, a pager. It would wake you up beeping in the middle of the night; it would take you away from your dinner or a wrestling match one your sons was in. You get used to changing your mental gears from eating dinner to being at a bloody crime scene or the emergency room with a crying victim. Starting work at two in the morning and going all day on pure adrenalin. Not even realizing you didn't eat breakfast, or lunch nor take your imaginary fifteen-minute break in the morning and the afternoon. Now I was in age where my cell phone had become my electronic baby sitter.

Ray Twohig was one of the best at putting together a legal defense. He was the best sword fighter I had ever seen. Sword fighting was an art and skill that Ray often referred to saying, "We are sword fighters not mud wrestlers." Ray was truly a sword fighter. He had received his Juris Doctor degree Cum Laude in 1969 from the Ohio State University College of Law. He then attended the Georgetown University Law School as an E. Barrett Prettyman Fellow from 1969 to 1971 in a graduate law program, which emphasized trial skills.

Ray had accumulated a wide variety of experience. He had taught at the Ohio State Law School clinical program for two years and was in private practice in Ohio until 1977. Then his work took him to the position as Assistant Federal Public Defender in New Mexico from 1978-81. Once Ray moved to New Mexico he was hooked. He had fallen in love with the state. Ray has been in private practice in New Mexico since 1977. He had practiced law for 40 years and with his 30+ years of private practice in Ohio and New Mexico, he had concentrated on criminal defense and plaintiff civil rights cases. He received the New Mexico ACLU Guardian of the Constitution Award in 1995 and the State Bar's Courageous Advocacy Award in 1997. He had been listed in

Best Lawyers in America for Criminal Law since its first publication in 1987.

Three months after my retirement, defense attorneys were calling me at home and asking me if I could come in and do investigations for them. I was lucky I have never had to advertise; the attorneys knew me, knew my work and knew how to find me.

The U. S. Department of Justice in New Mexico had charged eleven people with the death penalty. Attorneys were grabbing every private investigator they could. Ray and Jeff Buckles, another defense attorney, had been assigned one of the death penalty cases. Ray's office found me and asked if I could join them for lunch and to bring my resume. I met with Ray and Jeff for lunch and have been working with Ray ever since.

Ray knew the law and I knew investigation, evidence, interviewing techniques, and crime reconstruction. I had twenty-one years of law enforcement behind me and six years of doing defense work. My last eight years I had done child homicides and Crimes Against Children. The type of case that Ray was handing me was not new to me but the type of investigation was. The crime scene was going to be a challenge because they, the prosecuting team, had not done a forensic evaluation of the scene.

On the ride up to Moriarty, Ray filled me in. "We have a potential death penalty case. They are accusing our client of four murders. The young man we might be representing is Roy Buchner. His grandparents came to see me last night. They told me they believe their grandson couldn't do a thing like this and I believe them. When you meet them you will see what I mean. They are salt of the earth people and they believe their grandson is innocent. We have no police reports given to us yet. All we have to go on is the newspaper."

We had taken up the challenge of finding out the truth surrounding the Torreon Cabin Murders. The battle for the truth had begun.

18th Street Gang

IT WAS A MILD FALL IN NOVEMBER OF 1995 IN NEW MEXICO. During the 1990s, gangs were visible throughout the U.S. In Albuquerque it was no different.

The 18th Street was considered to be one of the nation's largest and most violent street gangs. They came from Los Angeles and membership was high in the Southwest as well as the rest of the country. Gang members committed assault, auto theft, carjacking, drive-by shootings, extortion, homicide, identification fraud, drugs, and robberies.

To join 18th Street, a member of the gang must recommend a member. Then upon approval of the member, the person is jumped or ranked in (a ritual in which the gang members may beat the new member in for a period of three to six minutes). The number of members ranking a person in depended on how many members were there.

The 18th Street gangs came from Mexico and Central America. In Albuquerque in the mid-1990s, the 18th Streeters existed all over the city in pockets of small groups in different areas of town. There was no major leader of 18th Street. Gang members would recognize each other by their tattoo XVIII or 18st.

The New Mexico Boys' School, the correctional institute for juvenile males, was located two miles north of the town of Springer, New Mexico. The New Mexico Boys' School was one of the state's oldest detention facilities with a history that dated back to 1909, when it was called the Raton Reform School. Today it is known as Springer Correctional Center or SCC.

In the summer and fall of 1995, the New Mexico Boys' school at Springer was home to Ben "Deuce" Anaya Jr., Woodrow "Woody" Nieto, Shaun "Sager" Wilkins, and Shawn "Popcorn" Popeleski. The boys all had two common denominators. They were all from Albuquerque and they all belonged to 18th Street.

Springer's boys' school was like a mini adult prison where strong bonds were created among the gang members. The members spent more time with one another than they did with their counselors.

Another 18th Street member was Roy "Eazy" Buchner. Roy belonged to the Westside 18th Street along with Ben Jr. and Woodrow "Woody" Nieto.

Shaun "Popcorn" Popeleski belonged to 18th Streeters in Rio Rancho, New Mexico. Shaun "Sager" Wilkins was 18th Street from the far Northeast Heights.

In the winter and fall of 1995, the 18th Street gang was upset at one of their members. Much like the Bill Clinton's rule of "Three Strikes," the 18th Street gang developed the same philosophy. They had their own "Three strikes Rule." If you made three mistakes with the gang, you were ranked out.

The first week of August, 1995, four gang members were arrested in Albuquerque. One of the gang members, Joseph, aka "Stalker," always used the alias of "Frank Gomez." This name belonged to Stalker and the gang respected Stalker's right to use the name Frank Gomez.

The second week in August four gang members hijacked a car. They took it to Arizona where the Arizona Department of Public Safety stopped them. When stopped in the car, Shaun "Popcorn" Popeleski was asked by the State Trooper, "What's your name?"

Since Joseph, aka "Stalker," was not there, Popcorn responded, "Frank Gomez."

The four members of 18th Street were all arrested. Popcorn was not the driver and was just a passenger so he was released. The other three were held for their parents to pick them up. They were aware Popcorn had used the name Frank Gomez. Popcorn had no right to use the name Frank Gomez. This was Strike One.

Popcorn had no place to live. He would stay at other members' houses until they got tired of him and kicked him out. Popcorn was hanging around the projects in the Northeast Heights.

One evening police had found Popcorn sleeping in a stolen car. "What's your name?" they asked.

Popcorn once again gave the name Frank Gomez.

When asked where he lived, Popcorn gave the address of Ben Anaya Jr.

He was asked, "What are you doing in this car?" The car had come back stolen. Popcorn knew it was stolen because he had stolen the car himself.

"I didn't steal the car, Dominic stole the car. I'm just sleeping in it. Dominic was the one who stole the car. I'll show you where he lives."

The police found Dominic in the projects and based on the information from Popcorn, Dominic was arrested for auto theft. The police were quick to arrest Dominic since he had prior arrests for stolen cars.

Popcorn was released. He had lied to the cops and it was easy to do. Popcorn was able to blame someone else for stealing the car and got away with his crime. This was Strike Two with the gang.

It didn't take long for the word to spread out that Popcorn was lying about Dominic. Popcorn was now a witness against Dominic. Popcorn was using the alias of Frank Gomez, the name that belonged to Stalker. Popcorn had now ratted and lied about a fellow gang member.

When Popcorn failed to appear for the arrest of Frank Gomez, warrants were issued to "Frank Gomez" at Ben Jr.'s house. Popcorn was hanging around Ben Jr.'s house and Ben Sr. believed Popcorn's real name was Frank Gomez.

The police later on stopped stalker. He gave them the name Frank Gomez as he did not realize there were outstanding warrants for Frank Gomez. Stalker was arrested and charged for the outstanding warrants. He knew it was Popcorn using the name Frank Gomez. This was Strike Three.

Ben Jr. had outstanding warrants for his arrest for burglary and probation violations. He had broken into homes and stolen guns. Now the gang unit, along with probation officers, were out looking for him. Ben Jr. was running from the police but Popcorn was running from 18th Street.

Ben Sr. was a former Marine and a well-disciplined man. He had worked as a heavy equipment operator at Kirtland Air Force Base. Ben Sr. had a nice home in the northwest part of Albuquerque. A wall surrounded his home with a fence on top with a locked front gate. In the front yard Ben Sr. would park his vehicles to make sure they were secure. He also had a small apartment in the back for his stepdaughter. Ben Sr. had known her since she was baby and took care of her.

Ben Sr. had built a summer cabin in Sherwood Forest. Sherwood Forrest, located in Torreon, New Mexico, was sixty miles northeast of Albuquerque, just next to the Cibola National Forest.

At the cabin, Ben Sr. had put a chain link fence around the property to keep trespassers off the land and away from the cabin. Ben Sr. had built the cabin out of 2 x 6's and placed insulation to keep the cabin warm. To supply water to the cabin, he had a fifty-gallon drum of water.

Ben Sr. installed security devices at the cabin. He would recall, "I had a wire mesh on the windows with two locks on them. As well as a personal gate (that) had a lock. The cabin had been broken into twice. I was trying to secure it."

Ben Sr. was a firm believer in security of his home and property. He had brought up his son in the same fashion. Security. Security. Security. Everything had to be closed and locked.

Ben Sr.'s home in Albuquerque was no different. Not only was the house surrounded by a large wall and fence, locked with a chain and lock, but the windows and doors had rod iron with locks on them as well.

Ben Sr.'s rectangle cabin in Sherwood Forest had a porch and front door. No other doors were built into the cabin. It had two bedrooms with bath, kitchen-living room combined, and a pantry between the two bedrooms. With the heavy winters, Ben Sr. built the cabin air tight to keep the cold out of the cabin.

The last week of November 1995, Ben Jr., his girl friend Cassandra, and her two boys, Matthew and Johnny, decided to go stay at the cabin. Ben Jr. was hiding from the law. Popcorn was also hiding from the law for outstanding warrants but he was also hiding from the gang. He knew he had three strikes.

Up to that point, no gang member had been to Ben Sr.'s cabin. Popcorn would be the first one. The last week of November, all five packed up in Ben Sr.'s charcoal grey Jeep and headed to the mountains. The only one Ben Sr. authorized to drive his Jeep was Ben Jr.

Ranking Out Of Popcorn

When the group returned to Albuquerque for Halloween. Cassandra and the boys went to her mom's house, Porfie Sedillo, to clean up and go shopping. Popcorn and Ben Jr. went to clean up at Ben Sr.'s house.

A young Hispanic girl, "Bonita" (meaning pretty), was so named for her good looks. Bonita had a small baby boy and lived in an apartment in the southeast part of town by herself. It was a place some of the gang members could hang out.

On Thursday, November 30th, Bonita was having a party at her house. Bonita had heard Ben Jr. was in town. They had known each other from midschool and were very, very close. Bonita called Ben Sr.'s house.

"Ben (Ben Jr.) we're having a party at my house. Do you want to come?"

"You know Popcorn is with me?"

"Ben you know they think Popcorn is a rat. They're going to rank him out if you bring him."

There was a pause on the phone. In the background Bonita could hear Ben Jr. telling Popcorn, "They want to rank you out."

Bonita feared for Popcorn. "I don't think it is a good idea. They are going to kick his ass."

By now everyone at the party knew Bonita was talking to Ben Jr. and Popcorn. They were yelling "Popcorn is coming. We're going to kick his ass."

Ben Jr. replied, "Popcorn said he don't care."

Sager jumped up and got in front of Bonita's face and yelled, "I'm going to beat your ass Popcorn and I am going to kick your ass."

Bonita could hear Ben Jr. talking to Popcorn. "I'll go, and you stay here." Popcorn refused to stay. "Bonita, we don't have a ride to your place. Can you pick us up?"

Bonita and her cousin drove over to Ben Jr.'s house to pick him up for the party. Both Ben Jr. and Popcorn got in the car.

Again Bonita said, "Popcorn they're going to kick your ass."

Popcorn who loved the adrenalin rush was pumped. "I'm going to the party, I can handle myself. I'm not a pussy, they can't kick my ass."

Bonita pulled up to her apartment with Ben Jr. and Popcorn. As she opened her apartment door, Sager came out swinging at Popcorn.

There were no words exchanged, just a powerful hit to Popcorn's face, sending Popcorn to the ground. Once on the ground, the 18th Streeters all jumped on Popcorn, kicking and beating him.

Ben Jr. stood back and watched the beating. He was not going to challenge the gang or their rules.

They picked Popcorn up off the sidewalk, bent him over a barbecue grill and beat him some more. Someone pick up a big stick and hit him in the arm. Nobody was stopping the beating.

Bonita, who was four months pregnant, jumped on the back of Popcorn. She yelled at everyone, "Leave him alone. That's enough."

Bonita herself took several hits before the gang members realized she was there. When they realized it was Bonita, they yelled, "Back off, back off."

The neighbors from the second floor above Bonita's were yelling from their balcony. "You boys quit fighting, leave him alone. I'm calling the cops."

The gang members responded by throwing rocks at the neighbors and breaking out their windows. The gang took off running, not wanting to be there when the cops got there. They left Ben Jr. and Popcorn with Bonita. Ben Jr. went into Bonita's bedroom and stayed there until the cops left.

Bonita had grabbed her phone and called 911, "Can you please send rescue here. Somebody hurt really bad."

Bonita and several other girls picked up Popcorn and spread him out over the picnic table. Popcorn was spitting out blood and holding his arm. When the paramedics came up to him, Popcorn told them, " I'm fine. I'm fine. Leave me alone."

Popcorn was now sitting on the table when the police arrived and asked, "What happened here?"

Popcorn told them, "Nothing happened. Leave me alone." Popcorn's elbow was hurting him and it was swelling up.

"You sure you don't want us to look at your elbow?" the Paramedics asked.

"No. I'm fine."

Rescue and police knew this was gang related and could care less. It was just gang business. Since Popcorn was not going to be treated rescue workers wrote no report. The police wrote no report—not for some gang bullshit.

Bonita's apartment manager did not take the ranking out lightly. Windows were broken upstairs, tenants were threatened, the police had been called and that was all it took. The manager wrote a report and gave Bonita a seven-day notice.

Bonita drove Popcorn and Ben to Lovelace Hospital's Emergency Room. Popcorn gave them the name of Frank Gomez. Since he didn't have any insurance, he was not treated and they left the ER.

Ben and Popcorn spent the night at Bonita's apartment. Bonita gave Popcorn some of her painkillers to help him sleep.

The next morning nobody said anything. This was not unusual for Ben Jr. but it was for Popcorn. Normally Popcorn was hyper and talked a lot of shit. This morning at breakfast Popcorn was silent.

Another of Ben Jr.'s girlfriend came over to Bonita's apartment, picked up Ben Jr. and Popcorn, and gave them a ride back to Ben Sr.'s house.

Bonita would later on testify, "After that beating the relationship between Popcorn and Ben changed. Ben was now calling Popcorn a leach."

Bonita would tell Ben, "Tell Popcorn to leave."

"Bonita, I feel sorry for him. He has no place to go."

"You know Popcorn is upset with you because you didn't have his back."

Popcorn stayed with Ben Jr. and Ben Sr. at the house nursing his wounds and taking the pills Bonita had given him.

Bonita saw Ben Jr. again that week. On Friday December 1, Ben called Bonita, "Do you want to go out to dinner?"

"Sure, that sounds good. I'll pick you up."

Ben took Bonita to Black Angus for dinner. After dinner Ben asked Bonita, "Do you want to get a room tonight?"

Bonita, who had a close relationship with Ben Jr., agreed. That night Ben Jr. and Bonita spent their last night together at the Luxury Motel on Central Avenue.

On Saturday the 2nd of December Bonita dropped off Ben Jr. at his dad's house and told Ben, "Give me a call." This was the last time Bonita saw Ben Jr. alive.

On Sunday Bonita found an eviction notice on her door.

On December 3rd Ben Jr. left his dad's house with Popcorn. They drove over to Cassandra's mom's house and picked up Cassandra and her two boys. On the way to the cabin they stopped and picked up Airie, Popcorn's girlfriend.

While Ben Jr. drove down the highway through Torrance County on the way to the cabin, a Torrance County sheriff's deputy pulled Ben Jr. over.

The deputy talked with Ben. "Where you headed to?"

Ben Jr. responded with his cool demeanor, "We're just taking the kids on a picnic to my dad's cabin in Sherwood Forest."

The deputy did not run Ben Jr. or Popcorn through NCIC (National Crime Information Center) but instead let them go on their way with a verbal warning.

Last Time Ben Sr. Saw His Son

On the afternoon of December 10, 1995, Ben Sr. showed up at the cabin. Ben Sr., being a concerned dad, brought with him pizza, cokes and food for the kids.

"Everything going all right son?"

"Everything is fine dad."

"I brought up a wax ring for the toilet. I noticed it was leaking. I also brought up a new dead bolt for the door. That old one is sticking."

Popcorn said, "I can put the dead bolt on for you, if you want to fix the toilet."

Ben Sr. gave Popcorn the lock with both keys to it.

The dead bolt Ben Sr. brought up needed a key for the inside and outside in order to lock the door. Ben Sr. also had door locks on the bedroom doors. The locks were on the outside and the push buttons were on the inside. If the bedroom door was locked you would need a key from the outside to unlock it.

Ben Jr. had permission to use his dad's Jeep with the one exception. Ben Sr. would recall, "I gave direct orders to my son to drive that Jeep. He was responsible for that Jeep and I told him he was the only one to drive it. Nobody else."

Before Ben Sr. left, he told his son, "I won't be back up here for a couple of weeks. I'm going on vacation to Las Vegas on Friday the fifteenth." With that Ben Sr. left his son and his friends. That was the last time Ben Sr. would see his son alive.

The Break-in At Ben Sr.'s House

On Tuesday or Wednesday, the 12th or 13th of December, Ben Sr.'s house was broken into. They stole shirts, jackets, guns, watches, rings, alcohol and money. When Ben returned home from Vegas, he found a set of keys to the cabin in one of his jacket pockets. Ben Sr. had left money in that same pocket. His hopes were that no one would find it. The money was gone but in its place were the keys to the new lock at his cabin.

Popcorn had lived at Ben Sr.'s house with his son for a while. Ben Sr. did not like Popcorn because he was always snooping around looking to see what was in his (Ben Sr.'s) home. Ben Sr. had a lock on his bedroom door because he did not trust Popcorn. When he returned from Vegas he could see where someone had put a knife near the lock and entered his bedroom.

That same day as the break-in, Ben Sr.'s stepdaughter saw the Jeep in the driveway. She also saw Popcorn and thought, "Oh Ben Jr. must be home as well." She would recall that she didn't think anything of it.

During the same time a large black garbage bag was left at the back door of Cassandra's mother's (Porfie's) house. Porfie would not find the bag for several weeks. A year after finding the bodies she gave the news media a statement.

"When I get lonely for my grandsons I go into their room where I have their clothes laid out. And when I miss them I go in there and smell their clothes. I have created a shrine in their room."

After reading the story in the newspaper, I began to wonder how Porfie got the clothes belonging to the boys. Cassandra had gone to the laundry and had washed clothes. There was a laundry basket in the back of Ben Jr.'s Jeep with some of Ben and Cassandra's clothes still in it.

On December 15, 1995, Popcorn was driving Ben Jr.'s Jeep. Popcorn had gone over to the Westside Community Center, where he met "Little Dreamer." This was Little Dreamer's first day of Christmas break from school, an easy day to remember.

Popcorn and Little Dreamer talked. "What are you going to do for Christmas break?"

"I would like to go see my aunt in Dallas," Little Dreamer said.

"You want me to take you?"

"Yeah, that would be cool."

Before they left, they stopped at Green Eyes' house to sell some guns.

Popcorn needed the money. Little Dreamer would recall, "Popcorn sold Green Eyes two rifles and a hand gun."

One would have thought the gang expert would have known who Green Eyes was, located him and asked him about the weapons and the time period of when Popcorn sold him the guns. By the time I got involved, Green Eyes had moved to parts unknown.

The Jeep broke down in Pecos, Texas, at the Holiday Day Inn. Little Dreamer contacted his Aunt and would recall, "Yeah my aunt sent us money to rent a room there and she gave us bus money to come home."

Little Dreamer had trouble with dates but a receipt found in Ben Jr.'s Jeep showed a Wal-Mart receipt dated December 19th at 7 pm.

In a Q & A with Little Dreamer, he said, "Yea. We got back on the twenty-first or twenty-second in the middle of the night."

"When did you see Popcorn last?"

"He spent the night with us and then left in the morning. I never saw him again."

"How was Popcorn acting?"

"Like he was running away from something."

Little Dreamer never mentioned anything about going to Arizona with Popcorn. Popcorn never mentioned he went to Arizona. Popcorn never talked about Ben Jr., Cassandra or the kids during the time he was with Little Dreamer.

Popcorn Is Arrested In Belen, New Mexico

It was unknown what Popcorn did or how he got to Belen. Popcorn was never asked what he did from the 22nd of December to the 24th. We knew he liked to steal cars to get around. No one from law enforcement checked for any stolen vehicles in that time period.

On December 24, 1995, Popcorn was in Belen at the Tabet Car Wash. Popcorn had a large screwdriver and was attempting to break open the quarter machine. The police were called for the break in. Popcorn who loved the chase, was arrested by a queen size female officer. There was no struggle and no running from this officer. Popcorn went to jail peacefully. Popcorn was booked into Valencia County Jail and was now using his real name Shawn Popeleski.

When Popcorn was arrested at the car wash his property was seized. Among the property taken were his clothes, keys, and a pager. Popcorn would stay in custody until March 23, 1996, when he would escape just as he had when he was in custody at Springer, New Mexico. On the 23rd of March, Popcorn went over the fence of the Valencia County Jail with Danny S... and Danny Si...

Popcorn and the two Danny's stole a car and traveled around in it. Then, once again, they led police on a high-speed chase in Albuquerque. Popcorn was once again arrested and booked into BCDC (Bernalillo County Detention Center) under the name of Frank Gomez.

Bodies Are Found

On April 14, 1996, Ben Sr. and his girlfriend decided to go to his cabin in Torreon. The snow had melted and there was a good chance he could drive to the cabin. Ben Sr. had gotten a large electric bill for the cabin and wanted to see if someone had left some electrical equipment on.

Ben Sr. had assumed it was his son who had broken into his home in December. He reasoned that Ben Jr. was too embarrassed to face him (his dad) and that was the reason he (Ben Jr.) had not contacted him.

What Ben Sr. was about to find was every father's nightmare. The front gate was wide open and there was trash all over the yard. There were dogs in his yard running around the cabin and barking at him.

When Ben Sr. reached his front door, the screen door was locked. He reached in the hole of the screen door and unlatched the eyehook. The dead bolt to the cabin was locked. With the keys he found in his jacket pocket he opened the door. Ben Sr. was greeted with a rush of hot air. The cabin was filled with hot air. He noticed the living room had been burned with scorch marks on the wall. The sofa had been burned and the cabin smelled of death. Everything was in shambles. A sofa chair was turned upside down, pictures on the wall were thrown on the ground, and trash was everywhere.

Ben Sr. looked over to the master bedroom and the door was closed. He saw the bedroom keys were hanging in the door from the doorknob. Ben Sr. opened the door to the right and saw somebody lying on the bed. He got scared and told his girlfriend, "There's a dead man in the bed."

Ben Sr. could not recognize his own son. With all the heat in the house, the heat had turned the skin on the victims a brown leathery color. Ben Sr. did not notice Cassandra on the floor nor the boys in the other bedroom.

Ben Sr. and his girlfriend left the cabin and drove down to his neighbors, the Elhers, and called 911. Ben Sr.'s first thoughts were that some African Americans had broken into his cabin and died.

Sherwood Forest fell under the jurisdiction of Torrance County Sheriff's Office (TCSO), a twenty-five-member department. Torrance County Sheriff Lyle was smart enough to know his department could not handle this type of case. It was obvious this was going to be a cold case. The victims had been dead for three to four months and the sheriff's department had no eyewitnesses, no evidence, and no murder weapon. After four months, the killer or killers were long gone.

His deputies had found a total of four bodies in the cabin. Two of them were Cassandra's boys, ages three and two, Johnny and Matthew Garcia. Ben Jr. and Cassandra both had headshots behind the ear. Cassandra had two shots in her. The first shot entered her right arm and then into her chest. When she had turned her head away from the attacker, the cold murderer shot her behind the right ear as well.

Sheriff Lyle knew they needed a good arson investigator as the cabin was in shambles and the living room had been set on fire. This case was going to require experts from the crime lab, an experienced group of homicide detectives, and an arson expert. Torrance County had none of these.

The District Attorney's office also sent out one of their attorneys to give advice and help with the issuance of search warrants. The Assistant District Attorney would be Mady Malka and she would work closely with the officers to make sure the prosecution would have an airtight case. The news of the murders in Torreon Mountains took off like a grass fire.

3

The Investigators Are Assigned

WHAT THE SHERIFF ASKED FOR AND WHAT HE GOT WERE TWO different things. The ADA on the scene, Mady Malka, thought this case needed the state police. They had the expertise to handle such a case. What Sheriff Lyle got, without his knowledge, was a total of two agents from the state police and one detective from the Albuquerque Police Gang Unit.

The total experience of all three officers was over forty years of law enforcement experience. The problem was that Agent Frank Jacoby from the state police had just transferred from narcotics to homicide, and the only homicide he had investigated was what Agent Jacoby called an "almost murder case" that turned out to be a suicide.

Agent Mike Fenner had just come back from polygraph school. He had never done a homicide investigation in his life. Officer DeReyes was from a gang unit with the Albuquerque Police Department. He had never investigated a homicide either. So among all three officers they had investigated a total of one murder that turned out to be a suicide.

Agent Jacoby and Detective Juan DeReyes came from the same school of thought—Jacoby from narcotic cases and DeReyes from gangs. You solve cases through snitches. Forget the facts. Just tell us what we want to hear.

What the sheriff wanted was for a crime scene team to come to the cabin and do a detailed search for evidence. The Department of Public Service (DPS) director at the time was Darren White, a former sergeant with the Albuquerque Police Department who had been brought over to be the Director of DPS. He had been brought over by the new governor at that time, Gary Johnson.

White thought that the cost of a forensic team would be too high and the department was making budget cuts. A forensics team would never be sent to the cabin. They had to rely on officers who were inexperienced in the proper collection and preservation of evidence.

At the same time, however, when Ben Sr.'s Jeep was located in Pecos, Texas, DPS Director Darren White thought flying an airplane with state police officers to Pecos, Texas, to look at a Jeep was appropriate.

They had also called for an arson investigator to come to the cabin. What they got was an ATF (Alcohol, Tobacco and Firearms) agent who could not handle the smell of death and forgot to bring a mask. When the agent saw a heater lying flat on the carpet he called the fire "accidental." The cause he determined was that a heater had tipped over and caught the rug on fire, causing the couch to burn. The agent would miss four other fires in the cabin.

The perfect storm was brewing. The media was now calling the Torreon Cabin Murders the worst in the state's history. Two adults murdered execution style and two small boys left alive in the cabin to die of starvation and dehydration. Everyone believed the two young boys must have gone crazy while they were dying and tore up the cabin.

"Who's The Baddest Mother Fucker On This List?"

Agent Jacoby was the primary agent in charge. To assist him was Agent Mike Fenner. Between them they had very little credentials in interviewing and interrogation and no previous homicide experience.

Ben Sr. in his first interview had told the state police, "My son is a member of the 18th Street gang. I last saw him with another gang member, Popcorn. I got warrants in the mail for his (Popcorn's) arrest under the name Frank Gomez at my house."

Agent Jacoby and Agent Fenner had no experience in working and dealing with gangs, so they requested a gang officer from APD (Albuquerque Police Department), and Detective Juan DeReyes was assigned from the gang unit to assist with the investigation of 18th Street.

Officer DeReyes had never investigated a murder case. Like Agent Jacoby, Officer DeReyes depended on snitches and informants to gather information and identify gang members and associates. No one from the investigation team knew what the word "corroboration" meant. Their belief was that two liars lying on the same subject made it truthful.

With the name Frank Gomez, aka Popcorn, it was not hard to find Popcorn. He was in custody at the Bernalillo County Detention Center (BCDC) for several charges that included auto theft, reckless endangerment, and alluding a police officer. If he had given them his real name, nine more felonies would have been added.

None of the officers knew or did backgrounds on Frank Gomez or Popcorn. The first thing Officer DeReyes did was to get a list of the gang members of the 18th Street. He used this as his investigative tool. Instead of gathering facts or analyzing the evidence, he used a list of gang members' names.

The list became known as the "Who's The Baddest Mother Fucker On This List." This was how they were going to solve the case. Just ask them (the gang members), "Who's the baddest mother fucker on this list?" Forget the evidence and the time line. Forget about verifying the facts and evidence with a statement or a confession. Just tell me, "Who's the baddest?"

On the 15th of April, 1996, one day after the bodies were found, the officers developed a theory. Forget the facts. Forget the evidence. Let's create a theory and then we can apply the facts to the theory.

The facts of the case as Agent Jacoby, Officer DeReyes and Agent Fenner had them were:

One: Ben Jr. had been shot in his sleep with a single .22 shot behind the right ear.

Two: Cassandra had been shot in the right arm. The bullet passed into her chest. A second shot was fired into the back of her head behind the right ear.

Three: There were two small dead boys in the bedroom. Since the OMI (Office of Medical Investigators) had not done the autopsies, the cause of death was unknown.

Four: There had been a fire in the living room and the cabin was in shambles.

The officers did not know the evidence in this case. They couldn't have. No crime scene team had been sent to the cabin. They had no one to explain the events in the cabin to them.

Forget The Facts and "Let's Have A Party"

On the 15th of April, 1996, the Office of the Medical Investigators had not completed the autopsies on the four individuals. Evidence or lack of evidence had not been reviewed. The officers didn't wait to gather any facts.

Somehow Agent Jacoby, Agent Fenner and Officer DeReyes must have created a theory. Maybe there was a party and there were alcohol, drugs and guns. Maybe Ben Jr. was shot because of the leadership of the 18th Street.

Agent Jacoby and Officer DeReyes never reviewed the crime scene or the autopsies. If they had reviewed them they would have realized there were no drugs in the bodies of Ben Jr. or Cassandra and there was no alcohol at the cabin.

Officer DeReyes and Agent Jacoby must have run the name Frank Gomez, aka Popcorn, and found that Popcorn or Frank Gomez was in custody at BCDC (Bernalillo County Detention Center). He had been in custody since March 24th, 1996, for auto theft. It would take three interviews with Frank Gomez pumping smoke up the investigators ass before the investigators would discover his real name was Shawn Popeleski (Popcorn).

One would have thought that one of the three would have requested a background check on Frank Gomez. Pulled police reports on him would have found that Popcorn had been arrested numerous times for auto theft, home invasions, using a false name, escape from Springer, New Mexico, and escape from Valencia County jail. They also would have discovered that he was found in a stolen car, used the name Frank Gomez, and blamed the auto theft on someone else.

One would have thought Popcorn's name would have been under the 'Who's the Baddest MF'. But we never got to see the list.

We Believe Frank Gomez

Officer DeReyes and Agent Jacoby went to BCDC to interview Frank Gomez aka 'Popcorn." They would interview Popcorn on the 15th, 17th, 18th and would refer to him as "Frank Gomez" as they had yet to realize that he was Shawn Popeleski.

Shawn Popeleski was born in Korea; his mother was Korean and his father was from Mississippi. His family moved to the US when Shawn was eight years old. Shawn's first language was Korean and Shawn had trouble in school and with the English language. Shawn was considered Special Ed. in school because of his language skills.

Popeleski developed the nickname "Popcorn" from either his last name or the bumps on his forehead that looked like popcorn kernels.

On April 15, 1996, Officer DeReyes and Agent Jacoby made their first visit to BCDC where "Frank Gomez" was being housed. The officers went into the interview of Popcorn, the last person who saw Ben Jr., Cassandra and the boys alive.

In a homicide case there are several key factors that comprise a forensic triangle and a good homicide detective follows that forensic triangle. Link up the scene, the person and the evidence. The other major component is transportation. How did the person get to and leave the scene?

A major mistake when you are interviewing a suspect in a murder case is to go into the interview without knowing the facts. That is just what Officer DeReyes and Agent Jacoby did. They literally went into the interview without knowing the facts. Frank Gomez was in custody and he was not going anywhere. Therefore, there was no rush to interview. They should have done their homework on the evidence and Frank Gomez first.

Popcorn started out by giving the officers numerous lies. His name, date of birth, social security number—all lies. His lies would continue throughout his statement.

"I was living with "Woody Nieto."

"My father's name is Jonathan Gomez."

"I am from Puerto Rico."

"The last time he saw Ben Jr., was in November or December."

"I dropped them off at Ben Sr.'s house and took the Jeep. (The logical next question should have been "So where's Ben's Jeep?" but it was never asked.)

"This is the first time I had ever been to the cabin."

"I don't know nothing about the fires."

"I dropped off Ben Jr., Cassandra and the kids at Ben Sr.'s house."

"I lived with Ben Jr., Cassandra and kids for over two weeks."

"Ben Sr. had come to the cabin to cut Christmas trees."

"Last time I saw Ben (Jr.) was November or December; it was in Albuquerque or the mountains."

And in the same breath, "We broke into Ben Sr.'s house. We took a bottle of JD only."

Agent Jacoby was so unfamiliar with the facts he asked Popcorn, "You guys went on a picnic?"

Popcorn was asked, "How long did you stay?"

Popcorn's response was, "Probably about a week, two weeks."

Popcorn would tell the agent, "Ben (Jr.) disappears a lot, but I've been trying to get in contact with him through my girlfriend, Airie."

Agent Jacoby told Popcorn they had found everyone dead at the cabin—another major mistake. They should have conducted their interview first, and gotten the information from Popcorn so it would have been untainted. They had told Popcorn about the fire in the cabin and thus they were providing information to Popcorn, something never done in conducting interviews.

"What day was it when you last saw Ben?"

"I'm not sure. It's when my girlfriend was with me. She'll probably know the day. I'll ask her tonight. I think it was before Christmas."

Agent Jacoby, "Were you camping out or in a tent or what were you staying in?" (*Agent Jacoby does not know the facts. He is asking about a picnic and now camping out in tents.*)

Agent Jacoby never verified any dates or times for the time period for being at the cabin. Just that it was two weeks. Another lie of Popcorn but neither Agent Jacoby nor DeReyes had started any type of time line.

"There were MRI (Military Rations) thrown around the cabin," Jacoby told Popcorn. This evidence the officers should have kept to themselves. But Agent Jacoby asked, "Did you see any MRIs around the cabin?"

Popcorn went on to give the description of Ben's Jeep. Popcorn would admit he had driven the Jeep, something contrary to what Ben Sr. said.

"Do you have any idea how they died, Mr. Gomez?"

"No, sir."

Popcorn admitted to Agent Jacoby that they broke into Ben Sr.'s house and had taken jewelry, money and alcohol. But Agent Jacoby never asked him when he broke into the house. This would have been very important to establish the events.

"Did you see any weapons up there?"

"Yes, we did. We had a 30-06, nine-millimeter, a bunch of .22's. Yeah. We brought them back down, though."

Agent Jacoby still looking for a motive, "Did you guys have an ongoing war with any other gangs?" *Agent Jacoby and DeReyes were trying to put their theory together.*

"Just the Westgate."

"Did you bring the guns down to sell them?"

"We sold some right there."

"Did you sell them to Ben's Dad?"

"I think so." *Yet another lie. They could have verified this with a phone call to Ben Sr.*

"So then you came back, what, like on a Saturday or Sunday?" *Instead of asking when they came back Agent Jacoby tells him when they came back.*

During the statement Agent Jacoby would jump around from the .22 rifle to where did you sleep? Then the dangerous question he informs Popcorn about.

"You guys didn't have a fire in the cabin, an accident with one of the heaters or anything like that?" *Again releasing information of the crime scene. This was a common factor with Agent Jacoby and Officer DeReyes.*

Popcorn's response was "No."

Popcorn tells Agent Jacoby, "I dropped off Deuce at his dad's house. And I took the Jeep." *You would have thought the next question would have been. "So where's the Jeep?"* But Agent Jacoby who had difficulties staying focused asked, "Did you guys get into a fight? Okay did you do it?"

"No, I didn't."

"By accident, drinking? Look, if it was an accident, it was an accident, okay?"

"Not that kind of an accident. I would never kill my homeboy, and all of my homeboys know that. That's one thing."

"So it's not like you got drunk and started shooting in the house and accidentally shot somebody?"

Agent Jacoby was trying to get a confession by asking Popcorn if he accidentally shot two people three times with one shot behind the ear of Ben and one shot in the chest and back of the head of Cassandra, then locked two kids in the cabin to die. And Agent Jacoby was asking if it was an accident.

Twenty minutes later Agent Jacoby would return to the accident. "You know, if you lost your head—and I know you said you didn't do it, but if you did, I'm ready to go talk to the DA on your behalf. I can't make any promises, but I'm telling you, if it happened by accident, you need to tell me, man. If you ever done anything in your life, man, you got to come forward now."

Popcorn said, "I know. I always come forward to the things I do. That's honest."

"I think you got a good idea who did it. Frank?" Agent Jacoby asked

Officer DeReyes must have been getting bored and felt he had to ask twenty questions in one questions. "Did you guys burn Westgate? Somebody knew that he was up there besides you and you're other homies. Who did you burn? You know what I'm talking about, homie. This man is here to help you, man. You ain't going to do it by yourself. You're not going to find out who it is because nobody is going to talk. So right now is the time to be straight up with us and tell us."

Agent Jacoby, married to Officer DeReyes' techniques, jumped in, "Yeah. We want justice, okay? Juan wants justice just like I do for the children, okay? Look, Ben was shot. Cassandra was shot, and the babies were left there to starve. They starved to death trapped in that house. Now, you believe in street justice. That's entirely up to you. We're interested in justice for these children and for your friend and for Cassandra, okay? This is the only system we know. All right? And right now I see you being up there. We have witnesses that saw you up there. Okay? We wouldn't be here talking to you if we didn't think that you might know something or even that you were involved some-how. So if you're scamming us—"

"I ain't scamming you."

"Let's start a brand new story right now, bro. Let's start a brand new story right now. Tell us the truth. It's going to come out soon no matter what."

Popcorn knew the officers wanted information on a fantasy war and he would give them one. "It's not just Ben. They ranked—Westgaters ranked in some vatos (slang for other gang members) named Popcorn, Deuce, Loco, Crow, Woody, some of the main ones, like one of the main ones from Eighteenth Street, and we kept on looking for them and the old ones got mad because we kept going to the West Mesa all the time. And then one day we started throwing down, and next thing you know we started capping, capping at each other. And one said we'll see, what comes around goes around, vatos, and we'd throw each other down. That's what we do."

"Let's talk about this war you guys were in." *There was no war going on. If there was Detective DeReyes from the gang unit would have known about it. The officer continued now with gang rivalry, which didn't make any sense to anybody. No gang member knew where the cabin was except Popcorn. Officer DeReyes, a gang detective, should have known none of this was true.*

Agent Jacoby said, "You had to know. If you're his homie, man, you got to know who he was beefing with, and you know who it is. Trying to take care of it with your homies by yourself is going to cause more problems, dude."

"How's that going to cause more problems?"

"Because you're going to end up doing time for it, man, and it ain't go-ing to help anybody. Is that what you want to do, man? Help us so we can get them bro. Why don't you help us? You can't do it from inside there. If you want to gangbang, you know, this was the price to pay, you know. You know that. And Deuce knew it, too. But the thing is what we're trying to do is we care about the kids, bro. These vatos who did it didn't care, and you know who it is. And you can help us right now by telling us who it is because this dude's own justice; he won't get his own justice when he does a pinta, and you know how that rolls when you go down in a pinta for doing some kids. It doesn't go very well, does it? You should know that. So why don't you tell us right now so we can go get these bros and get down to business and do it the legal way. Who was he warring with? Who is the vato? *Who do you think is the one?*" (This is what is known as the crystal ball theory. Just *think* of someone.)

"Just the vato from Westgate. That's all I can say."

"Which one?"

"Who did it, Frank?" Officer DeReyes thought by talking loud he would get an answer.

"I don't know who did it."

Agent Jacoby grabbed the list. "Who do you think did it, man? Who is the baddest mother on this goddamn list right here?"

"He ain't baddest if he's doing this bullshit."

Officer DeReyes said, "Well, who the hell is it who *thinks* he's bad? Huh? Tell us, bro. Come on, Frank. Come on, Frank. Who do you think did it, man?"

Agent Jacoby said, "I don't think anybody in this damn world is worth four people."

"Was it Wizard or Mammouth? Who was it, bro?" Again DeReyes thinks talking loud will help get a statement.

"My best guess would be Cosby."

"Cosby? Why? Why did you say Cosby? Did he hate Deuce that bad?" *DeReyes also thought repetition was good.*

"He hated me, too, though."

Officer DeReyes said, "No, bro. You're not hanging. You're being straight up. You're being a man. Because if this shit would have went some other way, right now what you're doing is helping us do this investigation. If you guys want to gang bang, bro, that's between you and them, man. That's the cost of doing business, man. But when it gets kids involved or somebody that doesn't know nothing, that's cold shit, man. Well, what did you expect, bro? You tried to backfire on him. He got pissed. You yanked him on the dope. I bet you, for all he wanted, maybe he just wanted to get you and Deuce and that didn't happen and the chavalitos were there and his vieja was there." *DeReyes was now going into his come to Jesus speech.*

"But how did he know we were at the mountains?" Popcorn asked.

"That's what I want to know. Who else would know where you guys were at besides Cosby and these guys? Who else knew besides Crow and—"

"Unless April, my girlfriend's friend April, met a Westgate and told them something about it." *I guess Popcorn forgot his girlfriends name was Airie.*

Agent Jacoby said, "All right. I need to have your word today, tonight, okay. And I know I'm talking a little loud, but I want you to understand me. Even from inside here at the jail you can get things done. You have got to leave these people alone because if something happens to them we're coming back to talk to you again. Okay? Let us handle this. Okay? Let us talk to April. You're just assuming now that she ratted off Benny and you because she's going with this Westgater. We don't know that for a fact. Okay? Now, whatever evidence she has to give us you'll destroy if you do something. Okay? Do I have your word that you won't do anything? Can you give us your word like an hombre, like a man?"

"I don't know."

For the next twenty minutes Officer DeReyes would give Popcorn the "come to Jesus" speech. "Don't mess it up for us, bro. We need to get this bro, man. If he still has the Cuete (gun) there, man, if you call out your boys he's going to dump them, man, we'll never be able to prove it and that won't solve nothing, man. We need to get this homeboy with the stuff. If he cops out to us, then even better, or if he gives us names of who did it, the actual trigger-man, then you're clean, bro. Nobody will ever know that you did it. All they'll ever know is that we talked to you. But if you put the word out in the street, and you know the word goes out fast, man, this bro is going to split town. He's going to dump the stuff. And nobody will touch him. He'll jam, man. If he's got that much bank, he'll split. Promise us that, bro. Just give us time, man. Give us time to do this. Let us do it right, man, for the familia. They want to see justice, too. All right? Come on, Frank. Come on. You got to do this, bro. Let us check it out, man. Let us check it out. Let us do our job and we'll go up there and we'll take care of business. Don't blow it for us, man. Like you already said, you already gone far enough with us, man. This gives us pretty good info at least to talk to this dude. Just hold on. Just sit tight, man, because all the homies right now are all upset. Everybody knows what's coming down. We don't need other people getting killed, man, especially innocent people getting in the way trying to protect this guy. We don't need that. Will you sit on it, bro? And then if you think of any of these names like April or something, you can contact this man and talk to him direct. You don't have to tell nobody nothing man. Just tell them that we talked to you about this case while you're here. That's all you got to say, man."

Agent Jacoby said, "I'm going to give you a business card, okay. Blank sheet of paper, not a blank but a lined sheet of paper with my name. As far as anybody is concerned, I'm your attorney. Do you have an attorney now? Do we have your word, Frank? Do we have your word, Frank, as hombres?"

"Si."

Frank Gomez, Hombre to Hombre

On the 17th of April officers returned to the Bernalillo County Detention Center (BCDC) to bend over and talk to Frank Gomez once again. In the beginning the officers were doing formal introductions but as time would go on that would soon stop. They would run out of tape, they would have malfunctions with their taping equipment. This did not make any sense to me—two officers two tapes, and two recorders. Then the ultimate would be, "We did not tape all the interview." Four people are dead the death penalty is looming in the background and the officers are not recording conversations.

Agent Jacoby said, "Okay. You didn't really have any dates, set dates, and today we wanted to put down some dates a little bit better, okay? You also had said then that you had come to town sometime during that period of time and had met with your girlfriend and had taken her back up to the mountains with you, and we want to clarify her name again and when she went up and so on and so forth. I'm just kind of introducing the tape right now so you don't have to answer anything right now. You also had told us at that time that you had strong suspicions that the murders may have been committed by members of Westgate gang because of some conflicts you had had with over some weapons and some drugs and that. Okay, sir. You also said at that time that there's a strong possibly that Donald Cosby might be involved together with some of his friends including Wizard and some other individuals that are on the first two tapes. Since that time we've been able to interview some more people and today I'm prepared to ask you some questions, specific questions about certain things. Are you prepared to answer those to the best of your recollection? What we've done, Officer DeReyes and I have done this morning is we've accessed a copy of your property inventory form from the jail. And is this the property that you turned in now that you were arrested because you currently are doing time here at the BCDC, right—on a separate charge, separate, unrelated charge. This is the list here and it shows here that you have a gray/blue/black on person clothing—that must be your clothing—a white toothbrush, a criminal complaint, miscellaneous papers and stuff like that, right? The miscellaneous complaint and papers, that doesn't include keys or anything, right? Okay. The name of your girlfriend that you give us the other day was what again?

"Airie." *Now Popcorn got the name right instead of saying 'April'.*

After all the speech Frank Agent Jacoby gets one word from Popcorn. This will be the same throughout the statement.

Agent Jacoby said, "And that's spelled A-I-R-I-E, no?"
"Yes."
Agent Jacoby moved back to the party. "Who was at the party?"
I had no idea what party Agent Jacoby was talking about. Unless they had to

have been talking to Frank Gomez before the tape came on. This was the first time the word party had showed up.

"There was Dreck Zenina 'Crow' probably Lawrence Nieto—'Woody,' maybe Jeremy Sedillo." (Jeremy Sedillo was Cassandra's brother.) "We shot a .22 rifle. We had four to five .22s, a shotgun, nine-millimeter."

Agent Jacoby said, "And when you came back down off the mountain to get your girlfriend, you said last time that you brought the weapons back down, right?"

"We kept the guns at Deuce's house," said Popcorn.

"How many rifles did you keep there?"

"Six or seven."

This conversation got too confusing for me at this point.

Agent Jacoby, "So you left all the weapons there?"

"We sold them going around to everybody."

Agent Jacoby said, "Okay, but wait a minute. You were down at Deuce's place. Deuce is Ben Anaya, Jr., right? And his place is really actually Ben Anaya, Sr.'s, home, right, on 62nd Street, right? Okay. You left six or seven weapons there, but then you come back and say you sold some, so what did you sell?"

"We sold a 30-06." *Bottom line Frank Gomez, aka Popcorn, sold a bunch of .22 rifles, shotguns, 30 06.*

Popcorn told them, "But I don't know who I sold them to."

After wasting forty-five minutes going back on forth on the .22, Agent Jacoby moves it back to the party. "Yeah. You said you guys were partying up there." *No it was Agent Jacoby who said there was a party.*

"Last time we had it was when my girlfriend, when we were all together when we first went up with my girlfriend. When we first, first went up, we partied long and then we came back down, picked up my girlfriend, and we partied again."

Agent Jacoby, "Who was it, you, your girlfriend?"

"Ben, Cassandra."

Agent Jacoby, "How about the second time when you came down to Albuquerque to get food or whatever. Did you guys throw another party?"

"No."

Agent Jacoby said, "Did you guys invite anybody else for a party or, like you said, Cassandra?"

"We wanted to. We wanted to party, but nobody wanted to."

Agent Jacoby said, "You told us the last time that when you partied you guys were smoking marijuana and drinking some alcohol and stuff like that, and you told us also that you thought it was sometime in December that you went up there. Do you remember now—you've had a couple of days to think about it. Do you remember what day in December it was? Was it the first week of December, the second week?"

Airie never mentions anything about smoking marijuana and drinking alcohol. I could not believe that neither one of the officers were pursing the Jeep, or the keys. Instead Agent Jacoby is telling Popcorn, "So you had nothing to do with the shooting, right?"

Popcorn played Officer DeReyes and Agent Jacob like a Yo Yo. Agent Jacoby and Officer DeReyes are trying to get a time line for December done with Popcorn. It sounded more like, Abbott and Costello's "Who's on First Base?" When it came down for Popcorn to give a date for being at the cabin he would go blank.

Agent Jacoby asked, "Was it the first or second week?"

"Not sure."

Agent Jacoby asked, "Did you go Sunday or Monday?"

"I don't know."

Agent Jacoby asked, "The same day?"

"Not the same day."

Agent Jacoby asked, "How many days?"

"Not long."

"You were there a whole week?"

"I think so. I'm not sure, though."

"Okay. Well all right. You took some food right?" *I was glad Agent Jacoby got that issue resolved.*

"Right."

"Did he (Ben Sr.) make more than one trip?"

"I think he made two."

"Two visits in one week?"

"Yeah, Not like right away. Like a day or two later."

"The first time you came down? Is that when you picked up your girlfriend?"

"I don't know. I'm not sure. It's just confusing."

"Was it December? How do you know?"

"Cutting trees for Christmas."

"Right."

"I think so."

Agent Jacoby asked, "How many days and night?"

"I don't know, I wish I could remember."

"Was it cold?"

"It wasn't that cold, it got cold a little."

"Was it cold outside?"

"It wasn't that cold."

Agent Jacoby astutely noted, "Then you came back before Christmas."

"I'm not sure."

Agent Jacoby asked, "How many weekends, Christmas, had you already been back? Most of us remember weekends. I know I do."

"I don't know. I party almost every day. I just don't know what day is what day, you know."

"But you say it was two weeks. What makes you think it was two weeks?"

"Just to say it was two weeks. The first week, I'm not sure. That's why I'm like—so much stuff happened that month. It's like weird."

Agent Jacoby asked, "Where were you for Thanksgiving?"

"Thanksgiving? I'm not sure if I was with Woody or—no, I was with Crow, Deuce. Josie is like a home girl, I guess."

Agent Jacoby asked, "Did he have to use a key to open the cabin?"

"I think so. I'm not sure. I think so."

"You don't know if he had keys?"

"I think he had keys."

Popcorn claimed they all came to Ben Sr.'s house and stole a bottle of Jack Daniels. They took showers and cleaned up. Cassandra and the kids also came down. All of this could have been verified through Cassandra's mom Porfie. But it wasn't.

Agent Jacoby asked, "What was he going to do? Was he going to stay in town? Was he going to go back to the mountain? What was he going to do?" *Four Questions in one was not unusual for Agent Jacoby.*

"He was going to go back up."

"He was going to go home? He was going to go what?"

"He was going to go back up to the mountain."

"He was going to go back up to the mountains. Do you know if he did go back up to the mountains right away?"

"Not right away."

Agent Jacoby asked, "What did you do then? You left with him and you thought that maybe Ben was going to go back up to the mountains with Cassandra and the kids? Is that what you believed, that would happen?" *I thought to myself, how do you answer shit like this?*

Agent Jacoby said, "But that's the same day you went to pick up your girlfriend and then took her up? Is that when you went shopping? When you guys came down to pick up your girlfriend, is that when you guys went shopping? And then when you went and left again, is that when you picked up your girlfriend and went back to the mountain, during that same time? Do you understand what I'm saying? Let me show you. You're saying that you went to the mountains, okay? This is a weekend. This is Saturday and Sunday, or whatever days. This is a two-day period, okay, or break. Even if it's a one-day break I don't care. You told us the last time you were here for two days, almost two days. You slept at Ben's one night. You don't remember if you stayed another night, remember? Okay. That's the break between your visit in the mountains. In here you're at the mountains and here you're at the mountains. Here you say is four days last time we talked to you. Your girlfriend was with you. I'm going to put an A for Aerie."

Agent Jacoby would go non-stop with his narrative and Popcorn would respond in three words, "I think so."

Officer DeReyes asked, "Who was with you when you got arrested for the stolen car on the charges that you're in now?"

"I can't say. That would be like killing myself right there."

Agent Jacoby asked, "How is it going to be killing yourself, if they all got arrested too?"

"They all got arrested?"

Agent Jacoby said, "You had nothing to do with that. I needed to ask you real quick while we still have some tape left about an incident where you were being referred to as a rata and you got in an argument. You got in a fight at a party when Ben was with you."

"Yeah. He was the one who was with me all the time."

Agent Jacoby said, "Okay. Well, did he back you up at the fight?"

"Did he back me up? He had to stay out. He had to."

Agent Jacoby, "Okay. Did you get pissed at him for that?"

"I didn't."

Agent Jacoby asked, "You didn't get mad?"

"I was the one who went to the party wanting to go and get it over with?"

On April 19, 1996, the officers finally discovered Frank Gomez was Shawn Popeleski. The Jeep was also located in Pecos, Texas. The officers must have been hot for the last three interviews Popcorn blew smoke up their ass. For the rest of the interviews they would blow smoke up each other's ass. We never got the interviews when the officers found out Frank Gomez was Shawn Popeleski. The officer decided it was time to bring in Agent Fenner, the polygraph expert.

Fenner, fresh from polygraph school, put Popcorn on the box. No more lies from Popcorn. They had him hooked up to the polygraph.

"Where were you born?"

"September."

"What?"

"Korea."

Popcorn had no problems with dates and times giving his background. Just troubles with dates and time when it came to the murder.

"What are you in jail for now?"

"Grand Theft Auto. I get adrenaline rushes from stealing cars."

"So you took your friend's name?"

"It was his fake name."

"It was his fake name?"

"Yeah."

"So you borrowed it?"

"Yes."

"When was the first time you went to the cabin?"

"The first time?"

"Yeah. You don't have to give me a date, was it a couple of years ago, or last year?" *Why wouldn't they want a date? At some point they should have started a time line. But they never did. Create a time line.*

"It was last year. End of November beginning of December."

"When did you last see Deuce?"

"Probably last August. When he came down into town. Albuquerque. We screwed up, we stayed together for a little while no, selling guns and stuff like that. And we kept it on the low down and then we would have movidas and split over here." *Popcorn just finished telling them they went to the cabin the end of November 1995.*

"In December?"

"And then I went to, what do you call it, Belen. Not just once, we came back like twice."

"You guys would commute back and forth from the cabin?"

"Right. And then we came back for the second or third time, I'm not sure. We split up no. When we split up I went to Belen. And then I went to Belen I got in trouble right away, no. And ended up with Henry." *Popcorn got them off the subject of the cabin. He also forgot to tell Fenner he went to Arizona to see his girlfriend in Ben's Jeep.*

"Let me ask you this Popcorn, who do you think did it? You know what from what you have been telling me, you were like best bloods. Do you suspect anybody of doing it? Who do you think." *They are back in their mode of, "Who do you think?" Agent Fenner must have attended the school of Crystal Balls.*

"I don't want to say."

"Do you think Sager did it, do you think, who do you think did it? Sager? Listen to me for a second, okay. In a minute we are going to go in there and run some charts. And you gotta pass that test before they are going to help you out, bro." *They are focused on Sager without any evidence, no corroboration, just tell it was Sager. They were into day three of the investigation and for the last two days tell us Sager.* "That is what is going to happen. We are going to talk about some things, look at me. I want to talk to you. I'll tell you something I very firmly believe in, okay. I believe the eyes are the windows to your soul. I really believe that. I think you can look into somebody's face and you can tell, by looking right into their eyes. If they are telling the truth or if they are lying, whether they are happy or whether they are sad. Okay." *Agent Fenner was now blaming Sager without evidence giving Popcorn the clues as to who they wanted to blame the murders on. Fenner had to have gotten the name Sager from the Gang Officer DeReyes.*

"Yeah."

"Okay so you suspect Cosby and you said Sager? Why do you suspect Sager?"

"That's what the detective like made me think?"

"Which detective?"

"Those two guys."

"The one from APD and Jacoby?"

"Yeah, they made me think."

"What made you think of Sager? Why would Sager go and kill Ben? He must have wanted him pretty bad, to kill Cassandra and the kids."

"I don't think it was like. Sager doesn't like. I thought we were cool because I did make a slip with Rascal. I don't know if you know about him or not? And what I found out is Woody thinks Tiny killed Deuce."

"Who told you that?"

"The detectives. They said that Sager..." *Later on we would find out we were missing this interview also.*

"And so since Sager is putting the finger on you, you think that maybe Sager did it and he's trying to put it on you to get the heat off of him?" *Mike Fenner was not listening now. He is trying to get Popcorn to believe "Sager is putting the finger on you."*

"I figured that. Because like Woody and Tiny came up to party." *So why didn't the officer go find Tiny and verify the fact they had been to the cabin?*

"Up to the cabin?"

"We made them follow us once or twice. We went up and before Sager left and I know that look already from Sager. Sager is dangerous. You can tell just from his looks. It's like hard to say. I don't. I feel that he was with it, but then again I don't. That is what I assume no, but I don't for sure I don't think it's Woody because he's one of the vatos. But what the detectives were saying, anybody could be a suspect. And I was like, maybe Shaun." *Sager is Shaun Wilkins. We never got this interview Popcorn was talking about nor were there any reports made by the officer.*

"And so you think Woody could have done it?"

"No."

"No you don't suspect Woody?"

"I don't know, it's like making me think. The detectives like make me think, and it's like hard to say."

"Is Sager the person you thought shot Ben Anaya Jr.?"

"He might have something to do with it." *From "no" Popcorn goes to "He might have."*

"Do you know for sure if Sager shot Ben Anaya Jr.?"

"No."

"Let me tell you something about you, what I see looking into your soul here through your eyes. Okay. What I think is you are the kind of person, you really don't have the stomach to kill somebody?"

Mike Fenner must have attended, "The Mind Hunter Class or the Soul Hunter Class of interviewing."

"I don't."

Then the World of the investigators stopped for twenty-two days. From April 19 to May 11, 1996, the world stood still for the three investigators. There would be no police reports, no tapes, no reports, and no interviews. The officers must have gone on vacation. Or were they talking to their newfound friends Frank Gomez, Shawn Popeleski, or Woody?

Then on May 11, 1996, more aggressive interviewing would take place. All we knew was that this was the next interview we got. There was no proper introduction on the tape, no date or time. We knew there had to be a previous interviews from the first part of the tape.

Jacoby at his Santa Fe office would tell us he was giving the original tapes to Mady Malka the ADA. I did not understand at the time. Why was Jacoby giving all the original tapes to Mady. The tapes Jacoby was talking about were the tapes of Popcorn and Woody. All the other taped interviews were tagged into evidence. Why wouldn't Jacoby tag Popcorn and Woody's tapes into evidence? The tapes instead were being given to the Mady Malka to decide how the tapes were to be used.

The other possibility was if Mady was going to successfully prosecute Woody, Shaun, Roy and later on Popcorn's only the false statement and false confession of Woody and Popcorn would be given to the defense teams. Mady knew Woody would have to testify according to his false confession. Popcorn would never take the stand in any trial and attorneys would be stuck with the videos of Woody and Popcorn.

Popcorn would be the last to be prosecuted.

If the State Police tagged in all the videos, they would have all been copied and turned over to us and there would have been a chain of custody on the tapes. By giving them to ADA Malka she could not be held liable for holding back the tapes (evidence). The District Attorney's office is given immunity from civil liability, whereas the State Police are not.

Woody's case would be a slam-dunk. How do you defend a false confession? Also at Woody's trial Shaun Wilkins, Roy and Popcorn would never testify. Only the tapes would come into evidence. Malka knew that Popcorn would never take the stand and testify and the state could bring in his false statement against Shaun, Roy and Woody.

April 19th was their last reported work on the Torreon Murder case. Then on May 11, 1996, the officers were up and running again. All of a sudden on May 11, 1996, the tale between Woody and Popcorn was getting closer.

From April 15th the officers were telling them, "There was a party at the cabin (and) there were drugs, alcohol, and guns." Now the rest of the facts have to be added in to include MOTIVE. The officers had to come up with a motive for the murder.

The first motive was to kill Popcorn. That's what they went to the cabin for. Then for some miracle Popcorn was spared. Then for some reason it turns to Ben Jr., Cassandra and the boys.

Second motive from the officers. "Sager" wanted to be the top man in 18th Street. But Ben Jr. was not the top man, so then how would killing Ben Jr. make "Sager" the top man?

Third motive: "Sager and Eazy" stole all of the guns and drugs from the cabin. Why was it the only one selling guns was Popcorn? Popcorn was selling guns to "Green Eyes." However DeReyes, the gang expert, could not find the name or location of Green Eyes to interview him or recover the stolen guns that may have killed Ben and Cassandra, even though they had been told he lived at 47th and Central. Jeremy Sedillo and Little Dreamer knew where he lived.

Popcorn and Woody were getting close to one story but there were many differences in the story.

The officers were playing a role. DeReyes was the talker and the screamer. Fenner was the good cop.

Somehow during the twenty-two day period where nothing is happening Popcorn and Agent Fenner had become close friends. Agent Fenner was now calling Popcorn Shawn. Popcorn was calling Agent Fenner, "Mike".

After twenty-two days since the first interview with Popcorn, they are back talking to Popcorn with no formal introduction nor date or time. We didn't even know where the interview was taking place.

"Face Down or Underground"

Fenner was now taking yet another statement from Popcorn. They had not gotten the facts the way the officers wanted from Popcorn.

"Shawn, why don't you start and tell me what happened that night, okay?"

"I went out to use the restroom."

"Okay, let's back up, okay. This is in December, right? About when in December, do you know? Do you know the date? Do you remember the day you guys ripped off Ben's dad? Was it before this or after this? It was after this obviously, right?" *When you ask this many questions in one, most people respond to the last question.*

"Maybe like days." *Popcorn was now playing Fenner like a Yo Yo on the date and time.*

"You were like just kicking back?"

"We were just kicking back. We didn't—Sager came back and just dropped by, no, just to see how we were doing." *Now for the first time Sager is at the cabin and he is there just to see how we were doing.*

"What time of day was this?"

"This was like—not too long."

"Was it night time yet?"

"It wasn't night time yet."

"It was in the afternoon?"

"Yeah."

"Early in the afternoon or late?"

"I don't know."

"Still daylight out?"

"I just woke up, no."

"You were smoking a weed?" *Who got stoned? This had to come from a previous interview. Fenner now had asked these questions previously.*

"All of us, all of us."

"So there was you, Woody, Sager, Deuce." *No mention of Roy 'Eazy.'*

"Deuce, he doesn't...he didn't like to smoke weed that much. He would drink though."

Okay, when they left, what time was it?"

"Not too long."

"Stayed an hour or two hours. Was it dark when they left?" *Fenner is saying an hour or two, not Popcorn.*

"No, it was still light."

"Do you know what kind of car it was? Was it Chevy, a Ford?"

"It was like a Trans Am and then something like that."

"A Trans Am or a Camaro or a Grand Am?"

"Looked like a Camaro."

"A Camaro?" *Now it is a Camaro.* "Who's car was it?"

"Deuce's."

"The Camaro?'

"The Camaro was Sager's ride, right?" *Popcorn had to make a guess.*

"That's what they drove up in?"

"That's what they drove up in."

"But it was a stolen car?" *Fenner told Popcorn it was stolen and Popcorn agreed.*

"Yeah. Deuce was gonna buy it, buy it. And I said, nah, I think it's too much money, man."

"So he was gonna buy it and you talked him out of it? And then what happened the rest of the night?"

"We just kicked back and watched movies."

"And then what happened, bro?"

"I was going outside to take a piss, no, because inside we couldn't take a piss because it wasn't hooked up. There wasn't any running water. I went outside, I went to take a piss around the comer where the cement ended, and

I was just right there. I knew it was Sager right away. He said, 'Face down or underground,' and then he pumped the gauge, no. And then the other guy—the light was on, no, the light was on outside. He's the only one that has an Eighteenth Street right there, not Eighteenth Street but one-eight right there."

"So you knew it was Sager by his voice?"

"Yes. I, I knew it was Sager. I just got…"

"You saw his eyes?"

"…just got down. I just knew it was him. I know for a fact. You could put on…you could disguise him, describe him to you. I could just tell it was him just by his voice."

"So you're outside taking a leak and somebody comes up behind you with a shotgun?"

No response. Popcorn just nodded his head.

"And what was the other guy carrying? There was two guys right?" *Popcorn never said two guys. Fenner did.*

"I'm not sure. I know it was a long gun, though, because…"

"A rifle?"

"Yeah, because he had his foot on my back, and then the barrel was right there…on my head. And…" 'What do you guys want?' And I mean I was all panicking. And I heard like five shots." *Woody said he had put a shotgun to the back of Popcorn. Not a rifle. If Popcorn heard five shots then Wilkens could not have shot the two people inside and hold Popcorn down at the same time.*

"Okay. So they put you face down on the ground?" *Popcorn would go on to use this quote, along with the other officer and the DA. They had found their theme for their trial.*

"Yes."

"And then one of them stays there with his foot on your back and puts a gun to the back of your head, and then the other one goes inside?" *Fenner had to know Popcorn said Sager. So Fenner changes it to "And then one of them."*

"See, after those five shots I was like kind of jumpy, and I go, 'Check it out. What's going on,' and he said, 'Don't move,' because I was trying to move around no, I was thinking of running. And then he just said, 'Just stay here,' and I said, 'I will, homie, I will I'll just do whatever, you know.' And they were just backing up and backing up, and I just kept on looking at them like that in the (inaudible), and they started right down, and I just jumped in the Jeep because I knew it was open, no. And I jumped in and started it, and just floored it and went back down the hill. And I know they were running because

I saw them on the end, no. Like the light was on, and I saw them then, I was going. They got in the ride. I saw the lights being on, they started to split. I turned and then on the middle of the dirt my Jeep turned off. It has problems sometimes, bro. It turns off when you like take the gas off, bro. So I tried to start it back up again. It took a long time, and they were gone. I had some guns in the Jeep."

"So you saw the guy you thought was Sager, was he the one that stayed out there on you, or is he the one that went inside?" *He should have asked if Sager goes inside who was left with Popcorn?*

"He's the one that went inside."

"So he's the shooter?"

"That's what I think."

"All right. So he went inside and you heard some gun shots, and then they took off running?"

"They didn't take off running. He just stayed like he was calm...calm. Through the whole thing he was like calm."

"You're talking about Sager?"

"The one who was on my back."

"Was it Woody?" (*Fenner knew the tale they have woven and now Popcorn is saying it was Sager. Woody is saying, "I was holding Popcorn down."*)

"It wasn't Woody. I would know right away if it was Woody."

"Was it anybody else you recognized?"

"No."

"I heard the thump. You could pretty much hear everything out there. And I just jumped in and started it and then backed up and then forwarded it and tried to get out of there. I had some guns, no."

"So they didn't park in the driveway?"

Popcorn just nodded his head.

"You told me a while ago when we were talking before the video came on you thought you heard keys in the door lock?" *We never got the tape of the previous interview.*

"Yeah."

"That was after the shots?"

"That was after the shots. I even heard some footsteps going back and forth."

"Like they were loading something up?" *Fenner was trying to get Popcorn to say they were carrying guns and drugs.*

"Like there were more people. I don't know if there was more people or

not, you know what I mean? There could have been more than two people."
Fenner needed to have Popcorn say there was three people there.

"But you only saw two for sure?"

"I only saw two for sure, and I know one of them was Sager for sure because he's the only one with one-eight." *This would change on the 13th of May interview.*

"Did you ever go back to the house?"

"I don't know."

"You don' know? You never went back after that?"

Popcorn again just nodded his head.

"Did you ever see the ride they got into?"

"I know for a fact 'cause it was the same kind of car."

"It was the same car?"

"It was the same car that they came up in."

"Was it the same car or was it the same kind of car?"

"It had to have been the same car."

"The same color?"

"Same color and everything. It was like reddish maroon, you know what I mean."

"How many did you see get into the car?"

"There was two in the car."

"So you only saw two get in the car?"

"Yeah."

"And that's—so as far as you know, there was just two people?"

"It could have been one, do you know what I mean? They jumped in. There was the driver and the passenger."

"Did they take anything out of the house that you know of?"

"No."

"How many guns did you have in the house? Sixteen, ten, twenty, thirty?" *How did Fenner know this?"*

"About twelve, thirteen."

"Twelve or thirteen. What kind of guns were they?"

"They were rifles. Some were hand guns."

"What kind of hand guns?"

"Some nine millimeter. One .22 was a sprayer gun."

"What's a sprayer, bro?"

"A Mack."

"Oh, like a Mack ten. Did they had—you are telling us that they had those black ski masks or were they—" *Fenner must be a mind reader, also he even chose the same color of ski mask as Woody did.*

"It was white."

"Was it black or white?"

"It was white."

"It was all white?"

"It wasn't all white. It had holes in it. It had like a bunch of holes, but it had like that part like that, you know what I mean."

"Okay."

"It came down like that though."

"Okay. But what was the color, what was the actual color?" *Fenner was still trying to get Popcorn to say black.*

"White." *No, Popcorn. Fenner's trying to get you to say black.*

"Like real bright white? Like your T-shirt? That kind of white?"

"It was like this kind of white."

"Okay. How about that other vato?" (dude)

"He had the same kind of mask on, the same kind of mask."

"Okay."

"The same exact thing." *Sounds like to me the masks were white. But they will change his mind.*

"From the way he talked. Was he buffed out? Did he look buffed out? Did he look skinny?" *Skinny like Roy Buchner.*

"He was tall as—tall as Sager."

"Would he fit the description of say Eazy? Is Eazy as big as Sager?" *Now Fenner is getting brave. He is giving names to Popcorn.*

"Yeah. kind of. Same size." *Popcorn guessed right.*

"But you recognize Eazy's voice, don't you? Would you?" *Second hint— say it was Eazy.*

"I think so. I didn't hear him—I didn't talk to him that much, so."

"Okay. But the voice that was telling you that was very like near to you, you know, you might have recognized it but you couldn't recognize it?" *I wondered, does Fenner listen to himself talk?*

"I would recognize it."

"If you heard it again, if he said those words, but you definitely know for sure that it was Sager because that's what you guys used to use in the car-jacking's?"

"Yeah."

"What happened after you got to town?"

"I looked at there. He wasn't there. I drove around like close to his pad, no, like around his area where he lived, because I know where he lives, pretty much. I looked out there and he wasn't around there. I looked at pretty much where he hung out. He wasn't there. I went to Joker's house. He wasn't there. So I just tried to kick it with them on the west side, the main west side. You know what I mean, because he comes down to the west side all the time. I figured then I'll run into him, no. I always had—I was always packed after that. After that, I didn't care. I was just packed and just wanted revenge, no."

"Did you go by Woody's house in the Jeep looking for Sager?"

"I even went by there."

"Did Woody see you or anybody see you there? Did you stop or did you just cruise?"

"Just cruised by."

"And he wasn't there? The car wasn't there?"

"No."

"How long after you got—how long after the shooting did you hook up with Little Dreamer and go to Arizona?"

"Two days, I think."

"So you looked for Sager for two days before you hooked up with Little Dreamer and took off?"

"Yea."

"You did the right thing bro."

Popeleski said, "I hope so."

"You did, bro. you did."

I guess Popcorn forgot to tell Fenner how he broke into Ben Sr.'s house and sold guns to Green Eyes on what he was doing with the laundry in the back of the Jeep? How the Fire started, how the cabin was turned into shambles? Or where he went after he escaped from VCDC (Valencia County Detention Center)? Popcorn also never mentioned that Roy "Eazy" Buchner was at the cabin.

They were going to have to do more interviews with Popcorn. He was not getting his role down pat. He needed more rehearsal time.

4

Estancia Court

I GLANCED AT THE NEWSPAPER HEADLINES THAT RAY HAD given me as he talked about the case. "From what I got, Roy is eighteen years old. He's a member of Eighteenth Street Gang on the west side. The grandparents are a very solid couple and have been raising the boy for the last couple of years. They said he was not capable of doing what he is accused of doing and I believe them. They are very sincere, very religious and have a lot of faith in their grandson."

I started off reading the *Albuquerque Journal*. "Owner's Son Found In Cabin." It talked about the location being sixty-five miles from Albuquerque.

The Torrance County Sheriff's Department was turning over the investigation to the Department of Public Safety (New Mexico State Police). The State Police had identified the bodies as Ben Anaya Jr. Cassandra Sedillo, and her two sons Johnny and Matthew Sedillo, age four and three.

Public Safety Director Darren White had stated at a press conference that the victims had been dead for over two weeks. *As usual Darren White was only off by three and a half months.* "We also have tons of evidence in this case," he had said. *As usual Darren White didn't realize they had none.*

On April 8, 1999, there had been a missing report on Cassandra Sedillo and her two boys. According to the report they were last seen in the company of a person called Popcorn.

The next article I read, "One Arrested in Torreon Slayings," had talked about a city man arrested and charged with four murders. "City Man Faces Four Murder Counts. Shaun Wilkins Reportedly Knew Victims in Cabin."

"Shaun Wilkins age nineteen was arrested without incident on Friday at an Albuquerque residence at six am. He is facing four counts of murder in the death of the Albuquerque couple and the two kids," said Darren White, Public Safety Director.

Police said Cassandra Sedillo and Ben Anaya Jr. were shot to death. Johnny Ray, age four, and Matthew Gene, age three, were left in the cabin after the adults had been killed. They died of dehydration and starvation. They had been locked in the cabin without food and water according to the Office of the Medical Examiner.

At a news conference late Saturday, Public Safety Director Darren

White, who loved the spotlight, had said police believed Wilkins knew the boys were in the cabin when the December shooting occurred. White said the police had *substantial evidence and a motive but would not release details. (For the next 18 months there would be no evidence in the case.)*

Now after reading four of the newspaper articles, I knew death occurred in a remote cabin in the Sherwood Forest. The victims who had been shot to death were in there twenties. Both had been shot in the head, execution style. There were two small boys, ages four and three, who had died of dehydration and starvation. There was another person who was with them and he was alive. They called him "Popcorn."

Arrested was Shaun Wilkins, along with Roy Buchner and "Woody" Nieto. All were members of the 18th Street gang. They had the key players and it appeared they (the prosecutors) were going to make the incident to be gang related since all the boys belonged to the same gang.

The newspaper continued to say that a State Police officer had described the inside of the cabin as "The place had been trashed like someone had gone in there like a tornado." He had noticed "scorch marks on the wall and the couch half burned."

Listening to Ray talk about the grandparents' trust and belief in their grandson, I told Ray, "Now that I'm a grandparent I would not want to believe one of my sons or grandsons would be capable of doing something like this. But over the years I have seen people do some bullshit and anyone is capable of doing anything. I have heard of Torreon, New Mexico, but have never been there. I am assuming it's in Torrance County."

"You're right about that. They're saying it happened in all places, 'Sherwood Forest.'"

As I read the articles my mind started to race. I assumed the young man was shot first as he was the biggest threat to the assailant. The female, asleep next to Ben Jr., had to have woken up when the assailant shot Ben. When she woke up, she had rolled off the bed, put her arm up in a defensive manner and was shot in the arm. The bullet traveled into her chest. After she was shot in the chest, she rolled over onto her back so as to not see what was going to happen next. The killer then put the .22 rifle behind her ear and shot her in the back of the head. According to the newspaper, the four people had been dead for some time, anywhere from two weeks to months.

The first thing that came to my mind is that it appeared to be an inside job. Two people shot while they were asleep. The majority of murders are simple to solve and they have an eighty to eighty-five percent solvability factor built in. You draw a circle around the victims and then who they associate with, their family and friends. From there you can develop a suspect. The remaining fifteen percent of murders break down to ten percent of the murders committed by a weaker acquaintance (i.e. a person you met in a bar) and the last five percent by a stranger. Stranger apprehensions are rare.

On the way to the courthouse your mind starts to think about the location of where the murders occurred, especially in a case such as this where the murders had occurred in the woods. There had to be a minimum of three shots or more and no one heard anything? Noise travels far in the woods. So how did two people in the woods get shot and none of the neighbors or their dogs wake up? How close are the neighbors? Didn't anyone know they were there?

How does one sneak up onto a cabin and not make noise, especially at night? Most forests I have been in are extremely dark at night. It is very difficult to walk, much less run in the forest without stepping on sticks or falling on rocks. How does one guy, much less four, walk up to a cabin undetected?

Ray voiced the same concerns. "We have a lot of unknowns here Maurice and my client claims he has never been to the cabin, much less knows where it is."

"Ray, what is going to be important is the criminalities report. They are going to have DNA, prints, hair, clothing, blood, and projectiles, you name it. They have to have some kind of physical evidence to back up their arrest. You just don't go out and arrest someone of this magnitude of a case without evidence. It doesn't make sense. According to the newspaper they don't have a weapon at this time. This tells me they should have done a minimum of five search warrants. Warrants were probably done on each one of the boys' houses along with our client and grandparent's house."

Ray looked over at me and argued back saying, "They don't need evidence. They have two eye witnesses to their case. This makes their case very solid."

"I agree Ray, but based on my experience I have had enough smoke blown up where the sun doesn't shine to make me a hot air balloon. I don't trust witnesses. It is whoever gets to first base first." It was my past experience with district attorneys that they always cut deals with snitches to get them to say what they want. After they get what they want to hear, they give the snitches what is known as "Sweet Heart Deals."

We could see the Magistrate Court House from the freeway. A small brown stucco building surrounded by sheriff's cars, State Police cars, and unmarked units. Media hounds surrounded the buildings with their satellite dishes sticking up in the air. All the usual stations were there: Channel 7, 13, and 4.

I noticed Rod Green with his usual cigarette and mike in hand, hair blowing in the wind. Rod was waiting for us to get there so he could get his fifteen seconds of us walking into the courthouse. Both the front and back doors were surrounded by law enforcements checking IDs and keeping everyone from entering the building. They were checking brief cases and padding everyone down for weapons. Security was high but I didn't see any gang members around the courthouse. There were more uniformed officers than anyone else.

As we walked past all the media and their cameras we headed for the side door. They knew who we were but Ray told them anyway. "I'm a lawyer. This is my investigator. We're here to see our client in private."

"We're going to need to check your brief cases and your person." After a quick check of our person and brief cases they escorted us inside to the small courtroom.

The magistrate judge was a retired State Police officer. We were not going to come close to winning in his courtroom. He was already seated behind the bench wearing his black robe. He looked up from the bench after recognizing us, "You have ten minutes to talk to your client then we are starting."

The only information we had was from the newspapers. Now we were just minutes away from going into a preliminary hearing to represent our client Roy Buchner on a death penalty case.

They had put Roy in a small room with no chairs or table. We introduced ourselves to Roy and the first thing out of his mouth was, "I didn't do anything wrong. I didn't do anything wrong."

"What happened out there?" we asked. "We need to know."

"I don't know. I wasn't even there."

"When was the last time you saw Ben?"

"I think it was some time in October."

"Do you know Woody and Shaun Wilkins?"

"Yes, we all hang out together."

"Are you part of Eighteenth Street Gang?"

"Yes, sir."

"What about Ben Anaya?"

"Yeah I know who he is. But I didn't do anything wrong, I didn't kill anyone."

"Do you know Shaun?"

"Yes."

"When was the last time you saw him?"

"Last month."

"Have you ever been up to the cabin they're talking about?'

"No, never, I heard about it but I have never been there. I heard Ben had warrants and he was hiding at his dad's cabin, but I've never been up there."

"Roy, are you sure you were never there? They are bound to have some kind evidence you were there."

"I'm telling you I have never been there."

"All right Roy, we'll deal with it."

"I didn't kill anyone."

We got a knock on the door. "Time's up counselor. Judge wants to start."

Going into the case cold and having to do a preliminary hearing cold is not uncommon in doing defense work. If you're lucky they may give you the arrest warrant or the booking information. In this case we got nothing.

As we entered the courtroom there were two small tables for the attorneys. The gallery was small and you could hear the breath of the media and the law enforcement officers behind us in the back of the room.

They had no electrical plugs within reach for our laptops. As I looked over at the ADA's table I could see three, three-inch binders on her table, along with her legal brief.

As I sat down I could recognize the officers involved in the case. They were the only ones wearing suits and ties. Each of them had three black, three-inch notebooks in their hands.

I knew it had to be part of the case file they had started. What I didn't see in the audience were any of the criminalistics officers, only the investigators. It appeared to me we were not going to hear any testimony on evidence today.

I leaned over and whisper into Ray's ear. "It looks like there are only investigators here and no criminalistics officers."

Ray looked at me and said, "Don't be surprised if the ADA is not hiding them in the backroom."

As we approached our tables the District Attorney handed us four autopsy reports marked as exhibits one through four. They belonged to Cassandra Sedillo, Ben Anaya, Johnny Ray and Matthew Garcia.

Ray got up and argued, "Your honor neither our client nor myself have received any discovery. We have no police reports, no recording and now what we were receiving was a report of findings done by the Office of the Medical Examiner."

It is a rainy day in New Mexico when the defense wins any arguments with a Magistrate Judge and today was no exception. It was going to be a hot day.

"The Court notes your objection and also rules your objection and will admit one through four. Any other preliminary matters?"

Madeline Malka the assistant District Attorney stood up and said. "No, your honor. I would request, however, that the court permit me to make a very brief opening statement."

Ms. Malka at one time had been a public defender and had now switched roles. I had worked with her on a previous murder case where she had represented the accused and she thought he was innocent. I was hoping she would be fair with this case. But personal involvement in cases changes a person and their outlook.

Madeline Malka known as Mady to her friends stood up and started, "Thank you. Your honor, it is my custom in cases of this complexity and magnitude. I like to make a brief opening statement in order that both the court and, the defendant and defense counsel may track what, what it is the State intends to do during this particular proceeding.

"This is a preliminary hearing, a probable cause. your honor, the State in its amended criminal complaint, which is filed against Mr. Buchner, stating in its opening paragraph that the above named defendant is charged as a principal or accessory, pursuant to Section thirty-one-thirteen [Sec. 30-1-13] New Mexico Statutes Annotated. A person may be charged with and convicted of the crime as an accessory if he procures, counsels, aids or abets in its commission.

"Finally, the State will call Shawn Popeleski. Shawn Popeleski is also an eyewitness to the events of this date and he will be called essentially to wrap up the rest of the picture for the Court. The defendant is charged with four open counts of murder. Two counts, two open counts of murder, two of these counts contain firearm enhancement. Cassandra Sedillo and Ben Anaya, Jr., both died of gunshot wounds. That's the firearm enhancement. Even though the firearm enhancements are not charged to counts three and four, the death of the two children. Those open counts of murder still will be tracked and the testimony of the eyewitnesses and exactly how the death of these two children came about.

"Essentially, what the witnesses will tell this court is that there were several people up at the cabin; they were 'partying' quote-unquote; they were doing some drugs; they were drinking some beer; they were smoking some weed. And sometime during the course of the day, the decision was made by both defendant Shaun Wilkins, who is not here today, and defendant Roy Buchner, to steal the guns and the drugs and to kill the people that were inside the cabin. They left, went down the hill, put on ski masks and gloves, came back up the hill, surprised Shawn Popeleski who was outside the cabin, they went into the cabin, and murdered the two adults who were inside. They committed aggravated burglary or homicide and finally, armed robbery. An inference can be drawn for purposes of a probable cause hearing under these circumstances, because weapons were used and because weapons were taken. They were taken by force. This was done while Ben Anaya, Jr., the son of the owner of the cabin was in control of those items.

"Finally, your honor, the evidence will show that the firearm was never recovered. But there was indeed a firearm, a .22-caliber handgun that was used. The ski masks were put away someplace and never seen again. The gloves were burned at a rest stop not too far from the scene of the crime. Count Ten is conspiracy and that speaks for itself. The defendant, Mr. Buchner, and his cohort Mr. Wilkins combined together, agreed to commit this crime."

I leaned over to Ray and whispered, "Ray, looks like the DA is going to present two eyewitnesses to the incident who will say they were at the cabin having a party. If there is a case based on witnesses then they should or will have the forensic evidence to support their witnesses. There should be prints on the cans, in the cabin, possible cigarettes butts with DNA or saliva on them or hair from the individuals who were in the cabin." Ray was going into his trial mode and I knew when to shut up and start typing. But maybe Ray was right. All they needed were eyewitnesses to the crime.

"The State will call Agent Tom Christian."

The clerk stood up and administered the oath, "Agent Christian, do you swear or affirm that the testimony you are about to give is the truth, the whole truth and nothing but the truth, under penalty of perjury?"

"I do."

"Agent Christian, could you state your full name for the record?"

"Thomas E. Christian, Senior."

"What is your occupation?"

"I'm employed as a New Mexico State Agent."

"Okay. At the present time, what are your duties with the New Mexico State Police?"

"I'm assigned to investigation and I was the Primary at the scene."

"And have you had the opportunity or did you have the opportunity prior to this particular case, to investigate other violent felons?"

"Yes, ma'am."

"Any of those felonies been homicides?"

"Yes, ma'am."

"Did you receive a call on April fourteenth, 1996, regarding a potential crime scene in Torreon?"

"I did."

"For purposes of the record Agent Christian, where is the crime scene located, in Torreon, the report indicates approximately four miles west of Torreon, into an area that is referred to as the Sherwood Forest Subdivision? And is this up in the mountains?"

"Uh, yes, ma'am."

"And is it in Torrance County, in the state of New Mexico?"

"Yes, ma'am."

"Did you get an opportunity to get a good look at the land, at the cabin and the land up there?"

"Yes, ma'am. I do have a diagram of the eastern area of the property which would include the residence and measurements of that area."

"Okay. Can I have that? May I approach your honor?

"You may."

Mady went up to the bench. "And I don't believe defense counsel has seen this; I haven't seen it so..."

Agent Christian continued, "I actually have a total of twelve different documents and one diagram..."

The ADA stopped the agent and before he could finish, "Agent Christian could I beg you, if the Court will permit, to just do a very brief sketch if you would, kind of a geological sketch of what the cabin and the roads incoming and outgoing look like?"

Agent Christian continued, "The arrow here indicates north. Uh, this is a fenced-in area, some chain link, and some barbed wire. This is, uh, this here is a concrete pad. And there's a walkway all round it. This is, uh, a porch area, a screened-in porch. The front door is located on the west-north corner of the residence. And then this area here is the residence itself."

"I'm sorry, is there any kind of a fence that surrounds that property?"

"There's a chain link and barbed wire."

"And does it surround the entire perimeter of the house?"

"Yes, ma'am. There is a gate, right about here. In the back of the property. And the front gate is up here."

"Okay. Now, is the house situated in a flat land or on the top of a hill?"

"It's on top of a hill."

"Okay. Describe, if you would, Agent Christian, the roads leading up to the house. What are they like?"

"Initially before you can get up to the top of the hill, there is an extremely rough road. Extremely rocky. Extremely difficult to travel by car. Not impossible, but difficult."

"And where would they come up in relation to the driveway if you would just point it out?"

"The driveway is here and you have the front gate. This is a dirt road here. I'm not even sure if that is a public access road, or it's a right of way. And you travel that road about two-tenths of a mile down to another dirt road which then travels this way, connecting with it here. And then that connects out all the way to the entrance of the Sherwood Forest, and then more or less to the main county road."

"Agent Christian after you arrived and observed the outside of the cabin, did you, did you enter the cabin?"

"I did."

"Did you enter the cabin with anybody?"

"Myself, Sergeant Branch, Agent Jacoby and Mike Granger."

"What did you observe inside in the cabin?"

"Immediately upon coming into the living room area, the couch appeared to have been somewhat consumed by fire. I would say probably at least half of the couch had been almost completely burned. There was scorchy, black scorch marks up one wall into a corner, up another side, and there was quite a bit of uh, scorching on the ceiling. There would been a window over here and there was only a partial remaining part of the curtain that had been burned and that was hanging. Whatever the curtain had been, it had been consumed by fire. There was trash and debris covering the entire living room, combination kitchen area, which is piled up all over the place."

"Was there, what you might call a pathway through all this trash and debris?"

"I never really recall looking for a pathway because there wasn't any specific clear area that I saw. There was just debris everywhere. It was like the place had been trashed. Like someone had gone in there like a tornado."

"Did you have to pick your way through the trash, inside the house?"

"Yes, ma'am."

"What else did you observe sensory-wise when you walked into the house?"

"It was a god-awful smell. I mean, it was, evident that there was something dead inside of the cabin."

"Did you finally find the cause of that odor inside the house?"

"Yes, ma'am."

"And where was that located?"

"This is more or less your kitchen area. This would be the living room. This would be bedroom number one, bedroom number two and this was a bathroom in here. Immediately coming into here, we entered bedroom number one. In this area right here, up against this west wall, there was a bed. And on that bed, there was a, what appeared to be an adult male individual lying face down with his arms somewhat in this position, tucked under his body. There appeared to be some form of trauma to the back of his head. I then observed a female on the east side of the bed here, lying down on the floor. She was in a face-up position and I believe, I can't recall which one of her arms was in an upward fashion, somewhat like that. She was clothed. It was a short and shirt set, kind of white and blue stripe. The male individual was only in boxer shorts."

"At that point in time, when you, when you first arrived, in that bedroom, did you find anything that could enable you to make an identification?"

"Shortly afterwards we discovered inside the second bedroom we entered, we discovered, a small male child lying on the floor. It was quite a bit of debris covering him, I want to say, from about the waist down. All kind of junk and debris. On top there was a bunk bed. He was on the floor, and there's a bunk bed immediately next to him and there's an upper bunk bed. We discovered the other child, lying face up on top of the bunk bed. Next to the bunk bed there was a windowsill right here. And on that window sill we located a New Mexico identification card in the name of Cassandra, and I want to say Eugenia or something like that, Sedillo."

"Thank you. Were the victims that you found removed from the crime scene that night?"

"I assisted in the removal of the bodies. The bodies were bagged. I did not assist in the bagging. I did assist in the removal of the bodies when they had been bagged from inside the residence where we positioned them outside. As soon as the ambulance arrived, we then transported the bodies out to the front gate here, to the ambulance personnel. The bodies were then turned over to them."

"After the discovery of the victims, Agent Christian, what did you do next?"

"Then we did quite a bit of photographing, and quite a bit of diagramming, taking measurements, looking for any items. We did find some shell cases in the bedroom here."

The ADA stood back up. "We want to reflect, I believe the witness pointed to bedroom two where the shell cases were."

"Yes, that's right. We did quite a bit of diagramming, a lot of photographing, that night."

"How many people, by the time you began to do the diagramming and the photographing, after the discovery of the bodies, how many people were assisting you at the crime scene?"

"There were at least, probably ten to twelve State Police officers out there."

"Agent Christian, for purposes of the record, who is the case agent?"

"Frank Jacoby."

"Was he present?"

"Yes, that's correct."

"Your first day, how long were you present at the crime scene?"

"We left the crime scene, between one and one-fifteen in the morning."

"And did you return to the crime scene?"

"I did, ma'am. It was the next afternoon. "We obtained a search warrant through the district court and we went back there to, locate in the daylight and see if we could locate additional evidence, going through the residence on the outside."

"So was some of the search done the previous day in the dark?"

"That's correct, yes, ma'am."

"Did anybody do any follow-up on the fire?"

"There was a ATF agent who had arrived at the scene."

"How many times would you say you went back to the scene approximately?"

"Five. Maybe six."

"And were all, were all of those returns to the scene for the same purpose of searching the house further or were there other purposes?"

"I went the first day, the second day we had to use the warrant. I went back a third time. We scoured the entire area, going down the hills on both sides, looking for anything. And then went up another time seeking some additional evidence out of the residence. At least, I would say, probably five, five times."

"Did, did you have the opportunity at any time to interview any of the people who live up there?"

"Officially, no. Unofficially, I do know a couple that live there I've known for many, many years. I have talked to them. I have not interviewed them in an official capacity in regards to this investigation. Other agents have interviewed them in regard to this."

"Was there anything else. Agent Christian, that you can think of at this point that you observed, that we have not covered?"

"On the male individual who was lying on the bed. There was trauma to the left rear side of his head. I noticed that his head, that there was pillows on his bed. And his head was somewhat, not completely on the pillow. Somewhat on the pillow, somewhat off. And he was in a face down position. And I was looking to see if he had been shot and fallen on the bed, I was trying to make a determination was there other blood splattered, any blood trailing, blood splatter in the area? And I didn't see any whatsoever, not on the carpet. I couldn't make the determination in the living room, due to there was just too much debris. But at the area of the bed, right near the front, there was no blood in this area, nothing to indicate a fluid. And then directly under the individual there was blood that had gone from the deceased to the pillow, then had pooled off to this side of the bed, traveling down to the mattress and the box spring and then pooled on the floor. And then the same was observed underneath the female, Cassandra, on this side of the bed. Outside I had notice a scuff area where it looks like someone may have been running then tripped."

"Agent Christian, did you notice anything unusual under the body of the child that was on the floor of the bedroom?"

"Yes, underneath him, after we cleared that debris, it appeared that there had been a fire. In that bedroom underneath the child. There was a scorch black charcoal type of debris."

"Were you able to make a determination visually as to whether or not that fire had touched the child?"

"What I could see, no, ma'am. It appeared that that fire had more than likely taken place prior to that child lying down. The child from the position I could see his body in clothing, there was no burning, or scorching of the clothing or of his skin. And when I observed him, he was face-up. I did not assist in his removal from the bedroom, so I can't tell you what may have been on the backside, but from his topside, from his clothing, everything I could see on the side and fore there was no scorching or burning of the clothing or of the skin of the body."

"Agent Christian, have you seen dead bodies before?"

"Yes, ma'am."

"These people appeared to have been recently killed?"

"The only thing I can say…"

Ray came out of his chair and said, "You can't ask him unless he's qualified to answer that by expertise, your honor. The time and, the death is certainly a matter of expert testimony, not lay testimony."

The ADA responded, "Your honor, if I may. If I may ask him a couple of questions, I think what I'm getting here is not necessarily whether he can pinpoint a time of death, but, given his experience as an investigator who has investigated homicides and has seen deceased before, I think he can make a determination that the bodies were not just recently killed, within a few hours prior to that. That particular point in time, I think that's what I'm getting at. If the Court will permit, uh, I'll limit it to that."

"I'll let you ask that."

"Thank you. Agent Christian, in your experience as a police officer, how many bodies would you say you have seen?"

"It's hard to put a number on. Probably close to a hundred or more."

"Have you seen people who have been recently killed?"

"Yes, ma'am."

"And you have seen people who have been killed or have been dead quite some time, over two weeks?"

"Yes, I have some. I have seen some decomposed bodies, yes."

"And, given your own observations, not necessarily of an expert, would you say that, that the condition of these bodies was closer to that one or to the bodies who were recently dead?"

"It was closer to the situation."

"Thank you. I'll pass the witness over."

I couldn't believe he did not talk about any evidence. No mention of whose blood was whose. No finger prints, no hair fibers, nothing except the .22-shell casing.

Ray picked up his laptop with his notes and went up to the podium. "Officer Christian what was your involvement in this case?"

"I've been involved in primarily response and assist."

"Did you ever learn how it is that these bodies were discovered?"

"My understanding is that Mr. Ben Anaya, Sr., is the one who reported the incident to the Sheriff's Department in Estancia."

"Before you came in here did you have an opportunity to review any materials? What did you review?"

"My police report."

"Is your report complete?"

"Is it complete, up to this date? No. I had an initial, supplemental report done and I have much more to do."

Ray stood up. "May I see that report?"

The ADA jumped up out of her chair. "Your honor, if I may. I haven't seen the report yet, but I am wondering. If I may for the record, and Mr. Twohig's benefit, one of the situations that arose with the investigation is with Agent Christian, who was at one time assigned to Albuquerque, magically became assigned to Santa Fe. And therefore his report goes through a different channel than the report. So I think that must have just become. Just gotten that. I know that Sergeant Branch is in charge of it has not given us a copy of it yet so. Mr. Twohig has the advantage here."

I thought to myself B.S. After working with the ADAs for this long of a time period normally they are there at the scene, they do the search warrants and arrest warrants. Ms. Malka would not have come to court today without reading or having a copy of the report, plus each one of the investigators had three notebooks with them.

Ray came back with, "Your honor, in order to have an opportunity to review this report, may I ask for a recess of half an hour?"

Ms. Malka was not about to give a chance to see that report. "Your honor, if I may. Pursuant to the Magistrate Court rules and pursuant to, uh, the policy of our office, which I have, put in writing to Mr. Twohig, he is entitled to all the discovery that he needs after the preliminary hearing. The State would ask the Court that the preliminary hearing not turn into a discovery proceeding. This report has not been made available to me. I haven't had the benefit of the report. I've had only the benefit of my discussions with Agent Christian and with the other officers. Mr. Twohig did not file a motion for production order. I would ask that the Court allow us to proceed with this preliminary. He can have plenty of time to review this afterwards."

Ray responded, "Then I'm not asking that the hearing be canceled, I'm asking that I have a short recess to review what looks like about three-quarters of an inch of material, in order to be able to effectively cross-examine this witness."

Ms. Malka was not about to give up the report. "And I'm asking, I'm suggesting to the correct act, that report goes beyond the scope of any direct examination that was presented. And therefore to effectively cross-examine the witness all Mr. Twohig needs to do is recollect what was asked by the State."

The Judge: "You're entitled to cross-examine based on anything that was brought out in direct. I don't see that your examination of that report is going to be of a nature that this Court should allow that continuance to be made available to you if you please during the preliminary hearing. I am going to afford a stay; you may proceed with your cross-examination."

Ray also was not giving up the fight. "I'm going to make this report as Defendant Exhibit A."

Ms. Malka: "And your honor, I'm going to object. I don't know that counsel move as submission, but I'm going to object to any motion as to the admission of that report as hearsay. Police reports are specifically excluded as hearsay in this code of evidence. Evidence as exhibits for exhibition purposes I have no problem."

The judge replied, "I believe this defense is Exhibit A."

Ray went back to the officer. "Officer Christian, now you said that you had some diagrams, some official diagrams. Do they show a lot of surrounding area in addition to the house itself?"

"Yeah, they show some of this area here. There were other diagrams that were done by other officers that would entail the entire property outlay."

"Where did you park?"

"Down here, sir. Where the road is in here, I parked right in here, sir."

"In the course of your investigation of this scene, you went into the premises. Were there people already inside in the house?"

"There had been people to my knowledge that had already gone inside, that is correct."

"And were there some already there when you went in?"

"When I got in, when I arrived here, there was nobody up here."

"When you got in the house, and you saw all the garbage and debris and that sort of thing all around, could you identify anything about the nature of that debris?"

"It was a lot of empty food cans. There were a lot of broken items. It just, it looked like someone had just gone through the place. And just tore it apart."

"And this fire that you saw was in the living room, I think you said. That is."

"Yeah, there was a fire. My observation and I'm not an arson investigator, but where the couch was in here, you see where the plants, you see where the heat had traveled up and scorched the ceiling and the walls. And we had checked these doors here, because we noticed inside the bedrooms on the ceilings there was no scorching, no black smoke, no soot. We noticed that when you look at the, the framing, if I can come over here, I'll show you real quick. Say this door here, there was soot damage here, and when you'd open the door here, it would come in here, and that's about where it would stop. So the doors had been closed at the time of the fire to prevent smoke from getting in. Or excuse me, getting into the bedroom."

"And both the bedroom doors were closed when you arrived?"

"I recall when, when we came in, was somewhat open. I don't want to say it was in a full position, but I don't remember it being closed. Where we had to fully open it. It was somewhat open. And the same thing with this bedroom door here. It wasn't open completely, but it was somewhat open."

"Do you have a record or information concerning who had been at the scene prior to your arrival?"

"My report will reflect that actually to the best of my memory there was a, a Detective Lieutenant Luis Henna, Marcus Harden, Susan Encinas, Jimmy Chavez, Sergeant Villanueva, Deputy Gallegos, Vivo with the Torrance County Sheriff's Department. There may be someone I missed. All my grand jury and deputy district attorney Malka. Those are the people upon my arrival. I arrived with Frank Agent Jacoby, Sergeant Branch, myself. New Mexico State Police officer Mike Fenner was in uniform and Sergeant Mike Garley with the Torrance County Sheriff's Department."

"Who was in charge of this scene?"

"For the Sheriff's Department, my assumption is Lieutenant Henna."

"What steps had been made to secure the scene?"

"At that point in time, to the best of my recollection, everybody was out here. When I arrived, I noted my arrival time and I took down the names of all the deputies, the district attorney and all mind that were present."

"Was there trash or debris outside the premises?"

"Yeah, there were beer cans, bottles, shell casings, that were discovered all around. We found, altogether we found three .22-caliber shell cases in what, appeared to be .22-caliber shell cases inside the bedroom here."

"You're speaking of bedroom number one?"

"Right."

"Where Mr. Anaya was found?"

"Yes. And then on the porch area here there was this screen. This is the door. Right here. On the window ledge, there was a shell casing from, uh, what indicated on the bottom of the shell casing, a .45 caliber. An empty, spent .45 caliber shell casing."

"Find any guns?"

"No, not to my knowledge."

"Now I notice you've done some of the diagrams you showed us."

"Yes, sir."

"Was the house locked when you arrived?"

"When I arrived, no, sir."

"Was the bedroom locked?"

"No, I don't recall, don't recall the bedroom being locked. Like I said, I believe the door wasn't fully closed, but it wasn't fully open. To the best of my recollection."

"Near the rounds that were located in the bedroom, did you see any sign of any powder or soot?"

"No, I can't say."

"And what was the placement of the rounds in the bedroom?"

"Okay. This the bedroom, again, to the arrow pointing north.. And on the east wall, we found a shell casing here. Excuse me, right, yeah, right here. One by the front door here, as you open in. Off the doorjamb. One feet, nine inches. And then to the south, one feet, five inches. Then we found one under the bed here. And then one over there, we found three spent shell cases."

"And they were all the same caliber?"

"From visual observation, I didn't do any marking or anything. They all appeared to be that of .22 caliber shell cases."

"All right, thank you, sir. Now you described a gentleman who was in bedroom number one. You said he was face down and his hands were under his body."

"The best I recall, the only clothing I recall on him was boxer shorts."

"Who did, who was responsible for that at the crime scene?"

"I don't know. You have to ask my supervisor." *As I continued to type I made notes there was no crime scene team at the cabin.*

"What injuries, if any, did you observe? And you mentioned something about there was some trauma to the left rear of his head. And approximately where in the left rear? Toward the top of the head?"

"Down behind the ear."

"Can you give us a description of some of the physical manifestations of that, please."

"Where I noticed it immediately was, on the feet and the toe areas, they really seem to shrivel up and they start. They lose any and all moisture in them. And that was one of the signs to me that they had been dead for quite some time. In my opinion, based on my experience. And that they hadn't been just recently killed."

"Did you notice that on all four people who were there?"

"The only two I had really taken direct notice of was Cassandra. I noticed it with her hand, with Ben Jr., with his feet. And then I want to be perfectly honest with you, with the children, I did not look or did not choose to look too much at them. Although I did."

"Was the scene videotaped?"

"It was."

"Was the scene photographed?"

"It was."

"Do you have photographs present?"

"No, sir. I didn't take photographs and I did not videotape. I did. I take it back. I videotaped the next day the outside area, but not the inside."

"Going to, the second person, that is, the second, the woman who you've marked Two, you said that the person in there was female and that she had certain clothing on. Bedroom number one sir?"

"Where Cassandra and Ben were found. Bedroom number two is where the two children were located."

"And the two children in bedroom two?"

"Correct."

"All right, looking next still at bedroom one, Cassandra on the floor, what position was her body in?"

"She was in a face-up position. One of her arms somewhat in this position, don't remember if it was a left or right arm. Like I said, on her back, face-up. With her legs pointing to the south and head to the north."

"What clothing were the children wearing?"

"The one on the top bunk bed was, naked from the waist up. It is my understanding he had no clothes on. But I did not. It seemed somewhat of a heavy blanket or a sleeping bag that was covering his lower torso. I did not lift it up so I don't know if he had anything. I was told he was naked. The child on the floor definitely he had on, it was a khaki colored pants, light pants and a yellow short-sleeve shirt."

"Did you see any bullet holes anywhere in the premises?"

"No not off hand, no, sir."

"And did you yourself participate in the search of the premises for items such as that?"

"That's correct."

"What items were recovered from the premises, sir?"

"Shell casings, we did some locate some paperwork. Baptismal certificates, social security cards, we did take some empty food cans. And at this point, that's about it. I can't recall. I mean there were some other things that were taken. I have a list of items that were removed."

"Did you discover any sign, any footprints, did you seize any footprints in the course of this investigation?"

Mady stood up. "Objection, your honor. Apparently counsel doesn't understand the Court's ruling. I think what counsel is doing, just asking the next question on his list. But what the State would ask the Court to do now is limit the defense to asking questions pertaining to the questions that were asked by the State. And, I think, I think an admonishment might be in order. Otherwise, I think I'm going to have stand up and object to every question the counsel, the counsel arrive at. I don't know how else to do this, your honor."

You could see the Judge's neck start to turn a bright red. "Counsel, we're not going to turn this into a four or five day fact-finding mission. This is a preliminary hearing. This is to determine probable cause. I'm going to sustain your objection and ask that you stick to cross examination based on direct testimony."

Mady continued, "Yes, your honor, I will do so and my objection to Court's ruling."

Ray asked the agent, "You have not previously interviewed my client, right?"

"That's correct, sir."

"Have you been present when he's made any statement about this matter?"

"No, sir."

"Thank you. No further questions at this time. I'm noting my objections to the limitations on the cross examination."

Mady stood back up. "Thank You. The State will call Agent Eric Lucero."

The judge looked over to Agent Lucero. "Agent Lucero, would you raise your right hand. Do you swear or affirm that the testimony you are about to give is the truth, the whole truth and nothing but the truth, under penalty of perjury?"

Mady looked over at the agent from her podium. "Thank you, your honor. Agent Lucero, could you state your full name for the record and your occupation?"

"Eric Lucero, I'm an agent with the New Mexico State Police. I investigate cases, criminal cases that are assigned by my supervisor."

"Agent Lucero, how did you become involved in this case?"

"I was assigned to assist Agent Frank Jacoby with the homicide up in Torreon."

"And as part of your assignment, your duties in this case, did you have occasion to interview Lawrence Nieto?"

"Yes, I did."

"And, how did this come about?"

"I contacted Mr. Nieto (Woody) in Santa Fe on the concept that additional information could be gained concerning the homicides in question."

"Agent Lucero, did you see Lawrence Nieto in the courthouse today?"

"I saw him earlier."

"When you interviewed him in Santa Fe, was he in custody?"

"He was in custody, yes, he was."

"And do you know what he was in custody on?"

"Yes, my understanding it, he was in custody as a material witness."

So that's how they did it. They are going to claim Woody was not under arrest for murder, just as a material witness. Therefore he didn't need a lawyer as he was just a material witness. After he gives his statement they could arrest him for murder.

"And was it your understanding at that time that he had been charged with any of the crimes pertinent to this case?"

"At that time he was not charged with any crime, as far as I know."

"You mirandized him at that interview in Santa Fe?"

"Yes, ma'am, I did."

"And did he waive those rights?"

"Yes."

"Did you at any time during that interview, or at any other time, promise Mr. Nieto anything?"

"No, I did not."

"How did you begin your interview with him after you mirandized him?"

"I think I told him that I, I wanted to talk to him about the incident in question and I wanted him to tell the truth."

"And in response to your first question, what did he tell you?"

"That he just said that he was willing to tell the truth."

"Did he tell you whether or not he went to the Anaya cabin in Torreon that day?"

"Yes, he did."

Ray stood up. "Objection. Statements are misleading. They are made hearsay."

Mady argued back, "Your honor, the State at this point in time has a motion to admit all of the testimony of Agent Eric Lucero, regarding the statements made by Mr. Nieto pursuant to 11-804B3. For that purpose, your honor, the State has supplied with State vs. Self and State vs. Puerta. The State is making this motion pursuant to the fact while this is hearsay, it is indeed an exception to the hearsay rule, and it is a statement against interest. That is a statement which was, at the time of its making, so far contrary to the declarant's pecuniary or proprietary interest or so far tended to subject the declarant to civil or criminal liability or to rendering valid a claim by the declarant against another, that a reasonable person in the declarant's position would not have made the statement unless believing it to be true. A statement tending to expose declarant to criminal liability and offer to exculpate the accused, that is, that is not relevant but I read it into the record, an offer to exculpate the accused is not admissible unless corroborating circumstances clearly indicate the trustworthiness of the statement. Your honor, essentially the rationale behind this rule is that nobody in his or her right mind makes a statement him or herself in a crime that is clearly a statement that implicates himself or herself in a crime unless that statement is true. Therefore, there is an underlying reasonable issue of reliability and if the Court will direct its attention to the case applied to by the State, the Court will note that essentially what we have here is a test that has to be used."

Mady continued, "This test follows the federal test. It is essentially a three-part test. The three-part test goes something like this: (1) for purposes of a statement against interest and for declarant unavailability, unavailable, that the Court must make the finding that the declarant is indeed unavailable. When a Fifth Amendment privilege is claimed, the declarant becomes unavailable and this Court has made such a finding. (2) on .... If the statement that is offered by the witness who heard the statement against the declarant's penal interest. In other words, does it so clearly implicate the declarant in a crime that under ordinary circumstances and without any coercion, would he have made a statement like that? The State admits that under these particular circumstances and what the State intends to do right now is to offer a tender to the Court. So that the Court can then make a ruling on this. That this indeed was a statement so far against Mr. Nieto's penal interest, that he would have never made such a statement unless it was clear and unless it was true. The third part of the text, your honor, is that the statement against interest can be corroborated in some way. That is the weakest part of the test, because essentially that goes to whether or not the State has offered to exculpate somebody. What we have here, your honor, is the interview that was done by Agent Lucero of Lawrence Nieto. The interview was done in custody. The custody occurred as a result of a material witness warrant. Mr. Nieto essentially knew he was that he was going to be questioned, he was placed in custody essentially for his own, his own protection and also so that the State could have access to him. He had not been charged at that particular point in time and when he made the statement, your honor, at the time he was making the statement, the State had no intention of charging him. At that particular point in time, however, and the State submits this to the Court as its strongest proof; this was a declaration against his penal interest. The statement so strongly implicated him in the crime that the State felt the need to charge him. What Mr. Nieto simply tender will testify to is that he was present at the scene of the crime, he went up from Albuquerque during the day, he partied with Cassandra, with Ben, with the children, with another witness, Shawn Popeleski. He went up to the house with the defendant and with his co-defendant Shaun Wilkins. They partied during the day; at some time toward the end of the day, a signal was given to Mr. Nieto to go outside. He went outside with Mr. Wilkins and the defendant. He was told at a certain time during the day that the reason that they were going up there was to 'blast Popcorn'. That's Mr. Popeleski. The decision was made sometime during the day by the defendant and by Mr. Wilkins to steal the guns and the drugs that were present in the residence. They had prepared themselves to do this by bringing weapons and masks with them, and also gloves. They went back down the hill; they stayed by the vehicle for around thirty minutes to an hour.

"At which time, Mr. Nieto was ordered to put a ski mask on by Mr. Wilkins. Mr. Buchner, the defendant, also put a ski mask on and put a pair of gloves on. Mr. Buchner and Mr. Wilkins armed themselves, Mr. Buchner with a thirty-ought-six, Mr. Wilkins with a .22 caliber, at least a .22 caliber handgun. Uh, Mr. Nieto was told to take a shotgun up the hill and he was given the assignment of 'blasting, blasting Popcorn.' They went up the hill, the three of them, the three of them wearing ski masks. Mr. Nieto also wore a ski mask. They encountered Shawn Popeleski (Popcorn) outside the residence, where he was relieving himself. Mr. Nieto was told to get rid of Mr. Popeleski outside the residence.

"He placed Mr. Popeleski face down on the ground, put his foot on Mr. Popeleski's back, put a gun barrel to the back of his head while the defendant and Mr. Wilkins walked into the house. Mr. Nieto then heard gunshots and miraculously, he let Mr. Popeleski go. However, as we observed, he saw the defendant and Mr. Wilkins taking guns out of the house, go back down to the car, running, moving quickly, loading up the car with the guns, loading up the car with the drugs. He then accompanied Mr. Wilkins and Mr. Buchner to the car where he took off his ski mask, they took off their ski masks and gloves, put them in the back of the car. They left. They destroyed the gloves by burning them at a rest stop or at an area not too far from Torreon. He observed the burning of the gloves... the tampering with evidence.

"He observed the putting away of the ski masks, didn't know what happened to the ski masks. He observed the loading up of the weapons; he heard the gunshots. The State would submit, pursuant to that tender, that this declaration is most certainly against Mr. Nieto's penal interest. He is not available and the State intends, at this point in time, to call also Detective Juan Areas and Mr. Popeleski to testify."

The DA had provided us more information than any witness had up to this point and she did it without looking at her notes. She was definitely driving the train.

Judge Jones was going to side with the DA. "The Court will overrule and note for the record, defense counsel's objections. It will allow the testimony of Agent Eric Lucero under the hearsay exception with declarant unavailable. And the State may proceed."

Assistant District Attorney Mady was very happy after she made her speech voicing the objection. This also told me she anticipated Ray Twohig jumping up on the hearsay rule and had come prepared. At the same time, I kept thinking to myself, what do we need Agent Lucero for? The Assistant District Attorney had just told the judge everything he was going to say. She had done all of this without a script. She was into this case and she was up to her knees in the shit. She had to have been present for all the interviews.

Mady was happy with her argument. "Thank you, your honor."

Ray got back up. "Will the Court allow me to voir dire (a legal phrase that refers to an oath to tell the truth) on the issue of what evidence of the statements actually being made to this, such as tape recordings, etc."

"The Court will allow you to voir dire."

Mady came back with, "The state will submit to the Court that there is a video tape recording of this particular statement. The State got access to it yesterday, observed it last night and this morning and most certainly will make it available to defense counsel."

"May I then request that (it)be made an exhibit rather than about the statement, preserving my objection to the statement itself."

It was apparent the ADA Mady did not want us to have or see anything. "Well, your honor, the problem with that is that we do not have a copy available right now to be made an exhibit."

I leaned over to Ray, "They have had this case for a month and half and never made copies of the videos. Are you shitting me?"

Ray argued back, "If the Court please, it would appear that what Counsel is saying is that the videotape, the best evidence of the statement itself, may contain other matters. The videotape itself will indicate a great deal more about the actual circumstances of the statement by showing the witness himself actually talking."

Agent Lucero went on to regurgitate what ADA Mady had argued to the judge.

Mady went on with the agent, "Thank you. Agent Lucero, did he tell you, did Mr. Nieto tell you whether or not he went to the Anaya cabin that day?"

"Yes, he did."

"Okay. And what time did he tell you he went there?"

"That he arrived at the cabin about three o'clock that afternoon."

The ADA continued. "And with whom did he arrive at that cabin?"

"With, Shaun Wilkins also known as Sager and, Roy Buchner, also known as Eazy."

"And did he tell you what the point of origin was, where they started from?"

"From Albuquerque. From the residence of uh, Mr. Lawrence Nieto."

Mady knew all the answers to her questions. "And did Mr. Nieto tell you why they were going to the Anaya cabin in Torreon?"

"Upon leaving the residence, Mr. Nieto believed they were going up there to party with Ben Anaya Jr."

"Did Mr. Nieto tell you approximately or at all what route they took to the cabin?"

"He said that they went east on Central from the residence of Mr. Nieto, that they had left on Rio Grande to 1-40 and 20 somehow or another they ended up on a dirt road which led them up to the residence of Mr. Anaya."

"And at any time did Mr. Nieto tell you that he had learned on what the defendant and Mr. Wilkins intended to do?"

"Yes, en route to the cabin, according to Mr. Nieto, Sager and Roy Buchner told him they were going up there to 'blast' Popcorn." *I started thinking to myself. Blast Popcorn, but instead they kill Ben and Cassandra in their sleep. Lock the kids in the cabin to die. How many theories do they have?*

Agent Lucero continued, "Mr. Nieto, stated later on in the day that they intended to steal the guns, the marijuana and cocaine that belonged to Ben Anaya Jr. In addition, again, to blast Popcorn."

Mady knew this was a small problem in the case. "Did he tell you why they wanted to blast Popcorn?"

"According to Mr. Nieto, they wanted to blast Popcorn, because they consider him to be a snitch."

"Did he give you any information as to what event caused him to be a snitch?"

"Apparently an incident occurred in Arizona between them. But he did not go into detail as to what had happened."

"What did Mr. Nieto tell you that he and Wilkins and the defendant did when they arrived at the cabin?"

"Upon arrival at the cabin, according to Mr. Nieto, he drank beer and smoked marijuana with Popcorn. At this time, according to Mr. Nieto, again, Buchner, or Roy Buchner and Sager apparently started cocaine with Ben Anaya Jr. and apparently they also viewed some weapons that Ben had."

"Did Mr. Nieto tell you who else was at that cabin?"

"Yes, he said, Popcorn and two kids that belonged to Cassandra."

"Did Lawrence tell you what time of the day he and the others left the cabin?"

"For the first time they left around nine o'clock pm that evening."

"Did Mr. Nieto tell you how he knew it was time to leave?"

"Yes, he said that, Sager, Shaun Wilkins, had motioned for him to go outside and he knew that that was a signal to go outside."

"For the record, your honor, Agent Lucero has made a gesture where he jerked to the left as a sign. To the right as a sign. It all depends on how he was sitting in the cabin, but basically made a motion for him to go outside with his head."

"Did Mr. Nieto tell you whether or not he'd used drugs that day?"

"Yes, he did. He said he had smoked marijuana and he drank beer. Okay. And at nine o'clock pm when he and Wilkins and the defendant left the cabin."

"What did they do?"

"According to Mr. Nieto they walked from the residence of Ben Anaya, Jr., down to the vehicle which was parked down the driveway."

"Okay. And how long did they remain at the vehicle?"

"According to Mr. Nieto, between thirty to forty-five, possibly an hour."

"What did they do while they were down there at the vehicle?"

"According to Mr. Nieto they put on black clothing. He specifically said Sager and Buchner put on black clothing and some black masks. And this point they, uh, they, uh, told Mr. Nieto that they were going to sneak up to the residence, blast Popcorn and steal the guns, cocaine and marijuana."

"And did Mr. Nieto put a mask on?"

"Yes, he did. According to him, he did."

"And did he arm himself?"

"According to him, yes."

"Did Mr. Nieto tell you what the defendant was armed with?"

"According to Mr. Nieto, Roy Buchner, he was armed with a thirty-ought-six rifle."

"And did he tell you what Mr. Wilkins was armed with?"

"Yes, he said he was armed with a .22 caliber semiautomatic pistol."

"And what was he armed with?"

"According to Mr. Nieto, he was armed with a shotgun."

"Did he tell you whether that shotgun was racked?"

"According to Mr. Nieto, Sager racked the shotgun, handed it to him."

"Did Mr. Nieto and the others encounter somebody outside the house when they got up to the top?"

"Okay, upon, arriving at the residence a second time, they noticed Popcorn, like you said, relieving himself outside of the residence. And at this point it … to Mr. Nieto. Sager told him, 'Go around the residence and put him on the ground and hold him.' And at this point they went into the residence."

"Okay. When you say. they, who went into the residence?"

"Buchner and Sager."

"And did Mr. Nieto remain outside?"

"He remained outside with Mr. Popeleski, or Popcorn."

"What did he do with Mr. Popeleski?"

"According to Mr. Nieto, he told Popcorn, 'It's me, Woody, get on the ground.' And basically just remain quiet."

"Did Mr. Nieto tell you whether he was able to observe anything that went on inside that, inside the cabin?"

"He was unable to observe anything inside the cabin, because he was outside with Popcorn. But he did hear something that happened inside the cabin."

"What did he hear?"

"According to him, he heard about eight shots come from within the residence."

"And at that point in time what did he tell you he did?"

"He basically fired that twenty-gauge shotgun in the air and told Popcorn to leave, get out of there. At which point, according to Mr. Nieto, Popcorn left."

"Okay. Did Mr. Nieto tell you whether he observed Mr. Buchner and Mr. Wilkins leaving the residence?"

"Shortly after Popcorn took off, according to Mr. Nieto, he saw Eazy, Mr. Roy Buchner, coming out of the residence holding his gun. And he also indicated that he saw Sager carrying marijuana and cocaine in his hand."

"Okay. Did he tell you about anything else that Mr. Buchner did prior to their leaving the scene of the crime?"

"According to Mr. Nieto, as they were leaving the residence, halfway down to the vehicle from the residence, Roy Buchner also known as Eazy, ran back to the residence and locked the door to the residence."

If Roy locked the residence where did he get the keys from? How was it there was a set of keys in the Jeep? How was it Ben Sr. found a set of keys to the cabin?

"What did Mr. Nieto tell you happened when they arrived back at the vehicle? Were they, were both Mr. Wilkins and Mr. Buchner carrying anything?"

"According to Mr. Nieto, Sager was carrying marijuana and cocaine and Eazy was carrying the gun."

"And what did they do when they arrived at the car?"

"They took off. According to Mr. Nieto, they took off. Sager and Eazy took off the masks and, threw them in the back of the car."

"Thank you. Did they make a stop anyplace at all? During the course of their trip back?"

"According to Mr. Nieto, they stopped at a rest area some distance away from the cabin and at this point, they burned the gloves, masks, burned the clothing.."

"Okay. Agent Lucero, do you know what if any ski masks were recovered in the investigation of this case?"

"My recollection they have not having been covered."

"And to the best of your knowledge, was the .22 caliber weapon recovered?"

"To my recollection it has not been found."

"Did Mr. Nieto tell you anything else about the events of the day at the cabin at Torreon?"

"Nothing, not offhand."

"Okay. Thank you, I'll pass the witness."

The judge looked over at Ray. "You may cross examine."

Ray got up and asked "Was a written statement prepared for Mr. Nieto's signature?"

"No, sir."

"Did he sign any statement?"

"He signed a waiver of rights."

"Do you have it with you?"

"Yes, I have it with me."

"And this was signed at one fifteen pm on May fifteenth, 1996?"

"Yes, sir."

"Who was present?"

"Me and Lawrence Nieto."

"Was anyone else present?"

"No. Not at that time."

"Was this the first statement Mr. Nieto made?"

"No."

"He had made other statements?"

"I had taken another statement from him."

"Was that prior to the one at eight pm?"

"Yes."

"Was he in custody at that time?"

"No."

"What did he say in that first statement that he took? That you took?"

"Okay, that statement was taken on April the twenty-fourth, 1996 in Albuquerque. At that point he basically stated that, Roy Buchner and Sager drove off to his residence in a maroon vehicle. At that time, stated that they had just come from the cabin and that, according to him, pulled some shit out there."

"Now, in the first statement, did he describe the vehicle?"

"He described a maroon-colored vehicle."

"Did he say what model it was?"

"No. He didn't."

"In the second statement, did he give you a more specific description of the vehicle?"

"He did say it was a black Trans Am."

"In the first statement did he acknowledge that he was involved in any way in any plans or coordination, leading up to the shootings?"

"No."

"Not arrested and brought in to custody by somebody?"

"He was, he was being held as a material witness but I don't know for how long."

"You know what his circumstances were at that time? When the last time he had slept, the last time he had ate."

"No, I didn't."

"You know if others had questioned him before you did?"

"I was aware of that ... Mike Fenner and I believe Detective Juan Reyes from APD questioned him on a prior occasion but I don't know exactly when that interview took place."

"When you questioned him was that part of the videotape?"

"Yes."

"Where is the videotape?"

"Right here."

"You reviewed them before you testified?"

"Yes."

"Did Mr. Nieto make other statements other than the one you've testified to here today, about the reason he was told that they were going to kill Popcorn?"

"No."

"Did he tell you of any discussion, between himself and Mr. Buchner and/or Mr. Wilkins concerning, uh, whether or not any of them were participating?"

"According to Mr. Nieto ... to the cabin and halfway out Sager and ... Sager and Buchner. That's what they had the discussions about how ... that's on the way driving ... right. Before they even got there to party, he said, according to him."

"Did he tell you he did not agree to participate?"

"He basically said that he did not want to participate and told them he did not want to kill Popcorn."

"Can you describe any discussion at that point as to whether they should or should not kill Popcorn?"

"According to Mr. Nieto, Sager and Eazy were still intent on killing Popcorn and they did not."

"When the signal was given, approximately what time was that?"

"He said about, uh, he didn't give me a time. But it appeared it was right around eight o'clock."

"That would be eight o'clock or nine o'clock."

"Eight o'clock or nine-thirty. He said basically at nine o'clock is when they left. And, uh, an hour later is when they left. So it would be about eight o'clock."

"Did he tell you the date when this occurred?"

"He said it was around January the thirteenth or fourteenth, but he wasn't sure." *I was taking notes on dates and times—by the thirteenth or 14th of January they were already dead. I was passing notes to Ray.*

"Did you or anyone else to your knowledge fix the time of death in this case?"

"I believe that they have been just around December sometime. I'm not too sure on that."

"So Mr. Nieto told you that this had occurred after the State contends it did occur. He said it occurred around January the thirteenth or fourteenth of January. In the course of your statement with him, did he explain to you how he fixed that date?"

"He didn't explain."

"Did he tell you what day of the week it was?"

"No, he didn't."

"Did he tell you of any other events that occurred on that day that may help you think?"

"No, sir."

"Did you discuss the time with him? That is the date itself with him, in your interrogation?"

"No, I didn't."

"Did he tell you anything about drugs?"

"He said that Buchner was carrying the guns and Sager was marijuana and cocaine."

"Did he say anything about drugs being ingested, consumed by any of the participants there that day?"

"Yes, he said that both Buchner and Sager were snorting cocaine."

"Did he say anything about himself?"

"Yes, he just said, 'I smoked grass, and drank beer.'"

"Did he say anything about his own consumption of coke?"

"No cocaine. Just the marijuana."

"Did he say that this was crack cocaine?"

"He called it soda. I'm not too familiar with the terminologies."

"Did, he tell you anything about the children being there that day?"

"Yes, he said that two kids that belonged to Cassandra were in the cabin at that time."

"Did he say he actually had seen the children?"

"Yes, he actually saw the children, spoke with the children. In fact, he claims that he shook hands with one of those boys. I don't remember which one he said, but he shook hands with one of them. According to Mr. Nieto, he was inside the cabin."

"And, did he give you any idea how much quantity of cocaine he himself consumed?"

"He just said that he drank a quart of beer on the way up and drank some beer. But he never gave an indication as to how much."

"Did he say where they were in the cabin during the day when this, during the time, prior to the time the signal was given?"

"He didn't say exactly where in the living room. Because, a living room, kitchen and three bedrooms, I believe. And they were in the living room."

"Did you ask him at all and did he say anything about trash being around the living room?"

"He didn't say anything concerning that."

"Well, did you ask about that?"

"No."

Agent Lucero did not know the facts or the evidence and we are now in May 15th and they still don't know the evidence.

"When you ask him did he say anything about whether or not there was any sign of a fire?"

"He did not give any indication about that."

"Did you, ask him anything about any signs of a fire?"

"I did not."

"Did, you ask him anything about whether they're during the course of the events, the shootings, etc. that you talked about, anyone set a fire?"

"No, sir."

"You said that he said that the decision was made to the take guns and drugs from Anaya. Did he tell you how that decision was made or who made it?"

"According to Mr. Nieto, Sager told him 'We're going to go up there, sneak up there, we're going to steal the guns, and we're going to take the marijuana, take the cocaine and we're going to blast Popcorn.' According to Mr. Nieto."

"When did Nieto say that Sager said that to him, in the sequence of events?"

"Okay, in the sequence of events, when they left the residence the first time, walked down to the vehicle, when they put on the masks, black clothing, armed themselves with weapons. As they were walking up, this plan according Mr. Nieto was what Sager said, 'This is what we're, going to do.' That was the plan."

"Did he report anything about Buchner making any statement at that time?"

"Not at that time."

"Did he tell you whose car they had driven up there?"

"According to Mr. Nieto, he said it was probably a stolen car."

"In the course of his statement, did he tell whose car they left in?"

"They left in the same vehicle, the black Trans Am."

"Did he tell you anything about what type of vehicles were already up there when he got there?"

"He only vehicle that he indicated was up there was a Jeep that belonged to Ben Anaya, Jr."

"Did he say that Jeep remained there, when he left that evening?"

"Mr. Nieto never indicated that. He just said that they left."

"Going now to the description that he gave you concerning what happened after they put masks on and went back up to the scene, uh, did he tell you where he himself was holding Popcorn?"

"Yes, he did."

"Where did he say that was?"

"To the north, northern part of the residence outside."

"And did he give you some, did he pinpoint that in any way. In any drawing?"

"No, he didn't."

"Did he march Popcorn from one place to another?"

"No. According to Mr. Nieto, as they were sneaking up to the residence, they spotted Popcorn relieving himself on the northern part of the residence. At this point, according to Mr. Nieto, Sager told him, 'There's Popcorn. Get him and … hold him down.' At this point, according to Mr. Nieto, he went around the residence, he came around, told Popcorn, 'It's me, Woody. Get on the ground.' And basically put his foot on his back and put the shotgun to his head and told him to stay there."

"So, in other words, Popcorn was held, according to Nieto, at the location where he was relieving himself?"

"Yes. That's according to Mr. Nieto."

"All right. Did Nieto tell you anything about the spacing of the shots?"

"He didn't say anything about the spacing; he said he just heard eight shots. According to Mr. Nieto, when they had left the residence they were back in the vehicle, saying that Eazy Buchner was laughing. And according to Mr. Nieto, Sager said, 'We got away with it.' And according to him, there were no more witnesses."

"According to who, Sager or Buchner?"

"Okay, according to Mr. Nieto, he stated Eazy was laughing because they got away with it and there were no witnesses. That's all I have on my report, on the table."

"Did Mr. Nieto tell you anything about how all three of them left together?"

"They left in a black Trans Am." (*Now the color is black and it is a Trans Am from a Maroon Camaro.*)

"You described him saying they had black clothing, is that correct?"

"According to Mr. Nieto, Eazy and Sager had black clothing."

"Did he himself have black clothing?

"According to him, he had on a blue mask."

"Did he say anything about the black clothing being destroyed?"

"According to him, they destroyed the masks, and I believe the clothing. I'm not too sure on that."

"You don't know whether he said they destroyed the clothing or not?"

"I don't know."

"Did he say what happened to the firearm that he had?"

"He did not give any information regarding knowledge about what happened to the weapons."

"Did he tell you anything about there being any discussion at all about whether to kill or injure, Ben Anaya, at any point?"

"According to Mr. Nieto, there wasn't any discussion about Mr. Anaya. Only Popcorn."

"Which rest area did he say they stopped at?'

"He didn't indicate which one specifically."

"Are there rest areas that exist between the location of the killing and Albuquerque?"

"I'm not familiar with that part of the country, if you will. But I believe that there are some places that could be considered rest areas."

"Did you take him out there to ask him to show you where this rest area was?"

"I did not."

"I have no further questions at this time."

Mady just showed us how to get in testimony of a witness without him testifying. We had no right to confrontation of Woody. Our biggest surprise was yet to come.

Mady stood up. "The State Will Call Detective Juan DeReyes"

The judge swore in the detective. "Officer DeReyes, would you raise your right hand. Do you swear or affirm that the testimony you are about to give is the truth, the whole truth and nothing but the truth, under penalty of perjury?"

"Yes, your honor."

Mady looked over at Detective Reyes with a grin. "Officer DeReyes, could you state your full name for the record."

"Juan DeReyes, I'm a detective with the Albuquerque Police Department, Metro Gang Unit."

"And how long have you been a police officer?"

"Fourteen and a half years."

"And what are your duties with the Metro Gang Unit?"

"We investigate, violent crimes committed by gang members and we concentrate on that particular area in the city or outside the city."

"Detective, this is a State Police case. How did you happen to become involved in it?"

"The Department of Public Safety requested through our chief of police that, the State Police had these homicides. They believed that it was gang-related. They contacted our department and they assigned myself as one of the task force."

"What is involved, in the task force?"

"We did field interviews with various individuals, witnesses, suspects, anybody that could provide us with leads or information regarding the homicides. We went out and talked to them."

"And did you have occasion during your, have occasion after you had been contacted by the Department of Public Safety to come into contact with Roy Buchner?"

"Yes, during one of our interviews."

"Detective, do you see Roy Buchner sitting in this courtroom today?"

"Yes, ma'am."

"Could you point him out to the Court?"

"He's between his attorney and the unknown gentleman here, wearing a black suit and a white shirt."

"Officer DeReyes, what's a moniker?"

"A moniker is a name that the, an individual uses on the street level, aside from his real name. The nickname or a different alias."

"What is Roy Buckner's moniker?'

"Eazy."

"Detective, do you know Lawrence Nieto?"

"Yes, I do."

"And what is his moniker?"

"They call him Woody."

"How do you know him?"

"Through some investigations our unit had conducted on a particular gang we had come across this individual before. And we have documented them as self-admitted gang members. And we have documented them through photographs and information and both documented the monikers and the real names."

"Officer DeReyes, during the course of this investigation, did you have occasion to interview Lawrence Nieto?"

"Yes, I did, ma'am."

"Where?"

"We interviewed him several times. One place was the New Mexico State Police headquarters on Carlisle. And the second time was at the State Police headquarters in Santa Fe."

"Okay. When you interviewed Mr. Nieto in Albuquerque, was he in custody?"

"No."

"And do you recall the dates of...?"

"No, I don't. Of any interviews."

"At the time you interviewed in Albuquerque, had he been charged with any crimes relating to this case?"

"No, ma' am."

"And, did he voluntarily interview with you?"`

"Yes, ma'am."

"At the time you were interviewing him in Albuquerque, was he free to leave?"

"At any time, yes, ma'am."

"Was he locked up in a cell for the interview?"

"No, he interviewed up in an office."

"Did Mr. Nieto tell you anything about the homicides in Torreon?"

"Yes, he did."

"And specifically, did he tell you who was up at that cabin with him?"

"Yes, he did."

"And who did he tell you was up at the cabin with him?"

"On the second interview that we had in Santa Fe, he told us that the individuals that were up at the cabin were Shaun Wilkins known as Sager, Roy Buchner known as Eazy, himself, and an informant."

"And at that interview in Albuquerque, did he say anything about the defendant being present?"

"The first time he did not. And the second time he did say he was there due to the fact that, he was in fear of his life."

"Okay, could you clarify that in fear of his life?"

"Based on the information that we've gleaned from our interviews regarding this case, Mr. Nieto felt that his life was in personal jeopardy due to the fact of his involvement in this case. Which is the defendant. And for that reason, he did not disclose the names at first, during the first interview. But he finally came through and did disclose it on our second interview."

"And did he place the defendant seated here at the scene of the crime in Torreon?"

"Yes, ma'am, he did."

"Thank you. I'll pass this witness."

Ray picked up his laptop and began his cross. "Detective, where were the dates of each of these interviews you had with Nieto?"

"I don't have that available."

"Why not?"

"Because. The State Police handled the reports. The interviews were conducted by the State Police. And what my particular assumption was to assist them in these interviews. And that is documented in their reports as well as my reports will also show when they're submitted. The same date."

They only had from April 14th to today to write a report and they had not done a report. This was hard to swallow.

Ray went on. "When you first talked with Nieto, you said it was in Albuquerque?"

"Yes, sir."

"Who else was present?"

"Agent Mike Fenner."

"You said at that time that he told you that people who were in the cabin included Wilkins, Buchner, himself and I think you used the term informant."

"That is correct."

"Is that the name he gave?"

"No, that's. Well, that's what I'm stating right now is 'informant.'"

"What name did he give?"

"I don't know if I can divulge that."

"I, I think it's okay. He's being called as a witness."

"Shawn Popeleski, known as Popcorn."

"You said that the Albuquerque statement was consistent with the Santa Fe statement. They were completely consistent then, is that what your testimony?"

"No, consistent in the context, with the exception of names, of placing the defendants there, because of the fact that I stated before he was impaired to drive ... and he felt that he had exposed ... on the street. That the individuals would be against him. And that was the only reason he ... back. But once we interviewed on the second time, he finally admitted the fact that Mr. Buchner was at the scene of the crime."

"Did he at any point tell you that the reason that he had not mentioned Buchner earlier was the fear that you just described?"

"Yes, sir."

"When did he tell you that?"

"On the second interview."

"And was that interview taped?"

"Yes it was."

"Was the first interview taped?"

"Uh, as far as I know, I think it was taped. I'd have to check."

"Who was present at the time of the second one?"

"It was, uh, myself, Agent Lucero and Mike Fenner."

"No further questions your honor."

The judge leaned over, "You may step down."

As the officer was stepping down they exchanged glances with each other and were given smirks of approval by the ADA.

The Dance With The Devil Begins

Mady was now calling her star witness. "The State will call Shawn Popeleski." *Little did we realize this was the first and last time we would ever get to talk to Popeleski. He would not testify in our trial. Mady had it all worked out, our second surprise was about to happen. Soon after our hearing Mady would charge Popcorn as she had charged Woody. This way Roy and Shaun Wilkins would never get a chance to confront their accuser. We would now have to challenge the videotapes we were given. Mady knew we could never cross examine a videotape.*

The Judge looked over to the witness. "Mr. Popeleski, would you stand please? Would you raise your right hand. Do you swear or affirm that the testimony you are about to give is the truth, the whole truth and nothing but the truth, under penalty of perjury?"

"I do."

"Thank you. Would you state your full name for the record?"

"Shawn Popeleski."

"How old are you, Mr. Popeleski?"

"Twenty years old."

"Are you in custody right now?"

"Yes."

"Why are you in custody?"

"I'm a witness."

This was not true. He had escaped from Valencia County Jail; he had committed a home invasion, stole guns, auto theft. He also had outstanding warrants.

"Prior to your being in custody, where did you live?"

"With Woody."

"Was that in Albuquerque?"

"Yes."

"Do you know somebody named Shaun Wilkins?"

"Yes, I do. He's known as Sager."

"Do you know somebody named Roy Buchner?"

"Yes, I do he is also known as Eazy."

"And do you see Mr. Buchner in this courtroom here today?"

"Yes, I do."

"Could you point him out for the Court? The witness has pointed towards Mr. Buchner, who is seated at defense counsel."

"Do you know Lawrence Nieto?"

"Yea. They call him Woody."

"How is it that you know Mr. Wilkins, Mr. Buchner and Mr. Nieto? How did you meet them?"

"Gang on Eighteenth Street."

"And did you know Ben Anaya, Jr.?"

"Yes, I did."

"How did come to know him?"

"Went to school..."

"What was your relationship with him?"

"Like a brother."

"And did you know Cassandra Sedillo?"

"Yes, I did."

"How did you come to meet her?"

"Ben's girlfriend."

"Did you know her children Matthew and Johnny?"

"Yes, I did."

"Were you staying with Ben Jr. and Cassandra and her children up in Torreon?"

"Yes, I was."

"And did you take care of the children from time to time?"

"Yes, I did."

"Mr. Popeleski, sometime in, in December, did Mr. Nieto and Mr. Wilkins and the defendant come up to the cabin in Torreon?"

"Yes, they did."

"Had they been there before?"

"Yes, they had."

"How many times?"

"Once or twice I think."

"Why did they come up to the cabin?"

"Just to party."

"And, that day in December, when they came up, did you party that day?"

The ADA never said a date and Popeleski never volunteered a date.

"Yes, I did. We smoked a little bit of marijuana, drink some beer, did some coke."

"During that day at some point in time, did Mr. Nieto, Mr. Wilkins and the defendant leave the house?"

"Yes, they did."

"Well, what did you do when they left?"

"Put on a flick."

"When you say." a flick," what do mean?"

"Whatever 'Sleeping with an Enemy.'"

I thought to myself how appropriate for this case.

"Okay."

"Boys in the Hood."

"And were the children awake at that time?"

"Yes, they were."

"And what did they want you to do?"

"Put on Pinocchio."

"After Mr. Nieto, Mr. Wilkins and the defendant left, what did Ben and Cassandra do?"

"They went into the bedroom to sleep."

"And were you watching the children?"

"Yes, I was."

"At some point in time, did you go outside to relieve yourself?"

"Yes, I did."

"Why didn't you stay inside?"

"Cause there was no bathroom inside. The water wasn't, didn't work."

"Okay. What happened when you went outside?"

"Two guys come around the corner. And one of them I know was Sager for sure. He told me on the side. He said, 'Face on the ground'."

"What did 'face down on the ground' mean to you?"

"We used that on our car jackings."

"Could you see, could you completely see either of their faces?"

"They had masks on but you could tell because it was like that, Sager ... right there."

"Okay. Did somebody put you face down on the ground?"

"Somebody put their foot on my back, they had a gun pointed to my head and then, the two of them went into the house."

"What happened, what did you hear, when they went into the house?"

"Five shots."

"You heard five shots?"

"Maybe more. It's my best guess."

"And the second person who went in the house. Not the person you've identified as Sager. Do you know who he was?"

"Pretty much."

"And who was that?"

"It's Eazy."

"Mr. Popeleski, how did you get away?"

"Pretty much didn't shoot at me. Pretty much listened to the person that was speaking to me."

"Okay. Do you know who that person was?"

"Yes, I do."

"And who was it?"

"Lawrence Nieto, Woody."

"Okay. Were you able to, when you were on the ground, were you able to see, physically see anybody going to the house?"

"No, I wasn't."

"What could you see?"

"Saw pretty much the ground ... the truck."

"What did you do, when you got up and got away, where did you go?"

"Into the truck."

"Which truck?"

"The one that they found in Pecos, Texas."

"What kind of vehicle was it? Do you remember? What make?"

"I'm not sure."

"Okay. But you said they found it in Pecos, Texas?"

"Yes."

"All right. Did you see anyone of the two people who went into the house do anything when you were going for the vehicle?"

"Running down to the car."

"Did you say running?"

"Did you see them carrying anything?"

"Guns?"

"Did you either hear or see anybody go back up to the house?"

"No, I didn't."

"Did you hear anything that you thought was strange?"

"No, I didn't. Maybe keys. When I was on the floor, maybe ten or twenty minutes. I hear keys that was the last thing that I heard."

"Okay. When you got into that vehicle, what color was it by the way, do you know?"

"Grayish-black."

"Okay. When you got into it, were the keys in it?"

"Yes, it was."

"What did you do?"

"Started it, and backed up, chased after them."

"And what happened?"

"It stalled out like it always did."

"Okay. Were you able to get it started again?"

"Yes, I did."

"Were you able to locate the defendant and Sager after that?"

"No. Tried to but he wasn't around."

"Were did you go after you left the mountain?"

"Tyrone's pad. That's where Sager always kicks it at."

"Is that in Albuquerque?"

"Yes, it is."

"And where else did you go?"

"Dropped by Shaun's neighborhood."

"Were you ever able to locate Sager and the defendant?"

"No, I wasn't. I figured they would be out on the West Side, so I kicked it ... just waiting."

"Did you go someplace else?"

"Yes, I did."

"Where did you go?"

"Arizona."

"And why did you go to Arizona?"

"To see my ex."

I couldn't believe what I was hearing his best friend and his girl friend murdered two kids left in the cabin to die, and he's going to see his ex in Arizona. Are you shitting me? He couldn't call 911?

"Who is 'Little Dreamer'?"

"That was the person that went with me."

"Did he go to Arizona with you?"

"Yes." *Little Dreamer denied going to Arizona.*

"And after Arizona, did you come back to Albuquerque?"

"Yes, I did."

"And then, did you go on to Pecos, Texas?"

"Yes, we did."

"Why did you stop in Pecos, Texas?"

"The carburetor broke."

"So what do you do after the carburetor broke?"

"We went to Holiday Inn and stayed there overnight and came back to Albuquerque."

"How did you get back to Albuquerque?"

"On a bus."

"Did you get arrested shortly afterwards?"

"Yes, I did."

"Do you remember the date?"

"It was on a Christmas Eve."

It amazed me Popcorn didn't know the date of death but he knew when he got arrested.

"And have you been in custody ever since?"

"Pretty much."

"When you say 'pretty much,' was there a short time period when you were not in custody?"

"When I escaped."

Popcorn never said when or where he escaped from and there was no reports that we would see about the escape.

"And did you get picked up again?"

"Yes, I did."

"Was it that same day?"

How did Mady know it was the same day. If Mady knew then so did the officers but there were no reports given to us or created.

"Yes, it was."

"Between the time that this happened in Torreon and today, have you spoken to Lawrence Nieto?"

"No, I haven't."

"Okay, I'll pass the witness."

Ray stood up and little did we realize this was our first and last time we would ever get a chance to interview Popcorn.

"Mr. Popeleski, did you give any statements before today about this incident to anyone?"

"No, I didn't."

"You never said anything to any State Police officers or any Albuquerque police officers about what happened that day?"

"Just detectives who questioned me and stuff like that."

"Which detectives?"

"Mike, Mr. Juan, Garret, I think that's his name." *Popcorn was calling the detectives by their first names. It was a stronger relationship than what he was testifying to.*

"Have they or anybody else promised you anything at all concerning what they would give you or do for you if you testified for the State?"

"No, they didn't."

"Has anyone granted you immunity from prosecution?"

"No, they didn't."

"Has anyone told you anything about what would happen to your pending charges?"

"No, they didn't."

"Do you have a lawyer on your pending charges?"

"Yes, I do."

"Who is that?"

"Trina Maes-Gorman."

"And where is that case pending?"

"At Albuquerque."

"And where did you escape from?"

"Valencia County, Las Lunas."

"Did they charge you with that escape?"

"Yes, I have." *Popcorn did not have good control of the English language.*

"And you have a pending charge then down at Valencia County?"

"Yes, I do."

"Who is your lawyer on that charge?"

"George Eichwell."

"But when did you escape?"

"A month and a half or two months ago."

"What was the date when this incident happened you testified to here today? I'm talking now about this incident out at Ben's cabin?"

"December. It was before the eighteenth I know that." *We were getting close to a date of death we thought but the date of death became a moving target for us.*

"You know it was before the eighteenth? How do you know that?"

"That's the week before Christmas Eve. Around that eve I was pretty much. Pretty much everywhere."

"So in that week, you're saying before the eighteenth. "How much before the eighteenth?"

"Not sure."

"You were staying up there with Ben in the cabin?"

"Yes, I was."

"You and Woody had lived together previously, is that right?"

"Yea."

"Where had you lived together?"

"Down on Sunset Road." *Now I knew that was not true. Woody lived on 62nd.*

"Had Woody ever lived with you and Ben up in the cabin?"

"No."

"Had he ever been up there before this one day he was talking about?"

"Yes."

"How many times had Woody been up there?"

"Once or twice, I think."

"Are you and Woody pretty tight? Or at least were you?"

"Yes."

"Are you from Albuquerque? In other words, did you grow up there?"

"I didn't grow up there but I know a lot of people there now."

"Where did you grow up primarily?"

"Korea."

"And then when did you come to Albuquerque?"

"When I was eleven. That's when I first, first came. And that's when I got ranked into Eighteenth Street."

"You got ranked into Eighteenth Street when you were eleven?"

"I did."

"When you were at Eighteenth Street, did you ever meet Roy Buchner?"

"Yes, I have."

"Did you ever commit any crimes with Roy Buchner?"

"No, I haven't."

"At Eighteenth Street, were there some people who were real tight with each other and there might be another group who might be tight with each other?"

"Yes, that's how it works."

"How did that work?"

"Works like. Criminal against police officer."

"Would that be one part of Eighteenth Street would be against another part of Eighteenth Street?"

"That's like ... not get along. It's not the same side, no?"

"You did get along?"

"We didn't get along."

"So you had conflict between the west side of Eighteenth Street and the east side of Eighteenth Street?"

"Yea."

"Did you see anything that looked like maybe there had been a fire around a couch?"

"No, I didn't."

"On the day that everyone was up they're partying that you described here, can you give us any idea how much before December eighteenth that was?"

"No, I can't."

"Well, you said that after this incident occurred, you came back to Albuquerque, you then went to Arizona, you went to Pecos, Texas, and then you were back in Albuquerque by the twenty-fourth, Christmas Eve. Is that right?"

"Right."

"How long were you in Arizona?"

"Came back the same day. Took a day real late."

"It was a one-day trip over and back?"

"Yeah."

"Were you still driving the same vehicle you talked about leaving in that night?"

"Yes."

"Who did you say went with you to Arizona?"

"Richard 'Little Dreamer' from Eighteenth Street."

"What's his last name?"

"I don't know his last name."

"Was there anyone with you, anyone who you talked to?"

"No, I just wanted to be by myself."

"Did you talk to Tyrone about this?"

"No, I haven't I just looked out. To see who was kicking on the outside part. I figured that he would be out. I waited for pretty long."

"Was this that same night?"

"It was."

"Were you involved in, any deals with Ben Anaya involving guns or drugs?"

"What do you mean?"

"Did you buy any with him? Did you sell any with him?"

"Yes, I did."

"Were you involved in any recently, shortly before this killing took place?"

"Maybe in October, that was pretty much the last one."

"Were you with Ben when he got stopped and got arrested? He got charged with some guns and drugs."

"No, I wasn't."

"When you and Ben were living up there at a cabin, did you leave the cabin?"

"No, I didn't. If I left, I'll go with him."

"What vehicles were out there?"

"Just the one was found at Bakerwells." *It was found in Pecos, Texas. Popcorn had a problem with the English language.*

"What kind of vehicle was it?"

"A four-wheel drive. It was a Jeep."

"Who owned that vehicle?"

"Ben Anaya's dad."

"And you got in the vehicle that night and left the scene of this shooting, correct?"

"Yes, I did."

"And you're the one who drove it to Pecos, Texas, correct?"

"That's correct."

"Why did you go to Pecos, Texas?"

"For Richard."

"I'm sorry. Can you explain?"

"For Richard. He wanted to visit his aunt. And I had..."

"Did you shoot Ben Anaya?"

"No, I didn't."

"Did you shoot his friend at the scene?"

"No, I didn't."

"When you were up there that night, after you left, did you think they were shot?"

"I didn't."

"Did you go in the house and look?"

"No, I didn't."

"Did you ever go back in that house after that?"

"No, I didn't."

"Did you report to the police that they had been shot?"

"No, I didn't."

"Why not?"

"I wanted revenge."

"You wanted revenge?"

"In fact I had a gun on me."

"What did you do?"

"Went looking for them."

"Who were you looking for?"

"Sager."

"Who did you talk to, looking for him?"

"Pretty much nobody."

"You didn't even talk to anyone at all? Did you tell anybody what happened up there?"

"No, I didn't."

"While you were looking?"

"No, I didn't."

"You didn't tell Richard?"

"No, I didn't."

"You tell Richard you were looking for Sager?"

"No, I didn't."

"You drove around, though in Ben's father's vehicle?"

"Yes."

"What are going to do if you found him."

"Cap m."

"What do you mean by that? Shoot him? Kill him?"

"Yeah."

"Is he is the only one you were looking for?"

"Pretty much."

"Why?"

"He was the only one that really.. He always wanted to..."

"He always wanted what?"

"Deuce's day flick."

"What do you mean?"

"Deuce. I could say like Sager is kind of jealous of Deuce."

"Deuce is who?"

"Ben Anaya. You studied your sheet, I mean you should know that."

"Why don't you explain it to us? Deuce was in what position?"

"That Sager wanted to replace him. He had some ... didn't he? Selling guns and selling drugs. Keeping on a ... and never get suspected or anything. But Sager would know certain people that he knew and he just wished. I think he just wished he would get things."

"So Sager was trying to eliminate Deuce so that he could replace him, is that. Is that what you think?"

"Yeah."

"Did Sager ever say anything to you to make you think that?"

"No."

"Did he describe the situation up there at the scene as partying all day. Were there any conflict between Sager and Deuce that day?"

"Wasn't."

"No conflict at all?"

"No."

"Did you see what kind of a vehicle Sager had?"

"Reddish-maroon."

"Reddish-maroon?" *Eric Lucero had just testified it was a Black Trans Am.*

"Yeah."

"What kind of car was it, do you know?"

"It's like a Trans Am. I'm trying to remember the name of it. You know."

"Whose was it?"

"Ben and Sager's. It was a stolen vehicle."

"Where was it parked?"

"Close to downhill."

"How close to the house, did you say?"

"Two hundred and fifty yards."

"Was it on a road?"

"Like right before you go up the hill, no. When you got in the vehicle, when you got in the Jeep, the four-wheel drive to drive away."

"What route did you take?"

"Took the same route except you like drive off, no? And then it turns in, there's a gate. The truck was right here; and then I backed it up and then drove out. Right. And then I try to go down. And that's when I f....'"

"Where did you get the keys for that Jeep?"

"It was in it."

"Did you have a gun with you at that time?"

"Yes, I did."

"Where had that gun been?"

"Under the seat, right there."

"What kind of firearm is that?"

"It's black. Twenty-two like that."

"Was it a rifle then?"

"Kind of, let me draw it."

"Looks like what you're drawing is like a cut-off rifle. Right?"

"It's not a cut-off. It's a black and white one."

"Where is that now?"

"Probably in the truck."

"You left there in the truck in Pecos? Is that right?"

"Yes, I did."

"Did you have any other firearms with you?"

"When I left there? A bunch."

"What else did you have?"

"Thirty-ought-six, thirty-ought-six, two forty-three, twenty-two, twenty-two, forty-five, nine. Probably another twenty-two, another two-four-three match up there. Almost all of them had bolts on it."

"Where were they when you left?"

"They were all in the back seat."

"And where did you get those?"

"They were in there."

"They were in the vehicle itself."

"Yeah. I can't tell you the person who would get ... That's ... no."

"Yeah. But those guns were there that night and you left with them in the vehicle, is that right?"

"We got in the truck, we got guns in the cabin."

"What was in the cabin? What kind of guns were in the cabin?"

"Pretty much the same except we had a sprayer too."

"What do you mean?"

"Tech."

"And how many firearms did you say were in the house?"

"Twelve or thirteen."

"While you were there that time and after Buchner and Shaun left, did you hear any sounds outside?"

"No, I didn't."

"Did you go outside to say goodbye to them?"

"Yeah, but I went right back in, shook hands at the gate and came right back in."

"After the shooting took place in the house, did you hear vehicles start up and leave?"

"No, I don't think I was. I was, was already in the vehicle that I was in."

"Did you see anybody run from the house before you got in your vehicle?"

"The Jeep, I mean. I heard footsteps. So I pretty much imagined they were going to leave. It is quiet up there and you can pretty much hear every-thing. I went down and then I saw two people get in the car. I know Sager was on that side because he has ... He threw that in. And then the other guy just walked in with a gun. Then they started driving off. Then I just rammed it down."

"Where were you staying in the house?"

"I was staying either here or here. On the couch."

"And where was it that you were told 'face-down on the ground'?"

"Right here."

"Outside the house?"

"Yeah, and right by the cement."

"Who told you 'face down'?"

"Sager."

"What were his words?"

"Face down on the ground."

"When he told. 'face down on the ground,' did he have a gun?"

"Yes, he did, I know I heard a click sound like a pump gauge."

"And, uh, did you see that that was him clicking?"

"I didn't see it was him 'cause I was like that, face down on the ground so I figured it was him, no?"

"Did you see Nieto around any, Woody?"

"No, I didn't. I just saw two people come out the same time. I didn't think it was really Woody, at the start, until I keep on thinking back and thinking. I saw them coming around the corner. They're pretty much the same size. The only person I could really think of the same size as Sager right there."

"Did you talk to Woody, or did Woody talk to you when you were face down on the ground?"

"I kind of talked to him."

"Where was he?"

"Had a foot on my back."

"And how is it you got up and went to the Jeep?"

"When they left? "Pretty much. I got on the corner over there, no? I can pretty much picture it all."

"All three left, is that right?"

"I only saw two. Two leaving. That maybe one was down already."

"What about the guy who had his foot on your back?"

"I see Woody."

"You saw him? And one other person, right?"

"Yeah."

"When they first came up to you, and you were taking a leak, how many people were there?"

"Two."

"Two? And one of them stayed there with his foot on the ground, on your back, is that right?"

"Yeah."

"And one."

"I don't know if it was one of them putting a foot on my back. I know it wasn't because it has to have been Woody on my back, didn't he? He's pretty much said. 'Don't worry; I'm not going to shoot, uh.'"

"He told you that?"

"Yeah. He told me that."

"And so you recognized his voice?"

"Yeah."

"And you knew it was him, standing there with his foot on your back?"

"Yeah."

"So then the two people who came up to you and one of them stayed there with his foot on your back, right?"

"Yeah."

"And only one went in the house, as far as you know?"

"Right?"

"Did you ever see three people up there at that time, around the time those shots took place?"

"Get this through your head, okay. I know it was three. Because two people when they came around from the corner of the truck was the same size. Sager is pretty tall, right? As you can see. Woody is pretty short as you can see. Okay? Now those two were not on my back. Woody was on my back. Those two I saw. And there's another person. I mean, does that make three? So I saw three people and that's my answer."

"Were the lights on in the house or off when they left?"

"On."

"Did you lock up the house before you, before you left?"

"I did." *Woody had accused Eazy of locking the door. But Popcorn had to say he had the keys as he used them to start the Jeep. If that was the case Popcorn had to have the keys.*

"At what point did the truck stall?"

"I was down the hill. It went around right there. It stalled out where it turns and begins."

"At the time you were in the house that night, was there a bunch of debris, trash, etc. around inside the house?"

"What do you mean?"

"Well, like wrappers, cans, a bunch of stuff on the floor like that, all over the house?"

"No."

"There wasn't? It was clean?"

"Yes, it was."

"And is it correct that you never went back to the house after you left that night in the Jeep?"

"I never went back."

"When the Jeep stalled, what did you do to get it started?"

"Put it in park and it started again, pumped the gas."

"It started right up?"

"Yeah."

"So it was just a second, just a few seconds when it stalled?"

"It wasn't a few seconds. I had a hard time starting it."

"Did you have to get out and do anything to the car?"

"No."

"You just put it in park, cranked it and it started up?"

"Yes. Sometimes like when it stalled out, I would have to get out and open the hood and put the gas in the little tiny round thing, you know."

"But you didn't have to do that, that night?"

"No."

"And, you knew the kids were in the house, is that right?"

"Yes, I did."

"Did you ever call anyone to say that you thought somebody got killed and those kids were in the house?"

"I thought they were dead. Right. When you hear more than five or six shots, what are you going to think, huh?"

"So that's what you thought and you never went back to look?"

"That's right."

"No further questions."

The Nail In The Coffin

"DEFENSE COUNSEL MAY PROCEED."

"We recall Officer DeReyes."

"Thank you. Officer DeReyes, when did you take a statement from the participating, take a statement from Roy Buchner?"

"When we located him at his work, and he was brought to the State Police headquarters and questioned."

"Do you remember the day?"

"No, I don't."

"And were you present when the statement was taken?"

"Yes."

"Was Mr. Buchner advised of his Miranda rights?"

"Yes."

"Did he make any statement at all concerning the incident?"

"Yes, he did."

"Did he waive his right to counsel under Miranda?"

"He never waived his rights. He just spoke about different generalities when we were trying to ask him the questions. And he never requested counsel at that time."

"Did he ever, say he wanted to speak to an attorney?"

"No, he just would make references that, we had the wrong guy and he was going to sue us."

"Was he in custody at that point?"

"No."

"Were you present at all or involved at all in his early, in the earlier discussion with him? "Prior to the time they got him at work and he came down."

"No, no, I was. That was the first time that he had actually, formally talked to Mr. Buchner. The other times I was not present."

"Didn't make any statement concerning Popcorn?"

"No."

"Did he make any statement concerning Sager?"

"No."

"Did he make any statement concerning Woody, or Mr. Nieto?"

"No."

"Did he make any statements in any way related to the incident involving the deaths of Mr. Anaya and the other people?"

"Yes."

"What statements did he make?"

"When myself and Agent Fenner asked him about if he was there at the cabin, he told us, laughing, that he was not and that we were, that we would be sorry if we would charge him with this because, he would sue the whole department and everybody and Agent Fenner asked him, 'Don't you care about the family?' And his response was, excuse my language, he said, 'Fuck the bitch, fuck the kids; all I care is about my homies.' And then we asked him what'd he meant by that, he went on just to laugh about the whole thing. He thought it was a joke. I got up and I told him, 'Look, this is a serious investigation. You're here to find out what information you might have. And you want to cooperate with us, fine. If not, we'll continue with our investigations.' His attitude was very nonchalant, very cavalier. And at that time, we just felt that this interview wasn't going anywhere and we didn't want to detain him any longer, so we told Mr. Buchner at that time the interview was terminated and that he would be returned to work and he was."

"And that's the end of the tape on which he spoke?"

"Yes."

"No further questions."

"Cross?"

"No cross, your honor."

"You may step down, Detective."

"Thank you, sir."

Mady stood up. "Your honor, I did say I have no further evidence to offer at this time, but that's partly because, my cross examination was limited in this preliminary hearing.

"Your honor, Count One of the complaint is an open count of murder with firearms enhancement. An open count of murder, as this Court knows, deals with each of the four different kinds of murder that are statutory in the state of New Mexico. First-degree murder and what the State says incorporated into Counts One, Two, Three and Four."

Mady went on to regurgitate the testimony of everyone who testified about all the facts all over again:

"There is more than ample evidence to bind Mr. Buchner over. We have the testimony of Lawrence Nieto through Agent Lucero and he was present at the scene; he was an eyewitness. And that he saw, positively, Mr. Wilkins and the defendant seated over there, Roy Buchner, walk into that house. And that he heard gunfire go off in that house; he heard up to eight shots. He saw Mr. Wilkins armed with a .22 caliber weapon; he saw Mr. Buchner armed with a thirty-ought-six weapon. They went into the house; he heard gunfire. Later on, there were four victims found in that house. He also testified that he saw people walking out of those house, out of that house carrying guns and drugs. He saw that man seated over there, Mr. Buchner, and Mr. Wilkins, the co-defendant, walking out carrying guns and drugs. Out of that house.

"You've got the testimony of Lawrence Nieto through Agent Lucero that Mr. Buchner, the defendant seated over there, laughed and said, 'We got rid of the witness.' Well, your honor, if that's not an admission, I don't know what it is. Now, your honor, the State can't submit to this Court that there's anything more heinous that doing that, when that defendant knew that there were two children in that house. And he locked the door. That was as good as murdering those children where they sat or where they slept. And of course, that is what happened. And that's the proximate cause of those children. They died of dehydration and starvation, your honor. They were left in that house three and four years old.

"And suffice it to say that two eye witnesses have identified both Mr. Buchner, seated over there, and his co-defendant Shaun Wilkins, as having gone into that house armed, having fired shots, having come out, having stated they got rid of the witnesses, having carried away weapons and drugs and then having left the scene of the crime.

"That covers the first four counts, your honor, and as the State has, has suggested to the Court, because we're not a hundred percent sure what happened inside that house, the State has charged these crimes as open counts of murder. The State submits, however, to this Court that there is ample justification for the State's charging a felony order.

"That leads us to Count Five and Count Six, aggravated burglary with a firearm enhancement, armed robbery with a firearm enhancement and aggravated burglary. You come to the house, you park, and you've got permission to be in that house. You leave that house and you go down the hill and you put on ski masks and you put on gloves and you arm yourself and you go back up to that house and go in and you blow the occupants away. You do not have permission to enter that house. However, what you do have is the intent to commit a felony when you enter that residence. That, your honor, is aggravated burglary. Firearms enhancement rings true. Shots are fired. Two of the victims die from gunshot wounds. Armed robbery. Maybe at sentencing that's going to merge with aggravated burglary, but for the time being, your honor, there's ample, ample evidence to support the contention that Mr. Buchner and Mr. Wilkins walked into that house armed. Armed with firearms. Shots were fired inside that house and items of value were stolen from that house. And that Mr. Buchner and Mr. Wilkins left with items of value stolen from that house.

"And they walked down that hill and they loaded those items up in their car and they left and laughed. The State submits, your honor, that there is more than sufficient evidence and definitely probable cause to support the charge of armed robbery with a firearm enhancement. Finally, your honor, we get to the, the, not finally, but almost finally, we get to the tampering with evidence counts. We have the testimony of Lawrence Nieto and the testimony of the investigating officers that they arrived at a rest stop or something that looked like a rest stop. And that Mr. Buchner and Mr. Wilkins burned the gloves that they were wearing. And Mr. Nieto has told us, through Agent Lucero, that they were wearing gloves. We have the testimony of Lawrence Nieto, who was with them, your honor, and left the scene with them and maybe is involved as fully as they are. But maybe not. And he has chosen to tell the police what happened. They left the scene. They had ski masks. They put them in the back of that car. Not only is the car missing, but also the ski masks are missing. Well, your honor, the State suggests to the Court that if they decided and if they had enough presence of mind to dispose of the gloves, then they certainly had enough presence of mind to dispose of the ski masks, as they have not been found. And Lawrence Nieto tells us that each and every one of them was wearing ski masks.

"Finally, we come to, to the weapons. Twenty-two-caliber handgun, one from Nieto's side. He heard the caliber when the shots were fired. That weapon was never recovered. That weapon was never found. And, your honor, search warrants were executed in this case everywhere. Everything was turned upside down in the search for that weapon. That leaves only one inference, your honor, supported by the evidence. And that's that the weapon was destroyed. Or sold. Or somehow or another done away with, so that it couldn't be found. Couldn't be tied to the crime. Finally, your honor, perhaps the easiest count of all and that's Count Ten, conspiracy. Well, we've got the testimony of two eyewitnesses. It was this defendant seated over here and at least Shaun Wilkins who got together and decided, somewhere along the line, that number one they were going to blow away Popcorn. Fortunately, Popcorn did not get blown away but the intent was there. And/or that they were going to go in and rob that place. Take all the money and the guns.

"Mr. Popeleski has told that there was a jealousy issue. Somebody wanted to be top dog and somebody wasn't top dog. Somebody wanted what makes you top dog in a gang, and that's the guns and the drugs and the money. How do you become top dog? You get the guns, the drugs and the money. And that was exactly what Shaun Wilkins intended to do and that was exactly what Roy Buchner intended to do. And they did. They went back into that house and took the guns and the money and the drugs and they agreed to do it. They had a plan. They were down at that car putting on ski masks and putting on gloves. That, your honor, is a conspiracy. Your honor it's difficult to say at this point in time since these people were masked and gloved, exactly who shot whom and who did what. However, we know that the two of them went into the house together. We know shots were fired; we know items were stolen and we know four people ... dead. Under New Mexico's Accomplice and Accessory Statute, your honor, that makes this gentleman seated right here, just as responsible for this crime as the man who pulled the trigger. Or it makes the man who went in while this man pulled the trigger just as responsible for the crime. And that's why this particular statute was developed. Finally, your honor, just as a note. We're dealing with witnesses here who are most unusual. They're members of gangs. Their credibility may be tested. And it may be tested later on. The language is different. The words used are different. The attitude is different, the demeanor is different. But, your honor, I submit to this Court that one thing is not different. Shawn Popeleski sat there in that chair and was unflappable. he told what he saw. Nothing changed his story. Not any questions that the defense counsel could have asked him, nor any of his own problems. And the Court could see how emotional, how upset and emotionally disturbed he was about having to testify ... he told the truth. State submits to the Court that there was sufficient credibility on the part of all of the witnesses. That there statements corroborated one another. They saw what they saw, your honor, they were up there at that particular point of time. And on that basis, I would submit to this Court that there is ample evidence to bond this defendant over on each and every count of this ten-count complaint. And I'd reserve the right to."

Ray stood up to argue, "The State should have been embarrassed to sponsor this bizarre tale. The tragedy is obvious; the facts are inescapable. And the two children are the most tragic of all. But the State has made a deal with the devil. And the Court saw the devil incarnate."

The Judge wasn't going to listen to arguing. "Mr. Buchner, it is the decision of this Court that the State of New Mexico has met probable cause and will bind you over for trial in District Court on counts one through ten. This Court believes that probable cause has been met. That will be the decision of this Court today. The Court will sign the bind-over order. Are there any further pleadings if any to take into consideration?"

Ray had one final request, "Judge if we could have five minutes with our client?"

"Five minutes and that's all."

We went back to out to the little hole in the wall and Roy was the first to talk, "What happening, what's going on, I didn't do anything wrong."

I could see Roy's wrist were purple from the handcuffs and sweat under his shirt. Ray talked first, "We're headed for district court Roy. They are going to be seeking the death penalty on you. We have our work cut out for us. We have reports and videos to go over plus the evidence they collected."

"But do I have to go back to that prison, I can't eat or sleep. All they do is yell at me."

"You're going to have to stay there Roy until we can get it in front of a District Judge. Right now you're one of the most hated persons in New Mexico."

"I know the inmates are yelling at me that they are going to fuck me up and kill me."

"We'll be up to see you first chance we get Roy."

"Ray, I see the Mady over there let me see if I can get some discovery out of her."

"Hey, Mady how you doing?" It was a good thing that I had worked with her in the past. "I know the discovery is not ready yet but I am assuming the video can be copied can I get copies of the videos and the tapes?"

"That shouldn't be a problem, stop by in the morning and ask for our investigator Levi to make you copies."

"Thanks Mady, I'll be there first thing." I should have asked, "why do you have the tapes and why aren't they tagged in?" but in the excitement of getting some discovery it didn't dawn on me. I had made a bad assumption the tapes were copies of the original and Agent Jacoby had tagged in all the originals like they are supposed to.

Ride Back Home

We made our way past the media and them sticking out their mikes wanting a comment from Ray. That was Ray's job, the media knew me by now and knew they weren't getting anything from me on or off the record.

They came up to Ray, "Why did he kill those people?" Ray, looked at them and said, "We don't know too much about the case right now. We believe our client is innocent. We will know more when we get the discovery from the District Attorney's office."

Over the years we had learned not talk to each other while walking to our car. Once we go into our cone of silence Ray asked, "What do think Maurice ... two eye witnesses."

"The witnesses I can deal with but it looks like DeReyes memorized those lines from Roy's statement, 'Don't you care about the family?' And his response was, excuse my language, he said, 'Fuck the bitch, fuck the kids; all I care is about my homies.' The DA has its opening and closing arguments the media is going to play it up, it's just another nail in the coffin."

"That just means we got more nails to pull."

"Still there's no evidence. Where's all the evidence? Darren White and the media keep talking about evidence. To me right now it's just a, 'he said, she said case' but in our cases, 'he said, he said.' It also appeared Popcorn and the officers were well coached. It is going to be interesting when we take Woody and Popcorn's statement. But we have a lot of work to do before that happens."

"You realize Woody and Popcorn are not going to be interviewed, Woody is being represented by Attorney Gary Mitchell. Popcorn is represent by Gorman. So all we can do is rely on the two statements on the videos they did. We're dealing with a confession and an eye witness."

"From what I heard today the time line is not that big, Ray. If Popcorn and Woody were eye witness, Roy and Shaun had to be present. So there has to be a time period they could all get together to commit this crime. No one testified as to a date. We need to narrow it down. From what I've got so far, Ben Sr. and Popcorn for sure were the last one to see them alive. If Ben Sr. was at the cabin December twelfth, Popcorn is arrested on the twenty-fifth and prior to that he was in Arizona. We have so far a thirteen-day window where the murders have to occur. Popcorn testified it happened before the eighteenth of December that's a six day window. Woody also said it was in January. Since no one knows the date of death, we're going to be a moving target. We also should extend the time line out to when they found the bodies April fourteenth."

"You're right, we need a tight time line, or else we're going to be a moving target."

"What I don't understand is why does it take them from April 15, 1996, to May 15, 1996, to get a truthful statement. Does not make sense to me."

"Maurice, I found out the attorney for Shaun Wilkins is Steve Aarons and his investigator is Troy Garrity."

"Don't know either one of them so we should have Regina set up a meeting with all the defense attorneys and figure out the best joint approach on this case."

"You're right, we should also think of drafting up a 'Joint Defense Agreement'. I'll also need your To Do List ASAP so we can get prioritized. We don't have much time."

"I know it's early but we need a speed letter from Mady. I want to get in and see that evidence." (A speed letter is a letter of authorization from the DA to us that allows us to view evidence being held by the police.)

"I still find it hard to believe they didn't present any solid evidence. No prints, no DNA, no nothing."

"It still early and you know DPS (Department of Public Safety), they are always behind by three months."

"Your telling me the state has the worst murder case in its history and DPS is putting the forensics on the bottom of their list. I don't think so. These officers can get anything they want. When I had high profile crimes the department gave me a gold card."

6

Getting Your Priorities In Line

I STARTED THINKING EVERYTHING IN THIS CASE HAS HIGH priority. "I need to get a good background on everyone involved and get my time line going so we can get a good idea where everyone was at between the twelfth and eighteenth and twenty-fifth of December."

I called home and told my family where I had been and the case I had got involved with. I knew Ray and I were going to be all over the news since we were representing the most hated men in New Mexico's history. The media was going to have a field day with this case.

"You realize Maurice that we're about eighteen months away from trial and were about the same distance in our death penalty case with Jason and the Sureno Thirteen case."

"That means I have only nine months for each case. I already have my 'To Do List on Sureno.' I'll get one started on Roy's case this evening."

This wasn't our first complex case and in order to make sure we were at our best with the little time I had, I knew what had to get done.

"I'll get started with our time line. who's who lists, evidence list, and our exhibit list. We should also do a time line on all the interviews and their meeting with Popcorn and Woody to see what we're missing."

"You know we're going to get the discovery in bits and pieces don't you."

"I don't worry too much about the discovery. I'd rather do my own investigation." After 21 years with law enforcement and the last eight in child homicide and serial crimes, I knew how to do my work.

"That's why I want to get started first thing in the morning with all the video. Part of my plan is while I'm going up to Estancia to get the tapes, I was going to go do a canvas of the area around the cabin. I like to get a look at where everything happened. We're already four months behind the investigation. I also want to stop off at APD records and start pulling reports on our client, Wilkins, Woody and Popcorn. I have a feeling it's going to take them a while."

"I'll have Regina get you releases for Roy to sign so we can start getting his educational and work records. We also need to set up a time to go visit with him."

"Make sure we get him some pencils and legal pad. He is going to get some homework assignments." I needed a list of names of gang members I can trust to make an introduction for me so I could gain the trust of the gang.

"Roy's grandparents are a good source of information. His grandfather was taking him to and from work in December. Roy was working at Orley's Hydraulics. We have our work cut out for us."

"This just means we get up earlier in the morning."

Ray and I had a unique working system. Ray is an early riser and I'm a night person. Ray is up at four am and I go to sleep at twelve or one am. I would do my work at night fax it to Ray so he has it when he gets up and we cover a twenty hour day.

I was well aware if we even stood a chance in hell in this case, not only did we have to mirror the work of the investigation, we had to out investigate them.

First of many trips to Torreon, New Mexico

That next morning I'm up early and driving back through the Sandia Mountains over Sedillo Hill down to Edgewood, into Moriarty. As I passed the courthouse, the building appeared to be closed. Memories of yesterday came back to me. Changing highways, I moved over to the single lane highway to Estancia. This highway always gives you time to think. It's 55 MPH on a sixteen mile stretch to the DA's office, a trip I would take many times.

When I got to the DA's office, Levi, their investigator, was already busy copying the tapes. I wanted to see what they had in their war room. I noticed a large box of tapes that Levi was reaching into, along with several three-inch binders on the shelf. Next to the binders were packages from Walgreen's. They were photos of the crime scene.

If I had hindsight I would have asked, "Why are the tapes here and not tagged into evidence?" I had assumed the State Police had made copies for the DA. The originals should have been tagged in.

"Hey Levi, are those the crime scene photos?"

"I believe they are."

I knew DPS didn't have a photo lab and had to take their photos to a drug store to get them developed.

"Can you take the negative for me and drop them off and I'll be willing to pick them up?"

"Let me check with Mady."

"I can talk to her Levi, why don't you finish what you're doing."

Mady agreed with me and told me she would have Agent Jacoby drop off the film and would call us when they were ready. "What about the binders can I get those copied?" I knew I was pushing my luck but it wasn't going to hurt to be told no.

"They are not complete yet, Maurice, I'd rather give you and Ray a complete set. We're still gathering up the reports. You know it's a big case. You also know, Maurice, that Levi has another six hours of copying don't you?"

I agreed, "I think I'll go over to the Blue Bonnet Café and get a cup while I'm waiting." The Blue Bonnet was a local bar and café in Estancia that served a mean green chile cheeseburger. On weekend the place was covered with bikers. I was one of them.

I left Estancia driving down Highway 55. It was a quick 15-minute drive to the small town of Torreon. The town of Torreon is a one store gas station and post office. To get to the Cibola National Forest and to the edge of the forest where the cabin was located you had only two roads. I noticed a old worn sign saying "Sherwood Forest Estate." That was my road.

As I followed the asphalt road it didn't take it long to turn to dirt. The higher I climbed the rougher the road became and the slower I traveled. I had a 1992 Camaro that would not make it up this road, so how did they drive a Trans Am up here much less race it down this mountain at night?

I also owned four acres in the Sandia Mountain's at a place called Cerro Heights. We had spent many a night on the land. At night the only light you get is from the moon and stars. This place is like mine. It gets pitch black when the sun goes behind the Sandia so you're lucky to see your hand in front of your face.

I made it to the cabin by picking my way past the rocks in the road. As I drove past the cabin I could see the crime scene tape blowing in the mountain wind. The eerie sound of silence in the air was the only noise from the trees. The gates were closed and locked.

Someone had already placed four crosses in the front yard. I knew well enough not to go into the property even though I wanted to. I knew the DA and DPS would be yelling I was tampering with evidence.

Looking around I noticed a cabin above Ben's Sr. cabin that had a perfect view of the cabin. I drove up to the cabin and the view became more spectacular. I love New Mexico. You go thirty minutes anywhere in the state and the view changes. Must be why they call it "The Land of Enchantment."

It didn't take long for the two big mixed dogs to come down the road to greet me. They must have alerted all the trees that I was coming up to their house. The dogs were growling at my tire as if they were starving for food. I noticed the name "Zenner" on the mailbox. From the looks of the property all they had was electricity. A large stack of a couple cords of wood were stacked up against the house. With that amount of wood it told me they had to use it for heating and cooking.

An outhouse with the Zia symbol on it was on the east side of their cabin. Next to the front door were two wooden chairs outside facing the west. The house was made of wood and stucco. The roof was an old rusty tin that gave the house some great character. The brick barbeque grill was near the back door.

Then reality hit me. I had to get out of my vehicle and now both dogs were barking and growling at me. Damn I hate growling dogs. I kept hoping someone would hear the dogs and would come out to greet me. It was not going to be my lucky day. I kept telling myself to look them in the eye. I stepped out and they moved toward me. Show no fear, hell, they could hear my blood racing through my bad leg that had been crushed while I was riding motors for the police department.

I just wanted to make a fifteen yard round trip to the door and back to my truck. I can do this. I reached over and grabbed my leather notebook as though I could use it to protect myself. Since it was made out of leather they would go for that and not me.

I got out keeping my notebook between me and the dogs. I walked to the front door. I knew no one was home but I wanted to leave my card. After what seemed like the 'death march,' I made it. I knocked on it, not wanting to look at my newfound friends behind me. I could now hear barking in the distance. They must have woke up every sleeping dog in the mountains.

No one answered the door so I left one of my cards at the front door and then looked around. Damn. What if they park in the back and go in the backdoor. I wanted to make sure they found my card. Now I had another round trip to make. I left my card on the back door and walked back to my car. I reached in the back and took out my camera.

I have learned over the years that P.I. work was no difference than being back in the department as a Field Investigator. I carry all my equipment with me, from cameras, video camera, measuring tape, black and red markers, and index cards.

I looked back at Ben's cabin and began to snap away. I could see the entire cabin along with the shed on the side of the cabin and the fence line around the property. I wonder if they could hear a .22 caliber if it went off at the cabin.

I could see the large ruts in the road caused by the tires of traffic moving towards the cabin. I heard testimony they had parked down from the cabin. I tried to spot the area they were talking about but there was no such place.

On the side of the road I could see where the water runoff caused small arroyos to be created. This small arroyos followed the road back into town. So where did they pull off? It would have been difficult for a Camaro or Trans Am to pull off to the side without getting stuck or bottom out.

I drove down the rough road to the first cabin after Ben's and there was smoke coming out of the chimney. Only small Chihuahuas running around the yard barking at me. This I could handle. I didn't get a chance to get out of my car when an elderly lady came out of the house and stood guard by her door.

"What do you want?"

I don't like talking from my car and I knew they were not used to strangers in the area.

"You from the fucking media?"

"No, ma'am, I am not them."

I have always been up front with people I meet. I have learned people love to talk and I was hoping I had found my Ms. Grafits from Bewitched. I took a wild guess.

"Are you Ms. Elders?"

"Yes, who asking?"

"My names Maurice, here's my card."

I had learned from an old time sergeant that you never tell people who you are and what you do until you get to know them. I had been working patrol on a early Sunday morning with Jimmy Hultz when he got dispatched to a loud party. A party at seven am. I thought there had to be girls there. "I'll cover you Jimmy," I said as we got to the parking lot of the apartment complex. You could hear the music from the fourth floor bellowing out.

We walked up to the door knocked with our baton so as not to hurt our knuckles. The music stopped. It was dead silence and then a voice yelled out.

"What do you want?"

Experience taught us never to stand in front of the doorway. Jimmy yelled back, "APD, we would like to talk to you."

"Give me a second."

The music stopped. We waited for him to open the door. Instead the sound of a thirty odd six filled the air not once, but three times. We stood there looking at each other to make sure we were alive. Then his voice yelled. "You got one hour to get the fuck out of here."

Jimmy looked at me and said, "What do we do?"

"We got fifty nine minutes to get the fuck out of here."

We went back racing to our patrol cars for back up. Sergeant Royce Keller could hear, "ten-3 (the air) 10-82 (the code for help). Shots fired." (10-3 shut the air down, 82 send cover)

Royce must not have been that far away because within seconds he was there. "Four hundred PD clear the air. Have the other units stand down, I'll advise."

"What do you have here?"

We told him what had happened at the apartment and how we approached the situation. Royce looked at us, "Hell let's go back up there and talk to him."

I thought, "Are you nuts. Let's get the SWAT team to come here and talk to him."

We went back to the same door. I could see the three holes and the fresh splinters pointing at us. The bullets went through his door and into the next apartment. The neighbors were peeking out of their doors and we motioned them to go back in.

Sergeant Keller wore a large graduation ring from "OU" (Oklahoma University) and he called it his knocker. We stood off to the side again and Sergeant Keller knocked. I kept thinking we done this before.

The familiar voice yelled out, "Who is it?"

Sergeant Keller responded, "It's Royce, son, I want to talk to you."

I could feel the sweat building up in my right hand as I held on to my forty-one magnum. Something was going to happen. I held it by my side, out of his sight. I wanted him to stay calm.

Then the door opened up and a young college male stood at the door. "Can I help you Royce?"

"Can we come in son and talk?" Royce gave me some of the best advice I ever got that day, "Never tell them you're a cop. Always use your first name."

After that day I was baptized "Maurice."

I got out of my truck and walked up to Ms. Elders hoping I would not call her Ms. Grafits.

I extended my hand, "My name's Maurice and I do private work for attorneys. I heard your name on the 911 call when the 27-1 call came out." (27-1 one was code for murder. I wanted her to know my background.)

"Oh yes, come on in. You know I used to dispatch for the S.O."

Like most people in New Mexico she always had food on the stove. "You hungry?" she asked.

I could smell fresh beans and red chile along with fresh tortillas. "I was just about to eat lunch, sienta se."

Without waiting for an answer I had a bowl of beans, with fresh grated cheese on top, covered with red chile and a tortilla in front of me.

She brought me some aluzumia tea with honey and asked "Do you want it hot or cold? This is a great herb tea that my grandmother used to make all the time. Here, some homemade jelly to go with that tortilla. You want some Fritos on those beans?" Without waiting for an answer she had already dug into the bag of Fritos and put a handful in my bowl.

After that we talked for a good couple of hours and she told me all about the Anaya's, how they would shoot those damn guns in the yard and scare the hell out of her dogs. They'd come down and bother her for water all the time.

She didn't know anyone was staying at the cabin. Most people live in the mountains for a reason: they want to be left alone.

"I didn't know there was babies in the cabin, you know with all the trees out here, sound don't travel all that well. My husband helped Anaya build that cabin. You know its air tight cabin. We have to make it air tight because we have some mighty cold winters."

"You didn't see anyone at the cabin?"

"Let me show you." We walked outside and she pointed back. "See you can't see the road or the cabin from here. And I don't leave the house anymore unless it's to the store."

"Did you get a lot of snow this winter?"

"Oh yea, hito, we had over two feet. It started in January, stopped around the end of February, but it was all melted by mid March."

"Did you notice any tracks in the snow going up to the Anaya's?"

"Nope. Just Ms. Zenner. You can tell when they go up to their cabin, they make several tracks so they don't create ruts in the road. But those god damn cops when they came up here, they tore out the road."

I gave her a hug and told her I would be back in touch. "You know you have to come and visit me. I don't have a home phone."

I loved small towns in New Mexico. Everyone is your abuela (grandma). I didn't tell her we represent Roy because I didn't need to hear, "Get the fuck out of my house. You're defending the devil."

I stopped at the store gas station in Torreon and went in and looked around. No video camera. Just a small country store. "Is there a phone here?"

"Pay phone right outside to your right."

"Do you know the Anaya's who live up in Sherwood Forest?"

"No, we mind our own business. You asking about those murders?"

"I am. Have the police been here to interview anyone?"

"No."

"Did you know the Anaya's?"

"No."

"They drove a charcoal grey Jeep."

"Nope."

"They were some small kids..."

"I read it happened in December, it's May now. If they were here I don't remember."

I paid for my drink, walked outside to the phone and copied down the phone number at the pay phone. We may have to get the records from that phone.

I drove back to Estancia and picked up the tapes to take home and start making copies for Ray and faxing him the information on Ms. Elder and the Zenner's cabin.

7

Hyakutake Comet

THAT NEXT MORNING IT DIDN'T TAKE LONG BEFORE MY CELL phone went off at seven am.

"This Maurice."

"Yes, this is Jean Zenner. You left your card on my door."

After advising Jean who I was she agreed to meet and talk to me.

"I work in Albuquerque at an auto shop near Wyoming and Central. If you want to come over we can talk here."

I was thankful she did not want a do a phone interview. I had learned you get so much more out of personal contact. It was not hard to find the business. A young middle age blonde was sitting in her office. I walked over to her.

"Ms. Zenner, I'm Maurice. I just talked to you on the phone."

"Oh yes. Come on in, let me close the door. Gives us more privacy."

"You live in Torreon?"

"Yes, I commute back and forth. We just love it in the mountains. We're from New York. Moved here a few years back and fell in love with New Mexico."

"Were you in the Torreon area in December nineteen ninety-five?"

"Yes. I was."

"You aware of the Anaya's cabin just to the east of you?"

"Oh yes we went down to the cabin the day they found the bodies. We talked to the S. O. officers. We didn't even know what had happen to those people. We felt so bad for those kids."

"When you said 'we' who did you mean?"

"Oh, my boyfriend was there with me. We gave the S.O. a statement."

"I read your statement, but I would like to ask you a little more about noise you heard."

"Yes. It was towards the end of March. I can't remember the name. It was the comet that was in the New Mexico area. But it was around the last weekend that you could visibly see it, where the tail on the comet was extremely visible. I was living up in Torreon. We didn't have the city lights and we could see it. It was incredibly beautiful."

"Now, do you remember the day of the week?"

"It was either a Friday or a Saturday night."

"What did you see besides the comet on that Friday or Saturday night?"

"I had gone to the outhouse. We didn't have running water. It was approximately ten-thirty, elevenish before I was retiring for bed that night. I was standing outside smoking my nightly cigarette looking at the comet. I heard loud music being played from across the cabin."

"Did you see anything from across the cabin?"

"Lights in the cabin when I meandered from the house to the outhouse."

"Which cabin was this that you saw lights and heard music?"

"The one across from me."

"To make sure, we're talking about the same one directly across from you? That was the Anaya's cabin?"

"Yes." *I could not believe what I was hearing. Someone was in the cabin was alive at the end of March 1996.*

"Did you see lights or hear music at any other time that day or after?"

"No. As far as the lights go, I never paid any attention, so I can't say whether lights had been on before, but I had never heard loud music up there before. That's what prompted my attention to look in that general direction."

"Did it seem very important at the time?"

"No, no. I did comment on it when I went back into the cabin and told my boyfriend. 'at least someone's having a good time this weekend.'"

"And when you say. music, was it—could you tell if it was a car stereo, a house stereo or..."

"I didn't really pay any attention to it as far as that goes. I would have thought that it was a home stereo just because of the fact that it was loud enough for me to be able to distinguish that there was music going on. I don't know. Stereos—some car stereos—"

"Did you happen to be at the scene on the day the bodies were discovered?"

"Yes."

"Have you ever been in the cabin?"

"Well, we didn't go physically to the cabin and witness the bodies or anything like that, but out of the people that were up there, it was Mr. Anaya, Mr. Ehlers, Mr. Ehlers' wife, who was home that day, me and my boyfriend and my brother-in-law and myself."

I had been on my computer checking for the comet when it popped up. Hyakutake.

"The name of that comet was Hyakutake. Does that sound familiar?"

"I don't know. I wasn't really paying attention. I couldn't be specific. I don't know the name of the comet."

"Now, according to the Expedia they said that it was most visible about March 25th."

"Okay."

"Would that pretty well coincide with what you were saying, late March?"

"I remember the comet. That's all I can tell you."

"And, of course, it was visible in April, as well?"

"Yes."

"Is that the only time you saw it?"

"We had watched it several times. March was the last of the best viewing."

"And according to them, what they're saying is that would have been the best time to see it, late March around the 25th. Is that pretty much what you're saying, in the late March area?"

"That's what I said."

"Did you see anybody at the cabin?"

"No. I can't see that far."

"You can't see it from that far?"

"I cannot see people from that far. We're talking ten-thirty at night. It's extremely dark there."

"Where is Ben Anaya's cabin located in reference to your property?"

"About a hundred yards."

"Just a hundred yards away?"

"About a hundred yards. I never measured it."

"Can you see their cabin from your cabin?"

"From certain parts of the property, yes. Not from my cabin, no."

"Can you see it from the outhouse?"

"Oh, yeah."

"How far—well, can you see it from your outhouse?"

"I wasn't standing at the outhouse when I was looking at the house, no. I was standing on the driveway between the outhouse and my house."

"Can you see it from there?"

"Yes. In the day time."

"So you can see from the driveway between the outhouse and the cabin?"

"Yes."

"Did you see any movement around there?"

"No, not that I noticed."

"And you said you saw lights?"

"Yes."

"Where were these lights?"

"At the property of the Anaya's."

"Where in the house?"

"Outside of the house. I don't know."

"Which window are you looking at then?"

"I just glanced in that general direction. I didn't go over and investigate anything. I'm not a nosey neighbor. I was standing in the driveway when I was looking at the cabin. When I heard music and I glanced over—"

"And you didn't see anybody moving around the cabin?"

"I wasn't looking for anybody, no."

"Did you see a party going on?"

"I didn't see anybody."

"What was the weather like?"

"You know about the weather in February. It was harsh, harsh snow, about two-and-a-half feet? Plus mud, I have a four-wheel drive truck specifically purchased for living up there. We got stuck."

"In March is it pretty muddy up there, too?"

"It was probably dried up a little bit, but there was still some spots in the road."

"Now, a normal car would have had trouble moving up there?"

"My mother and sister parked down the hill and walked up. The ruts are so bad, the cars bottom out."

"So a car having been up there would show evidence of being there?"

"Yes. There would probably be holes on the bottom of it."

"I don't think I have any other questions Ms. Zenner. Here's my card again. I've got your phone number if I need to get hold of you."

"Well I don't know if I was any help or not. Just being honest with what I saw and heard."

I walked away. Maybe I should go back and verify her story. There was a party at the end of March in the cabin with dead people. I got on my phone to the office.

"Regina, let me talk with Ray."

"Yea, Maurice."

"Ray, I just talked to the Ms. Zenner. She's owns the cabin just above the Anaya's cabin."

"Did she see anything?"

"Are you sitting down."

"Yea, I'm at my desk."

"End of March of this year there was a party at the Anaya's cabin."

"What? Are you sure?"

"Hyakutake helps us out with the dates."

"The comet?"

"Yup, that's what fixes the date and time for the party."

"You're telling me there was a party at the cabin with four dead people in there."

"No, I'm telling you what the neighbor told me. I'm the messenger."

"How positive is she? Did she see people there?"

"She's a smoker having her last cigarette at ten-thirty or eleven pm. She just heard the music and she comments to her boyfriend, 'at least someone is having a good time tonight.'"

"What the hell going on there?"

"It's New Mexico, Ray. Probably ghosts. We have everything else in New Mexico. Aliens. La Llorona. The humming noise from Taos. Why not ghosts in Torreon, New Mexico."

"By the way Regina set up a defense meeting for the attorneys and the investigators so get it in your calendar. Also State police called. Your photos are ready to get picked up. Also Regina needs some dates from you to set up Agent Jacoby's statement."

Review of Ben Sr.'s Statement

After reading Ben Sr.'s statement I sent the following fax to Ray:

Ray,

The following information is from Ben Sr. when he arrived at the cabin.

The screen door was also locked he had to reach in and unlock the screen.

The dead bolt to the front door was in a locked position.

The TV VCR was on.

The power for the house is in the bedroom. He saw another set of keys in the bedroom door.

Ben Sr. had two sets of keys at the cabin. One of them was kept in the dresser drawer in the same room where Ben was.

The other set must have been the one with the Jeep keys.

The bedroom doors and pantry all have locks on them.

Cassandra has two kids and they should have been with Ben Jr.

Missing is Ben Sr.'s 1976 Jeep Wagoner charcoal grey.

Last time he saw it was before Christmas.

The house was trashed.

The front gate was open.

Ben Sr. and Ben Jr. had a falling out in December.

Porfie told Ben Sr. someone took her VCR and left a bag of kid clothes at her house, this was around the 15th of Dec.

On the same day someone broke into his house and stole jewelry, guns, money and booze.

Ben Jr. did not have a drug problem. He smoked dope.

Ben Sr. daughter saw the Jeep at the house around the 15th or 18th of December.

The only person she saw was Popcorn.

He had bought Ben Jr. a cross and necklace at Santuario de Chimayo. (that was the one Ben had around his neck)

Ben has a .22 still in his leg. Ben Jr. accidently shot himself.

The only gun Ben had was a 357.

The other person who hangs out with Ben Jr. is Popcorn. They met when they were locked up.

At the time of the interview Ben Sr. did not know his son was dead.

Ray, if the 15th is true then to me the murder already has happened. Date of death is between the 12th and 15th. I don't believe Cassandra or Ben Jr. would have to break into their own parent's house and steal from their own family. Popcorn was the only person seen. My Time Line is now becoming a living document.

    Maurice

In November of 1996 we finally got to interview the lead investigator Agent Frank Jacoby. The last time we saw him was May 15, 1996. The bodies were found April 14, 1996 so now they have had a little over seven months to do their investigation. I thought this was more than enough time to get their time line done, their evidence gathered, the labs to do their forensic work.

I was looking forward to interviewing the lead agent. We also had a little over five months and received nothing by way of forensic requests or any evidence linking our client much less any of the other suspects.

It took me three days to get ready for our interview with the agent. We decided to do it at his office. Based on previous experience it was best to do the interview at the agent's office. This way he couldn't tell us, "Oh I must have forgot it in my office."

We started the interview at one thirty pm and went past six pm. Two Deputy DAs showed up, Ms. Malka and Mark Trujillo.

"Could I have your full name and occupation, please?"

"Frank A. Jacoby. I'm a law enforcement officer with the Department of Public Safety, the State Police. I'm an agent. I'm a senior patrolman."

"Can you summarize your assignments in the State Police since that time?"

"I did approximately three plus years in uniform, until about nineteen eighty-seven, as a patrol officer. In nineteen eighty-seven, I was assigned to the Narcotics Section headquarters here in Santa Fe, and I remained there until June of nineteen ninety-five."

"How is your present position?"

"I'm responsible for taking information on crimes and so forth, receiving information, investigating that information, developing reports, basically investigating the violations of the New Mexico statutes."

Frank had a habit of saying "so on and so forth" so much I nick named Frank 'Mr. So Forth.'

"Now, to your role in this case, are you the primary assigned agent in the case?"

"Yes."

"To clarify a couple of details at the scene, who did the forensic work at the scene?"

"Sergeant Branch, myself, Tom Christian, and Lawrence Murray, who's another agent assigned to Criminal with us here in Santa Fe. We did inventory, took pictures, and so forth. Christian later did the diagram. I made assignments as we went along, in concurrence with the sergeant's direction, as well. And then additionally, the second day, we had Mr. Larry Renner, who was a forensic person from the crime lab here at headquarters, go to the crime scene and look at different deposits on the walls that we thought might be blood. We had him evaluate those for presence of blood and so forth."

Larry Renner is an excellent forensic person and is excellent in processing crime scenes. After talking to Larry we found out all he was called out for was to examine the blood in the bedroom.

"On the second day, I did not go back on. I spearheaded the investigation in Albuquerque. I don't have a list of those names readily available."

"Did you follow up on the various different things that were processed, either by Renner or others, to determine what tests or evaluations were done of those things? By that I mean the blood, the fingerprints, any DNA, any work like that?"

"Yes, I did. I have reviewed all the lab results as they came in, and I believe they're all in. I checked with the lab this morning, and it seems like we have everything that they evaluated."

When Jacoby said this, what he meant was they only found fingerprints in the Jeep, because they never looked for any in the cabin.

"Do you have any fingerprint reports?"

"Yes, we do. They're in the lab. I gave them to you in discovery, in all the lab forms, results. I did make some more copies, though."

"Do you have handy what lab information you think you gave us, so I can make sure."

"This is all of it here. I made that this morning. You can have that, if you'd like."

"The material you have just given me has a number of reports in it. They appear to be dated April and May of 1996. Are there any more recent lab reports than these April and May 1996 ones?"

"Not to my knowledge, and I accessed these copies from the lab this morning."

They don't have any in their folder, and I can't recall any other items that are being processed at the time." *I couldn't believe what I was hearing. Five months into the case and they came up with only fingerprints from inside the Jeep. No DNA or fingerprints from the cans found at the scene. The only fingerprint found was from the firearm expert, who examined one of the guns. They should have had him examine the guns after they fingerprinted the guns.*

"Do you know of any that are being processed anywhere else other than the State Police laboratory?"

"No, sir. All items were to be processed here."

"Do you know if any request has been made to compare the latent prints recovered from the Jeep Wagoneer with fingerprints of anybody?"

"Yes, I made a request to compare those to Richard Munoz."

"Have you made any request to compare those with Shawn Popeleski?"

"I can't recall, probably based on the fact if I did request that, even on Richard, being whether or not I have even requested it, because they both admitted to having been in the Jeep."

When someone like Jacoby says, "I can't recall," the real answer was NO I did not. I couldn't believe what I was hearing. Jacoby had never gotten DNA, body samples (cranial hair, pubic hair, clothing from jail in Belen). Jacoby has done nothing to eliminate his star witness.

"But you don't recall whether you did or didn't make that request?"

"No, I don't, now that you remind me of that, the reason being, of course, that they both admitted having been in the Jeep."

"Did you make any requests, make any comparison with any other person of the latent prints found in the Jeep?"

"I can't recall right now."

This meant NO. A good investigator would have wanted to know who else was in the Jeep. What amazed me was Darren White, the Public Safety Director, could not afford to send out a forensic team but he sent out the State Police in an airplane to Pecos when the Jeep was discovered.

"Where would your documentation likely be?"

"I'm looking at it right now."

"Do you have a separate file in which you maintain the requests that you have made for laboratory comparisons or evaluations?"

"Yes. Here's a copy of the one we submitted on the Jeep itself, for processing. But to your question, to address your question on whether or not I specifically asked for anyone's prints to be compared to the latent found in the Jeep at this time, I can't recall if I had. And if I did not, that's based on my reasoning that both Shawn Popeleski and Richard Munoz admitted having been in the Jeep, and the Jeep was not believed to have been taken by the perpetrators."

"Does the fact that the Jeep was seen by several different people in March of 1996 cause you to think that possibly someone else's prints might be in it, other than the two men you have identified, Munoz and Popeleski?"

"Those are just allegations. Those have not been substantiated, those sightings, as you indicated, in March. I don't know that we substantiated any of those alleged sightings."

Ben's Jeep was seen several times after Ben was murdered. Popcorn and the Jeep were in Pecos, Texas. In December of 1995. The employees of the hotel verified the Jeep was there from December to April of 1996.

"Wasn't there a deputy sheriff in Santa Fe County who claimed to have seen the vehicle and copied down a license number?"

"I didn't talk to him. I think someone spoke to him. It's probably in one of the reports. You'd have to speak to that agent."

"Did you see the report?"

"I can't recall." *The answer was NO Jacoby.*

"Your information, according to the reports we've been provided, is that the vehicle was taken to Pecos, Texas, and left there at some point in December; is that correct?"

"We believe sometime in late November or December, yes. I believe in December, but..."

"And your belief is that both Munoz and Popeleski went down there in the vehicle and left it there at that time?"

"According to the information that they have given us, and information from the hotel itself, it seemed to fit."

"Did you request or obtain, from any State Police officer, to obtain logs of the Torrance County Sheriff's Department indicating a sighting of that Jeep by a Torrance County deputy sheriff in March of nineteen ninety-six?"

"I think that the agent that may have handled that was Tom Christian. He has a pretty lengthy report. I believe you have a copy of it provided to you in discovery. I'd have to refer back to it and see if, in fact, he's the one who did that."

"What method do you use for recording statements?"

"There's no usual method. Depends on the circumstances. If I feel we need to do an audio, we'll do audio. If we have the capability to do video, we'll do video. If the person doesn't want to go on tape for some reason, I'll handwrite."

This was the worst homicide in the state's history and Jacoby is telling us, "If I feel the need to do an audio." Jacoby wanted me to trust his notes. No way. Jacoby must have gone to the FBI where they are trained not to tape record statements or confession. Just trust us. Jacoby did not realize there was a very good jury instruction if they did not record the statement; any issue about who said what must be decided in a manner in favor of the defendant. It was hard to believe Jacoby was playing this game.

"What is your practice with respect to your notes?"

"It all depends. If I'm able to write a report right away, immediately after, let's say a day after, whatever, once I generate that report, I keep a rough, and I give the main report to the secretary to type. Once it comes back and clears, then I get rid of that copy. I make a fresh copy for myself. The notes I usually just destroy. In this case, I started a bit of a diary from the very first day in chronological order. There are some dates where there are no entries because nothing relevant occurred, and there was a time when I stopped taking notes because, for some reason, I didn't—interviews were being done either on audio or video and I didn't take notes."

"And then when you take notes, let's say, of a witness statement, let's say you interview someone, and you do it with handwritten notes, in this case are you keeping those notes?"

"I have them with me."

"I'd like to request that they be preserved, and I'd like to request that they also be produced for all witnesses who have been interviewed in connection with this matter."

Ms. Malka said, "I'm going to probably—well, I'm not one hundred percent sure. I think that the personal notes or the rough drafts kept by an officer are not discoverable. I'll look into that, Ray. I believe that the report that is synthesized from the notes is what is discoverable, but I will look into that."

"All right. But will you agree that they'll at least be preserved so that the issue can be addressed by a court or by counsel?"

"Certainly."

"Are there other witnesses whom you have interviewed for whom you have not yet made a report?"

"Yes."

"Who are they?"

"Mr. Richard Munoz, Mr. Daniel Silva, Mr. Daniel Saiz. I'll have to look at the other name. There was one other person. I can't remember this lady's name offhand. I don't know if I have it. If you bear with me just a second. This lady's name escapes me. She is the girlfriend to—here we go. I found it. Letitia Dominguez."

"Whose girlfriend is she?"

"She's girlfriend to Daniel Silva."

"And so just those four different people have been interviewed by you without reports; correct?"

"Mr. Popeleski was interviewed again. I met with him sometime in July, also, of this year, and interviewed him one more time."

"Was that a taped interview?"

"No, it was not."

"Who else was present?"

"Just myself and him."

"Where did you meet him?"

"Where he is incarcerated."

"Do you know of any other agents who have met with him and interviewed him in connection with this case?"

"I don't know of any other agents that may have interviewed him. I would have known—the only thing we have done is that Mike Fenner did transport him one day to a preliminary hearing."

This wasn't close to the truth. Fenner had Popcorn driving him around for over eight hours and never told anyone on May 13, 1996.

"Would that be one of the preliminaries in connection with this homicide?"

"Yes."

"And Letitia Dominguez—what was the date of her interview?"

"Six twenty-five ninety-six."

"What about the interview of Daniel Silva?"

"The same."

"And Daniel Saiz?"

At the time Jacoby knew who Saiz and Silva were as well as Letitia. We were under the assumption they were just gang members. We had no reports on them.

"And what about Mr. Silva and Mr. Saiz? Are they in custody?"

"Sir, I don't know. They were at the time. They were both at the Valencia County jail."

There were still in custody in Valencia County jail. They did not provide us with Letitia's address so we would have to find her on our own. Jacoby did not want us to talk to her or to Saiz or Silva.

"I notice that on the reports that we have, most of them have names of witnesses but don't have their addresses. Do you have their addresses?"

"No, but I will get those addresses for you. The agents that were assigned to these leads, it was their intent to get addresses and so forth."

"So the cover sheet, then, is the only record of the address that you maintained?"

"Unless that agent doing the interview has maintained some notes on their own, where they might have an address written down. And what I'll do is make a request through the chain of command to all the officers that were involved. We'll make the request for any addresses they may have, phone numbers."

"All right. Do you not, in your office, computerize any aspects of your investigative files or work?"

"I don't."

"And then you thought possibly the lab may have a tracking system in their computer program?"

"I do believe so, because I have been in there looking for a case, and they'll access by name on the computer and give you a file number and so forth. But I don't know how extensive that would be."

"You gave us the names of several for whom you haven't completed reports as yet. Do you have any for whom you completed reports and nonetheless retained the rough notes?"

"No, I rarely ever take handwritten notes, statements, from people, so I don't have any. And I don't have knowledge of anybody else having those kinds of notes."

"But what I'm talking about is your own notes of interviews you did with witnesses."

"Yes, of course."

"Other than the tapes of Archuleta and Setina, you have got, I see, several tapes with you."

"Videotapes, yes, sir."

"You don't have any audiotapes?"

"I have these audiotapes here, the ones that we have not transcribed, and of course, they'll be made available for you. The transcription on the interviews with Popeleski, they were audio. And the videos are here, and you have been given copies of those. I do retain all the copies of all the transcripts we provided you, both on Popeleski, and Shaun Wilkins, and Nieto. I have those."

"Can you just run through the list of the ones you do have there?"

"Popeleski's have been done, and you have transcripts."

"And the videotapes. Can you run through which videotapes are there? I want to make sure I have all of them."

"Okay. I have the original homicide crime scene video by Torrance County. And then I have an original videotape by Lawrence Murray. I have three duplicates here, but I have the homicide scene by Frank Jacoby, the one I just mentioned by the SO, and the one by Murray. They're all condensed in one tape here. I have Shawn Popeleski, four fifteen of ninety-six. Interview. I have an interview four fourteen ninety-six on Richard Munoz.

"And I have one for Lawrence Nieto dated five thirteen of ninety-six. Ms. Malka has the original on the interview with Nieto."

In all my years of working in law enforcement I had never heard of the DA's office being in charge of the original taped interviews. In looking back, if the officer would have hid the tapes they would have been libel. But if the DA does something such as hiding tapes, they have prosecutorial immunity.

"Popeleski? But you have a copy of that one, I believe. So I need to make copies of Munoz, and I believe you also do not have—from looking at what we've provided for you, we may not have the one on Shawn Popeleski on five-ten."

"I believe that's right."

"I'm going to mark this so I can get you copies."

"Mr. Twohig, now, when you did the transcriptions of tapes, what has happened with the tapes? Where are they kept after that?"

"I have them."

"You maintain those?"

"I have them. As a matter of fact, Frank Gomez, five thirteen, and Lawrence Nieto are right here. I have one in here for Nieto on seven sixteen ninety-six. I mean four seventeen ninety-six with the interview, but transcription on seven sixteen ninety-six. So I keep them."

Jacoby withheld the information of two interviews on the 5/13 of Nieto. He had to have known of the other tapes the DA Malka had, and why did he give her the original tapes to hold on to?

"Could you go through whatever other tapes you have and just tell us what they are? I just want to double-check what we have received against what you think you have provided."

"Okay. I'm going to open these, so I'm right on the money as to what I'm saying, okay? Let's see if I have any others here. Four fifteen of ninety-six, April fifteen, nineteen ninety-six, for Frank Gomez."

"That's the tape and the transcript. You keep them both together in an envelope, then; correct?"

"Yes, and you have copies of these."

"Yes."

"These two tapes, one is on Shaun Wilkins, four eighteen ninety-six, and Lawrence Nieto, five thirteen of ninety-six. And Lawrence Nieto, four seventeen of ninety-six. And to the best of my recollection, that's it." *Jacoby continued to lie. Jacoby referred to only one 5/13/96 tape of Woody.*

"We also note from testimony at the preliminary hearing that an Albuquerque police officer by the name of DeReyes was involved in this case."

"Juan DeReyes, yes."

"Well, when we first started the investigation at the crime scene and learned, of course, that Mr. Ben Anaya, Sr., was the owner and he lived in Albuquerque, our investigation took us there. After interviewing Mr. Anaya and his girlfriend and other individuals, we quickly determined that his son, the victim, Ben Anaya, Jr., may have been involved in the Eighteenth Street gang. Realizing immediately that we were out of our element, as far as being out of our area, like Albuquerque, we needed the assistance of local authority. Plus given the fact that a gang might be involved, we solicited through their command structure assistance from the gang unit and Mr. DeReyes was assigned to us."

"Did he, as someone who was assigned to this investigation, make separate reports, to your knowledge, of his activities?"

"Yes, he did. As a matter of fact, I have a copy of one of his reports. I don't have it with me right here. I don't know if he generated any other reports that he might have in his custody, but he may have."

"I don't recall seeing DeReyes' report. It's a very short report. It doesn't say much, but I will get it for you." *In a mouthful Jacoby can tell us I don't recall seeing DeReyes report. But it's a very short report, it doesn't say much.*

"What role did DeReyes have in the investigation itself? I mean, how you would you define his role?"

"I can't speak for DeReyes' experience, but we did learn early on that he had spent some time with the gang unit and had been around the police department for quite a while, and was very well-respected by his people. The role that he played was that he made available for us, information relative to the gangs, as to who they were, nicknames, where they lived, addresses, and so on and so forth. They have a computerized information database which he accessed for us, and knew where people lived, knew how to track them down, the associations, who to ask to go find a certain individual. So he provided a lot of basic information to track down people."

"Did he tell you anything about his familiarity with any of the defendants in this case, his prior familiarity?"

"Shaun Wilkins. Willie Nieto. He knew them quite well. I don't know what kind of interaction they may have had in the past. I do know that all these individuals appeared in their database."

"Did DeReyes participate in the investigation actively?"

"Yes, I would consider his participation active, as far as being asked to do certain things like do some interviews, because of the rapport, the language on the street, the fact that these individuals did know him and wanted to talk to him. But as far as making decisions on the investigation, he did not make any decisions."

"Who made the decision to videotape the interviews that were videotaped?"

"I prefer to do interviews on videotape, because—well, most of us are visually oriented, and it just has more—you can see facial expressions and so forth. So basically, it's my decision, but we concurred. And early on we decided we would do video when it was necessary or viable."

"Did the district attorney's office have any role in the investigation?"

"The only role I think the DA's office played was that Mady went to the scene the day of the discovery of the victims, made a conscious decision to request State Police do the investigation, and then she later assisted me—she did not enter the crime scene. She later assisted me in putting together search warrants and so forth, motions, different kinds of motions and so forth that she needed to do."

"Did she or anyone else from that office attend the briefings?"

"She may have attended some discussions, especially when we had a question of a legal nature. Especially when we had concerns of a legal nature."

Jacoby failed to mention she was also the custodian of all the tapes of Woody and maybe Popcorn.

"Who generally conducted the briefings?"

"The briefings were informal, and we preferred them that way, so that everyone would feel like they—no idea was outrageous."

"Did you obtain any telephone records in the course of the investigation?"

"We did quite a few requests for telephone calls, and we have quite a few responses. They're upstairs in my office. They're very extensive. I have not been able to even make headway with those records. The majority of responses are such that long-distance calls and so on and so forth can be accessed to a different carrier and so forth, so that they're not—of no consequence. But if you would like to review those, it's going to take quite a while to do that."

"We would like a set of copies."

"Sure."

"Were any requests made on the toll phones in the vicinity?"

"Not to my recollection, no. Somebody may have done that without me knowing, but—phones in what vicinity?" *This told me Jacoby did not check the pay phone at the store in Torreron*

"Do you recall being present during the interview of Popcorn on the fifteenth? At that time he was using the other name, Frank Gomez?"

"Well, yes. The first initial interview, I was present. I think we have a transcript of that."

"Yes. Was Officer DeReyes there as well?"

"I believe so. I'd have to look at the report."

"On the transcript of that interview, there's a reference to a list being shown to Popcorn. Do you have that list?"

"I don't know what list."

"It appeared to be a list of gang members."

"It might be generated out of the entire—I do remember seeing it, and Juan DeReyes would have access to that, and I think he'd be the only one authorized to release that."

"But he was showing it to Popeleski during that interview; correct?"

"If that's the list that they were referring to, yes."

"That's a list that he himself brought to the interview, not something you provided him?"

"You'd have to ask Juan DeReyes about that."

"At this time I request that the State provide all the tapes that exist in the case and simply locate them and collect them, rather than us having to take the statements of each one of these separate agents associated with the investigation. I can put that in writing, if you like." *We were never provided a list of all the tapes.*

"Yeah. From talking to Mr. Anaya on the first day, I believe, he had—I'm sorry. It should be in the reports, how that came about. We learned early on that Popcorn was an associate of Deuce, which is Ben Anaya, Jr. We pretty much suspected that this Popcorn might be Frank Gomez, because Mr. Anaya, Sr., had received a letter at his address belonging to Frank Gomez, from the courts. So we deduced that Popcorn and Frank Gomez may be one and the same. So that kind of helped when we got information that there was someone in jail by the name of Frank Gomez that may be a Popcorn, put it together for us there. So the name Popcorn popped up from different sources, some of which are probably documented, some of which are just in somebody's mind somewhere."

"Did you ever find out if there was a real Frank Gomez and Mr. Popeleski was just using his name?"

"Yes, there is. In fact, I believe he admitted it on one of the transcripts. He admitted that he borrowed his name. He had done some time with him or something."

"And did you or any other agent, to your knowledge, discover how that dead bolt lock was actually locked? In other words, who locked it the last time the cabin was used by anyone?"

"No, because I don't think that was possible, because according to Mr. Anaya, when he opened the door and discovered the bodies, there was no law enforcement around. He then gave the keys to Mr. Ehlers to open the back gate, the little lock, and Mr. Ehlers discovered then that the chain itself had been opened on that back gate. In other words, the lock would serve no purpose. I don't believe that any law enforcement ever established whether or not that dead bolt was locked." *Ben Anaya Sr. told him the door was locked.*

"But some dead bolt locks, as I'm sure you know, will lock from the inside and the outside, so that a key is necessary to unlock it on the inside, rather than just a switch of some sort."

"That's right."

"Did you ever locate the clothing Shawn Popeleski was wearing at the time of his arrest on December twenty-fifth, nineteen ninety-five?"

"Did I ever locate his clothing?"

"Yes."

"That he was wearing?"

"Yes. Or do you know if any State Police officer or anyone connected with this investigation did so?"

"I don't recall. I don't have possession of that clothing. I don't know if maybe it's still at the jail. I don't remember requesting it."

"It's never been examined, then, and compared with dirt, blood, or other fibers associated with the crime scene, has it?"

"Not to my knowledge."

"I will request that the diary kept by Agent Jacoby be provided a copy to us. Well, let's go through it. You mentioned, then, Agent Jacoby, that you made kind of daily notes, if there was activity that day, in association with this case; correct?"

"Yes."

"What kind of notes did you make, for example?"

"They're just handwritten."

"But I mean, like, if you had a witness you were going to interview, would you make a notation?"

"No. I have nothing to hide here. Any leads that he might give, description of his son, and so forth. We were trying to identify the body. Those kinds of notes."

"I misunderstood your description. When you examined the scene, did you ever find, let's say, a stash area where guns apparently were kept or could easily have been kept, that was a hiding place?"

"Well, there's any number of places in that area where guns may have been kept. Obviously, the attic area and so on and so forth. Any one of the bedrooms. Naturally, we did not find the house in the condition that it would have been when they—before the incident happened. I'm sure there's plenty of space. That house is pretty big."

"Did anyone, such as Popcorn or anyone else you talked to, describe a stash location for firearms, where they were kept by Mr. Anaya?"

"I can't recollect that. I can't recall that. I do remember that Popeleski did mention the fact that weapons were being kept in the Jeep, some of the weapons were being kept in the Jeep."

"Have you ever—you being the State Police, or any investigator—to your knowledge identified anyone who bought any firearm from Popcorn?"

"Not to this date. We're still trying to work on that, and the investigation is actually still continuing on those matters."

"Did he inform you as to who he sold any firearms to?"

"He mentioned the fact that someone had seen some weapons, a gentleman by the name of Green Eyes, and he may have sold him some right before they went to Texas. Agent Lucero, I think, makes mention of that in his report."

"Well, according to this interview, Sedillo said he went to the residence of Green Eyes and then gives the location and said he only knew him by his gang name. I wondered if that was it, or if you're talking about a separate statement Popcorn made concerning Green Eyes. Do you know?"

"I'm trying to remember. I can't answer that at this time. I would be guessing."

"Do you know if anyone who used the name Green Eyes, was referred to as Green Eyes, has at this time been identified?"

"That's possible, but I can't confirm that. I'd have to look at some notes, because Richard Munoz also knows a gentleman by the name of Green Eyes. He may have given me a name. I just do not recall."

"But that's the only lead you are pursuing at this time on someone purchasing a gun from Popcorn?"

"Popcorn, yes, of a name. Popcorn stated to us in some of our conversations with him—which are probably not documented, because it was just conversations—that they were in the business of stealing guns and selling guns. So they sold guns, you know. And he had to sell some of the guns to make the trip to Texas. But he didn't mention, from what I can recollect, any names right now."

"But he's indicating, then, that the guns from the Jeep, that he described as being in the back of the Jeep when he drove away were sold in the Albuquerque area before he went down to Pecos?"

"He didn't sell all the guns. We discovered some of them in the Jeep, as you can tell by the evidence. He said he had sold some guns before he left. We do know that he also traveled to Arizona. I don't know that if he—that he didn't sell any in Arizona, and that he didn't sell any in Texas. We do suspect that he took Ben Anaya's .357 magnum, which he stole from him and Deuce had stolen from his father early on in December, had taken that to Texas according to Richard Munoz. He had seen a gun matching that description in the Jeep. What became of that gun, I don't know. Popeleski did not reveal that, what became of that gun. So he may have sold some in Texas, New Mexico, and Arizona."

"But there have been none recovered at this time?"

"Yes, sir."

"No, and according to Mr. Popeleski, there were quite a few."

"And also, in his subsequent interview that you did that we don't have yet, he confirmed that those guns were in the Jeep at the time he left the cabin?"

"Yes."

"But they had simply been stored in the Jeep?"

"Yes, had so many guns, they just kept some of them in the Jeep."

"When do you anticipate completing your reports that you have mentioned?"

"These are being put together on one report. I'm about halfway through it already. So all the ones I mentioned are part of one report. I anticipate by the time it goes to the secretary and everything for typing, I would say the second week in December, if not sooner."

"I don't see a record of videotapes taken into evidence. I'm talking now about, say, rented videotapes, purchased videotapes, movies, you know, videotape movies."

"On the second day, we had requested that the second group seize VCRs and so on and so forth, and I believe some tapes were taken then. I'm not quite sure if they were or not, but I believe there were some tapes around that should have been taken into custody. I'd have to look at the evidence control sheets and see if they were, in fact, taken. This morning, while reviewing these, I did see that the VCR was entered."

"Have you had a chance to review the evidence logs to determine whether any tapes were seized, any videotapes were seized?"

"No."

"Have you located any indication of any of the videotapes being seized or otherwise logged into evidence?"

"I don't see any of it, any indication of that right now."

"At the time that the videocassette player was seized, was there a tape in it?"

"You know what? I don't know. You're asking me questions that I'd have to review that lab work that was done on that, to see if that existed. Is it relevant to something?"

"It is. It's relevant to the time of death. That's why I was curious."

"For the rental time?"

"If there was a rental of the videotape and it was the one in the machine, it might give some additional insight into the time of death."

"That would be a benefit to all of us, but I do not recall that, sir, and I'd have to look at what was submitted to the lab. I did not submit the VCR myself. I'd have to go through that and see if there was something stuck inside or something like that. I don't have any paper on that right here right now."

"Who made the decision to leave whatever property, tangible items, et cetera, were left at the cabin once the crime scene was abandoned?"

"No. You can't take everything, naturally. We don't even have storage space for half that stuff. If it showed—at least if we perceived that it didn't have any evidentiary value, we would leave it. Basically, on the second day, whoever was in charge made a decision, probably Sergeant Baughman. And I later went to the cabin at least one other time, again went in with permission, and looked around, just in case we missed something. I didn't find anything that I thought of value, so I didn't seize anything additional. So I made the decision then not to seize anything else."

"When did you go on that next trip?"

"I can't recall. It's in my notes. It will be in that report that's forthcoming. Tom Christian went with me, as a matter of fact. I can give you a date. I do have it logged. It was sometime after, though. I don't remember the exact date. We can get you that date."

"All right. Was it after the family had disposed of some of the property, thrown a lot of the junk away that was out there?"

"No. It was before. On the second day, what happened was, they cleared the house completely. Everything went outside. The first day we were very meticulous about not disturbing too many things. The second day they went through it very precisely, including a number of agents. Most of the stuff was left outside then. When I went to visit the cabin was just a few days after that. That stuff was still outside."

"Have you issued—you being, I suppose, the state Police associated with the investigation subpoenas for evidence?"

"Yes, to obtain any evidence."

"At one point, I believe a debit card of Cassandra Sedillo's was seized, an EBT card."

"Yes."

"Have you been able to determine the dates and amounts and locations of the usage of that card?"

"Yes. It is in records somewhere. I don't believe that I have it, if it's not in someone's report. One of the agents was assigned to research that. It should be in one of the reports."

"I don't recall seeing it in the report. It was one of the questions I had. That's why I wondered."

"Yes, it was determined there is a last date of usage, but I don't know what that date is."

"Has a document been obtained reflecting, like, a printout from the usage of the card?"

"I don't recollect. That agent may have it in possession, but I will check on it."

"A couple of last areas that involve things that we thought would be there that we have not yet seen. One is there's a reference to a tape of an interview with Mr. Nieto, that began on April seventeen, 1996, and there was some malfunction in the tape. Is that tape available?"

"That's the one where side A recorded, and side B would not record for some reason. That's that tape, I believe, the one I have with me. Because the transcript ends abruptly, I believe. That's why, because it malfunctioned."

"Is the remainder of the interview available in some form?"

"I think we ended it right there, because basically we had learned everything we needed to learn. We may have talked a little bit after that, but I don't recall any notes, keeping any notes on it."

"Well, in that interview, there's a mention, interviewing Woody—and this was on, as we understand it, April seventeenth, around seven-thirty in the evening, there was a mention of a maroon car. I believe you're the one asking him, or the interrogator said, 'You guys went up there in a maroon car.' Where did the color of the car—where was that learned from?"

"We had already known about the car, because, well, you know, you have it in the report. I'm liable to say something that—those statements are in there, but the colors had both been mentioned by Popeleski, who believed the car to be maroon or black or dark-colored, and Nieto himself had said that Shaun had come over to threaten him in a maroon car at one time at the house where he was living, 405, whatever, 59th, I believe. So they're in the transcripts where this color came up."

"And there was a mention of a Camaro parked in front of Woody's house."

"Yes. That's the same car that they believed to be the real dark maroon or purple car."

"Same vehicle?"

"Yes, which Wilkins had been driving."

"Can you clarify how the date of December eighteenth has been fixed as the probable date of the homicides in this case?"

"Do I say that somewhere?"

"It's in the information in this case, and it was in the initial complaint in the case."

"I think what happened there was that in the process of interviewing people and setting dates down on the time line, Mr. Ben Anaya had said that it was possibly around the fifteenth—at first he said fifteenth—of December that he had gone up there and took them food. He then retracted and said the tenth, about the tenth, because he remembered it was a Sunday, and so on and so forth. And then Popeleski, of course, and Munoz were in Texas the twenty-third, is when they rented the room in Pecos, Texas. And some other information that I can't recall right now—it may be in the reports—which kind of narrowed it down, narrowed the time around probably the eighteenth, as the central dates. But it could have happened anytime from, let's say, the eleventh through, let's say twenty-second, twentieth, of December."

"Has there been any verification of Popcorn's trip to Arizona?"

"Oh, yes, of course."

"Is that verified?"

"Well, we have the receipts, copies of the receipts for the motel, the bus tickets, which Mr. Moya has already seen."

"That's the Pecos ticket. I'm talking about his trip to Arizona."

"Oh, Arizona, excuse me. Popeleski told us about it, and independently. Munoz had not had contact with him. Richard Munoz, on my interview, also told me about his trip to Texas. I mean, to Arizona, excuse me. And also I believe one of the agents requested some information out of Arizona on some other matters pertaining to Popeleski, and Popeleski, of course, had said he went to visit a girlfriend but didn't give a name or address or anything like that. So Richard Munoz also said that they did go to Arizona, stayed there whatever time it took to travel to Winslow, I believe, and then left for Texas almost immediately, coming through Albuquerque."

"But has there been any corroboration of those two statements? By gas receipts, by anything of that—"

"Didn't find anything in the Jeep that showed Arizona, that I can recollect. They're independent statements. I mean, two individuals that haven't seen each other for months, you know, gave that statement."

Munoz never stated he went to Arizona with Popcorn.

"But when you speak of corroboration, you're just saying two people who apparently have not seen each other; right?"

"Uh-huh."

"You don't have any idea whether they have talked on the phone or not?"

"There's no way to know that, other than the fact that when I have met with Shawn Popeleski, the last time, when he was in jail, probably around July, something, I got a list of phone numbers that he had been calling from the jail. You have to call collect and so forth. Mr. Munoz's phone number does not appear on that list. So he had not called him from that location."

"We'd like to request that list of phone numbers, too, as well, to determine who has been called, and any information that's been obtained from Arizona authorities relating to the Popeleski—which you referred to a moment ago that another agent has obtained."

"If you haven't already obtained it, yes."

We never got the list.

"Did you learn the date of the incident that Popcorn was assaulted in Albuquerque? You mentioned his arm was broken or injured."

"You know, many people, other people, that were interviewed by different agents knew of that incident, but no one could really put down the date. We do believe that it's sometime in November, around the fifteenth, I think, as some people mentioned, but we haven't been able to confirm it. A lot of the names that were mentioned are first names only. Nobody seems to know the address."

"Didn't Woody tell you in his statement that it happened on December fifteenth?"

"He may have."

"A couple more background things. What homicides have you investigated in the past?"

"I'm currently working on one now that happened after this. We treat all our cases where a person has died unattended as a possible homicide. And in uniform, I had a suicide—appeared to be a homicide, turned out to be a suicide—in Las Vegas. And prior to this case, coming aboard with Criminal, we had an individual who died also in Las Vegas. They treated it as a homicide, found out that it was self-inflicted injury during a domestic; and the Torreon homicide. I have been involved in other aggravated assaults and so forth."

"But since you joined Criminal Division, Criminal Investigations Bureau, this is the first homicide you investigated?"

"It's the first confirmed homicide, yes."

"Well, I'm inquiring because I'm dealing generally with an experience base, and I'm trying to inquire into the experience base, especially since this present one is an ongoing investigation. Which homicide is it that you're investigating?"

"Well, it's at the penitentiary, and I'm not going to give you the name. It's ongoing. If I may add for the record, though, I did not manage this investigation into the Torreon homicide by myself. We had experienced people giving me a hand. The sergeants both have had the experience in homicides. The lieutenant, all the agents there, Lucero, Fenner, have all been in longer than I have. The briefings, so on and so forth. So I have not had the final say on everything we've done."

"I also would like to request the time sequence you indicated had been put together. You mentioned, I believe, also in your testimony there's a written time sequence. I request that we obtain it."

"Did I say it was written? Did I say it was written?"

"I thought you did say it was written."

"I said we hadn't established one, but we can put one together for you. It wouldn't be a problem."

"There is no written time sequence at this point, as far as you know?" It had only been seven months since the bodies were found.

"No. As far as I know, not one that we would present to the Court. In my notes you'll see some dates here and there. But we don't have one established that we're ready to go to court with. So when we establish one, we'll provide it for you."

"All right. We'd like even the interim time sequences, because they may have a bearing on the sequence of the investigation, as well. So we'll request those, as well."

The interview ended with the agent. Ray and I had one-hour drive back home to talk about the case.

"What do you think, Maurice?"

"Bottom line Ray, they are calling it the worst homicide in the state of New Mexico history and they have not got any forensic evidence. The agent keeps telling us they are testing but no results. You would think their lab would have this case as a high priority. Also if you noticed they sent Larry

Renner to the scene but no report from Larry. That is not like him at all. They did not send up any other forensic experts to the scene. They did no luminal, testing, no fingerprint collection, no time line."

"We're still dealing with eye witnesses, Maurice. I agree so far they have no forensics but that doesn't mean they're not testing."

"They've had seven months on the evidence to get things tested and they have no results. Let's get a speed letter from the DA and see if we can get a look at evidence they collected so we can do our own evaluation. Jacoby said he's got all the results back already, and they have nothing."

"I'll ask the DA in the morning for the letter as well as the list of the other items we didn't get from the agent."

"We got all the photos from the State Police, Torrance County S.O. and Office of the Medical Investigators. They are tough to deal with. They gave them to us in four by five's. I've been using a magnifying glass to get close details of the inside of the cabin. It's like looking for a needle in a haystack."

Ray had seen some of the police photos. "How did the cabin and the yard get so trashed?"

"I've got no idea I understand. The S.O. is blaming D.P.S. and vice a versa. I don't believe two small young boys who are dehydrated and starving would have had the energy to have done all of that. But I did see on the news where the TV stations were reporting with film coverage of people cleaning out everything from the cabin. We need to get into that cabin Ray before they do anything else to it. What I don't like is Jacoby never did any corroboration of Popcorn or Woody's statement. They never checked to see when any vehicles were stolen. Mode of transportation to a murder scene is extremely important to investigators."

I had started my own time line:

November 30, 1995:
    First event of Popcorn and the gang. Popcorn is ranked out of 18th Street.
    Party was at Bonita's house.
    Eighteenth Street ranks out Popcorn over a stolen car, using the name of Frank Gomez twice, snitching on a fellow gang member.
    Wilkin's was the first to hit Popcorn

December 8, 1995
    Cassandra used her EBT card at 5900 Fortuna NW. (They were still alive.)

December 10, 1995
Ben takes food and a dead bolt lock to cabin. (They were still alive.)

December 11-18, 1995
Shaun Wilkins is arrested and in custody at BCDE (Bernalillo County Detention Center)
Roy is at Motor Vehicle Department Ck. 562 Make an exhibit out of check. Wilkins is in custody until the eighteenth of December. Could not have been at the cabin between those days.

December 15, 1995
Porfie and Ben's Sr. houses are broken into. Bens Sr.'s Jeep is seen out in front of the house. Popcorn is seen out in front of Ben's house. Ben Jr. would never have loaned his dad's jeep to Popcorn to drive to Ben Sr.'s house to break in.

Woody statement from April 17, 1996. Homicide could not have occurred.

December 23, 1995
Popcorn and Little Dreamer return from Pecos, Texas. Spend the night at Dreamer's house.

December 24, 1995
Popcorn leaves Little Dreamer's house to Belen, New Mexico.

December 25, 1995
Popcorn is arrested in Belen.

March 24-25, 1996
Party at the cabin. See Ms. Zenner's statement.

April 3, 1996
Shaun Wilkins was at Woody's in a stolen car. Maroon Camaro. Officers are accusing Wilkins, Roy, and Woody using this stolen car in December.

April, 14, 1996
Ben Sr. finds bodies.

April 17, 1996
Statements of Woody. (Stolen car. They were at my house two weeks ago.) This would have put it back to the 3rd of April.

Looking for Alibis

I had also found out Roy worked the entire month of December at the hydraulic shop in Corrales. The owner who paid some of his lower employees in cash for tax purpose did not want to say Roy was there every day.

But Roy's supervisor liked Roy and stood up for him. "Roy worked every day from the day after Thanksgiving to the middle of January. His grandfather dropped him off at eight am and picked him up at five-thirty pm every day. I don't know where he was on the weekends but all the rest of the time he was right next to me."

I had to get the reports and jail records on Wilkins and Woody. I wanted to put those times into the time line.

I finally had a chance to look at my phone and check my messages. The first one was from APD records, "Maurice your Prints Screens and reports are ready. Bring a check for three hundred fifty dollars."

Second message: "Maurice your photos are ready to be picked up they are at the Walgreens by Richard Road in Santa Fe. I don't know the cost so bring a check."

Third message: "Maurice this is Dan Burrola give me a call 'hito' when you get a chance."

Fourth message: "Maurice this is Doug Case, Roy's supervisor. Call me."

Fifth message: "Maurice this is Bubba give me a call. By the way no stolen Camaros or Trans Am in the months of October, November, December, or January. Found one in March taken from Press Hospital. I'll get you the case number. Good luck."

Sixth message: "Maurice this is Margaret, Roy's girl friend, can you call me please."

Seventh message: "Mr. Moya this is Benita, I heard you were looking for me my number is _____"

Eight message: "Mr. Moya, this is Airie's father, I heard you're looking for my daughter. She is no longer in the state of New Mexico. Please don't call back."

Ninth message: "Maurice this is Wayne from the OMI's office returning your call."

Damn. I need a secretary and a bottomless checkbook. I figured the reports and photos had a high priority and the rest of the calls I can make on the road to Santa Fe to pick up the photos.

I had a stack of reports from APD and jail records to go through. I thought I could read them and put them in chronological order at the same time while driving to Santa Fe.

One hour later I look up from the reports and I see the Cerrillos Road exit the main highway into Santa Fe.

Santa Fe is my birthplace and my father's birthplace. In the Plaza hangs my great, great grandfather's shield from Spain. The ladder climbing the castle wall underneath the shield displays the name "Moya."

My dad and grandparents owned most of the land off Canyon road and Camino Delora behind the church. My grandmother took care of the Cristo Rey church and we always felt this was her ticket into heaven.

Both my grandparents are buried in the church's front yard. By working at the Cristo Rey church my grandmother assured a place for her and my grandfather in the yard.

The area was known as the Acequia Madre. The Santa Fe River follows Alameda Street. I could never get lost visiting them. My father built several homes in that area in the 1950s and they are still standing today. I wanted to go by and reminisce but there was more work to be done. I went into Walgreens, gave them my name and the clerk gave me a nasty stare.

"You want these photos?"

"Yes, do they have my name on them."

"You represent those baby killers."

"No, I came to pick up the photos."

"Gas chamber is too good for those boys."

"How much do I owe you?"

"If it was up to me I would triple the charge. You have fifteen rolls here, you realize that don't you?"

"How much do I owe you?" I handed him my credit card.

He stared at it, "So you're that PI who represent the devils. How can you defend them after what they did to those babies."

I could tell he saw the photos when they came out and may have made a extra set for him. "Can I please have the photos."

He slid them over to me knowing I could not carry all of them. "Do you have a bag for them?"

He handed me a bag, "You put them in. I don't want to touch them."

I wanted to start looking at the photos of the scene. But I held back. I didn't want to get them out of order. (Being a Field Investigator I knew photos are taken in sequence.) I looked into one of the bags of photos, "No Negative."

We were not going to be able to blow up photos for details. They were all 4 x 5's. Great, now I have to find my mom's magnifying glass to look at the crime scene photos.

On my way back to Albuquerque I called Ray to brief him. "Ray, I picked up the reports from A.P.D. (Albuquerque Police Department) and the photos of the crime scene from Walgreens in Santa Fe. I also fax you a copy of my notes on Ben Sr.'s statement."

"Did you get a chance to look at the video or the recording of the statements on Popcorn and Woody?"

"No that is going to be a three day job."

"We need the recording so we can get them transcribed."

"I know. I plan to tape record them as I'm viewing them. I'll drop off all the tapes minus the Crimes Scene, Woody's and Popcorn's."

"I thought that was all them."

"No, they did about twenty other interviews. Some of gang members, but mostly people on the outskirts. So I don't need them yet."

8

Little Dreamer

I REACHED INTO THE BOX OF TAPES AND GRABBED THE CASSETTE tapes and started listing to interviews as I drove back to Albuquerque. I saw the name 'Little Dreamer'. He was the one who Popcorn picked up and took to either Arizona or Pecos, Texas. I pulled out my pen and pad, put it next to me and started taking notes while I was driving south on I-25. I was able to get his phone number and address written down, hoping I could understand my writing when I got home.

"When did you first meet him?"

"You mean Popcorn?"

"Yea."

"Been a while."

"Did you go on a trip with him?"

"Yea, we went to Pecos, Texas. In his Jeep."

"When did you see him?"

"Christmas break the fifteenth of December. I saw him at the Center by my house." *I remembered that was the day Ben Sr.'s house and Porfie's house were broken into.*

"Was it a black Jeep you were in?"

"Yea."

"Who was he with?"

"Green Eyes. He lives at Forty-seventh and Central by the fire station."

"Did you see any guns?"

"Yea, I saw two rifles and a handgun. He sold them to Green Eyes."

"Do you remember what day you left Albuquerque?"

"No."

"Why were you going to Pecos, Texas?"

"We weren't, we were going to my aunt's in Richardson, Texas."

"Did you stop anywhere?"

"Wal-Mart in Belen."

"We found a Wal-Mart receipt in the Jeep date December nineteenth at seven pm."

"Yes, sir. I guess so I don't pay much attention to time."

"How long did the trip take?"

"Just a couple of days."

"Did he ever talk about Ben, Cassandra or the kids?"

"No, sir."

"When did the Jeep break down?"

"When we got to Pecos and my aunt send me money for a room. Oh yea, and a bus ticket back to Albuquerque."

"Did Popcorn come back on the bus also?"

"Yea. We got back on the twenty-first or twenty-second in the middle of the night."

"When did you see Popcorn last?"

"He spent the night with us and then left in the morning. I never saw him again."

"How was Popcorn acting?"

"Like he was running away from something."

"We got a credit card in your aunt's name. The receipt is dated December twenty and twenty-one for the Holiday Inn."

"Yea, that's when we stayed there."

As I listen I kept going back to the dates. The 15th, two burglaries, and a trip to Pecos. Popcorn testified he had gone on a day trip to Winslow, Arizona. That would have been on the 14th. The murders had to have occurred then on the 12th to the 14th. Ben Sr. saw his son on the 10th. So where were Woody, Shaun and Roy on the eleventh through the 14th? If we could narrow down the events of December 11 through the 14th it would help. So how long did it take the two boys to die, four or five days at the most. That would put the time of the boys' deaths from the 11th through the 16th of December.

So why don't Popcorn and Woody know the date of the party? And if death did occur on those dates? The 10th was a Sunday, the 11th on a Monday, the 15th would have been on a Friday and Popcorn is seen in the Jeep.

Based on my training, I knew how memory recall works. Memory recall has three parts to it. "Primacy" effect is the memory's first recall. If a person is given ten words the majority will recall the very first word. With "recency," the last word given in a list of ten will be recalled. "Saliency" is the third type of memory. For example, things that stand out such as one of ten words that appear in color would stand out. And saliency relates to a very important event in one's life.

These murders of four people would have stood out in one's memory. There is no way in hell either Woody or Popcorn would have forgotten a day when four people were murdered. Especially when it was the death of their best friend, and his girlfriend. Both Ben and Cassandra were shot in the head execution style. How could they forget the slow death of Johnny and Matthew Garcia by starvation and dehydration?

All these events meet the qualifications of memory recall. Primacy, recency, and saliency would have affected Woody or Popcorn's recollection of that information. This is a day that would have gone into their memory like Pearl Harbor and the assassination of President Kennedy.

Woody is saying January or February when he thinks they happened. Popcorn just doesn't know when the murders occurred.

Jeremy Sedillo, Cassandra's brother

I reached into the box. Cassandra's brother Jeremy was interviewed on tape and I found the label marked Jeremy Sedillo and put it in my tape player.

"What is your name?"

"Jeremy E. Sedillo."

"Are you the brother of Cassandra?"

"Yes."

"Did you ever go to the cabin?"

"No."

"When did you see her last?"

"Just before they went to the cabin."

"Did you know Popcorn?"

"Yea. I saw him with Ben."

"When did you see Popcorn last?"

"When he was at Green Eyes' House in December." *According to my time line this would have been on the 14th or 15th.*

"Did you talk to him?"

"Yea, I just asked him where my sister was and he told me she was still at the cabin." *Popcorn had lied to Jeremy. Cassandra was dead so why didn't Popcorn ask about Wilkins?*

"Was there talk about guns?"

"Yea, Popcorn was trying to sell some guns to Green Eyes."

"What vehicle was he in?"

"In Ben's black Jeep."

"Did you get in it?"

"Yea, but it wouldn't start."

"Have you seen Green Eyes?"

"No he split. He moved out of that house."

There had been no mention of Green Eyes. With a nickname like that you would have thought the gang expert would have found him. It was possible Popcorn could have sold him the murder weapon. I kept telling myself the cops have to know this.

Porfie Sedillo, "She's my first born."

My mind went back to the highway as I was passing Tramway exit. Rush hour traffic was backing up on the southbound on I-25 as usual. I had twenty minutes before I would be home so I pulled Porfie's tape out. I could not imagine what she went through. Losing her only daughter and her two grandson, all at the same time.

"How do you know Cassandra?"

"She's my first born. We were best friends. She was always there when I needed her. She lived with me in Albuquerque."

"When did you see her last?"

Without hesitation Porfie answered. "December seven, nineteen ninety-five. She told me she was going to the mountains with Ben and would be back for Christmas."

"Did you know Ben Anaya?"

"Yes, he was with her."

"And the two babies?"

"Oh, my Johnny, he was—he was so full of life. He was the man in charge he took care of his little brother. He was very smart, he was a smart little boy. We would play hide and go seek and read, watch movies together, go to the zoo, and to the park to play." *I started choking up listening to the tape and Porfie's voice talk about her daughter and the boys.* "Johnny knew all the lines to the Lion King and all the Disney movies."

"What about Matthew?"

"Matthew was the same. Always with his big brother. Always copying him. He would love to sing all the music from the Disney movies."

"When did you see Cassandra last?"

"On the weekend we would go to the store. And I would take care of the boys. After that December I never saw her or the kids anymore. Around the middle of December someone broke into my house and took my VCR."

The tape came to an end and I didn't realize I was parked in my driveway. My wife came out and asked me, "You going to stay in your truck all night?"

I got out of the truck and grabbed my best friend. (My grandkids gave that name to my laptop since I always had it with me.)

"You hungry? I got dinner warmed up for you."

I didn't realize I had gone without lunch and I only had a tortilla and jelly all day long but I wasn't hungry. "No, thanks I got to get some notes down for Ray."

It was hard to concentrate after listening to all the tapes coming home. I looked around for some distraction. My wife asked me, "Did you get hold of Steve? He's been calling you. You have a handball game tonight."

I had forgotten all about it. It was Monday at seven pm and Wednesday at seven pm for the last twenty-five years and it was handball night. I started playing handball in the empty boxcars at the railroad yard. We would leave a crack in the door to let the light in and play four wall handball. Later on we would sneak into the chicken cage at the YMCA on Central and we would play until they kicked us out. We would climb the chicken wire in the back that stopped the ball from going over and collect the handballs that were stuck in the wire so we could have a ball to play with. I met Steve at the Fraternal Order of Police where we had to share the courts with the racquetball players. Competition was always tough all the way up. The old guys had fastball serves and could put so much spin on the ball you didn't know where it was going.

I left for the game.

"Hey Steve, how's it going?" Steve was a second-generation shoe re-pairman and his father owned the Hoffman Town Shoe Repair. Best place in Albuquerque to get your boots and shoes repaired. Steve took care of all my boots for me from my traffic boots to my cowboy boots.

"I saw you and Ray on TV."

"Did I look good on it?"

"Yea, it looks like you got your hands full. My dad knows Dan Burrola from the VFW. I never met him there but my dad knows him." Steve like most men my age had seen action in Viet Nam. Steve was awarded the Purple Heart and carried it proudly on his license plate. And like most Vets, he never talked about the war.

"We got doubles with Ben and Bruce tonight."

I was glad we had a doubles game as my ankle had swollen up on me from being on my feet all day. When I put on my high tops tennis shoes along with my air cast I could see my calf and ankle were twice the size. Steve noticed my limp.

"You okay? You might want to stop by. I can check your lifts on your left foot." Steve was aware of my injury and would create lifts in my heels a quarter inch in the inside and on the outside so I could walk level.

"I'm a little sore so why don't you take the front court and I'll stay in the back court and if the ball comes off the back wall, I'll let you take it."

Bruce came walking down the hall with his normal two extra large wristbands, his eye protection and the handball gloves he must have had for the last twenty years. "You guys ready?" as he started clapping his hand hard.

Bill was behind Bruce and also twelve inches shorter than Bruce. For whatever size Bill was he made up in speed and picking up the low shots. Bill's trademark was the rag he wore around his head. They were both engineers for Sandia Labs and like Steve and I they had been playing for over twenty years. It was a hard game to give up.

Bill looked over at me, "You guys have that Torreon murder case, don't you?"

"Yea, I do."

"After all those years with violent crimes, how do you do it? I know you did child homicides all those years, but dead babies."

"That's why I'm here Bill. Let's play."

"I know you don't carry a gun but aren't you concerned about getting hurt?"

"You know what concerns me Bill? It's the media. The media tears up our client's, they show the worst picture of our client they can find. Like the mug shot they get from the jail. They run stories about the murders over and over. By the time we get to trial our clients are guilty. The public feels once the arrest is made they must be guilty. Then we go to the prelim hearing and they are bonded over. Same thing. They must be guilty. My fear is trying to get a fair trial for our client. If our client looked like Brad Pitt, Tom Cruise, or Matt Damon, they would be found not guilty in a heartbeat. I don't care what the charges are. When you don't have charismatic clients it is tough to sell their innocence. It doesn't matter if your client was living at Mars at the time of the incident, four out of twelve people on the jury will say he was there. The majority of jurors have their minds made up after opening arguments. Half the time the jurors are not paying attention in trial and they forget eighty-five percent of the testimony. Instead of taking notes they are drawing on their notepad. They spent time staring at our client and judge him by the way he looks or does not look at them. That scares the hell out of me. Most of them feel they have to do justice to the victims and convict someone. The two star witnesses against our client are videotapes. We don't get the opportunity to confront the accuser. We get to ask the videotape questions. How's that for American justice. They can believe lies without evidence. Let's play. I feel the need to hit something hard."

I got home and went to my hot tub to soak and try to take the aches out of my back, butt, and my left leg. Bill had spun off the back wall, caught the ball, and then had tossed the ball like a major league pitcher. The ball was speeding down the left alley of the court. I had tried to give him room but he nailed me in the back of my calf. My bad leg. Now I had a large purple donut on my calf.

Working Two Cases At Once

I finally got home and to bed and closed my eyes trying to get some sleep, knowing I had to get up early. But as soon as I fell asleep the cramps in my leg woke me up. Now it my leg's turn to fuck with me. It seemed like every thirty minutes it woke me up with a cramp in the back of my calf. Normally I don't drink, but I thought it was time for my friend Jack Daniel's to slow my muscles down.

I took the afternoon flight on Southwest into Los Angeles, grabbed a rental car and headed north on the 405. I had to get back to work on the "Sureno 13" case. The bulk of my work was taking me into East LA's Echo Park, right off the 101, home of the three-inch glass plates at the gas and grocery stores

Originally Echo Park was the movies' spot for the *Three Stooges, Charlie Chaplin* and *Laurel and Hardy*. Famous painters such as Carlos Almaraz painted at the park. Echo Park was deep in history being next to Hollywood. The movie *Me Vida Loca* had been filmed there. The movie described the "Latino Gang Culture" in the neighborhood. I left my cowboy boots at home for this trip.

I had presented a seminar at UCLA on "Violence and Homicides Among Hispanics" and felt comfortable off the 405 and Wilshire. The Hampton Inn was a good place for me to stay. It was not that far to East LA.

It was only two pm when I got into my room. On the way to my room I stopped at one of the local Taco Wagons and grabbed me a Carne Asada Taco and took a Mexican bottled Coke and a couple of extra limes to go to my room.

I had with me my recorder and several of Woody's tapes. I found the Nieto interview with no date or time on it. I put my earpieces on and lay back in the king size bed with pillow under my left leg to bring the swelling down.

9

I Want A Lawyer

"WE NEED TO TALK BRO."

"I know."

I could recognize Detective DeReyes and Woody's voice.

"Again and it might not be nice. It's all your choice. I'm tired of talking bro. Because I have, is some serious shit on you bro. Very serious. And the only way it's going to help you bro is if you tell me what went down when you and Sager went up to the cabin."

"I've already told you."

"No, no, no."

"I'm telling the truth."

"Don't go there bro."

"I want to talk to my lawyer."

"You want to talk to who?"

"My lawyer."

'You want to talk to a lawyer about what bro?"

"About whatever you guys are trying to blame me for, fuck that I ain't done shit. I didn't go the fucking cabin. I'm telling the straight up truth. The straight up truth. That's my word for life. I'm not gonna lie. I'm telling the straight up truth."

"And you're not trying to protect somebody?" *DeReyes changed the subject from Woody wanting a lawyer.*

"No, I'm telling the straight up truth. I'm telling the straight up truth."

"I ain't blaming you for anything bro. Why are you saying that?"

"Because you say I'm lying."

"I'm asking you bro?"

"I'm telling you the truth. I'm telling you the damn straight up truth, I want my lawyer."

"Why do you want a lawyer present if you're not being charged?"

"No, because you guys are blaming me, man?"

"We're not blaming you. I'm trying to explain to you. Have you been charged with anything man?"

"No, but I'm telling the straight up truth and you don't believe me? I'm telling you the truth."

"Are you?"

"Yeah."

"Are you going to give up Sager, bro? Give him up bro. And do your time." *If Woody is not being charged why does DeReyes tell him, 'And do your time.'*

"I didn't go to no fucking cabin."

"Who did?"

"I don't know, I'm telling you the straight up truth. You guys just don't fucking believe me man."

"Who was there bro?"

"I'm telling you, I don't know man."

"You told us before that Sager did it."

"Yeah, I didn't say he did it. But he came over and said."

"And said he was in."

"Yeah, I'm telling you guys the truth."

"You also said too that when he came over to your home he had some dope, and he had some rock. Did he ever tell you where he got it from?"

"He didn't tell me nothing sir. I'm telling the straight up damn truth."

"Well I think somebody's trying to do you bro?"

"Do me what?"

"Trying to take you down, but it's not us."

"It's not us, yeah right, ah whatever, fuck it."

"What's gonna happen to you bro? What's gonna happen to you Woody?"

"I don't have the slightest idea. Fuck it, I'm straight up the telling the truth."

"Who else had gone up there with Sager?"

"Roy that I know of that day."

"That day of what?"

"That day that they came over to my pad, with Roy Buchner."

"He told you Roy Buchner? You'd swear on that bro?"

"Yeah."

"You'd go to court on that?"

"Yeah, I'd go to court on that."

"You'll testify? You'll testify?"

"That he was there at my pad that day?"

"That he was there at your house...that he was there with Sager in a stolen car and that they went up to Ben's cabin. You would testify to that? You would say that?"

"I'd say that."

"You would say that?"

"I would say that they came to my pad."

"They came to your pad, they told you were up there. They told you that."

"Yeah. I'm telling you guys the truth."

"But you would say that in court?"

"Whatever's ever, no."

"You would say that, bro? Well, that's interesting you knows bro, because as it stands, as it stands now, you're the one that's going to place Sager up there. Aren't you?"

"Whatever."

"Yes or no?"

"Yes, sir, if you want me to."

"No, I don't want you to bro, I'm asking you? Yeah, I'm asking you?"

"Right, I'm saying."

"Are you going to change your story on me bro?"

"No, I'm telling you the truth."

"Okay, well let's stay with the same story. Sager and Eazy went to your house in a stolen car, what car?"

"That one, that one guy drives that purple Camaro."

"Okay. And what time did they come to your house?"

"Around nine o'clock."

"At night or in the day."

"At night."

"At night, and you know it was Eazy, you are positive it was Eazy? Si or no?"

"It was dark."

"Did you go cruising with them?"

"No, I didn't go cruising with them."

"Why would they came to your house in a stolen car, bro?"

"I don't know."

"Okay, and what did Sager do? Sager and Eazy jumped in the car with you guys?"

"No they were in their car."

"They were in their car?"

"Yeah."

"And your girlfriend would be able to verify this?" *You would have thought*

164

DeReyes would have verified this. He would have found out the stolen car happened in March of 2000.

"Yeah."

"What did you say?"

"I didn't say nothing, man."

"If your mind is clicking right now bro, how come you woke up, I must have touched some nerve there, somewhere."

"Because you guys are trying to blame me."

"No, no, it's not us bro. I'm telling you what I know. And haven't I been straight up with you from the beginning?"

"Yeah. And I've been straight up with you too."

"Well, that's what I'm trying to find out, bro. Because in the course of my investigation there is a lot of stuff that has come up and your name, homeboy, has come up again."

"Whatever, you know."

"And I know you Woody, you're a lot smarter than what a lot of people give you credit for. Don't they. You know what's right and you know what's wrong. Don't you?" *Woody was Special Ed with an IQ of 68.*

"Yes, sir."

"And you know what is right when you make a movida with your homies and you know that something is going down and you want no part of it. Right?"

"Yeah, I'm telling you the straight up truth, they were there."

"And this situation here you know is not right what happened to Ben. Don't you?"

"Yes."

"And you know that one of your own homeboys could be responsible for the death of Ben. You know that don't you?"

"I don't know."

"You don't know, but you think it."

"Yeah."

"And you think that something went down. And you suspect one of your homeboys. Who is that homeboy that you suspect? Tell me?"

"I'm telling you straight up."

"Who? Sager. Sager. Why bro? Why Sager of all the homies? Why him? Convince me bro."

"What?"

"Convince me, man. This is your last chance bro, convince me Sager is the one that did it."

"They came over to my pad."

"Give him up, bro."

"They came over to my pad saying that they went over there and then about three weeks later they found them dead." *That fit the time line in that the car was taken from a lot at the hospital in March of 1996.*

"Who told you that? That they found them dead."

"The news."

"Oh, the news okay. So then did you snap then?"

"Yeah."

"And what did you feel then bro, when you found it was them?"

"I found out that it was them."

"And why would you think it was Sager?"

"Because he told me that he went up there."

"That he went up there, him and Eazy?"

"Yeah."

"Did they tell you what they did?"

"They didn't tell me nothing, sir. Like I told you all the time."

"Okay. So then two weeks later from the time that they went to your house in a stolen car, him and Eazy all of sudden the next thing you know, on the news Ben is dead. And you snap? You snap and said something is wrong here? Did you ever talk to him about it?"

"No, I didn't talk to him, sir."

"Did you see them again after that?"

"Yeah, three weeks later after he came by and showed me you know."

"The money and…"

"The gun."

"And the gun. And then what did he say?"

"He didn't say nothing. He just came by."

"What did he say? What did he tell you?"

"Just that I did it. That's it."

"You told me, remember what he told you? What did he tell you?"

"He told me well I think he said, he told that I did some shit now. And I think I've got all kind of trouble. And that's all he told me you know. Then we'll I'll talk to you guys later on. And then he left no."

"Didn't you say that he said I did something up at the cabin."

"No, I didn't say that. He told me yeah, he said I did some shit up there, no. I did some shit up there and he showed me the fedia and then he said well I'll talk to you later no. And that was it."

"And did you put two and two together then bro?"

"Yeah, two and two."

"So why didn't you tell your homies about it?"

"Cause."

"Why didn't you call the cops? And say hey, drop the dime on them and say you know what I think I know who killed Ben Anaya. Why didn't you do that Woodrow? I thought Ben was your homie?"

"He is but."

"So why didn't you drop the dime on them bro? Why have you kept this in you man? What do you owe Sager, bro?"

"Nothing."

"You don't owe him anything? You're scared? You're afraid that he'll kill you, bro? Did he ever tell you he would kill you?"

"No, but I already know he's loco."

"That he's loco, huh? And that's the only thing that has ever kept you from saying anything, right? And that's what's kept you alive up to this point, que no? If you act like nothing's happening and you don't act like you know or suspect him, he ain't gonna bother you is he?"

"Yeah."

"Do you want to put him away, Woodrow, for killing your homie?"

"I ain't telling you nothing."

"Do you want to see him go away, bro?"

"Yeah."

"Because you know he did your homie? You know it? You know it in your heart, huh? That jerk right there wasted your homeboy and those kids, que no? You know that? Let it out bro?"

"I'm scared. Me and him we're like family."

"He's locked up. How's he going to touch you bro? Does he have that much connection? Who would he contract bro? Who would he contract?"

"Eazy and Marcus."

"What do you say we pick up Eazy and Marcus?"

"Huh?"

"What happened if we picked them up?"

"Then."

"Just move out."

"Where would you go?"

"Probably to Taos, or something."

"To Taos."

"I've got family there."

"Yeah, that would be good. Do you think Eazy did it with him?"

"I don't know for sure."

"Do you think that Eazy would be there maybe not pull the trigger but he'd be there."

"Yeah."

"Why would he not pull the trigger?"

"Cause, they're homies, you know they're close."

"Him and Sager. Did Eazy like Popcorn? If Popcorn was there at the place when they did the shooting do you think they would kill Popcorn too? Both of them?"

"I think so."

"Serio? No witnesses huh. What did you guys use to use when you guys would car jack a car bro?"

"I didn't car jack, I wasn't a car jacker."

"Never. Did he ever tell you when he would car jack a car?"

"Huh uh. No he'd just show up."

"Okay, Sager told you. Did he ever tell you what he would tell them to do?"

"No, he. I don't know if he helped them out but..."

"The pair of them on the murders, no?"

"Yeah."

"But that's what turned up Johnny right? They killed that girl for nothing, que no? Just for the hell of it? Do you think Sager would do that to you bro? Why?"

"Cause he knew what Ben was to me."

"Did he hate Ben that much?"

"And Popcorn knew about it."

"He hated Popcorn? What better person to blame them, no? Did he hate Ben enough to try to do that? Did Ben have the bank bro?"

"I don't know."

"Did he have a gun?"

"I know he had guns."

"He had the movidas, so he had the bank. And Sager wanted to do that, didn't he? And that's why you're telling me now Woodrow that him, that Sager would be the shooter, no? And that you failed to come forward because of the fact that you were afraid of this guy, because you're afraid that he might kill you too?"

"Yeah."

"Are you gonna pin him up bro, in court? Or are you gonna back down? You gonna be a man or are you gonna stand up? Are you gonna stand up to him, are you gonna pin him up, or you're not? Or you going to be cooking out?"

"I don't want to be killed see."

"Say it bro? We'll help you. We'll help you bro. We'll get you a new life. You'll get out of town. Cause I'll tell you right now Woodrow, I got three felonies on you right now, homie."

"What?"

"A drive by. A drive by, bro, tampering with evidence."

"Never did no drive by."

"You did a drive by."

"No I didn't."

"Who did it then?"

"I don't know who did it, but."

"Then why are you bragging about it homie?"

"I didn't do it. I ain't bragging about it."

"You were telling estorias with your homies and you told them you did a drive by. Who did it then? Who did it? Just tell me who did it bro? Who did it, Woody?"

"Who did what?"

"Who did the drive by?"

"I didn't do it."

"All right, well if you didn't do it, who did?"

"Sager and Weasel."

"Sager and who?"

"Shorty, and uh."

"Shorty's in Springer now, isn't he? Shorty used to live on the west side huh? What did they say?"

"That they were going to the west side."

"Why?"

"They were going to shoot a Westgater even."

"And instead they shot at the gang unit's car? Or house bro?"

"At the car."

"What did they use?"

"Tech, two thousand."

"What kind of a house? Was he a shooter? Otra ves? No? Do you know whose house that was bro? It was my house. That was my crib, bro? That was my house, my familia, that's personal bro? I don't go to your pad, I don't go to anybody's pad unless its business. And I don't fuck with anybody in mi chante. Respecto."

"That's what I'm saying."

"You broke that respecto, bro. You broke that respecto right now. Coming into my house and did that shit. And I always knew, I suspected someone and I've been looking, bro. And I found out who it was and I wanted you to tell me who that person was. Because I knew you knew about it. And you're gonna pin this dude up bro. You're gonna pin them up. Not only on the homicide of your homie but you're gonna pin him up on the drive by, him, Shorty and Weasel. Where's Weasel at now?"

"On Trujillo Street. Damn, now I'm gonna get killed."

"You ain't gonna get killed bro."

"After these guys get out, no."

"I've got protection for you bro."

"I've got a family."

"That's right. And you better think about your family bro. Because right now the homeboys doesn't give a shit about your family. He don't care about you. He doesn't care about anybody. All he cares about is Wilkins. He's implicated you bro. He said that you were up at the cabin. Now what kind of homeboy is going to tell on other homeboys like that. Especially you Woodrow."

"He's gonna kill my family, bro."

"Then why is he going to say it?"

"He'll say anything."

"Then why is he going to fuck with your family bro? Why are you going to let him do that Woodrow? He's a bad seed bro, he needs to be put away, no? He's brought down Eighteenth Street hard hasn't he? He knows what Eighteenth Street should have been, que no?"

"Yes."

"When you've got beef with somebody you take care of it. And that's gangbanger to gangbanger, que no? Because when you mess with other people and you mess with five-O it ain't gonna go away."

"Exactly, sir."

"And it's not going to go away with me. And I'll tell you right now Woodrow, if you're telling me the truth when I get Weasel, Shorty and this asshole right here and they tell me you're involved, I'm gonna take you down bro."

"Yes sir, whatever."

"But for right now I'm gonna give free up. And you're gonna owe me big time Woodrow. Because I'm gonna keep your ass alive."

"I don't care about me, I just care about my family."

"Well you better tell them, your parents and everybody in your chante right now. Because with that bro on the loose you better start running homes. And that is why you need to tell me now. What that son of a bitch has done. Everything that he has done, that he has told you, you need to tell me now."

"Whatever's cool no."

"Tell me bro, keep telling me."

"What I told you."

"He did the drive-by's, he did some car jacking. I want to know where he has the guns bro? Who is his connections to the guns?"

"I knew that he had those at his pad."

"So he can stash them, sell them, bury them. Where do you bury the guns, bro?"

"Huh?"

"Did he ever tell you where he would bury?"

"No, sir he never told me, sir."

"Have you ever been with him when he's burying some stuff?"

"No, sir."

"Do you know for a fact, bro that him and Eazy were up at the cabin and they came down that day and told you that something happened up at the cabin?"

"He said that him and Eazy went over there."

"That what? He did some shit?"

"That he did some shit."

"Yeah, and then he went and partied over at the park."

"Yeah. And then after that all of sudden you didn't see him anymore and the next thing you know Ben is dead."

"Yeah."

"And you started snapping, didn't you Woody?"

"Yes."

"Why have you waited this long, bro?"

"Scared."

"You were scared, no? You must have a lot of strength bro, on Eighteenth Street?"

"Huh?"

"Does Eighteenth Street like this stuff?"

"I don't really know, he's crazy no."

"Then why haven't you guys wiped him out?"

"I don't know."

"Why haven't you got rid of him? Wiped him out and said you're too nuts, man your bringing too much heat into us. You need to leave."

"He never comes down. Its always night."

"You guys know where to find him. Why don't you guys ever wipe him out, you guys wiped out Popcorn, no? You guys jumped him out?"

"Not me, I didn't."

"Sager and them did at the party didn't they? Popcorn thought he was getting his butt kicked huh, for shit on Rascal, huh. And that wasn't it, huh. He was getting ranked out by them, wasn't he?"

"Yes, sir."

"And that's why Eighteenth Street didn't want Popcorn around because of Sager, huh? See he's got some very bad views. To make Woody scared of him and a lot of other vato's that we've talked to. He must have some major stuff, bro. Is he connected to the or the Diamond Boy? I don't think you wanna go down bro. I think you know what the right thing is, que no?"

"Sure, sir. I'm telling you the straight up truth, no."

"Well I'm gonna see how straight up you are bro? I'm gonna see it. Because I'm gonna pick up Sager. And I've got some shit on him. I mean some good scandal. What you told me now, the fact that you suspect him of being the killer in the homicides and also doing the drive by at least I have something now. But it ain't gonna end there, Woody. Because you're gonna have to be a man and you're gonna have to go to court and you're gonna pin them. And you have to pin them hard. And you're not gonna have to worry about what he thinks of you or what. Because he ain't gonna touch you, bro. Because he's gonna be locked up for a long time when I get finished with him. And you're gonna be gone, bro, you're gonna disappear. Am I right, Woody?"

"Yes sir."

"And I'm gonna give you that chance, bro. Weasel, Shorty and Sager are going to down on something. I had to sell my house, bro because of that. Had to move my family, because of that. How does that make you feel, bro? Because they came by my pad, and did a drive by, your own homeboys? Westgate? Kind of messed up, huh? Well I had my kids there bro. And a chicken shit dude, came by my house just because he couldn't find Westgate, and did that. Those are real homies, those are guys you don't work with. A bunch of cookies. And if you want to be associated with them like that bro?"

"I don't."

"Maybe because you snapped, no."

"Trying to be good, no. Like keep an eye on babies, no."

"If she really wants to get out bro. Well I'm gonna get apiece of paper for a total statement. And you're gonna give me a statement on your word that Sager, Weasel and Shorty did the drive by. Just like you told me."

"All right."

"And, you're going to also say in that statement of all the other stuff that you know that Sager and Eazy went up to the cabin in a stolen car, and that is how you're going to prove yourself bro. Because when I go to court on this and present that. They're gonna ask me for that, they're not gonna ask me my word, or your word. They're gonna want to see it on paper. Because if we're gonna help Woodrow they're gonna want to know Woodrow is telling the truth. And if Woodrow is willing to put his butt on the line and pin that dude. Because that's the only way it's gonna happen and that's the only way they're gonna keep you alive, bro. Do you understand that?"

"Yes sir."

"Then after that Woodrow, you're gonna lay low. You are going to make yourself very available to us. And when we need to talk to you, we need to know where we can find you bro. We don't want to go looking for you."

"You'll find me every time at my pad."

"That's right and that's where we want to find you. That's where we want to find you. Okay?"

"Just this statement and then you'll take me home, sir?" *I thought to myself, in four hundred and forty years you will go home.*

"Yeah, and if the State Police have something else that they need to talk you about and they will. Cause like I said bro. If you're dissing me on this and you are involved in this I can't help you man. You're on your own."

"I'm telling the truth."

"Whether it be on the drive by or it be on the homicide. This is your time right now bro, to tell me. Cause as I say you come clean, you say the truth."

The tape just ended. They had hammered Woody, yelling, and DeReyes talking ninety-five percent of the time. Woody had asked for a lawyer but was denied. Woody thought he was going home after he signed the statement.

I went back to the part: "And you have to pin them hard. And you're not gonna have to worry about what he thinks of you or what. Because he ain't gonna touch you, bro. Because he's gonna be locked up for a long time when I get finished with him. And you're gonna be gone, bro, you're gonna disappear. Am I right, Woody?"

Popcorn "Face Down Or Underground"

I was getting tired after hearing DeReyes talk but even though the clock said 11 pm I was on MST and it was only 10 at home. I looked at the rest of the tapes to see which one had the shortest tape. It was marked "Interview Popeleski."

I put it in the recorder and like most, we got no formal introduction and it just started off like the Woody tape.

"And then what happened the rest of the night?"

"We just kicked back and watched movies."

"You had a VCR? You watched them on tape? And then what happened, bro?"

"I was going outside to take piss, because inside, we couldn't take a piss."

"There wasn't any running water?"

"I went outside, I went around the corner where the cement ended and I was just right there. I knew it was Sager right away. He said 'face down or underground' and then he pumped the gage, no. And then the other guy, the light was off so the light was on outside. He's the only one that has an eighteenth street symbol, not an eighteen street but one-eight."

"Right."

"That's how I knew it was him. I know his voice, I've been around him for a long time."

"So you knew it was Sager just by his voice?"

"I knew it was Sager, I just got down."

"You saw his eyes."

"I just knew it was him, I know for a fact. You can disguise him but I can still describe him. I could just tell it was him by his voice."

"And so you're outside taking a leak and somebody comes up behind you with a shotgun?"

"And what was the other guy carrying? There was two guys right?"

"I'm not sure, I know it was a long gun, bro, because."

"A rifle?"

"Yeah, because he had his foot on my back and then the barrel was right there on my head. And I said what do you guys want. And I was all panicking. And then I heard like five shots."

"Okay. So they put you face down or underground? And then one of them stays there with his foot on your back and puts the gun to the back of your head and then the other one goes inside?" *Mike was helping him fill in the facts. But Woody was saying Popcorn was not there and Sager put the gun to his head.*

"Yeah. After those five shots I was like kind of jumpy. And then I said go check out what's going on and he said don't move because I was trying to move around no. I was thinking of running. And he said just stay still and I said I will homie, I will. And then I said I'll just do whatever no. They were just backing up and backing up and I just kept on looking at them like that. And they started on the way down. And I just jumped in the Jeep because I knew it was open, no and I jumped in and started it and just floored it and went back down the hill and I know they were running because I saw them on the end. Like the light was on and I saw them on the end. I saw them when the lights beamed up. They started to split, and then I turned and on the middle of the dirt my Jeep turned off. It has problems sometimes, bro. It turns off when you like take the gas off bro. And then I tried to start it again. And it took a long time and then they were gone. And I had some guns in the Jeep."

"And so you saw the guy that you thought was Sager, was he the one who stayed out there on you, or is he the one that went inside?"

"He's the one that went inside."

"So he's the shooter?"

"That's what I think."

"So he went inside and you heard some gun shots? And then they took off running."

"They didn't take off running, he just stayed like he was calm, calm. You know through the whole thing he was like calm."

"You're talking about Sager?"

"The one who was on my back."

"The one who was on your back? Never got excited? Did you recognize his voice?"

"No."

"Was it Woody?" *Mike was determined to help Popcorn.*

"It wasn't Woody. I would know Woody right away." *Popcorn's testimony at the hearing said it was Woody.*

"Was it anybody else you recognized? So then what happened after you heard the shots?"

"After I heard the shots I just kind of jumped. And then he says 'don't move' and I said I'm sorry, I'm sorry bro. I didn't want to get shot."

"Okay, so after the shots, he told you not to move, then what happened?"

"He just started backing up, I was laying low. I'll just stay still, don't worry, don't worry, I'll stay still. And then I know they were running cause I heard it. You can pretty much hear everything out there. And I just jumped in and started it and then backed up and tried to get out of there. I had some guns."

"So they didn't park in the driveway? You told me a while ago when we were talking before the video come on you thought you heard keys in the door lock?"

"Yeah."

"That was after the shots?"

"That was after. I could hear some footsteps going back and forth."

"Like they were loading something up?"

"Like there were more people. I don't know if there were more people or not, you know what I mean. There could have been more than two people."

"But you only saw two for sure?"

"I only saw two for sure and I know one of them was Sager for sure. Because he's the only one with one-eight"

"And you recognized his voice?"

"And I recognized his voice. Big time, he's the only one who could say 'face down or underground.' That's what we used on all the car jacking's."

"And so you had pulled car jacks with him before?"

"Yeah."

"And you knew that was his movida? That is what he told you to do?"

"We did all together."

"And that's how he did it, on the ground face down."

"Face down or underground."

"So you took off after them?"

"Yeah."

"Did you ever go back to the house? Do you know if the door was ever locked? You don't know, you never went back after that? You chased them down? Did you ever see the ride they got in to?" *Mike must have taken lessons from Agent Jacoby on how to ask questions.*

"I know for a fact that it was the same kind of car."

"It was the same car?"

"It was the same car that they came up in."

"Was it the same car or the same kind of car?"

"It had to have been the same car."

"The same color?"

"Same color and everything, like reddish maroon."

"Okay, so let me get this straight. As I understand it, you come out of the gate in the Jeep, because the Jeep is parked inside the fence right? But the gates were open?"

"Right."

"So you come out of the gate and you go down the hill right in front, right straight out and they are running down the hill in front of you. Where was there ride parked?"

"It was just going up the hill. Here's the fence right here and they were parked like right there."

"So they were parked in the drive way or in that road that goes up to the drive way?"

"Yeah."

"So then you saw them jump in the car?"

"Uh huh."

"How many did you see get into the car?"

"There was two in the car."

"And so you only saw two get in the car?"

"Yeah."

"So as far as you know there was just two people?"

"It could have been more, you know what I mean. They jumped in, there was the driver and the passenger. He just threw the gun and the other one just jumped on in with the gun. I just tried my best to go after them."

"But then the Jeep gave out? How long did they have you on the ground?"

"For a long time, it seemed like it happened fast, you know what I mean."

"Uh huh. Do you know if it was like five minutes or ten minutes or?"

"It was like ten minutes."

"What did you have in the house? You had a TV, VCR, did you have a stereo? Did you have drugs?"

"We had drugs."

"Okay you had marijuana because you were smoking mota, right? How much marijuana did you have?"

"Just a little bit." *Compared to Woody they had a pound.*

"Dime bag?"

"More than that."

"More than a dime bag? Half pound?"

"Close to that."

"About a half a pound? Did you have any rocks?"

"Yeah."

"How much?"

"Two pill bottles, full." *Woody never mentioned bottles of pills.*

"Big pill bottles? About how many rocks, do you think?"

"I don't know."

"Okay, how many guns? You said you had two in the Jeep? But you got to keep those, right they didn't take those?"

"No, we had a bunch in the Jeep. We were loaded up in the Jeep. We had some in the cabin though too. We have a bunch of guns. "

"Okay so did you get, did you have all the ones in the Jeep or did you just have two in the Jeep? Did they get any guns out of the Jeep."

"They didn't even touch the Jeep."

"Did they take anything out of the house that you know of? How many guns did you have in the house, ten, twenty, thirty?"

"About twelve, thirteen."

"Twelve, thirteen, what kind of guns were they?"

"Rifles, some were hand guns."

"What kind of hand guns?"

"Some nine mm's, a forty-five, one was a spray gun."

"What's a sprayer, bro?"

"A mack."

"Like a mack ten? Did Ben have any guns in the bedroom with him? Did he sleep with a gun or anything like that? Not that you know of? Did you have anything else of value in the house? You had some mota, did you have any crank? Any powder, soda anything like that?"

"We had some soda?"

"How much?"

"About six ounces."

"Six ounces. Do you have any questions? You are telling us that they had those black ski masks, or were?" *Where did Mike get this information? Popcorn had never mentioned masks before.*

"It was white."

"Were they black or white?" *Popcorn had already said white but Woody said black so it appears they were trying to move him to black.*

"It was white."

"It was all white?"

"It wasn't all white, but it had holes in it, it had like a bunch of holes but it had that part like that, you know what I mean. It came down like that."

"Okay, but what was the color, the actual color?"

"White."

"Like real bright white? Like your T-shirt, that kind of white?"

"It was like this kind of white." *They couldn't get him to say black.*

"How about that other vato?"

"He had the same kind of mask on. The same kind."

"The same kind?"

"Same exact thing."

"When he was telling you to keep on the ground, did he also use the term, 'face down underground' or he was just like kind of real low key?"

"He just said don't move, you know what I mean. He was."

"Was he Chicano?"

"You could tell he was Chicano by the way he talked."

"The way he talked. Was he buffed out? Did he look buffed out, did he look skinny?"

"He was tall, taller than Sager."

"Would he fit the description of say Eazy? Is Eazy as big as Sager?" *Mike was now telling Popcorn Eazy was there.*

"Yeah, kind of."

"But you would recognize Eazy's voice, don't you? Would you?"

"I think so. I didn't hear him that much."

"But the voice that was telling you that was very new to you, like you might have recognized it but you couldn't recognize it?"

"I would recognize it."

"If you heard it again, if he said those words? But you definitely know for sure that it was Sager, because that is what you used to use on the car jacking's. Nobody would know that?"

"Nobody knew, because we wouldn't talk about it. He would tell the little homies that you know what I mean. But the other homies like Deuce's little brother Gremlin, Rascal and that would be it."

"But when you guys did your car jacking's, that is what you told your victims, 'face down or underground'?"

"He's the one that made it up."

"He's the one that made it up?"

"Yeah."

"And he had a gage?"

"He had a pump gage."

"That's what he drew down on you with?"

"Yeah I heard that click, click, you know what I mean. You know when you hear it."

"You know."

"And so I was like okay face down underground, I was like hey man, I know who this is."

"You knew right away."

"I looked and I said ay I know who that is. I thought I was gonnna die. I really did think that I was gonna die, you know what I mean."

"Because of the fact that he didn't like you?"

"Because of the fact that I ratted on his homies, you know what I mean."

"After all that happened and you took off in the Jeep trying to catch up to them. What happened, where did you go after that, when you couldn't catch up with them?"

"I couldn't catch up to them. I got more gas, no. I jetted."

"Where did you get the gas?"

"From the gas station."

"In Torreon?"

"Yeah."

"Was it still open?"

"Yeah."

"It must have been, huh?" *You would have thought Mike would have checked the gas station to see if they were open that late.*

"I left. I started like going to pads, no. I went to the projects to check it out and I just like drove by. And then I looked cause that's where Sager first goes, the first place that he goes to."

"Right."

"I drove around like close to his pad, you know, like around his area where he lived. Because I know where he lived. I looked out there and he wasn't around there. I looked at pretty much where he hangs. He wasn't there. I went to Joker's house, he wasn't there. So I just tried to kick with them on the Westside. Cause she comes down from the Westside all the time. I figured I would run into them, no. I was always packed after that. After that, I didn't care. I was just packed and ready."

"Did you go by Woody's house in the Jeep looking for Sager?"

"I went by there."

"Did Woody see you, or anybody see you there? Did you stop or did you just cruise?"

"Just cruised by."

"And he wasn't there, the car wasn't there?"

"I even went to Andrew's house when he lived on 57th. His little brother saw me, I took him out cruising with me." *So where were the reports on Andrew? They had to interview him.*

"Uh huh."

"I was just driving angry. Packed heat all the time, from them on. And that was it."

"And you never saw Sager again after that?"

"Never saw him."

"And you still haven't seen him since then?"

"Yeah, I saw him maybe outside the window."

"And he was with Woody that time? Is that the incident you told us about?"

"Yeah."

"How many shots did you hear in the house?"

"Five."

"Sounded like five? Was it bam, bam, bam, bam? Or just bam, bam? Or were they real quick? Was it a long space between any of them?"

"They were quick."

"Five real quick shots?" *After a month Fenner still didn't know the facts that there were only three shots fired.*

"They were quick."

"How fast? Just kind of go bang, bang as fast as you think they were?"

"I'll just. I jumped on the first no. It was a loud ass noise. I jumped and he goes don't move. And he stands on me and pointed it more and I was like alright, man don't shoot. I was all scared, I was all shitting bricks. I mean what can you do when you have a gun to your head, no. And then I'm like now, this is my second time. Andrew had already pulled a gun to my head. And believe it or not, even if you got stories or not, he really did pull a gun to my head. I felt like man, this ain't Andrew, I can't talk him out of it. I don't even know this vato, I don't know if I know him. I know Sager. But it ain't Sager who's got the gun on my head. And so I knew I couldn't talk him out of it. I was just scared. I didn't know what to do."

"Okay. How long after the shooting did you hook with Little Dreamer and go to Arizona?"

"Two days, I think." *Now I knew they were working without a time line and they still didn't have a date of death.*

"So you looked for two days for Sager before you hooked with Little Dreamer and took off? I think we've covered most of the information that we need. You did the right thing bro."

"I hope so."

"You did, bro, you did."

Where was the beginning of the audiotape? They're cutting off the beginning of the tapes on us. Now I couldn't go to sleep. I looked back in my bag and found a tape with Woody's name on it.

Police Interview With Lawrence Nieto "Woody"

We finally had an introduction. "It's five pm. It's May the thirteenth, 1996. I'm here with Detective Juan DeReyes with the Albuquerque Police Department and Lawrence Nieto."

"Yes sir."

"Also known as Woody."

"Yes sir."

"Woodrow."

"We've been sitting here talking for about an hour and a half, haven't we?"

"Yes sir."

"But we were in another office?"

(I stopped the tape. Where's the other tape if they have been there for an hour and a half? We're missing the first tape of May 13, 1996. This was sounding like Woody is confessing.)

"Yes sir."

"And we've been talking about the homicide in Torreon, right?"

"Yes sir."

"Why don't you tell me what you know?"

"Well first of all, um, Shaun Wilkins also known as Sager, and Roy Buchner, Eazy, also known as Eazy. Went to my house and told me let's go to the cabin over there no. And I told them no, I didn't want to go no. And he said come on let's go, no. So we went up there, parked right by down the hill.

"And then we went and partied, kicking back drinking a few beers. I went outside to take a piss and I just heard like eight rounds so I went back in and checked it out and told them what happened, no. And he put a gun to my head and said hey don't say nothing. And then he told me, Shaun Wilkins, Sager, and I like tripped out and then I had like tears ay. And they were just loading all kinds of stuff. Weed and the two eight balls and all kinds of guns. And that's all seen. We bailed and we stopped at some little rest area and they burned the gloves inside the trashcan and they kept on telling me on the way. Don't be saying anything because I know you're too good with the rats. And I don't want to end up killing you, or killing you. And they just kept on telling me. And so they dropped me off and then they went their own way. About two weeks later, ay, Shaun came by and showed me a wad of money. And just Roy Buchner just passed by my house. That's all."

"We're gonna back up and go through it a little slower this time? So they came by your house?"

"Yes."

"When was this?"

"Like sometime in January." *You had to be shitting me. Woody is now saying January.*

"It's been quite a while though, four or five months ago, or whatever?"

"Yeah."

"Okay, and what time of day was it?"

"Midday sir."

"Around noon, a little later?" *This was a good clue to Woody to make it later.*

"A little later, around three o'clock."

"Okay, and who was there? Besides you at the house?"

"My mom and my dad and my grandma."

"Was your girlfriend?"

"No, nobody was there just them."

"Okay, and they wanted you to go to the cabin?"

"Yeah."

"Did you want to go?"

"No, I didn't want to go."

"Why?"

"I just wanted to stay home and be with my family and just kick and drink there."

"What kind of car were they in at your house?"

"Black, Camaro or Trans Am." *I remembered his testimony. It was a maroon Trans AM.*

"Whose car was it?"

"He said it was his girlfriend's, but I thought it was stolen."

"What made you think it was stolen?"

"Because he was always in stolen cars."

"Did he have keys?"

"Yeah there were keys to this car."

"So you didn't want to go up to the cabin, but they talked you into it?"

"Yeah."

"So you went up to the cabin."

"We went up to the cabin and we parked like down the hill and we stood there partying with them."

"Okay and then you walked up to the cabin?"

"Yeah, I walked up the hill."

"Were the gates locked?"

"No, the gates weren't locked."

"And so you walked in."

"We walked in."

"Did you notice what kind of vehicles were there at the drive way?"

"Um, I really just noticed the Jeep was there."

"Who's Jeep?"

"Deuce's."

"Deuce's Jeep was there? Anything else?"

"Nothing else, that's it."

"Who was there at the cabin?"

"Cassandra, Ben and the two little kids. And we were just partying then."

"Just partying? You didn't see Popcorn?"

"No, Popcorn wasn't there." *Now I knew I was not going to sleep. Popcorn wasn't there? This was too good to be true.*

"Isn't that kind of weird, because Popcorn lived there?"

"Yeah. But he wasn't there unless he seen Sager and then like ran or something no."

"And so you, Sager, or Shaun Wilkins, Eazy, and you know him as Roy Buchner?"

"Yes, sir."

"Cassandra?"

"Yes sir."

"Ben or Deuce?"

"Yes sir."

"And two little boys?"

"Yes sir."

"And all you guys belong to what gang?"

"Eighteenth Street."

"And so you just stayed there partying? What kind of partying did you do. I mean when you say partying what were you doing?"

"Smoking weed and drinking beer."

"Okay. And so you were smoking weed and drinking beer."

"Yes sir."

"Was Deuce drinking or what was he doing?"

"Smoking weed and drinking beer."

"And Cassandra?"

"I don't know she prefers drinking."

"And Sager?"

"Sager was on soda, had a soda and smoking weed and drinking beer."

"Whose drugs?"

"They were there and so I guess Deuce's."

"Deuce's? And what was Eazy doing?"

"The same as Sager."

"And so they were taking on some pretty hard stuff?"

"Lineas (lines of coke) and stuff."

"So you didn't take any drugs with you?"

"No."

"It was all there?"

"That's all I was doing, smoking weed and drinking beer."

"How much weed was at the house?"

"Like about a pound, no."

"About a pound?"

"About a half a pound less than a pound. We were smoking a lot and we got all stoned and drinking beer."

"And did you see any crack?"

"No, I didn't see any crack I just seen soda, ay."

"How much coke?"

"Two eight balls that I seen."

"And then just beer?

"Just beer."

"What kind of beer?"

"Budweiser."

"Budweiser? Bottles, cans?"

"Cans, ay." *This was strange, there were no cans of Budweiser beer found at the cabin.*

"And that was all there when you got there?"

"Yeah."

"So then after a while how long?"

"It was about three hours. I just went outside and took a piss and then that's when I heard all the gunshots and I went in. And said what the fuck is going on, no. What's up ah? He just put the gun to my head and said shut up, don't say nothing. And I just like. *"Now Woody is saying they put the gun to his head. Popcorn just said they put the gun to his head. Must be the ghost of Torreon.*

"Where did you go outside to take a piss?" *I thought Popcorn testified he went out to take a piss.*

"Right there on the side of the cabin."

"Hold on. So you went outside to take a leak?" *Sounds like Woody had lost his script.*

"Yeah and that's when I heard it. And I just went in and said what the fucks going on?"

"So you come out the door and go to the right or to the left?"

"Straight out the door and down. And I just like."

"And then you heard the shots and go running back in to see what the hell is going on right?"

"Yes sir. I told them what's going on, ay? And he just put the gun to my head and said don't say nothing."

"Who put the gun to your head?"

"Sager." *There it was. The mystery was solved. Sager was a ghost and could be in two places at once.*

"And then what happened?"

"We just went down the hill and they were carrying stuff down the hill and then we just went back."

"You didn't carry anything out of the house?"

"I didn't carry anything."

"They didn't tell you hey, load up with this shit and take it?"

"No I just went down there with tears in my eyes."

"What did they take from the cabin?"

"Just the guns and the weed and the soda."

"How much guns, how many guns?"

"Five ay."

"Five? Or five that you saw?"

"I seen five."

"When Sager put that gun to your head, I'm sure you got a real good look at him right?"

"Yeah, it was that twenty-two ay."

"Describe the gun to me?"

"It was like a Colt twenty-two." *Sager must now have the capability of changing from a shotgun in Popcorn's statement to a .22 in Woody's statement.*

"Was it short or longer?"

"It was short and he just cocked it back."

"And so it was a semi-automatic?"

"Yeah."

"And what about Eazy did you ever see his gun?"

"No, I just seen him with the thirty-odd six."

"A rifle?"

"Yeah."

"How were they dressed?"

"They were dressed, Sager was dressed in like black Ben Davis with a white shirt. And Eazy was dressed black Dickies with a muscle shirt."

"Do you remember their shoes?" *Asking about the shoes and not about the cabin. I could not figure out how they were doing their interviews.*

"No, I don't remember their shoes, sir."

"Were they wearing masks?" *Wait a minute. I just heard Popcorn saying they were wearing black and white masks.*

"No just gloves."

"What kind of gloves?"

"Like leather ones, ay, black and then like brown ones."

"Both?"

"Sager was wearing leather ones."

"Black leather?"

"Yeah."

"And Sager was wearing or Eazy was?"

"Like a brown, dickie blues."

"Were they like leather or like nylon?"

"Cotton or whatever."

"Okay. So then you guys went back to the car and got in the car?"

"Bailed."

"Where were you?"

"I was in the back seat."

"And?"

"And we bailed and we went to."

"Sager was driving?"

"Sager. And then we went to the rest area and they burned the gloves and they just kept on telling me on the way."

"Did you guys just come back straight through?"

"Yeah."

"To Albuquerque or did you go to Belen?"

"Just straight through into Albuquerque."

"And it was the first rest area you came to?"

"Yeah, we just burned it."

"Was it on the highway?"

"Yeah, I think it was on the highway. And then they just took me home and."

"Do you know where that rest area is now?"

"Maybe."

"You guys didn't take the Jeep?"

"No, we didn't take the Jeep."

"Tell me when you guys were leaving the house did somebody close the door?"

"Yeah he closed the door."

"Who did?"

"Eazy, he locked it."

"What did they do with the keys?"

"I think they just threw them out on the highway sir."

"On the way back into Albuquerque? Did you see them throw them?"

"Yeah, I seen him like launch them."

"But you don't know where?"

"I don't know when. I just went home and then."

"They haven't said nothing to you?"

"Nothing."

"They haven't given you any money?"

"Nada."

"Guns, or anything, nada?"

"Nothing."

"They haven't bribed you to keep your mouth shut, they just threaten me?"

"They just threaten me and tell me keep your mouth shut and don't say nothing."

"You said that Sager was wearing some black pants?"

"Ben Davis pants."

"Ben Davis pants with a white shirt?"

"Yes sir."

"What kind of white shirt?"

"Just a regular white shirt."

"Not a t-shirt?"

"Like not a t-shirt, like fruit of the looms, it was just a regular white shirt."

"Was there any blood on it after?"

"There was nothing on it."

"There was nothing. What was Eazy wearing?"

"Black dickies with a muscle shirt."

"Black dickies and muscle shirt, what color?"

"Just a white one."

"The one that he always likes to wear?"

"Yeah."

"Okay. Now when you heard the shots, how many shots did you hear?"

"I heard about eight?"

"What did you think when you heard the shots?"

"I just tripped out, no? And I just, when he put the he put the gun to my head I just tripped out most."

"So you walked in from taking your piss?"

"And I said what's going on and they were already coming out and just put the gun."

"From the front or the back yard?"

"From the front."

"Oh you went?"

"No I went to the front to take a piss on the side."

"Oh okay."

"And then I like went back in."

"Right."

"And just like now that I heard the shots I was taking a piss and then I went back in and that's when he told me don't say nothing and he put the gun to my head and tears just came down."

"They were carrying stuff down?"

"The guns and stuff."

"The guns and the mota, and the cocaine. Did you help them carry anything down?"

"No, I just went down there because I was like all tripped out, man."

"Right."

"Cause they like put the gun to my head."

"Did you think of running?"

"No, I just thanked God and stayed cool. I just went back to the back seat and I just thought. They just kept on telling me don't say nothing. Dude, don't say nothing."

"Who kept saying 'don't say nothing'?"

"Sager."

"Why?"

"Because my brother's a rats and shit."

"And then?"

"And then he just kept on I'm gonna kill no, don't say nothing. That's what he kept on telling me on the way."

"What was Eazy saying?"

"Nothing, just a smile like always."

"Were they acting weird when you guys went up to the cabin?"

"They were acting like usual."

"Lettial?"

"They were kind of buzzed, ay."

"Now when you say that guns came out, where did they get these guns from?"

"I don't know."

"You mean you never saw them?"

"I never seen them."

"You didn't see them when you got in the car?"

"No, I didn't see them in the car."

"Did you see any guns in the car?"

"I didn't even see nothing."

"When they picked you up and all that?"

"They just showed me the twenty-two."

"Who did?"

"Sager."

"When they first picked you up? What do you mean?"

"When I got into the car he had it on his lap and he showed it to me."

"As soon as you got into the car?"

"When I got in the car it was on his lap."

"And what did he say?"

"Let's just go up there and party with them."

"You didn't think nothing of it?"

"I didn't think, I didn't think at all."

"Did Eazy show you a gun?"

"He didn't show me nothing."

"After you guys go up there, he already has a gun, so you know he's got a gun on him, right? And you guys go up there and start partying, about what time would you say you got there?" *Man I wish Mike would ask one question at a time.*

"We got there around four."

"Around four. And then after that you say three or four hours went by?" *Where was Mike getting this information from unless it came up in the earlier interview. The interviewer has yet to ask for a date or even a day of the week.*

"Yeah. Four hours went by."

"And everybody is doing heavy coke?"

"There was no coke man. I was just smoking weed, me and Ben."

"You and Ben were? And Deuce had coke right?"

"Yeah."

"And he gave these guys the coke and they were doing lineas, you said? How many?"

"Easily, like three or four."

"Three or four lineas? After they did that were they smoking more grass?"

"They were just smoking and drinking and stuff."

"Okay you went outside, took a piss, came back you hear the shots, they're coming out and you're going in. You say what happened? They put the gun to your head. Sager tells you?"

"Don't say nothing. He just told me like that."

"And?"

"They were carrying stuff and we went down there."

"Now when you were inside there you said you were inside the living room. While you were standing there and Sager put the gun to you and you turned looking around. Where did you see Ben's body at?"

"I seen like in his room, ay. Like I don't know."

"The bedroom or something? *"Agent Jacoby had to help Woody say bedroom. But he never did.*

"Yeah sort of like."

"Was he on the floor?"

"Yeah, I seen him on the floor, ah and then I like tripped out and I just went out running outside, no. And just went to the car and then just on the way he kept on telling me, don't say nothing, don't say nothing, don't say nothing. I won't man, I won't man." *I knew that was a lie. Ben died in bed.*

"Where was Cassandra? Was Cassandra next to Ben or?" *Agent Jacoby is still trying to give hints to Woody.* "Cassandra next to Ben?"

"I didn't even see Cassandra. I just glanced like that." *If Cassandra was there when Ben was shot, why didn't Woody see her?*

"Did you hear the kids crying?"

"I didn't even hear nothing, man. I just stayed in a state of shock. All that stuff, I just took off like outside."

"So when that happens you get in the car they keep telling you not to say nothing because they'll kill you. And now you're afraid for your life because of what they just did. Right?"

"Yes sir."

"Okay. So then you go to this rest stop, you?"

"They burn the gloves."

"They burn the gloves, they get back in the car and they take off again."

"They took me home. And they went on their own."

"And they went on their own? After all of that that you knew what had happened, right, you were there when that happened. Why didn't you ever call the police?"

"I was scared."

"Why?"

"Because I thought they were going to kill me, bro."

"And when you heard it on the news, you knew what went down right?"

"Yeah."

"Why all of a sudden like say for instance now you're trying to come forward with this information?"

"I'm tired of remembering."

"It's been bugging you, right?"

"Yes sir."

"And you know that this is wrong, for them to do that. Right?"

"Yes sir."

"And when we first started talking to you, you knew that from the beginning that eventually that we'd come around again, right?"

"Yes."

"And you knew it was another diez y ocho doing another diez y ocho, right?"

"Yes, sir."

"This life is pretty wicked, no?"

"No, it's bad."

"It's awful."

"It's bad."

"And you know that if Eighteenth Street would have been the way they originally set themselves up a long time ago, this never would have happened, right?"

"No."

"Why do you think he did it bro?"

"Ssshhh."

"What is your?"

"Just to get the drugs, or something, you know. Maybe somebody told him to do it. Or might have been."

"Do you think somebody put him up to it?"

"No reason to."

"Why do you say that?"

"Maybe he did a bad drug deal or something, I don't know."

"What about Ben? Did Ben know somebody else?"

"Maybe, with the drug dealers, it went wrong, or something, I don't know to tell you the truth."

"Or do you think that Sager wanted to be the man?"

"Yeah. Probably."

"Does he have a lot of stokes?"

"What do you mean by stokes?"

"You know he had the guns, he had the bank, you know he could make the movidas here and there, for diez y ocho and other gangs, no?"

"Yes sir."

"If the Westgate or any other gang needed a gun that was a connect, no?"

"Yes sir."

"And you were there when those connects were made, right?"

"No, I wasn't there. I just heard about it."

"You just heard about it?"

"I just heard about it, I wasn't there for the connects, sir."

"Okay, and you've been truthful, right?"

"Yes sir."

"What you have told me is going to pin Sager? And see he's right now sitting in jail thinking about at all of this. Thinking that we don't know nothing. So we are definitely on the right track, right?"

"Yes sir."

"And you know that?"

"Yes sir."

"Do you still fear for your life, Woody?"

"Not really, I'm like kind of."

"Relieved that it's over with, yeah?"

"Yes sir."

"All you want to do is take care of yourself, your family?"

"Yes sir."

"And you can honestly say in a court of law that Sager and Eazy were the killers?"

"Yes sir."

"And you have nothing to do with it?" *They had minimized Woody's role.*

"Yes sir, I didn't have nothing to do with it."

"And that the only reason you held out was that because they had threatened to kill you too if you ever say something?"

"Yes sir."

"Do you know what Ben and Cassandra were wearing when you left to take a leak?"

"I didn't snap sir."

"Were they getting ready to go to bed, or?" *Agent Jacoby still trying to give clues.*

"Ssshhh. They were just kicking back relaxing, watching TV."

"How was Ben dressed?"

"He was dressed regular, not all gangstered out, ay."

"Is Ben Deuce?" *Agent Jacoby knew Woody didn't know the answer and changed the subject.*

"Yeah."

"But what was he wearing that day, was it hot or cold in the cabin?"

"It was pretty fresh in there."

"Did you guys have any heaters or anything on? When you guys got there were the kids anywhere around?" *Agent Jacoby knew he didn't want to go the physical evidence in the cabin and quickly changed the subject. In all the interviews, the evidence was never a subject of the interviews.*

"I guess they were just playing around, I didn't."

"You didn't hear them come into the living room when you guys were partying?"

"No. They were there asleep or something."

"When you say that you guys went in the black Camaro or a black Trans Am, did it have tinted windows?"

"Yeah, tinted windows."

"Did it have any wheels on it?"

"No, it didn't have any wheels on it, it just had regular wheels."

"Just stock."

"Yeah."

"And there were keys in it?"

"Yes sir."

"Did you see when you were in the car, did you see any other stuff in the vehicle that would tell you that it belongs to a chick? That car belongs to a chick? You know?"

"It was just all clean."

"It was clean? Was it a real shiny black, a prime grey?"

"Primer black, ah."

"Like if somebody took care of it? Did you ever see that car before?"

"No, I'd never seen it before."

"And he said it was his girlfriend's?"

"Yeah, he said it was his girlfriend's."

"What girlfriend was Sager dating at that time?"

"Salina."

"Do you know if Salina has a car?" *I had found Salina in Bullhead City and none of this was true.*

"I don't know to tell you the truth, sir."

"When you asked him…this is your girlfriend's car, what girlfriend? Did you ask him that?"

"No, I didn't even snap. I just. I didn't want to go at first. They just kept on telling."

"Was it an automatic or a stick?"

"An automatic."

"Did you guys play some sounds or anything like that?"

"The music."

"Were you pretty comfortable?"

"I just kicked it in the back."

"You just kicked it in the back, smoked some mota on the way up there?"

"Yeah. I drank a quart on the way up there."

"When you guys were driving up there did you stop anywhere?"

"No we just went straight up."

"Where did you get the quart from?"

"My mom had bought it for me earlier, no. That day. So I just took it."

"And they weren't drinking when they were going up there?"

"They were buzzed no, but they weren't all that buzzed, you know what I'm saying."

"Did they say what they were buzzed on?"

"No just, I didn't even ask. They were just buzzed."

"So it was an automatic, huh? Did you ever see that gun again?"

"That twenty-two."

"Yeah."

"About two weeks later."

"He came by?"

"He came by."

"What kind of car was he driving then?"

"A little blue one, no."

"What kind of car?"

"A Cavalier, or something like that."

"A Cavalier, whose car was that?"

"Sshh, I don't know. It probably was stolen."

"What did he do with that twenty-two?"

"He said he had it at his girlfriend's house."

"That's where he kept it."

"Yeah."

"Do you think at Salina's huh?"

"You mean at Salina's, what happened?"

"No, it was at Salina's house as far as you know?"

"That I know of."

"Did Salina know he had a gun?"

"Yeah, she knew."

"Does she know what went down up there?"

"I don't know if he told her or what, I don't know to tell you the truth sir. Because after that they didn't like really come around."

"Did Sager brag around about doing that?"

"No, he didn't even say anything, he just kept it to himself."

"He'll come bro? Because he knew that his homies would smoke him didn't he? The homies were upset about all of this, weren't they?"

"And he didn't even go the funeral either? I went both places."

"Did he go to the rosary?"

"Yeah, he went to the rosary."

"Was Salina with him?"

"No."

"Don't you think that a homie is a homie, you go to the rosary and you go to the funeral. Did Eazy go to the rosary?"

"Yeah, he went to the rosary but not the funeral."

"Didn't that strike you funny, bro? That you were there for both of them, no?"

"Yes sir."

"Why did everybody want to blame Popcorn, bro? Who started that scandal? Sager?" *By this time I wanted to scream at Agent Jacoby. More compound questions for Woody. Leaving Sager as the last question to answer.*

"Probably, yeah."

"He wanted to cover his tracks, huh? He'll come...you went along with it, bro?"

"I was scared, no. I told you."

"I think that should just about wrap it here. Okay. I've got about one-ten pm."

I looked over at the clock. Midnight. But again I thought, nah, it's only eleven. I can listen to one more.

10

Shaun Wilkins' Statement

AGAIN, NO FORMAL INTRODUCTIONS ON THE AUDIOTAPE, JUST a starting point. Did these three officers know this was a death penalty case? Four deceased people needed justice. Officers are "Truth Seekers and Fact Finders not Case Makers."

"You think you're going to BCDC? Maybe not, huh." It was DeReyes again. *I groaned to myself.*

"Fuck it, ah. That's what you say. It's not like I'm gonna die."

"You're gonna die, but not by us. But by your own homies."

"Oh yeah."

"You're bad, like Sager. Did they give you your rights when they picked you up? And what did you tell them?"

"I'll come and talk to you guys."

"Have you waived your rights?"

"I didn't waive them, no."

"Do you know the difference between waiving your rights?"

"Yeah."

"You've been arrested before, right?"

"Yeah."

"So when they picked you up, what did they say? What did they tell you?"

"That I have the right to have an attorney. I had the right to my silence. And that I could stop this anytime I want to."

"Right. So what do you want to do now?"

"We'll talk."

"We're listening, we're listening bro. It's your turn to talk, bro. We already know the whole story. So you tell us what happened."

"I didn't even know what happened. All I know about is that a homeboy died and you think we killed our homeboy."

"You've seen this before right? Do you know what these are? These are called photo arrays."

"I know that."

"That means when you get arrested. I know why you got arrested for this. Because the hickey is still on your neck. Do you know what I'm saying.

Okay, anyway, check it out bro. When we do these is so we show them to people. And they say yeah, he's the one that did it. Because we want to make sure. We want to be positive that we have it. Do you know these people?"

"I don't know the bitch or the kids, but I know that homeboy."

"Homeboy, huh? Is that what you called him that night? You should be embarrassed man. Who do you recognize in this photo array, here? Oh your friend."

"Roy Buchner, Shaun."

"Shaun what?"

"Shaun Wilkins."

"Why do you think you're here bro?"

"Cause you guys ain't got shit."

"Of course we have."

"Yeah right, and I'm gonna prove that I didn't do nothing."

"Yeah and I'm gonna prove it?"

"You ain't gonna get nothing. You guys don't have a fuckin' clue who did this."

"Really, so enlighten us Eazy. Since you're the man."

"No, I wish I knew too, bro."

"Really. Because you guys would be blasting that person now too wouldn't you?"

"Not me, I don't gang bang."

"You don't. You're a working man?"

"Yeah."

"I don't think so. Your dad must be really proud of you huh?"

"I don't know. I haven't seen my dad in years, bro."

"I don't blame him bro, because if I had son like you I tell you I would be pretty disappointed."

"You brought me in to talk, so now let's talk."

"You think we're gonna talk to you now."

"I already talked to my attorney."

"You got an attorney. Now you answer me this, why would get an attorney if you don't even know what you're being charged with?"

"I know what I'm being charged with. You guys think I went and killed my own homeboy. What the fuck is up with that, hey."

"That's what we want to know."

"You're wrong."

"Well then clear your name bro."

"You're wrong, brother, you're wrong."

"Well then tell us, tell us why we're wrong."

"I didn't do anything. I've never even been to that cabin or nothing, man."

"Ha, you're living in a fantasy world, homie. Because you see this file right here. This file is full of an accumulation of effort. Let me tell you about something I found out. Have you ever seen this before? We get a lot of pictures, we get a lot of information about Eighteenth Street. This is all the vatos. How do you think I got this?"

"I don't know."

"Do you think somebody gave it up to me? Do you think somebody said, 'here you go Detective Reyes.' I got this because people owe me. And when you owe somebody bro, like you owe somebody."

"I don't owe anybody."

"The homie that gave this up he's in here because he owed me."

"A ratta."

"No he ain't a ratta. You know what I had respect for him because you know what when I nailed them he was man enough to admit it."

"I don't have respect for no one I don't know."

"Oh really, do you think that respect comes because you think that you deserve it?"

"I grew up where you have to earn respect, bro."

"That's right bro. That's right. And I grew up in the barrios way before you were even born, see."

"And?"

"And it's the same way. And that's why homeboy did it, because he has respect, bro."

"Yeah."

"And what I'm looking at right now is just a little punk that thinks he knows everything because he's been hanging with the bros. And that he knows everything and that he needs an attorney because he doesn't even know what he's being charged with. "

"I know. You guys will try and fuck me."

"Really."

"Might as well have an attorney."

"For what?"

"Because you guys are trying to fuck me."

"We can do it every day."

"Well do it."

"We jack you and watch you every day. So when we charge you and so you can exercise your rights. And right now you're not being charged with anything, are you?"

"No."

"So why are you sweating it, bro?"

"I ain't sweating nothing. I came here on my own free will."

"Good."

"Good."

"Okay you are here on your own free will. You want to clear this thing up so that way the 'hura' will not mess with the wrong guy again, then enlighten us, Roy."

"About?"

"Well you tell us what went down. And you tell us who did it. That you think."

"One day I saw my home boy on the news and I was totally shocked."

"On the news?"

"Yes, my mom called and my sister called me and told me."

"And that's all you know?"

"And that's all I know. And then the 'hura' got me. That's all I know. Did I enlighten you?"

"No. Sager wasn't home."

"Sager didn't do it then."

"Yeah, but you know who did it. That it was you. Because it was the two of you up there. Which one was it, was it you or was it?"

"I wasn't up there."

"Stay with that one bro. There are so many people who have never been there. That don't know shit. Framed by fuckin' society. Apparently you think that the way you react to it."

"Because it's all jacked up, bro."

"The only way of thinking is your way of thinking, huh? Somebody gets out of line and your fuckin' killing and leaving the little kids there to starve to death."

"I wasn't out there."

"Oh that's real manly. That's like something I would give respect for. Kill an old lady with a gun and leave two little kids to starve to death. Now that, now that could earn you some respect."

"You know what for anybody that thinks that. I don't give a fuck about the girl and the little kids, man."

"I know you don't."

"I don't even know who the fuck they are."

"Oh that makes it all the better, doesn't it?"

"The only one I care about is my homeboy fuckin' Deuce. Hey."

"Oh really was it a lot of fun putting the gun behind him."

"I don't know who did that."

"Your homeboy did it. Sager. You did too."

"Yeah. You guys don't have no clue."

"Oh no, well if we didn't have a clue, bro. You wouldn't be sitting in the hot chair right now."

"You guys don't know."

"We do know. We're just watching you and Sager. We are watching a young punk who thinks that we don't know. And we're gonna pin him. Locking him up."

"You guys can't know anything."

"Because you know what. That's a trip. You think that tie and that stuff makes you look cool? Do you think that you're Mr. Cool Vato with the women or with whoever, with the homeboys."

"I'm just another person out there."

"No you're not bro. You're another person who can't take responsibility for his own action."

"I do take responsibility."

"No you don't. Because if you did you would be taking it now."

"Yeah."

"You'd be taking it now."

"For what?"

"Because you're going down, bro."

"Fuck it."

"It's not my life? It's your life."

"My life."

"That's right."

"So don't worry about it."

"That's right. Oh, I won't bro. Because I know if we don't get justice. Somebody else will do the jerking for us. That's what you think right now. You're a little pretty boy."

"I ain't no pretty boy."

"Wait until you get into the pinta bro."

"I ain't going to the pinta."

"Oh really. Let's talk lawsuits, Mr. Lawyer. Let's talk lawsuits. When did you pass the bar?"

"I'm gonna take it now."

"Yeah, you look like an attorney. Do you have a bachelor's degree?"

"I'm gonna get one."

"Don't practice law without a license right now homie."

"I ain't practicing law. That's why I got me a lawyer."

"Really, who's your attorney?"

"I don't know."

"You don't know."

"I called him last night. My mom called me and said to get an attorney."

"Why? Why would she call?"

"Because it's Mother's Day."

"She tells you every Mother's Day to get an attorney."

"As a matter of fact, I want an attorney right now."

"I'll be right back."

"You better have a lot of money. Because you ain't gonna see light. You're such a bad boy. Just like Sager. Sitting there crying. Have you seen Sager cry?"

"Yeah."

"Really, when? You don't cry, because you're bad."

"I've already lived my life."

"Really, you haven't even lived. You don't know what life is all about."

"You can't say that, you can't judge me. You don't even know me."

"I don't want to know you bro. This is business. Strictly business. Whatever you do in your personal life."

"Yeah."

"My job is to put gangsters away like you."

"I got me a job, I don't go out gang banging. You can get my hours for the last fuckin' couple of weeks. Because I've been working fuckin' forty-eight hours a week. I've got my shit together. And I get off this now and I'm getting the fuck out of here." *Roy was right. The officers didn't do any backgrounds on their suspect.*

"Yeah."

"Yeah."

"Oh well that's good. I called the other jailhouse lawyers ... there and say you were framed boy. Don't even think about it bro, because it ain't gonna happen. You're dreaming, you're dreaming."

"Yeah."

"That's the big thing with all the gangsters around here always saying let's get arrested or let them arrest us. So that we can sue the city."

"I didn't want to get arrested. I was at work when you got me. You go and talk to my manager, go and get my work schedule."

"We don't care about your work schedule, homie. That has nothing to do with what we're talking about." *You have got to be kidding me. Work schedule and background. I always thought that was police work.*

"I guess the system does work, huh."

"No, it doesn't. Not for you homie. You think it does. Because you know what, man. Before you even existed in this world I grew up and I saw a lot of shit. It don't matter bro, it's the same shit. All these young pee-wees all these young wanna-be's thinking they know everything. And they know the law."

"I know the law."

"You don't know shit."

"The 'hura' don't know shit."

"Oh really. That's right. To put you down bro. I've got a few simple words for you bro. The black dickie pants and your tank top bro."

"You don't know nothing."

"Really. Well you look like a gangbanger to me, bro. You're gonna have a lot of time to do, a lot of thinking where you're going bro. Oh yeah. You're the material type that they want to see."

"I guess so. Even the probation officer told me to go to school."

"I'll tell you right now. In order to be an attorney. You can't have any felonies."

"I don't have any felonies."

"Oh really, you will now. You might as well forget about practicing law. You can only be jail house lawyer."

"Yeah, yeah. You're funny."

"I'm very funny. That's the same thing that Sager told me and look where he's at. What do you think that Donald Cosby told me and now he's doing fifteen years. He told me the same thing. You ain't got shit bro. You ain't got nothing, bro. I didn't do nothing bro. Hey I just pinned him up for fifteen years. And he was calling me every day before he went on that transport van to PNM. Let's work out a deal bro."

"I ain't done shit."

"Really, I'm glad. Let's just see how long you hold out bro. I don't think anything you've ever seen in a cell in BCDC will ever compare."

"What about it?"

"I'm just bringing it up. That's nothing compared to the pinta bro. You're walking into a big old world. You'll be fuckin' crying for mama. Mama get me out of here. I did my time in the military. I went to Saudi. I was fighting for everyone. Including a dirt bag like you."

"That's your thing, no."

"Yeah, that's my thing, bro. Because I have the balls to do it and stand up for what I believe in. You don't."

"I bet your parents are proud of you too."

"No bro. I'm proud of myself. Because I know what I'm doing. And this gangbanger life that you lead. And try to make the girls and make them think how bad you are. With the drugs, with the guns with the drive by's. Oh yeah, that's so bad, that's coward shit."

"I ain't never done none of that shit."

"Oh really, you don't have guns. Never had any guns bro?"

"Nope."

"Never? Really?"

"Was I convicted of it."

"Let's be proud of all this."

"Was I convicted of any of it."

"Let's be proud of people like you. Let's be real proud that we have outstanding citizens like you. Out there on the street, protecting our interests. Saying how proud we should be to have such a wonderful person like you."

"What are you going to do with all the crimes that I have."

"Oh we can't find them."

"Oh okay."

"You know what, right now at this point, I don't care what you did up to this point. Because you're gonna be gone for a long time. I'm gonna say case closed. Homeboys gone. Like I told Sager. I got another page about Sager to add to his rap. This ain't shit homie, I still got a file on your ass. A couple of car jacking's, a couple of armed robberies. All kinds of shit. And you know it. He told me last night. Well just tack them on. Oh yeah, I'll tack them on. If I were you, I would be the first one to talk and get my ass out of trouble. Why don't you tell me right now? Sometimes there is an advantage to being the first guy arrested on something."

"How do you figure?"

"Because you can tell your story before anyone gets to tell theirs."

"I don't have no story to tell."

"Let's talk. You'll be the first one. Where do you work at?"

"At Jewel Osco."

"Oh, Jewel Osco, yeah. Which one?"

"The new one."

The interview went on for another thirty minutes but there was no more relevant information. I looked through the tapes and found the Shaun Wilkins interview.

Shaun Wilkins "Sager" II

"So where did you screw up Shaun?"

"I didn't do nothing."

"Where did you screw up bro?"

"I didn't do nothing?"

"I told you we're past that point bro. We were past that the other day. We told you we'd come back with a warrant and what happened?"

"You said."

"Huh."

"You know what I think, I think somebody's lying to you and I'm telling you guys right now it's my line and I don't care."

"I think what happened is that you screwed up, you left somebody, you screwed up, you took somebody with you. You know what you screwed up and you talked about it, bro. You fuckin' talked about it. I thought you were smarter than that Shaun?"

"I didn't do shit, you swear I did, but I ain't got nothing to lie about. You know I'm going to court."

"I hope you do."

"And you know what I'll tell the truth, and I'll win this case. God knows, God knows."

"God knows, you did do it, okay? God knows you did, I know you did."

"I've never been to the cabin, and if anybody says that I have then they're lying to you."

"Oh, the other 27 people that saw you at the cabin."

"Oh, now it's 27 people that saw me at the cabin."

"I don't know how many there are Shaun, but several of them know you were there. Several. This is just bare bone. Bare bone. So you really don't know what's up. This is what you should know. What you don't know is what else was found out. You screw up bro."

"I didn't do nothing."

"You fucked up, you fucked up."

"I didn't do nothing."

"Face down, underground. Boy that's slick. Your gonna have 30 years or so for that."

"I didn't do nothing, man."

"You're gonna have, I don't know maybe not 30 years left. What's the appeal on a death penalty case. About ten or twelve. You'll have plenty of time to think about it though. In fact you'll have plenty of time to hear all about it. But of course, we want to know your side of the story Shaun. Because there is two sides here bro. There's two sides to every story. People don't get killed for no reason."

"I didn't do nothing sir. I ain't got nothing to tell you because I didn't do shit. I ain't got nothing to tell you. You guys arrested the wrong person. I'm telling you right now."

"Yeah, yeah."

"You guys just arrested me just to get somebody to blame for it."

"Yeah, that's all we're doing, you're absolutely right, Shaun. "

"I know."

"We ain't got nothing else to do but pick on you no, that's it. That's the only thing we've got. Well the fact is bro, you did it. Oh yeah, you get to keep them, in fact you should frame them, bro. You should fuckin' frame them. We'll put them right here."

"What's that?"

"That's a search warrant for your mom's house."

"I want to read it, I'm allowed to read it. Hey, I'll bring this shit up in court. I'm allowed to read what I want to read this is my shit. I can read it. I don't give a fuck. This shit is coming up in court, trying to deny me of my shit."

"It's just a standard search warrant, bro."

"All right."

"They all read the same."

"All right."

"Haven't you ever seen a search warrant?"

"I get to keep these in jail right?"

"You get the affidavit, bro. No, the affidavit is not here. This is just a standard search warrant."

"That is what I was trying to tell you a while go."

"You've seen search warrants. They all read the same, no?"

"Yeah."

"The affidavit is not here bro."

"I've never seen that before."

"They all read the same. Next time I try and tell you something, listen bro."

"Okay, well don't be grabbing shit from."

"Bro, sit down. Relax, fucking relax, okay."

"I didn't do nothing."

"Just sit there, were not gonna bang heads in here about whether you did or didn't do it. We've discussed this before, haven't we?"

"Yeah."

"We have and you know where I stand on it right?"

"I know where you stand on it."

"You can stand there and say I didn't do shit from now until the time hell freezes over."

"I know sir, I know sir."

"Okay, Shaun, okay. Just listen to me."

"I prefer to go to jail, I don't want to talk to you."

"Listen to me for a second. I'm not asking you to talk to me, I'm asking you to listen to me for a second. Okay bro?"

"All right, I'm listening."

"Let me put this away, just relax, be calm."

"I'm relaxed."

"Are you? Okay. What do you think? What do you think about this. This is not some bogus piece of bullshit. That you don't go and get a district."

"I don't know how the fuck you guys are using shit like that."

"You know what?"

"I didn't do nothing. You guys don't have nothing on me because I didn't do nothing."

"Listen to me okay? And we're not going to go and get something like this on the word of one person. Are we?"

"No."

"I'll tell you right now, you think I'm the kind of guy that would go and sign my name on the bottom of a warrant on the word of one person?"

"No, you wouldn't."

"You're right I am not that kind of person. I'm not asking you if you did or not right now. I'm asking you to listen. Here me out. Is that fair enough?"

"Yeah, that's fair enough."

"I'm telling you that it is not on the word of one person. I'm telling you straight up your bros have been giving you up. Okay? And that is, I'm telling you, they're not just giving you up on this, they're giving you up on drive-by's, they're giving you up on jackings, car jacking's, they are giving you up on everything. You know what the time has come for them to cut you out, bro. That's what it is. You know what I'm saying. You know how it is in a gang. Right? When you get a liability."

"But a lot of shit they are telling you, I didn't do. But I know that other people did."

"Listen to me, okay Shaun. I'm not asking if you did it right? We got back to that. Okay listen to me. The fact is that you know how it is in a gang. Don't you?"

"Uh huh."

"When somebody becomes a bigger liability than they are an asset. Do you know what a liability and an asset is? An asset is what you can do for the gang and a liability is what you do against a gang."

"I know."

"Do you know what I am saying? Now when you become a bigger liability for what you do against a gang then what you do for it. What happens? You get ranked out, self-preservation, bro. No, right?"

"I don't know what that is."

"Self preservation. You know what that is. Protect number one. Is that not the way the gang should be?"

"I want to man."

"Listen, listen to me."

"That's not my nature, ay."

"I'm not asking you for anything. I'm just asking you to listen. Am I asking you to snitch anybody out?"

"No you're not."

"Have I asked you if you did it? No. I'm asking you to listen. Okay just sit there, sit back relax and listen."

"All right."

"Okay, chill."

"All right."

"You know how it is when you become a liability. When you fuck up what happens? What happens? Gangs protect themselves. Right? They fuckin' protect themselves. They protect each other. They protect themselves. For some reason. Now, I don't know what it is. Whether it is the death of Deuce, I don't know if it's your association with other gangs. For whatever reason, bro, your own gang, Eighteenth Street, diez y ocho, right? They have decided that you are a liability, bro. They are snitching you off, bro. And it's not like one guy has done it. It's not just like one, bro. It's not like one. We've had two this morning. This morning, two. That shit you was bringing up about the drive by. That came up this morning and it's come up in our other interviews. Remember I told you were not gonna come after you on the word of one person. Because one person is going to cut their losses and leave right? Right?"

"I don't know."

"The problem is that there is more than one person out there. There was more than one person out there."

"Where?"

"At the cabin, bro."

"I was never at the cabin."

"Listen."

"You can say whatever you want. I know where I was."

"Did I ask you if you were at the cabin?"

"You just said I did the shit."

"Listen Shaun."

"You guys are treating me like an idiot."

"Shaun, Shaun, look at me bro. You can swear up and down and I'm not asking you if you were there. Did I ever ask you if you were there?"

"That's what you're telling me."

"I'm telling you what we know."

"I don't want to talk to you."

"I'm telling you this is what it is. Okay."

"I want a lawyer." *Every time one of them asks for a lawyer DeReyes finds a reason to stop the conversation.*

"I'll be right back bro. I'll be right back, you wait right here. Let me see where he's got that stuff, I'll be right back."

"All right."

"Okay Shaun, they're gonna go and get him. He'll be back in a minute. We'll find out what all he's got on you. I know what we've got on you. I know that you're going down for the murder. And I'm not gonna argue with you okay. I'm not gonna discuss it with you. I'm telling you for a fact. I'm telling you straight up. One to one. Man to man. Remember, have I lied to you yet? Did I tell you, you passed your polygraph or you did this or you did that."

"What do you mean?"

"Have I told you anything that is not true?"

"I don't know."

"Do you know if I have told you anything that is not true?"

"I don't want to talk to you."

"No I have not have I. The fact of the matter is that you're going down on this. This is not a problem anymore. This is nothing, nada, okay. I ain't worried about this. I don't know what he thinks. He read it, he even tried to read the search warrant without the affidavit. He's hungry for information."

"No, I want to read it so I can see all the shit you guys are lying about."

"You want to know what we know."

"I don't care who tells you that."

"Whose house is that where you live at?"

"That is my mother and father."

"Then you've got no business reading that affidavit."

"I don't know how you got that search warrant to begin with. They told me that is my stuff that I can read it."

"You can, you can have it."

"They gave it to me, that other detective."

"I don't care, you can have it bro. It has nothing to do with you, you are not the owner of the house. It has nothing to do with you. I tried to explain it to you but you don't want to hear it. You want to be hard headed. He seems to be having a memory lapse. Just like he did with that other stuff we were talking about. And then when the stuff came up with the stabbing, it's like oh okay. Yeah, yeah."

"You guys get 30 or 40 guys to surround me to see if I'm gonna do shit."

"Hey bro, think about it. How do you think you got back on the street? You know how you got back on the street?"

"How?"

"Because I put it there. I didn't have to put that 30 or 40 or 50 or 100 people on that arrest warrant. When I made that up, and gave it to the judge. He asked me about it and I said I want in there and he said why. Because I want him to go to jail and I want him to bond out. You know why, judge, he's gonna commit more crimes."

"I don't give a shit. I've stayed at my house every day."

"I know what kind of clothes you're wearing every day."

"I know you guys have."

"But I'm gonna tell you right now. I'm gonna tell you right now. We picked up some vato from your barrio today and he ratted you."

"He can't rat about nothing."

"Well I'm sure you've never done anything. You know what they told me, they said they are going to go and pin you up in court because I told them you think you're a hard ass and a bad ass and you think you're a leader and they said, challe bro. He ain't no leader, he's just a man."

"You guys are lying, cause there ain't no leader in Eighteenth Street."

"Oh no."

"No there was never leader and never will be."

"Oh, you've been around for a long time, huh?"

"No, not that long."

"Were you around when Happy Homes were around bro?"

"I wouldn't talk bro."

"I would, I know who ran him out. Eighteenth Street. That's where it all starts. In the pinta, no. Because the same thing that is happening to them is happening to you. Somebody ratted them and that is why they are. They didn't put themselves up. You guys went and lied and shit and said that guys on the shotgun. You guys showed him paperwork that I wrote. You know what I'm saying, I'm bringing that shit to court too, that I wrote statements."

"Did you?"

"Oh that's what they said."

"Did they show that, did they show you statements anywhere?"

"I don't know."

"Whose shotgun?"

"I don't know."

"Big shotgun or little shotgun from Westgate?"

"No. I don't even hang around with Westgate."

"Well which one, what's his name? What's his real name?"

"You know who I'm talking about."

"And you gave him statements?"

"No, he's saying that you guys gave him statements that I snitched on him."

"Wait a minute I'm getting confused here. You already told us you don't want to talk to us but yet you're talking to us. And I gave you your rights."

"Right so you know what."

"And so if you want to talk about other crimes that you're gonna be charged with."

"I want a lawyer, and if I want a lawyer then you have to stop talking to me right now, because I want a lawyer."

"Really?"

"I know my rights."

"Then invoke them."

"I will."

"Because you can sit here and I can talk all I want."

"Okay well go ahead."

"And as long as you keep talking that is legal. Mr. Lawyer. And I'm telling you right now bro. I got you on ten felonies."

"That's what you say."

"That's right I know. I'll make sure I tell the judge that, and the jury that you didn't do it. But I have a lot of people that are going to be lining up in the stand pinning your butt right up oh yeah by the way we want you to know that he didn't do it, because Shaun Wilkins, AKA Juan Diego Sanchez, AKA Juan Sanchez, has never been arrested in his life, but yet your honor, let me think. Assault on a police officer, hmm, burglary, tampering. Do you want me to go on bro? Because I've got your rap sheet right here with me. But you never did anything homie. You're a happy go lucky type of guy. You're just straight up. You're a model citizen. And I'm gonna tell you, I've got you cold. And your homie dissed you off. And I told you when I see you again Shaun I was gonna have something. And here we are aren't we? I've kept my promise twice. Do you want to go for a third time, fourth time, fifth time? I'll tell you I'll keep coming as long as you're still there. But on this deal you ain't gonna be there. You're gonna be bye, bye. And I'm gonna close all my cases saying he's bye, bye. But he didn't do it. Shaun's last words. He didn't do it, rest in peace. Rest in peace."

"Uh huh."

"Diez y ocho, Sager. You're a pussy bro, you're a coward. You think you're a bad dude, you think."

"I don't think I'm bad sir, you guys."

"Wait a minute, I thought you didn't want to talk to me."

"I won't then."

"Shut up then. Just listen. Since you're mister bad in invoking your rights. Do you know what the Fourth Amendment is? Do you know what the Fifth Amendment is? The Sixth, the Seventh?"

"I plead the Fifth."

"The Fifth. Really."

"Isn't that when you don't talk."

"Okay. Then shut up."

"Well then quit talking to me if you're not supposed to talk me once I want a lawyer."

"Really, oh no, no, no."

"Yeah."

"You've got it wrong bro."

"That guy right there told me not to talk to you guys without one."

"Really."

"Don't worry, my sister is going to get me a good lawyer."

"Really."

"And you know what, my brother-in-law is a cop too. He's a military police."

"Oh yeah. Yeah. Yeah. Big time military policeman. He's gonna help you out of this."

"I didn't do shit."

"Your loser bro, you use people like you used Salina."

"I didn't use Salina."

"Oh, yeah. Let's go back to the rosary party."

"What about it, I didn't hook up with no one."

"Yeah."

"I was walking from Nine Mile hill. I swear to God. We were walking from Nine Mile hill."

"Yeah."

"That's where a lot of people go is Nine Mile hill."

"Nine Mile hill. What did Looney say old Marcus had said? Hey bro, now you're a player, he's my man. I said right, he's your man he just burned you."

"I ain't no player and I don't cheat on my chick."

"Really, you don't. Okay, you don't. You don't. And what is the terminology that they use, pathological liar I believe. He tells this stuff so much that he actually believes his world. Your world is crumbling before you my man. And no matter what you say or how you say it or how many jailhouse lawyers tell you oh yeah. Invoke this, oh yeah they'll do this. When you hit BCDC. It ain't gonna help you, bro. It ain't gonna help you one bit who you know, who you blow and you dove. Because you are a dead man, my son. Yeah, yeah you are, bro. He had this same look on his face, remember. Over there when he was doing the test. And then he started crying and we have it on tape. I want to play it in court. Do you want to see the type of pathological liar this guy is. Let's roll the tape and you make your decision. How a guy this guy can say 'I never did nothing, I never did nothing' then all of a sudden he's crying five minutes later. Tears are rolling down his Eighteenth Street eyes."

"I never committed a violent crime. You guys are trying to blame me for something I didn't do."

"That's another one, that's right. Yeah, that is the other one. You were surrounded. He just invoked his rights a while ago, right? Did he."

"No, I didn't invoke my rights."

"So why do you keep trying to be a lawyer, are you practicing law without a license?"

"I know I didn't invoke my rights."

"Are you a lawyer?"

"I know did invoke my rights."

"Well then why do you keep talking if you're doing that? I can talk I've got ten felonies. I can talk all day long because these ten felonies are some major stuff. Shooting from a motor vehicle into an occupied dwelling, fourth degree felony. Aggravated assault on a police officer, third degree felony. Attempt to commit murder, on a police officer, second degree. Tampering with evidence. And your homies are with you. I guess Westgate wasn't around that night so you decided to do it. And your homies are with you. Conspiracy, tampering same charges. Oh yeah, Shorty, where did he live. He lives off of? Yeah I know where he lives. He's up in Springer thinking he's gonna get out on his charges, not. Because I'm gonna make it a personal thing. I'm gonna take another warrant out there and say by the way Shorty, you thought you were getting out, guess what? You ain't homie. But Sager didn't do it. He said you did and then see what happens. Sager never does nothing. Sager is just a nice guy. You think you got problems, you've got major problems. Because there ain't no lawyer gonna touch with this one. Ain't no lawyer gonna try to help you because of your record. And you can get your sister, your mom, your brother everybody to come up with million dollars to hire a lawyer to even try to take this case. And you know what they're going to do. They're gonna say I don't want this. Huh uh. I don't want this at all. Get yourself some other rinky dink lawyer. And you're gonna get some little chicken shit lawyer that doesn't know shinola from brown to wax. Oh yeah, I can help him. You know what's gonna happen bro. They're gonna plea your butt. They're gonna plea you and either way you're gonna do the time for the crime. And when they get finished with that, your gonna do the time for Bernalillo on my charges, consecutive. Not concurrent, consecutive. Do you know the difference between those two words their Shaun Wilkins? Yeah I bet you don't. Because you're a lawyer, you should now that, because you know all your rights. You don't. You just think that scares people. You've been watching TV and you hear your jailhouse lawyers. Well let me tell you, all these jailhouse lawyers that tell you don't do this, don't do that. Why are they still in jail? Because they are stupid, they don't know. It's the guys on the outside that have beat the rap. That are still on parole and probation that yeah they know the system, now. That's why they are still on parole and probation with bracelets and shit. Yeah those guys know what's going on. They know that when they went to the pinta they said I didn't do it. I got framed. And those boys said ah meda, chavelita. Ven para chavelita. You're gonna be somebody's chavelita, homey. You think you got problems, now. You're gonna have it worse. Because you've never been to the pen. You think your little world over here is bad. Mr. Bad Sager. You ain't seen shit bro. You ain't seen shit. They're gonna eat you up. No matter what you say, or how you do it. Your gonna be stroking somebody. And if you don't believe me. This man right here does a lot of investigations in the pinta. And he's seen it all bro. And I know a lot of pintanetos that say they never ever want to go there. But then there's those crazy ones that love it. They like getting fucked. They like being chavelitas. They come out with their tattoos as a sign of manly hood. Bullshit, they're a bunch of girls. Because if they were men they would face up to their facts, and then face up to their crimes and the victims that they screwed over. That is what a man is being about, Shaun. And you ain't got the balls to face up to it. Because you don't know what it is to be a man. You can sit there and play this little I didn't do it routine. Till your face is blue, because that's all you're gonna be is blue. Yeah that's right. I've got you cold."

"No you don't."

"Oh yeah I do, bro. You think I don't. But I'm not giving it up. I'm gonna be telling you the little bits and pieces just to let you know that I know. That I'm gonna eat you up, bro. It is my mission to do that. My job and I get paid for it. APD Gang unit is not done with you Shaun Wilkins, Eighteenth Street Sager. Because there is no more Eighteenth Street homies. There used to be at one time. They're a bunch of punks right now. Thinking they are Eighteenth Street. And I know that for a fact. Cause you're not gonna have to stroke me bro. You're gonna have to do it with your own barrio. They're the ones that are going to take care of this. I didn't do it. Shank, shank."

"I didn't do shit."

"Face down or underground. Very nice. I talked to one of your victims. Man, you're bad bro. You are bad. You are so bad. You thought Popcorn had it bad. Man you don't know what you have. But you didn't do nothing Shaun. You're a good angel. You're the kind of kid that every parent wants in its house. Her house. Constantly fighting, cops being at the house. Your mom was worried, not about your safety right now. She didn't say oh how's mi hieto. He didn't do nothing. You know what she was worried about bro? What the neighbors would say. Oh please could you put those guns away, what will my neighbors think. And I said lady, you need to wake up. Because your little hieto brings it upon himself and brought it upon you. And your step dad seems like a really guy like he's tried. He said I knew this would happen. Someday, somehow, I knew this would happen and I said sir. I feel sorry for you because I know you tried. I've read the report. Shaun's not new to the system. He's been in and out of the system since he was a kid. He's got something to prove. And at everybody's expense. To your marriage, to his friends or anybody. He's got the biggest ego that you will ever find that is going to get him either killed or it's going to get somebody else hurt. But he's not a man because he can't face up to it. He's not a man. And your mom just sat there and just looked me and she wanted to cry and I said lady I'm sorry and I hate to tell you this. Shaun's been lying to you. Whatever's he's told you. You're gonna find out what kind of son you really have. Because everybody in the world is going to find out. Not just your neighbors. Everybody in this city and the state. But you didn't do nothing bro. You're a man. Just like Salina, telling you that she loves you. Oh yeah. Salina did he treat you good? Well no. Who paid for it Salina? I did. Really? Where did he take you for Valentine's Day? Nowhere. Where did he take you for your birthday? Nowhere. Must have a lot bank accounts for everybody else but not you. He's always with his homies. He'll come? I thought he was your man? Do you know what? Do you know what you do? Yeah she looked down just like your looking down because you ain't got the guts to look me straight in the eye. Oh yeah, bro, yeah, you're bad. You're so bad, bro. Because what you're doing now is exactly what people with a guilty conscience do. Can't look at other people in the eye. They can't do anything they deny. And they lie, thinking there is some way somehow they are going to find somebody to believe them. I can tell you right now there ain't nobody that's gonna believe you. No matter how you cry, how much you squeal, chiquita. You're bad. You're bad, Eighteenth Street, can't even look. Such a man."

"I don't want to, I despise you."

"I know you do. You know why? Because of what I stand for. Because I put bad people like you in jail. And that is my job. I have morals, you don't. I have a job and I do it well. Because people like you need to go away because all you do is prey on innocent victims."

"Yeah."

"Now you're talking to me."

"Do you want me to talk to you or do you want me to shut up. Do you want me to talk to you."

"Are you going to invoke your rights?"

"No, I'm not gonna invoke my rights."

"I don't want to hear bravado. I want to hear a man talking. You despise me all you want. It doesn't matter, it doesn't do one damn-fucking thing. All it does is just prove my theory."

"It's not just because you're a cop I despise you. There are cops too that are cool."

"Oh yeah. I'm one of the coolest cops around. You just don't know that. You've crossed my path and you've crossed it very hard. I never jack people up at their house unless I have to do business. Nothing personal, its business. You break the law you're gonna find me at the door. That's it. That's it. It's a business just like your gang banging. It's a business bro. Your swinging, your guns, your drugs. It's a business. I've been around longer than you. You don't think I know you're nothing but 18 or 19 years old. You don't know shit, man. You think you do. You don't know nothing. You haven't lived until you've died and seen your homies go down. And I'm talking in other fashions, not in gangs. Gangs are for cowards, that's why they have to hang in gangs. Because they don't have the balls to be a man and stand up for themselves and say you know what I don't need these guys I can do it on my own. I don't need to prey on innocent people and rob them and break into their house. That is why gangs are so trendy right now. So hip. Because everybody needs somebody. Everybody needs something to hold on to. Because they ain't getting it at home and they ain't getting it where they're out. It's low self-esteem. Talk back to your lawyer, bro. You think I'm an asshole, well that's your opinion. And I can tell you I know a lot of gangbangers worse than you bro. Worse than you that I have treated better because they hold up to it and they were man enough to admit it."

"Yeah, you've got me cold bro."

"Yeah right, yeah okay. I'd see them on the street and what's up man. How's your family. Are you staying out of trouble. And you know what out of a few they would say yeah. I snapped. That talk you gave me. You jacked me up for the last time. I snapped. Now I've got a family, I've got a kid. I'm gonna take care of business and they are doing good. They've got more class than you've got underwear bro. And these guys are big time gangsters. Eighteenth Street, you're nothing bro. Next to Serenio. You guys are fuckin' pee wees. You guys are little chavalitos. They told me the same thing. But they are all doing time, that they're paying, the bad boys. They want to be bad. They can't do it by themselves they have to have the homies to back them. Go killing people. They gotta do it because it's the thing. You have to blast somebody because they dissed them. They dissed them bro, blast them. Yeah that's a manly thing to do. Isn't it? To do drive-by's. Why don't you just go up to the door and say you know what bro, I don't like you. I despise you. Let's throw down. Kick my ass, oh well. I've been there bro, I'm a scrapper. I don't need a pistol or a navaja. You don't like me you throw down bro. That's the way I settle it. I don't do that chicken shit drive by or a car jacking. Face down or underground. That is very manly. Very manly. Yeah you're bad bro. You're a fuckin' badass dude. What did that homie, tell us Mike today. That he had corazon, that he had heart. I have respect for that dude. He's bad. I had respect for that vato, man. There's been a couple that have come through here. I have respect for them vato. You know they get caught in bad places. He told me the same thing that this vato is telling me. I ain't done shit. Afterwards he shook my hand and said you know what bro. You know what you have to do and it's just your job and I said that's right. And you do what you've gotta do, bro, it's your job. But when our paths cross, man give it up Sam, whoever's right. You can lie all you want."

"I ain't."

"You're right Shaun. You were right about the other crimes you did. And all the homies that turn your ass in were also right because they ain't going down for your bro. They are going to say fuck him. Huh uh. They are smart enough to know being a bad ass Eighteenth Streeter has been the road. Because there is no Eighteenth Street anymore. And you know it. All these little want to be's. That's what you are is a want to be, bro. You think that you grew up the gang."

"You don't know shit. I grew up in sports."

"Oh yeah, then why are you in here homie. You look like a good baseball player or basketball."

"Football."

"Football. Look what happened to Keno Brown, homie. Remember Keno. He was bad, bro."

"I know Kareem."

"I know them too, I know all of them, all of them. And they had some ability bro and look what happened. They wanted to be a homie. They wanted to do the drugs. They wanted to be rolling in the bucks. And what did they do? Look at where they are not now. Either dead or on the run in the pinta. Why? Because they lost faith in themselves. They lost hope and that is what you are losing, bro. And that is what you're grasping right now. You're losing faith in yourself and you're blaming me and you're blaming him and everybody else for it. We're wrong, we don't know what we're talking about. You didn't do it. You didn't do it. You can go like that bro and sit in front of a jury and say I didn't do it. I didn't do it. Homie, after homie, after homie is going right there and saying I didn't do it, I didn't do it. I didn't do it. And each time you say I didn't do it bro, you lose faith in yourself. You lose hope. You've run out of hope. And that's is why you're just hanging on to that thread man. Right now you're on thread Shaun and you know it."

"Yeah. You think so."

"You've got your life together, yeah I know."

"I've been trying to get my life together."

"Then why do charges keep coming up if you're trying to do that. Shaun. Why do crimes keep coming up that Shaun Wilkins. Wait a minute I must be mistaken I have the wrong Shaun Wilkins, here. Or am I speaking to Juan Diego Sanchez, today. Is that it bro? Schizophrenia. Did you ever try to kill yourself Shaun? Never? So why are you using other peoples name. Is it the thing to do? To get somebody else in trouble. Afraid to be man enough and say arrest me officer, my name is Shaun Wilkins, Sager, Eighteenth Street, diez y ocho, down bro. You don't have the guts to do that do you? And so you have to use other peoples name. Yeah, look down, bro because that is faith and hope slipping away. Yeah, I know that look. Cop it out bro, because that is exactly what you're going to do in court and the people who judge are going to say 'wah, wah' and you're gonna say I didn't do it. Homie. You're weak, bro. You're a weak chavalita. Keep saying I don't know, I didn't do shit. Every time you say I don't do shit. You're not convincing me. You're just trying to convince yourself."

"I don't got to convince you."

"You're just trying to convince yourself, just building up it up in your-self. That's it, that's all there is, man."

"You guys are stupid."

"Yeah, but that the last guy that told me that, he got fifteen years on his hands, Donald. Hi, he got, told me the same thing. That I was stupid. Look at where he's at homie. I must be really stupid to put somebody away for fifteen years, huh. And you know what he was calling me every day. Homie, I want to talk, I want talk, don't set me up. Talk to me, talk to me bro. And I said you know what you had your chance and I came one time when he called and I said tell me what you know, Donald. Tell me what you know, help me and I'll help you. Oh no, bro, do you know Sager oh no, who's that, bro? I don't know who he is. There's his picture right there? I don't know him, bro, I must have the wrong Sager. Mike was there. And I'm going, do we have the wrong guy? And I said ok, you don't know nothing bro. Have a fun time and grand. See ya. Beep, beep, beep man messages up the ying yang, until the day they transported him. Give it up Donald, and he did. He gave up Beronice, his old lady. And I did her on some drugs. And you know what she told me the same thing you were telling me, bro. You're wrong. I'm gonna do this, I'm gonna call the DA. I'm gonna do you, I'm gonna do this. She went to internal affairs, bro, she tried to nail me. They laughed at her, they said, you know what. Your complaint is no good. You're a drug dealer. We've got you cold. He got you with four bags of crack. Big old rocks, man. Two bags of cocaine. Soda. And over $2,600.00 in cash. I got her bro, and I got her connection too. Took his ass down. Guilty, straight to BCDC. Say hi, to Johnny. And they all tell me the same thing. See you in diagnostic homie. Put you in and then lock those doors. That's the last thing you're gonna see homie. Deny it bro. Deny it three times and make yourself believe it. Because in the end it ain't gonna help you because when all these pinta's are in the prison and county, oh yeah bro, you got framed. You ask them yeah I did, did you to bro? Because we're both here. Did you get framed? Yeah bro, I got framed. No bro. That's not how life goes. That's how the life of a gangster thinks. Does his crime and gets away with it and gets bad. Gets bad. Gets bad like Wilkins does. And when the shit hits the fan he cries oh yeah. Like you cried and I'm gonna show that tape in court and say this is the type of person you're dealing with here. This is the type of personality that he has."

"So."

"The people are gonna stand there and look at you and they're gonna go look at that and they're gonna go 'but he didn't do it. Bro'. You didn't do it. Yeah. I'll be here bro. A front seat. Front seat every fuckin' day. Watching you squirm, as this world gets closer and closer. Watch your family disappear one by one. Try to raise that big money that the attorneys are going to rape your family for and they're gonna pin your ass to the ground. Because it's gonna take big money bro, and you ain't got it."

"Yeah, you don't know my sister."

"Yeah, yeah. We do know your sister and you have a big military policeman guy."

"I got two sisters."

"Oh you do bro. Yeah, I know. I know more about your family than you do Sager."

"I doubt it."

"That's right. I'm stupid. I don't know that. Why are you sitting there bro, with handcuffs and why am I not? You don't know? Because you're stupid."

"Because I'm being framed for something I didn't do."

"What did I just say, framed? Framed? Deny it three times. Denied it three times."

"Whatever."

"Your family is going to being paying out bucks after bucks. And you know what those attorneys are real good about that. Their billing department works every fifteen days. Every fifteen days, bro. Every fifteen days they send out the bill. We filed this motion, we talked to the client on the phone. If you've ever paid for an attorney you'd know that. I don't know whether you have or you haven't. The fact is the big ones pay. You know why because they get a check every fifteen days. Pretty soon we're refinancing the fuckin' house. Pretty soon we're selling the car. Pretty soon were working overtime. Somehow I just can't picture your step dad working overtime, to get you help, bro. I can't I mean. Maybe he will. Maybe. But I just can't picture it. Not in my mind. I don't see his mom sending him a care package in the pinta. Those chocolate chip cookies will be good. Hershey alley is more like it. Oh yeah. You still have a long way ahead. Pretty sad no. You have a long ways to go."

"You don't scare me bro."

"I know I don't because you're bad."

"No, not because I'm bad. You just don't scare me because I know what I know."

"Yeah."

"And I know what I did and didn't do."

"Yeah. We know that. We're just not telling you all. How many times have you been served with paperwork like that?"

"I don't know. I never have."

"Never have?"

"Not one like that. Well I've had one at my house, or a search warrant."

"Search warrant. They're bare bone bro, you know why? Because when you go to court the discovery gets you. But that ain't shit bro. That's just says we know. And the judge says you know. The fact is that they come in here one at a time. Does Sager know? Sager knows. He knows what he knows. That is why he is sitting over there. He didn't do shit. He knows what he knows. And he thinks that it's deal time. When it comes down to it they're gonna say. Bro, man I took your mom's house. I took all her fedia. I took your dad, whatever your sisters got money. Yeah, whatever."

"Whatever."

"But you know what ever. They're gonna plea you. Give it up."

"But, I didn't do nothing."

"Well fuck it. I'm his attorney, your honor do you want plea him to. Bye. And then Shaun's gonna sit there. I didn't do it bro. I've been framed. And then the lawyer says by the way Kathy, or your sister, you owe me some money. And since Shaun is going bye-bye. I'm putting a lien on your house or whatever you put up. And ah, I want it. Because he is no good to me now."

"Wow, wow."

"Do you know who a prime example is? Don Cosby. Do you know his attorney? Anthony? Ayala. Mr. Liberal, the man for the inmates. Guess what happened to him when we slammed Donald Cosby. Anthony was at the DA's office and he walked in and he walked up to me and the DA and he said good case. I can't do anything can I? And I said no you can't. You're not gonna plea him down are you? And we said no we're not. He needs to go bye bye. Donald is a bad boy. He needs to learn on his own. He's eighteen, he'll go to prison and be out by the time he is thirty-five years old. Wasted. Molested. Everything. And he goes, okay. He wants to talk now. And go gee, Anthony. I remember when I came to you when your guy that didn't do these drugs and the drive-by's and all this other stuff. I came to you and I said, let's work a deal here. Tell me what he knows and I'll give him skeena. He told me the same thing that you're telling me. 'Hey, you don't know nothing bro, you're stupid.' Later, we'll see ya. I'll be back. I'll be back, homie. They were calling me bro. I became the man. Because all of a sudden now, they realized that I was right. This stupid guy must have knew something. Because when it came down to nut cutting. And we started talking to Donald. Anthony said, sorry Donald, but you don't need this and you're going there. And there is no money because you're not on the street swinging bro, so you can do whatever you want with them. Their detectives and Donald is calling the pager, bro. Help me out, bro. I'll talk, I'll talk. I'll give you my connection. I'll do this, I'll do this. And I said I don't want your connects bro. I don't need you now. You had your chance. Now you go and do your time like a good little boy. But you didn't do it see. You didn't do all that hard stuff. And I was there when they transferred him down by PNM. I sat in my car with a Coke and he came out see and I said remember me bro. Because you had a quevrada with me. You might not like me for what I do or what I stand for. But I'm always fair. And I've always been fair and I gave you a quevrada. One time only and you fucked me on it. And this is what you get. And so now you've got to take it like a man and do your time. And your old lady is going to be following right behind you, bro. He said I don't care, she's a freak anyway. Okay I said that is your problem, that's your wife bro. Only you can say that. I won't diss your wife. But you can. He stepped out to that van bro. And he looked back and he looked around like this and he looked at BCDC and he looked around. He knew that was the last time he was going to see freedom. And he started crying. Donald. He's a fuckin' hard ass motherfucker. You know him. He's hard-core, man. He's hard-core. But I've never ever seen him. With all the stuff that I've got on Donald. He never cried, bro. Never. And that day he cried, bro. And I looked at him and I said bro, you had your chance. Now do your time. But he was framed, bro. He thought that people like me and his homies were going to take the heat. Bro. Oh yeah."

"I ain't got nothing to worry about."

"I know you don't. Not from me."

"No, I mean from no one."

"Then you must know so much information, Shaun."

"I don't know shit. That's why I ain't got nothing to worry about."

"Okay."

"You guys are trying to get something out of me that I don't know nothing about."

"Just like I was trying to get information from your homies that they didn't know about. And they gave it up. And from Donald and from the vato's on my list. That said I didn't know shit. We know what we're doing, we're just harassing them. Because they're gangsters. Yeah. It's a business. The cost of doing business. And I got all the money in the state and in the world to take you guys down. I don't have to worry about where my fedia comes from. Whatever it takes. It's there. It's a priority in this nation, now. You guys are diseased and you must be removed. And no matter how much tough you guys think you are. There is always somebody in the wind. A girlfriend, a homie, a mom, a sister that can't take it no more. And gives it up and says, crime stoppers, he's here. Come get him. And it's always the girl. But you didn't do it Shaun."

"Nothing to worry about."

"Nothing to worry about? That's what's gonna come your way. The path is getting dark. Just about now. Just about now. Face down or underground. Yeah, the jury's going to hear that one. And they're gonna say, oh yeah. Who developed that? That's him. Sager did. That's what we used. And they're gonna say. But he didn't do it bro. He doesn't do nothing. He doesn't do nothing. We have the wrong man. And the judge that signed that order is going to be looking at you and saying, they were right. All the people are right. And now what I have to do. I have this man's life in my hands. And not matter what you say. He's gonna look down on you and he's gonna say, you didn't do it, Shaun. Guilty. And all your victims are gonna fuckin' have a party. While Shaun is being lead away in shackles. PNM."

"What's PNM?"

"Penitentiary of New Mexico. Get used to it, bro. It's gonna be your next PO box."

"I thought it was like the gas company or some shit."

"Yeah, that's the next step for you bro. PNM. Writing to the ruka's write to me, ruka. I have a homie locked up, I love you. While they're fucking your friend. I love you honey. Yeah. I was at work, that's why I wasn't home when you called, honey."

"Yeah right."

"I need some money, I need some money for some cigarettes. Or I need some money to pay up before I become a chavelita. Chavelita. Those tatts ain't gonna get you shit in there bro. Not one fuckin' thing. Those boys have been there too long. They're animals. They are animals. And you're fresh meat. Fresh, white little meat. Welcome to Cell Block Three. Oh yeah."

"Ooooh."

"Yeah, that's what you're going to be doing bro."

"I ain't afraid of you guys."

"Oh really."

"I'm not."

"Oh okay, but your victims were, huh."

"I don't have no victims. I ain't never killed no one."

"Oh, okay, okay."

"I ain't never killed no one."

"Face down, underground, bro."

"No, just because I've said that before and I've done that. So people can just tell you that I said that or what?"

"People now."

"Yeah, that's what you told me."

"Ha, ha."

"Yeah, that's what you told me and that's what it says in there."

"Really, really?"

"Really."

"Do you know how to read?"

"Yeah."

"That's good. You're gonna have a lot of time for reading, bro."

"Really. I don't want to talk to you no more."

"So quit talking, man. Suck a dick. I ain't gonna be the one doing that."

"I doubt I will either."

"That's what you think, bro."

"I know it."

"That's what you think. I say ah, what do you think we ought to do with him now. I think we ought to take him and put him in cellblock three, no. Let's see if he doesn't suck any dick. By tomorrow morning, that's what I think. I guess we ought to take him down to BCDC. No, you know who's down there right now? I'm sure there is people that have already called in."

"Oh yeah, cool."

"There's news on."

"Yeah, they heard the radio."

"Oh really. Yeah. The man who killed two little kids. This is Sager. Killed his own homeboy. He's bad, two little kids. Stolen cars. That is what those car jacking's were. You know what I mean."

"What do you mean?"

"Face down, underground."

"Cartoon, man. You're like a cartoon. I ain't gonna be sucking anything. Haah."

"Yeah, they're gonna like that, they're gonna like that little 'haah.' Do that again bro. Do that again."

"Haah."

"Muenica, chiquita. What about the boys in the PNM. Oh that's the gas company right. That's right the gas company. They're gonna pull dick out, and say yeah, check this gas out brother. Have you ever been up north? Oh yeah, yeah. They're are wicked, bro. It's wicked. Fuckin' intense. Please phone home. I've been up there man, it's a wicked place. It's full of people who didn't do shit. I don't know if you've ever talked to any of them. But none of them have ever done shit. And they are all framed."

"I know. All of them."

"There is a guy up there who killed this old lady. He didn't do shit. He's convicted of killing an old lady in Clovis and his granddaughter. Burned the house down. Hundred, sixty-seven or one hundred ninety seven years, I can't remember. He's doing the death penalty. Do you know Tony Anaya? Do you know the governor? Community guy. You know what, big old guy. Big old guy, pulls into an ex-girlfriend in front of a little guy. But what he didn't realize is that this little guy has been sharpening shanks. Yeah, no. Kind of an equalizer, right. He took three of them off. But he didn't do shit. He didn't do nothing. One hundred and ninety seven years. What did he have to lose. He's not quite sure why he's there yet. Tony Anaya has been governor for what ten-twelve years. He's still not quite sure why he's there man. What is your point? Yeah. Oh Shaun wants to go to jail so bad. I can just hear him tonight going aaah. How are you doing Shaun? Are they you doing you yet? About this time next year. Exactly. Next spring. Don't worry about it baby, they don't have nothing. Well how much money is going to cost to get you out this time? How much am I going to have to fork out this time?"

"How much am I going to have to bond out this time?"

"No bond, fool. No bond. His sister bonded him out. No it wasn't. It was what's her name, Salina's mom."

"It wasn't her mom."

"Really, that's what Salina told us. But I guess she's a liar too, like you. You've got her lying too. That's all right. She's just a freak, anyway. But that's the lie she'll be following in your footsteps, because I got her on two felonies. Brother, she's next. And I said it in front of your mom and she looks at me and she goes 'he doesn't know what he's talking about, oh yeah right.' Oh yeah right, when she gets the d-home. That's right she's just seventeen. That's the girl that gets to go to the d-home. And the judge says oh yeah, okay. That sounds like a winner. But she didn't do nothing either. You ought to see her boyfriend. He doesn't never do nothing. Yeah, Salina is gone too."

"Uh huh. What is happening here? Oh yeah they're stupid. They don't know what they're doing. Yeah buddy. Leave the door open. It's getting kind of stale in here man. Cheap beer, cheap brain."

"You guys ain't got shit."

"Yeah, I know Shaun."

"Everyone of you guys think that everyone is lying."

"Prove us wrong."

"I'm gonna try."

"Okay."

"I'm gonna try."

"I'll be the first man to shake your hand when you do bro. I'll say yeah you were right Shaun. But I'm doing my job. And then you tell it to your homies, and they walk out that door."

"I ain't got no homies."

"I know you don't bro. You don't know."

"I know I don't."

"And they know it."

"I never did. I have some true friends that are true friends. Not my homies."

"What about Bruce?"

"Bruce is a homie. Just a homie. But there are certain things you've got between true friends and a homie."

"Yeah."

"I didn't know Bruce, you guys act like I've known him forever or something."

"That's what he told us, bro. That's what he told us you were trying to be. A big brother I guess, I don't know. He was out gunning for you, homie. Did you know he's got a rap sheet."

"Who?"

"Bruce. He tried to throw down with a sheriff's officer. He wanted to go to jail bad, because he was gunning for Sager. Yeah, I know. We do know that. We're gonna take you down. Do you want to put your t-shirt on the desk? I need my stuff in my car. We're gonna get some pictures. Do you know what? Scanning photographs. I used those composites and stuff on a couple of armed robberies on Guerro."

"An older guy?"

"Yeah. Killed him for honor. You gonna believe me or your lying ass?"

"My lying ass."

"Fuck you."

"Haah."

The tape started making a scratching noise and it took me out of my trance. The last 15 minutes sucked, as it was all DeReyes talking to hear himself talk. I looked over at the clock. Ah shit, three AM but only two AM Mountain Standard time. I rolled over and fell asleep.

After three days of hanging out at Echo Park, Montebello and Commerce City it was time to catch the Southwest flight home. Since I had been up late I had gone on line and picked up an A Pass. I wanted a seat in the emergency row so I could stretch out and work on my laptop.

I got to my gate and found a chair next to a power outlet and plugged my laptop in. These batteries on the laptop sucked. They lasted maybe an hour if you were lucky. I had to get my notes out to the attorneys.

I got on the plane, went to the emergency row and grabbed a window seat. Then I heard, "Ladies and Gentlemen we have a full flight to Albuquerque so please put your luggage in the overhead."

I did not want to hear that. I looked at the passengers coming down the aisle. I had two empty seats next to me and I did not want a person of heavy stature sitting next to me. Sorry.

Then I saw him, two-piece business suit with a white shirt sticking out everywhere. As he put his bag and jacket in the overhead I could see large pockets of sweat under his armpit. I started thinking to myself, "Not here please God not here."

He went past me and I sighed a sigh of relief. Then it felt like the plane had tilted to the left. And there she was, Shamoo's Sister. I knew I was dead meat. I thought maybe if I pretend I'm asleep she won't sit there.

I felt a nudge on my shoulder, "Sir, could you help me with my bag. I can't get it into the overhead." Now in the middle seat was a large purse with all of her goodies filling the bag to the top. I got up, went to the aisle and helped her with her bag. "Oh, thank you, I was hoping to get a seat in this aisle. They are so much more comfortable you know." Oh great and she is also a talker. I kept praying the stewardess would be brave enough to tell her she was too heavy to sit there. No prayers were answered.

"You going to Albuquerque?"

"Yes, I am."

"Do you live there?"

"Yes, ma'am."

"I'm going to visit my sister. She lives in Los Ranchos. You know where that is? We haven't seen each other in years. She has this cute little adobe home with apples trees in the back. She lived there now for over ten years. I don't understand how she can live in a desert. Do you know where Los Ranchos is?"

I had flashbacks of Officer DeReyes and Agent Fenner talking to me. I just looked at her and smiled and shook my head.

It didn't stop her. She kept right on going. "I hope no one takes the middle seat they make this chairs so damn small. I play sodoku, do you like to play?" She showed me her puzzle, "They are so much fun."

I could see three mistakes already but I thought, don't even go there. I just smiled and shook my head. The plane hadn't even left the gate. It was going to be a long trip back home.

My wife picked me up at the airport. Since I had carry on only, it was just as easy for her to pick me up at the departing planes. I didn't have to go downstairs with the mob. I just walked out and there she was.

"Did you get everything done?"

I did not like LA. Eight lanes of traffic always full. Every car owns the fast lane and they are all doing 60 MPH. Takes you four hours to do a one-hour interview. Parking is at a premium and gas is outrageous.

"I did for the most part."

"Have you seen the news?

"Nay."

"The news has been all over about that Torreon murder case. They have set a date for Woody's trial, it's two months away. They claim they are going to be able to convict him with his confession. What I don't understand if he's innocent why did he confess?"

The hardest case to defend is a false confession case. "You have to understand Woody has a marginal personality. They took numerous statements from him and provided him with details of only their theory. They spoon-fed him and Popcorn with their facts of how it happened and not the facts from the cabin. When there's no evidence false statements and confessions are needed to solve the crime."

"How you going to prove that? He said he did it, so how are you going to undo it?"

"I'm hoping I can show it by proving none of the boys were there except Popcorn. Roy was working during that time period eight to five then going home. Shaun was in jail from the eleventh to the fifteenth of December. I don't know where Woody was."

"Oh, Ray called the house and he said for you to call him when you come in."

I called Ray. "Hey, Ray I'm back in town. What's up?"

"Woody's trial is in two months so we have a defense meeting tonight at the Western Bank building with all the teams. I need you there at six pm and bring your notes and the photos."

Six pm came really fast. I had known Gary Mitchell for some time. Gary was one of the best trial lawyers in the state. I didn't know Steve Aarons or his investigator but we had talked on the phone before but never met.

We all found ourselves on the eighth floor with the windows looking toward the South Valley. I could follow the river south toward El Modelo. It has been there for years run by the Garcia Family from the South Valley. They have the best tamales in the state. The still wrap them with cornhusks and by hand. I knew what I was having for supper. Just get me out of here by 7:30 pm.

Ray got everyone's attention. "Maurice, why don't you bring everybody up to speed on what you've done?"

I said, "We all know they spoon fed Woody and Popcorn. I have gone through most of the tapes. I don't believe they are giving us all the tapes. The tapes start without any introduction, start in the middle of the interview and then they just stop. The officers are blaming it on faulty equipment. I'm doing a time line of Woody's tape to see what all are missing. I sent Ray a fax with the dates and times of missing tapes and he's going to contact the DA."

"Don't forget the ghosts of the cabin," Ray said.

"I found a witness who lives just above the Anaya's cabin. The lady was outside on March twenty-fourth or twenty-fifth using the outhouse, smoking her nightly cigarette when she thought there was a party at the cabin. She didn't see anyone but there was lights on and music playing."

"How reliable is she?" Ray asked

"My opinion, very reliable."

"How does she put the date of March twenty-fourth or twenty-fifth?"

"The Hyakutake Comet was at its brightest and she was watching it."

"Did she see any aliens coming or going to the comet?"

"Does this mean they were alive all the way up to the twenty-fifth of March?"

"Boy, if they were there this changes everything." Steve Aarons was pumped over this information. "We have to slow this train down and get this developed. I didn't see any of this in the discovery. How did you find her?"

Gary Mitchell leaned forward, putting his large arms and shoulders over the table. "That's mighty fine for you folks, but I got a death penalty case coming up in two months and my client gave a confession. What am I going to tell the jury? Woody made a mistake and it was the ghost that killed those people?"

Ray said, "I agree we have to slow the train down, we need more time to get a better handle on this case. I believe we have innocent clients here."

"That's all fine and dandy, guys. But I have a fucking confession that all the DA has to do is hit 'Plays on the VCR and Woody is fucked. I have to put him on the stand and tell the jury what he confessed to, in order to save his life, I will do it." Gary like the rest of us had some strong feelings about the death penalty in New Mexico. This case had the potential of four people being executed.

"I am going to trial in two months come hell or high water."

Gary was one of the best trial lawyers in the state. They would say if you want to find or talk to Gary he is someplace between Farmington and Hobbs, New Mexico, driving his truck listening to preliminary tapes of witnesses.

"What else do you have Maurice?" Ray was pushing for the information.

"I found police reports and jail records for Shaun. He was picked up and arrested on the eleventh of December and released on the fifteenth. The last one to see Ben Jr. was his dad on the tenth. Popcorn was seen at the Anaya's house on the fifteenth with Ben's Jeep. Popcorn so far is the only one with the keys to the Jeep and the cabin."

"Maurice, all the DA is going to do is move the time of death until he can put all the boys together. The date of death is a moving target for us. Lopez can pick any day he wants. The judge doesn't care."

"Well he has picked the twelfth of December and Shaun was in jail."

"We need to set witness statements up. Each one of us is going to get a shot at all the officers and witnesses. I suggest we share all statements and investigations with each other."

Ray chimed in, "Steve since Gary is going to go first let's file a joint motion for the transcript of the trial. It is going to be too costly in time and money to attend the hearing."

I still couldn't believe there was no evidence. "We need to keep pushing the evidence from the cabin. There has to be forensics."

Gary looked down at me. "Maurice, I believe they did this for a purpose. They are not going to analyze any evidence if it hurts them. They don't want to know the truth if it gets in the way of their case. Hell that's probably why they didn't send up the crime lab. All this shit about the cabin means nothing to me. I have a god damn confession. I am dead in the fuckin' water."

"Last thing. Mode of transportation. They have the boys in a stolen Trans Am, Camaro, or Chevy from black to maroon to purple. I checked with auto theft and there were no stolen vehicles matching that description in the metro area of Albuquerque. Woody was right in March of '96 that there was a Camaro, color maroon, taken from the parking lot of Presbyterian Hospital and recovered in front of his house the middle of March. I talked with Salina, Shaun Wilkins' girlfriend. She did not have a Camaro or Trans Am in December of '95. In one of Woody's statement he tells DeReyes the Camaro was stolen in March. DeReyes then takes that Camaro and takes it back to the future in December of '95. It is a very rough road for a Camaro or Trans Am to travel the road to the cabin. And if you believe Woody and Popcorn, they have to travel this road under the influence. In the statement to DeReyes Woody is telling him that Wilkins and Roy came over in a stolen Camaro. I found that police report. It was in March just like Woody said. And according to DeReyes they went from March 1997 back to December 1996. Kind of like 'Back to the Future.'"

"Is that it?"

"You would think, on a confession and statement that Woody and Popcorn gave the mode of transportation would be important to locate for evidence. To verify that Woody and Popcorn were telling the truth. Just like the guns they claim they stole from the cabin. The officers have not located one person, Shaun or Roy that they sold a gun to. Yet they have it from Jeremy and Little Dreamer, that Popcorn was selling guns to Green Eyes and had guns in the Jeep. They claim they were drinking and doing drugs at the cabin but no evidence in the cabin or in the tox report on Ben or Cassandra. Ben Sr. said his son does not do hard drugs. I believe him."

The meeting ended with everyone wishing everyone good luck.

Two days later Ray is calling me, "Maurice what did you stir up?"

"I didn't stir up anything."

"I need you to come over to office so we can meet on this matter."

We had a lot to go over. Ray was getting anxious, "You know Woody is going first. He is the easiest one for the DA to get a conviction on. Woody is going to be tried in Estancia. That means Aarons gets a change of venue and so will we. I understand Aarons is having his trial in Socorro. We will wind up in Sierra County, "T or C" Truth or Consequences. They are targeting Roy and Shaun for the death penalty. Woody didn't kill anyone. Popcorn was a victim that leaves them with Shaun shooting the two adults and Roy locking the cabin killing the kids."

"This case is highly complex. All we have are those tapes to fight. We can't get much cross from them. They didn't do any forensics and I agree with Gary that the forensic evidence would have shown they were not there. This case has the potential of six victims if they convict Roy and Shaun."

"I also got a call from the DA. They are under the impression we are going to claim those people in the cabin were alive all the way up to the end of March. They have a posse out looking for Ms. Zenner as we speak. They want your taped conversation with her."

So much for the circle of trust at the meeting. We have what Officer DeReyes would call a Rata among us.

"Only me and you knew for the last month. At the meeting the word got out and someone snitched us off."

"Well the DA is now asking if we're are going to be filing a notice of Alibi for Roy. Aarons did based on the jail records of Shaun. And now the DA has moved the date of death from the twelfth though the eighteenth when Popcorn left town. Now they can put Shaun in the mix."

"Well then we have the time line narrowed down from the twelfth to the eighteenth but Popcorn had the Jeep on the fourteenth or the fifteenth. I believe Ben Jr. is dead and Popcorn is at Ben's house so how do they figure those days?"

"I guess the DA forgot Little Dreamer said he left with Popcorn on the fifteenth of December. So if Shaun is in jail from the eleventh to the fifteenth the homicides didn't happen in that time period."

"We knew this would happen. They are going to change the date of death to stretch over a time period now."

"Gary faxed me the State's second prosecution list of witnesses. I'm going to fax over to you. Check their list against our Who's Who."

"I'll look it over tonight and fax you in the morning."

"I hired Eda Gordon to help us with the jury selection and mediation for Roy if we have to go through the death penalty phase."

"Good. I like to work with Eda but I am praying they don't get that far. The Burrolas have started a prayer group for the victims as well as Roy and Shaun. Let's pray it works."

11

"Blow Flies"

THAT NIGHT I WENT HOME AND LOOKED OVER THE WITNESS list. There was name I never heard of, P. La Scala. I looked him up on Google. I started a memo to Ray.

Ray,

It looks like they are bringing in the "pig guy." That's what I call him. He used to be on a show on the Discovery Channel with the Pig Doctor. He would kill pigs, put them in his back yard and study the maggots that developed on them from the eggs of blowflies, then study the growth of the eggs over time. La Scala is into entomology, the study of insects. He is sometimes called out on murder scenes to determine time of death. He has a master's degree in entomology. He belongs to the Entomological Society of America and he works with the Bernalillo County Sheriff's Office (BCSO) in Grave Recovery and Verifications Experts (GRAVE).

Somehow he can make a determination if a victim was moved, and how long ago the victim was murdered. Forensic entomology is the study of insects as applied to criminal cases. It sounds as if they're going to bring him in and talk about what happens to bodies after death. I had read a mystery novel called *Blowflies*. These flies are also cadaver flies. His work is also published. I believe they are going to use him to establish date of death in the cabin.

When I was over at OMI, files were collected along with some eggs off one of the boys. I bet he has those eggs and is going to be talking about what attracted the blowfly to the decomposing flesh.

These blowflies go through a particular life cycle. It's called complete metamorphosis. The post-mortem interval can be determined through the examination of these particular stages of deformity of this particular species of fly.

I looked up blow files in New Mexico and our mountains. Guess what. The only time they exist in the mountains—from the 12th of December to the 18th. I guess they don't like Ms. Zenner seeing the ghost at the cabin at the end of March. That along with Shaun in jail is why the DA changed the date of death. You're right. He does believe we are going to change the date. If that's what they believe, let them chase a fart in the wind.

Maurice

The Missing Client

I had called down for reports from the Valencia County sheriff's office on Popcorn and I was told they were ready. Now this type of work I didn't mind. I would get a chance to ride my Harley Davidson to Los Lunas and enjoy the ride through the Isleta Reservation and Bosque Farm area.

Riding my motor has its advantage as I can park up close to the buildings. The undersheriff in Valencia County was D. C. Jackson. He was a retired State Police captain. D. C. was also a Harley rider.

D. C. and I also rode with the Blue Knights motorcycle club. D. C. had also belonged to a hot rod club. He was one of the finest men I knew.

After I picked up the report, I came out of the building and noticed several of the deputies standing around my bike. "Dam good looking bike Maurice. I see Bubba's signature on the back of it. He did one hell of a paint job on it."

D. C. looked over at me. "Where were you for the Doug Henson ride? We missed you." Doug was a retired US Attorney who enjoyed motorcycles and was killed during a ride. Every year we had ride in his honor.

"Been tied up with Sureno Thirteen and the Torreon Murders."

"Oh, yea. Did you find your client yet?"

I had no idea what he was talking about but I was going to play along.

If you stay quiet long enough they will talk. "I heard they caught him in Pecos, Texas all over again. Doesn't he listen to you and Ray?"

"I guess not."

"Yea, we had to go haul his ass back to Valencia County again and he kept screaming all the way, 'Call Juan, call Mike. I'm working for them.'"

"You mean Popcorn?"

"Yea, he's your client isn't he?"

Now I know how to do interviews and interrogations. "What did you mean when you said 'again'?"

"Hell we had to haul his ass back here when he escaped over the wall with those two charters Danny Si… and Danny S… They're the ones who stole that dump truck from Belen, got into a high-speed chase into Albuquerque, and killed those people on Broadway and Lead. They ran the truck into the news car, the ones from the TV channel."

"What do you mean Pecos again?'

"Hell Maurice, you got a 'Tasmanian Devil' on your hands. I don't see why you are representing him." *I just looked and listened, knowing D. C. was not going to stop ragging my ass.* "You mean you don't know he did a home invasion in Rio Rancho, stole a bunch of guns, and took off in the old man's car? Picked up two juveniles, females, and took them to Pecos and got pulled over by Texas D.P.S."

"You mean Popcorn?"

By now the deputies were all having a good laugh. Kicking the dirt and spitting out their tobacco. "Who else do you think we're talking about? You represent him and you don't know where he is or what he's been doing?"

"When did he escape from here?"

"Hell you don't know that either? Come on in let me show you a video of him and his two friends going over the wall."

As we went into his office I could see D. C.'s trophy wall and his commendations. He had a right to be proud of them. In the corner of his desk he had a photo of his hot rod and underneath it, it said, "Rest in Peace."

D. C. had a prized hot rod. His cat found it a great place to sleep. D. C. hated that cat for leaving all of his cat hairs all over. D. C. covered his chrome plated V-8 engine with a rug to keep the cat off. One day D. C. took it for a ride and forgot to take off the rug. The rug got caught on fire and burned up his car. D. C. still has the cat.

"What's with the empty space next to your car D. C.?"

"It's for the cat if I can ever catch him."

D. C. reached into a drawer full of tapes and pulled one out. "Can I see that D. C. There was the date, March twenty-third, 1996 escape Popeleski, with two Danny's."

"You never seen this?" D. C. put it in his VCR and played the tape for me.

I watched the video. There were three inmates walking out the recreation door. Then they moved over to the northeast corner of the yard and went over the chain link fence.

"You talked about a second time that Popcorn was escaping?"

"Yeah, you're going to have to check with his probation officers on that."

"Who's his P.O.?"

"State Police officer Mike Fenner and Levi Lovato from the DA's office. I guess he just took off. That's when he went to Rio Rancho, broke into the house, stole some guns, money and the guy's car."

No wonder the DA kept claiming he didn't know where Popcorn was and that he was not in custody. Popcorn was out committing more crimes. The DA never told us any of this. Agent Jacoby, Fenner, or Levi never wrote a report about this.

It turned out that the District Attorney Ron Lopez and the State Police had contacted three District Attorneys where "Popcorn" had outstanding warrants for his arrest in three different counties. The warrants had been dismissed and Popeleski had been placed on phone supervision to Levi Lovato, an investigator for the District Attorney's Office and Sergeant Mike Fenner from the New Mexico State Police with the only condition that he not leave the state and stay in contact once a week with Levi or Fenner. It was no wonder they couldn't find him. He was breaking into people's houses stealing guns, cars, picking up 14-year-old girls and going back to Pecos, Texas where the Jeep belonging to Ben Anaya Jr. was found.

Popcorn never called or checked in with Agent Fenner or investigator Lovato. Neither Lovato nor Fenner wrote a report indicating they were supervising Popcorn and the fact that he never called in. The DAs in the three counties were never notified Popcorn had continued his crime spree. But the one person who had to know was the ADA Mady Malka, the engineer for putting the case together. Malka had to be the one to broker the deal with the other three DAs.

"Where's the two Danny's now?"

"Oh, we caught them. They're back in custody here at the jail."

"V.C.S.O. (Valencia County Sheriff's Office) brought Popcorn back this last time. Do you have the paper work from Pecos on his arrest?"

"Sure do. Do you want copies?"

"Yea, it would save me a trip."

"Do you want the police reports from the home invasion in Rio Rancho as well as copies of the Pecos PD and the escape video?"

"I sure do D. C. Can I also go back there and visit them?"

"Yea that will give me some time to make all these copies."

"Where's Popcorn? You said you brought him back?"

"Don't know. Mike Fenner and Levi Lovato the investigator from the DA's office came and picked him up. Why, is he gone again?" D. C. said it with a smirk.

We never saw any reports for Fenner or Lovato as to their involvement with Popcorn. It was as if none of these events were ever happening. ADA Malka was going to make sure no one was going to find out their involvement with Popcorn.

"We kept asking the DA to set up an interview with Popcorn. The DA would say, 'He's a protected witness. We don't know where he is.' By the way Roy 'Eazy' Buchner is our client. He is locked up with Shaun Wilkins in Maximum Security at the North facility in Santa Fe."

"Who's representing Popcorn then?"

"He has three public defense attorneys, from three different counties. Well four attorneys counting the ADA Malka."

I went back to the cell where the two Danny's were being held. I asked them, "Are you the guys that went over the fence with Popcorn in March of this year?"

"Yea. Who are you?"

"I do defense work for attorneys and I'm involved with the Torreon Murders. Where did you go after you escaped?" Both of the young men had numerous tattoos on them, shaved heads. But no Eighteenth Street tattoos.

"You work for the defense ese?" Danny S.... asked.

"I do. I represent defendants. I'm looking for information on Popcorn."

"What for?"

"All I want to know is where did he go after you guys escaped? I don't care about your charges I'm just dealing with Popcorn."

"You know his name's not Frank Gomez don't you?"

"He lies a lot, I know his real name. It's Shaun. He told the police you guys high jacked a car from a family."

"No way, that dude's a liar man. He told those people, 'on the ground or underground' and they got out of the car. We just watched him."

"His statement said you guys did that."

"No. You can check with my Ruca (girl friend). We went to her house when we got out of here then..."

"Who's your girlfriend?'

"Lettia. She lives in Belen."

"You got her number?" Without hesitation he gave it me. "You can check with her, we're not lying ese."

"Where did you guys go?"

"Popcorn was driving, right. He took the back way from Belen to the mountains, you know that road to Mountainair. Then to some cabin."

"You know where Torreon is?"

"Yea, look we didn't know those babies were dead in there, okay."

"What babies and what cabin?"

"I don't know. Popcorn was driving. Look man, we're not getting involved."

"That's not my goal. But you sure about what you just told me?"

"Samone ese. That dude was tripping out at that cabin."

They escaped one day before the party at the cabin. It was Popcorn and these two that were at the cabin.

I found my "Ghosts." They were at the cabin on the 23rd. Ms. Zenner was off by one day but I could live with that.

I got back on my bike and drove down to Pete's Mexican Restaurant in Belen for some chicos and beans. (Chicos are dried corn kernels that are roasted and dried.) They also make some of the best "flan" around. (Flan is fantastic custard.) That's what I like about my job as I can find all the great restaurants in New Mexico.

There I could sit down and call Ray with the information I got from the Valencia county sheriff's office.

I was still talking to Ray when they brought my order over to me. Later on the waitress returned, "Can I warm this back up for you?" I nodded my head. I was still talking with Ray, telling him about Popcorn being on probation, home invasion, going back to Pecos with guns. "In December of ninety-five Popcorn had guns in Pecos, Texas. Now he is taking more guns to sell in Pecos as he has a connection in Pecos who is buying guns from him."

"Maurice, we need to stay focused on this case, not Popcorn's charges."

"You don't understand Ray, March twenty-third Popcorn escaped from Valencia County Jail and returned to the cabin. He went back to burn the cabin down. He was the ghost that Ms. Zenner heard on the night of March twenty-third."

Where In The World Was Woody Nieto?

Woody's trial came and went. The media was all over as expected. Woody was found guilty of all four murders and sentenced to four hundred and forty years. Woody would never see daylight again. Gary won the death penalty phase. Woody got life without parole. It was considered a win.

Agent Frank Jacoby had on his wall below the headlines, "Woody Nieto found Guilty" and the sign read "ONE DOWN TWO TO GO." I thought to myself, Not on my watch Frank, Not on my watch.

That weekend I had a message from one of the girls who knew Woody. "Maurice this is Jannesa. I know you've been looking for me, could you please call me?" I called her that evening from my home so if needed I could take notes on my best friend.

"Hello."

"This Janessa?"

"Who's this?"

"This is Maurice, Janessa. I've been trying to get hold of you."

"Maurice, I feel so bad about Woody."

"We all do. I believe he is innocent, he didn't kill anyone."

"I know he's innocent."

"What do you mean Janessa?"

"I didn't know the dates those people were killed until I read it in the paper. They said the murders happened between the twelfth and eighteenth."

"That's what they are claiming."

"Woody was with me, Laura, and Polita in Juarez, Mexico, during that entire week. On the way back we broke down in Ruidoso, New Mexico. My mom had to come and pick us up."

"Where are you Janessa?"

"I'm not at home and please don't tell my mom."

I meet up with Janessa at her friend's apartment. "Hi Janessa. Why didn't you get back to me sooner?"

"My mom didn't want me involved in these terrible murders. She thought Woody, Roy, and Shaun were all guilty. We felt so sorry for those babies. But Woody couldn't have done it. On those days he was with us. My mom will tell you she picked us up from Ruidoso when our car broke down and she brought us home."

As I went over the story with Janessa I asked her where they stayed. She gave me the name of the hotel in Juarez where they checked in and the name the room was under. While they were in Ruidoso, Janessa had used her EBT card at the store to buy food.

"We left on the twelfth of December and stayed in Juarez until the fifteenth. On the way back the car was giving us trouble so we went to Ruidoso to my aunt's house. My mom can verify that day. I went over to the house to get some clothes to take with me."

"Can you get me a copy of the EBT card?"

"I think so but, can you call my mom, she's not talking to me."

"So when did you get back."

"I think it was Saturday the sixteenth or Sunday the seventeenth but my mom will know for sure. Woody would have never done anything like that. All of us girls trusted him. That's why we took him with us."

I thanked her and called Laura and Polita and they gave me the same story. I needed an adult to verify their story. The DA might make mince meat out of the young girls. Agent Fenner, Agent Jacoby and DeReyes might get them to confess that they were at the cabin with Woody.

I found Laura's mom an attractive blond lady with blue eyes, great figure and very well dressed. This is a witness a jury would believe in.

"They went to Mexico on the twelfth of December. I remember Janessa came over and got some clothes."

"How do you know the date in December?"

"I picked up Janessa's step sister at the airport on the ninth. And Janessa had not left yet. It was three days after I picked up her sister that they left and I know they came back on the eighteenth."

"Do you know where they were?"

"You mean when they called me? They were at my younger sister's house in Ruidoso."

"Janessa said something about your check book?"

"Oh yea. I use it as a calendar. I am always underlining and marking dates. See I circled the twelfth of December. That's the day they left. Then see I underlined the seventeenth at 11:30 pm when they came back."

I couldn't believe it. Woody was not even in town. I was right, they cannot put all the boys together. The week of the 10th through the 17th Shaun was in jail, Roy was at work and Woody was in Juarez. The only one available was Popcorn and he has no alibi. He was with Ben and Cassandra.

One would think with three out of the four young men not present during the time of the murders a judge, a jury, or the DA would say, "Houston we have a problem." Instead the cases would go on and fifty percent of the jurors would believe they were there.

Fenner, Jacoby and DeReyes had gotten a false confession out of Woody and a false statement out of Popcorn. They never asked where anyone was in the month of December. If Woody told them he was in Juarez and Ruidoso, why didn't they follow up on it? They were not interested in where the boys were. They had their minds made up.

Then they turn Popcorn loose to Agent Fenner and Lovato to be his probation officer. And Popcorn goes out and commits home invasions, car jacking, picked up juvenile females, and is stealing and selling guns in Pecos, Texas. They never tell anyone he was cut loose to Levi and Fenner. This is their reliable informant.

I was still missing something. Something just didn't fit. I had gone over all the tapes we had. All the statements we had. Looked at the crime scene photos over and over again. What was I missing?

It was difficult to go see Roy. They had him housed in 6 North at the Santa Fe prison. All high-risk inmates are housed in 6 North. Six North is located on the west end of the prison. You learn your lesson well when you go visit 6 North.

Inmates are housed underground in single cells. Each cell door has a mail chute where food, letters, or other small items can pass through. Roy and Shaun were the worst of the worst. They had left the two boys to die of starvation and dehydration. The inmates along with the guards were out to get Roy and Shaun.

The word was out that there was a hit on both Roy and Shaun. Roy and Shaun had not been convicted of any crimes yet, but they were being housed in the worst conditions in the prison. Mady Malka would claim she put them there for their own protection.

When Agent Fenner and Officer DeReyes personally took Roy and Shaun to prison, Officer DeReyes kept explaining in detail how both Roy and Shaun were going to be raped and forced to suck a dick and how they were going to be beaten every day.

When Roy and Shaun were brought into the prison, Officer DeReyes was yelling to make sure everyone in 6 North could hear, "Make way for the baby killers, Make way for the baby killer." Officer DeReyes and Agent Fenner were proud of themselves because they were going to make Roy's and Shaun's lives miserable.

Roy and Shaun had no rights in a state prison as they were county inmates being housed by the state. They could not complain about anything. The guards at the prison knew who Roy and Shaun were. They were going to get special treatment while at 6 North.

Their cells were 6 x 12, no TV, no radio, no books, no writing materials, nothing to do twenty-four hours a day, seven days a week. They were given one hour a day in the dog cage, a six by ten yard heavy gauge chain link around them. But both Roy and Shaun were concerned for their safety with hits on them and they refused to leave their cells.

For the first few months Roy and Shaun ate off the floor. The guards considered them dogs and dogs eat off the floor. They would get their tray of food through the mail chute. The tray would come in at high speed not giving Roy or Shaun the opportunity to grab it.

Every inmate was allowed cleaning materials to clean their cells. Roy and Shaun were not state inmates so they were not allowed to clean their cells. Due to the constant threats being received, Roy and Shaun were also afraid to shower.

Inmates are given one phone call a week. They are brought a phone, handed through the mail chute for fifteen minutes.

It was hard to go visit Roy. You park a half-mile from the facility and you had to make sure you did not back in. The tower guard must see the license plate to your car. If you back in they will tell you to go back and turn your car around.

You walk through the usual metal detector without your shoes. You are buzzed into the first door, go through a second door, down the stairs, past a third door to a large visiting room, then past the attorney visit rooms, around the corner and into a locked segregation room. There are two plastic chairs with a block wall between you and your client.

Anything you pass to your client must go through the guard. No food or drinks are allowed.

Prisoners at 6 North wear a bright yellow uniform with the name of the prison on their back.

They took Roy out of his cell with his ankles shackled, chained around his waist and handcuffed to the chain on his waist. The prisoners call it the penguin walk.

I could hear the chains being rattled coming down the hall and stopping on the other side of the door. The guard opened the door, looked at me and reminded me to stay on my side of the wall and no touching the inmate.

Without any ventilation the room contains a stale smell of old body odor built up over the years. Roy came into the room, went to his chair, and looked over the wall at me, "You got to get me out of here Maurice, I'm going crazy here. I can't sleep they are constantly yelling at me, they're going to kill me."

"Roy, I know Ray is filing a motion for reconsideration of placement for you, but to be honest with you, don't hold your breath."

"But I didn't do anything. I have never been to that cabin."

It was hard to talk to Roy he smelled so bad. His hands were filthy and his nails were long with black dirt under them. I could see the dirt building up in his ears.

"You're going to have to hang in there Roy. It's going to take time to get you out of this place."

"Maurice, the guards show you the death house as we walk across the yard to get here. They keep telling me that's the only way out of here for me.

Did you get to Orley's, did they tell you I was at work the entire month of December?"

"I did Roy. They verified you were at work the entire time."

"Then why won't they let me go? I didn't do anything."

"They have two eye witnesses, Roy, that are saying you and Shaun did this, Roy."

"But that's not true, I haven't ever been to that cabin."

"DeReyes is making a big thing about what you said about Cassandra and the kids."

"I said that because DeReyes got me mad. He was talking shit about Ben, I didn't like it. I never met Cassandra and the kids. I feel sorry for what happened to them. But Ben was my friend and DeReyes kept talking like he didn't care about him."

"It looks like we are number three to go to trial. Shaun is going to trial in couple of months, then we'll be up. Ray got them to move the trial to Truth or Consequences."

"They're going to convict us aren't they Maurice? They gave Woody four hundred and forty years. They're going to give us the same."

"It's not over Roy. You have to believe that. I believe you're innocent but we've got a long ways to go."

"Woody lied Maurice, I was never at the cabin, I heard about it but I have never been there. My fingerprints and DNA are not at that cabin."

Over the months Roy and Shaun would deteriorate on us. They would not get any sun, they were losing weight, they were losing their social skills from not talking to anyone, they were losing their hair, and they were turning grey on us. If it hadn't been for the family members who would go see them they would have given up on life.

Three Dimensional Crime Scene

Sherlock Holmes comes to life: *"You will not apply my precept," he said, shaking his head. "How often have I said to you that when you have eliminated the impossible, whatever remains, however improbable, must be the truth? We know that he did not come through the door, the window, or the chimney. We also know that he could not have been concealed in the room, as there is no concealment possible. When, then, did he come?"*

After finding out Woody was out of town, I went back to those photos again. I knew them by heart. I gave up looking at them at midnight and went to bed. Not to sleep, just to go to bed.

All we had to work on were the small four by five photos given to us by D.P.S. They were shot with a 35 mm camera and we did not have the negatives to blow up.

I had been using a magnifying glass to look at all the details in the photos. I could see military style matches on the floor. I could see several burnt marks on the rug in the cabin. After looking at all the photos several hundred times I could see the cabin in my sleep.

In looking back at the diagram done by Agent Christian I notice he had missed the storage room in the cabin. I could see in the storage unit shelves. There were several voids on the shelves, same size and shape as the paint cans in the boys' room.

The paint cans found in the boys' room had the same V pattern on them. The DA had claimed it was the boys who did all of this. To me the two boys were incapable of creating those patterns. They could not have climbed up in the pantry and removed the cans.

The boys could possibly have climbed up to where the cupboard was. But the window was not within their reach. I found the living room curtain had been taken off and placed in the kitchen. The large sofa chair had been turned upside down and no soot was on it. Someone had turned the it over after the fire.

Nothing looked right in the cabin. In the boys' room there had been three 1500-watt heaters left on. Could the boys have carried them into their room and turned them on, then placed the paint cans with the V pattern near the heaters?

If the boys had no food or water in their systems they had to be weak. Also the bedroom door had been kicked in then pulled back and placed on the wall. I doubt if the boys could have kicked the door in and then placed it on the wall.

Could it have been possible with the locks on the bedroom that the boys were locked in the bedroom? Could someone else have done the damage to the door?

On the night of the tenth of October of 1997 I could not sleep. The photos of the crime scene would not get out of my mind. I knew the photos like the back of my hand. And they were like flash cards flashing over and over.

Then it came back to me, from a Sherlock Holmes book, "In solving a problem of this sort, the grand thing is to be able to reason backward. That is a very useful accomplishment, and a very easy one, but people do not practice it much. In the everyday affairs of life it is more useful to reason forward, and so the other comes to be neglected. There are fifty who can reason synthetically for one who can reason analytically."

I had to think of the crime scene backwards. As the photos flashed I started to see the crime scene for the first time in three dimensions. I had never seen a three-dimensional crime scene before, a two dimension, yes.

I can see Johnny Garcia on the floor in the bedroom. I started picturing him under the clothes. In my mind I lifted the clothes off Johnny. I could see Johnny dressed only in a yellow shirt. I picked him up and suspended him in air just below the clothes. Now I was looking at the burned spot on the rug.

Now I knew the sequence of events through Johnny. Autopsy report: no burn marks, no carbon monoxide in the blood, throat, or lungs. Johnny died before the fires. Johnny had to be placed on the burnt spot after he died. I started going back to when the cabin was neat and clean and the first facts started to emerge. I saw the curtains back on the windows.

I got out of bed, turned on my laptop, and started writing down the sequence of the three-dimensional crime scene as it entered my mind.

Below is the fax I sent to Ray Twohig:

Ray,
We have a three dimensional crime scene and we can prove it with the evidence at the cabin. We know the following facts to be true.
Event One.
We know Ben Jr. and Cassandra were shot and killed first.
The two boys were still alive.
The killer or killers left the boys to die of starvation and dehydration.
Event Two.
The boys die of starvation. Five days after the death of Ben and Cassandra.
After the death of the two boys, someone or some persons returned to the cabin.
If the cabin was locked, the person would need a key to get into the cabin.
At this time Ben Jr.'s body was moved from the original position of his head onto the pillow.
We know this from the blood on the pillow and the blood on the floor along with the position of Ben's body where it found.

Ben's body at the time of death was on the pillow. He was moved down toward the bottom of the bed.

If you notice on the photographs and the videotape, Ben's head is to the left of the head of the bed and off the mattress.

If you look at the pillow you can see where the original position of Ben's head would have been moved after death.

During this same time period the blood in his body had not solidified.

We know this because blood had drained down to the floor.

The blood flow from Ben Jr. does not match up to the blood on the floor.

There is now a fire in the living room and the fire in the boys' room may have been started at this same time period.

We know this because there was no fire or smoke damage to the boys' bodies at their time of death (see autopsy).

The boys' bedroom door was kicked in from the outside, knocked off its hinges and placed on the side of the wall.

The open window in the boys' room. It is possible the boy on the top bunk may have opened the window above his bed and vomited.

But someone or one of the boys may have closed the window afterwards.

The blinds in the house had also been in the down and closed position. (You need a magnifying glass to see this.)

They have smoke damage to them and they are partially melted.

The blue curtain that is in the kitchen belongs in the living room.

The fire goes out due to no oxygen. The cabin does not burn. The window in the boys' room had to be closed or their door was shut.

Event Three.

Someone or some persons returns to the cabin.

One of the boys is now placed on top of the burned portion of the rug.

The burnt portion of the rug was done after the death of the boys. In event two. Covered with clothes.

Unknown persons returned to the cabin ransacked the cabin.

They turned over the sofa chair.

Unknown persons kicked the door to the boys' room open.

They removed items from the storage or pantry left a candle burning to cause a delay fire.

Attempted to create the second fire in the boys' room, by using the fumes from the paint and the three 1500 watt heaters.

Upon returning the boys were picked up placed on the burnt spot of the rug covered with clothes.

I need to get the electric bill as I do not believe the heater were on in December 1995. (Believe the heaters were turned on March 24, 1995 when Popcorn escapes.)

I believe the Third Event happens when Popcorn escapes for Valencia County Jail on March 24th.

The keys to the cabin. There are only two keys to the cabin. Ben Sr. had one to open the cabin. The killer needed a key to keep getting into the cabin. So then how did Roy get a key to lock the kids up in the cabin?

From a Sherlock Holmes book: *"In solving a problem of this sort, the grand thing is to be able to reason backward. That is a very useful accomplishment, and a very easy one, but people do not practice it much. In the everyday affairs of life it is more useful to reason forward, and so the other comes to be neglected. There are fifty who can reason synthetically for one who can reason analytically."*

12

Test the Fact Against the Three Dimensional Crime Scene

RAY CALLED ME BRIGHT AND EARLY, "WE NEED TO TALK ABOUT your crime scene theory Maurice. Can you come into the office this morning?"

"I sure can. I'll be there in thirty minutes." I was still awake from working on my crime scene theory and I was anxious to meet with Ray and get started.

I went into Ray's office and felt like I was Officer DeReyes as I couldn't stop talking. "We have more than one crime scene at the cabin. We also have two separate fires from two different time periods. I can prove the killer came back twice after the deaths and used a key to get into the cabin.

"Ray, we have paint cans being opened and the kids couldn't have done it. The cans were moved from the pantry into the boys' room after the first fire. We have Johnny Garcia on top of a burnt spot on the carpet, yet he has no burns to his body or smoke in his lungs. We have three large heaters carried into the boys' room along with the paint cans. The crime scene is a gold mine, not a disaster site. We can prove the killer came back twice after death. Ben's body was moved after he was shot. The blood on the floor does not match up with the blood flow. You can see where his underwear is bunched up when he was moved down toward the foot of the bed."

"Maurice while I agree with you, you cannot do it all. The DA hates you already for being a pain in their ass. We need to get some other experts involved. You can't testify to everything you're telling me. Tell me who you would like to bring in?"

"I'm ahead of you Ray. I have calls into Ron Metzcar, a retired APD Crime Scene Expert. He is the best in evidence collection and gives great testimony on the stand. I have a lunch meeting with Tony Anaya, not the Governor, at Barela's café this afternoon. Tony is a retired Arson Investigator from the Albuquerque Fire Department and he's one of the best around. He is very good on the stand and is fantastic at his work."

"Who else? You said three."

"Dr. Alan Watts."

"The physicist?

"I love that little Englishman."

"What do you anticipate him to testify to?"

"Knowing Alan Ray, he is worse than me. He can testify to everything. You've seen his resume. British Government, Ministry of Defense, Atomic Weapons Research, Nuclear Weapons, Behavior of High Explosives, High powered lasers."

"I know his resume Maurice. What can he do for us?'

"I know that damn sofa chair could not have been turned over by the kids. Alan can show by physics they could not have turned it over. The blinds that were in the living room. The boys could not have gotten then down and then put them in the kitchen. More important, the paint cans. I know you're tired of me telling you and telling you the same thing over and over. The blood flow pattern from Ben Jr. The fact that the body was moved after death. We have a treasure chest of evidence to work with. The sheriff at Torrance is blaming the State Police for fucking up the crime scene and the state is blaming the sheriff. Hell, it was Popcorn who fucked up the scene. He was trying to burn the cabin down and destroy all the evidence."

"All right. Go talk to them and see what they say."

Getting Tony Aboard

I had known Tony most of my life growing up in the Well's Park area where basketball was the way of life. Tony was a star in his day at Valley High School playing three sports. Tony also played on our summer league basketball team. We were known as the "Freedom Riders."

Tony had joined the Albuquerque Fire Department about the same time I had joined the Police Department. We remained friends and had developed mutual friends. One of my favorite characters was Detective George de Lao. George had gone to Arson School with Tony. When he returned from Arson School the department in their wisdom stuck him with me in the Child Abuse Unit.

George had joined another abused unit, working under abused conditions with abused vehicles. There was eight detectives assigned to work out of the Children Youth and Family Department. Since we were no longer housed with the city, but with the state, we were our own janitors. Our vehicles were old blue and white cars with the emblems scraped off and tar on the roof where the light bar was once attached.

George came to the unit with a new old car. It looked like a real unmarked car. George was very proud of the fact that it was his. George and I had a running battle, "Best Scam was No Scam."

George would walk around the office twirling his keys around, telling us, "You want to ride with me? You want to take my car?"

I thought it was time to pull a fast one on him, so for the next month when I went to get gas for my car I took along my five-gallon gas can. I would fill up my car plus five gallons into the can. I would then park next to George's car and three times a week I would add fifteen gallons to George's car, but he didn't know that.

At the end of the month we had to turn in our gas usage and mileage. George was getting a hundred miles to the gallon. "George, come in my office." Sergeant Tach had called George in.

"What's the deal with your car?"

"I don't know Sarge. I'm just not burning any gas."

"Take it the police garage and see what they say."

I could hear the conversation from my desk, "Wait up George I'll go with you." I had to see what was going to happen.

George drove his car into the garage and Red the mechanic came up to him. "What can I do for you guys?"

"My car is not burning any gas. I haven't put in more than five gallons of gas a week."

"What do you think I should do George?"

"I have got no idea, I just know I'm not burning gas."

"Well how many miles you doing a month?"

"Close to two hundred fifty and all I put in was eight gallons."

"And this is a bad thing?" Red looked at George. "Leave it here George. We'll look it over." With that Red walked over to the other mechanics and they all started to grin and started slapping each other on the back.

I went with George to pick up his car the following day. Red came up to George. "Nothing wrong with your car George. Get it out of here."

For the next two weeks I did the same thing with the gas. "Sarge, I don't know what's going on, I'm not burning any gas. The garage is telling me there is nothing wrong with it."

After that I figured George owed me gas so then I started siphoning gas out of his car, five gallons every Monday, Wednesday, and Friday.

George was back at the yards, "I am burning gas like crazy."

Red looked at George. "What do you think I should do George?"

George just shrugged his shoulder and walked away. When George got back to the office I left the five-gallon can under Marvin's desk. I had logged myself out of the office for the day. I could scam them both with one scam.

Next morning I came in George was just sitting there at his desk. "What's up George?"

"Someone is fucking with me."

"What you mean?"

"Someone has been putting gas in my car and now they're taking it out."

"You have any ideas?"

"Yea I do. I came in to work early this morning and looked around. Look what I found under Marvin's desk." George pulled out my red five-gallon gas can.

"I knew it George, I thought it was Marvin. You know him. He always thinks he can get away with it. Just because he has that innocent baby blue eyes look. You can't let him get away with it George, you got to get him back." Best Scam is No Scam. And that's the end of that story.

I walked into Barela's Coffee Shop and found a table outside in the patio away from everyone and tucked myself into the corner. I took out my photo album with the photos of the fire on the first pages and then placed A.T.F. Bangsten's report in the back of my folder so the gold letters A.T.F. would stick out.

When Tony walked in we gave each other the usual three pats on the back with a hug. "Man it's been a while since I've been here. This place doesn't change."

"This is the only place I have my meetings. This way I get good food and work done at the same time."

I closed the binder with the photos when the waitress brought me my usual bottle Coke. I knew Tony was trying to get a glance at the notebook.

"You got that Torreon Murder case don't you?" I nodded. "How can you defend those ass holes after what they did to those babies?"

"I think they're innocent Tony."

"Get the fuck out of here. I saw the newspaper and TV."

The waitress came up to our table. "Usual Maurice, medium menudo, red chile, lots of onions and a tortilla?"

Tony looked up at her, "Make it two."

The waitress smiled and left. "This case has been ruled complex Tony. They don't know the date or time of death. They have two star witnesses that have mental problems. In the confession the cops are doing 90 percent of the talking. We can prove two of the boys were somewhere else on the alleged dates of death. There were fires in the cabin that none of their witnesses ever talked about. Someone came in after the deaths and tried to burn down the cabin."

"Are those the photos from the cabin?"

"Yea. Do you know some Arson dude from A.T.F. by the name of Bangsten?"

"No. Those guys do maybe one or two fires a year, so I don't see them much."

"Well A.T.F. has made some outrageous remarks."

"What do you mean? Are those the photos? Let me see them."

As Tony looked at them I continued to talk. "He said the heater caused the fire in the living room. Then he said there were two fires in the cabin."

"He's full of shit Maurice. Look at these photos of the heater. These heaters have a automatic shut off valve. When they tip over they shut off. The heater was the victim of the fire, not the creator.

See this carpet. It has clean lines around it. That means there was an accelerant poured on the rug. This leg on the sofa chair is where it started. You can tell by the alligator marks on it. It burned the hottest. See how the smoke went up the wall. The sofa chair caused that. Sofa chairs are made of petroleum and they burn hot and fast. But it only burnt for a short time period then it went out due to lack of oxygen. You can see that on the couch portion that didn't burn. The cabin must have been airtight because the fire put itself out. Look. There are at least three more locations of fire."

"Well his report says..."

"Let me see his report." Tony took it out of my hands and must have found what he was looking for. "This report is bullshit. I don't think he ever went through the cabin. I bet he couldn't handle the smell and didn't take a mask with him."

I had Tony hooked. "You think you can help us out?"

"This is wrong. Can I keep his report and borrow those photos? I want to take a closer look at the photos of the fires."

We tried to eat but Tony kept going through the photos. "Look at that sofa chair. It was turned over after the fire and there's no soot on the bottom."

"Can you help us out?" I asked again.

"Hell yes, this is wrong. When can we get up to the cabin?"

"We have been asking the DA the same question and they keep stalling us. But I will get Ray to push them."

Now I had to go convince Ron and Alan to get involved. I knew I wouldn't have any problems with Alan as he was my Dr. Watson, the most logical man I know.

My Little Short Englishman

If I was stranded on an island and had my choice of people to be stranded with, one of them would be Alan Watts. Alan is one of the most amazing people I have ever met. I have often considered Alan as "Mr. Watson." Being into physics, Alan is aware of everything around him. In testifying I have heard Alan say, "It may surprise most people, but almost everything in the world is governed by physics. Even my speaking to you now is governed by physics. My tongue is producing sound waves. This microphone is picking up electrical signals."

I called Alan and got his ever-cheerful English accent. "Dr. Watts speaking."

"Alan, it's Maurice. Are you busy?"

"No, just sitting here watching the telly and drinking a spot of tea."

"I'm on my way over. I might need your help."

I knew it would not take much for me to hook Alan. All I would have to say was, "I need help on the Torreon murders."

I got to Alan's house and went inside. I gave Vicky, Alan's wife her usual hug. "Saw you and Ray on the news quite a bit Maurice. You guys are catching hell from the media." She didn't wait for answer. "Sit down Maurice I'll get you some tea, crackers and some tasty lemon cheese."

Allan was sitting on the sofa. "I hope you're going to ask me to help you with the Torreon murders. I have been so interested in them. I have followed the case in the news but I don't trust them. They only give you a one or two minute blip."

"You're right, Alan. I do need help. I have an ongoing dispute with Ray about some half-gallon paint cans and a sofa chair along with some other evidence. The DA in Woody's case said the kids opened the paint cans, turned over a sofa chair, started fires, all kinds of crap. I told Ray it was all bullshit and Ray tells me to prove it. So here I am. Plus I have some other problems with the crime scene and the statements that were given. No one has ever corroborated the statements and the evidence."

"What kind of paint cans, half gallon you say?" I knew Alan was hooked. "I think I may have some. Now the problems as I see it. Can the kids create the opening in the cans by using their force only, correct. What's the opening devise? Do you know? How much did the boys weigh?"

"The DA is saying a screwdriver was used to open the cans and the boys weighed between twenty and thirty five pounds."

"You know Maurice starvation and dehydration would have made the boys very weak, don't you think." Without waiting for an answer Alan went on. "I think I may have some gallon paint cans and screwdrivers. Step into my lab."

We went into Alan's garage where he did his experiments. He found a half-gallon can of paint. "This size the right size, Maurice? Let me see those photos of the cans and screwdriver. Ahh, yes it looks like this is the same size of screwdriver."

Alan picked out a screwdriver and said, "This should do. Let's go borrow Vicky's bathroom scale. She never uses it anyway."

When we went in Vicky looked over and smiled at me. "You know you can't trust the doctor."

I smiled in agreement.

"All right. Let me get my tripod and video camera and we'll be ready to test the cans."

We walked back into the garage and Alan sat the scale on the floor. Then he got the paint can from the shelf. He placed it on the scale and backed the scale from three pounds to zero while the can remained on the scale.

"Now we are at zero weight. We will now put the camera to watch the scale because there is no way our eyeballs have the speed to watch it."

Alan then got the screwdriver and placed it in the same location as in the photos. Then he started to apply pressure to the can. Alan is five foot seven and weighs close to a hundred and seventy pounds. After a while Alan had his entire body over the can and his face was turning red. Then I heard a loud thud and it was over. The screwdriver penetrated the lid.

"Well let's put the camera on the telly, Maurice, and see what we've got. I have to put it on slow motion for you, Maurice. I know how your eyesight is not that fast," he said with a smile.

As the tape rolled Alan started talking to me. "What you didn't see Maurice was I was pushing so hard I was almost lifted myself off the ground while balancing on the screwdriver. Ahh, there it is." Alan stopped the tape. There was 125 pounds showing on the scale.

Alan looked over at me with a grin. "Now how much did you say the kids weigh, twenty to thirty-five pounds?"

God, I love my job. Alan was hooked. "I brought you over your own set of photos and police reports. Also my memos on the case so you can catch up with us. One other thing, the flow of liquid is also the science of physics?"

"It is, but what does it have to do with this case?"

"I want you to look at the blood from Ben Jr.'s wound. The blood on the bed and the blood on the floor, and tell me the flow of liquid is not consistent."

I knew once Alan got his teeth into it he was going to able to do so much more. Alan was going to be great on the stand. He was a teacher of physics and did it in a manner everyone could understand.

Ron Metzger Retired Crime Scene Detective

The following day I met with Ron Metzger at his house. Ron was a Field Investigator who worked with me back in the day. Ron stayed with the program moving up to the Crime Scene Team and then retired from the lab at about the same time I left.

"All right Maurice, it sounds like you need something from me or else you wouldn't have called me."

"You're right Ron, I need help. I can't do it alone."

"Don't tell me. Torreon."

"All right I won't tell you. Can we sit down and talk."

"You know Maurice this is the worst crime in the state's history, don't you?"

"Someone once told me that."

"No one has ever starved two kids to death in New Mexico. Now what do you want me to look at and what do you want me to do?" I could tell Ron did not like the taste of this case.

"You know Darren White right."

"Yea, he used to work for APD and after the new governor is elected Darren is appointed from Sergeant to the Director of Public Safety."

"Darren claims a financial reason for why he did not send a crime scene team to the cabin. No forensic evidence was collected."

"How much would it have cost to send up a three man team to do the work? I keep hearing them say they have tons of evidence."

"Oh yeah, just ask Agent Jacoby. They collected all kinds of items but no evidence. They claim they are still testing evidence but Jacoby doesn't know what evidence is being tested or when it will be done."

"So what is it you think I can do?"

"All I want you to do is look at the photos and examine the evidence. See how they did things and if they did it the right way. I want to know what they missed."

Ron looked at my notebook with the photos. "Are these the photos from the cabin? Couldn't you get them any smaller Maurice?"

"I've been using my mom's magnifying glass to look at them. Ron, give me a break. This is what the DA gave us and we don't have the negatives."

We sat on the porch outside and Ron started flipping the photos over. "What happened in this cabin?"

I went over my theory with him, showing him the photos of Johnny and Ray Garcia along with the autopsy reports. Ron started taking notes like any good officer. "I understand your problem. Let my look at it without your help. I don't want your theory to fuck up mine. I'll give you a call in a couple of days."

Two days later Ron called me, "Maurice, when can we get up to the cabin? I want to see it in person."

When Did the Three Fifteen Hundred Watt Heaters Come On?

Located in the bedroom where the boys were, there were three fifteen hundred watt heaters. Based on Ben Anaya Sr.'s statement, one of the reasons he went up to the cabin was the large electric bill he had received. I felt the heaters were turned on in March 24th so now how do I prove that they were turned on three months after everyone was dead?

I went to Technical Vocation Institute and found their top electrician.

"Mr. Arco, my name is Maurice and I do criminal defense work. I was wondering if I could talk with you and see if you could help me."

"What can I do for you Maurice?"

"I need to know how you figure out usage of electricity."

"Well by doing calculations of loads which determines the amount of power or wattage that a dwelling would use, and that's based on the type of appliances."

"So if I can get you the electrical reading from a Co-op what else would you need?"

"The electrical box, that little thing with the number on the little wheel would help. That would tell us the kilowatt hours."

"I think they pulled that off the cabin."

"You talking about that cabin in Torreon, aren't you?" I thought to myself is there anyone who does not know about the cabin murders?

"Let me explain. I got some information that there were three fifteen hundred watt heaters turned on and left on. I want to know if we can tell when they came on."

"Do you know how many kilowatt hours was used in that time period?"

"Yes sir, 3,356 hours. That was the total. The month of January and February were 696 hours and 622 hours. That leaves us with 2734 Kilowatts for the month of March and fourteen days in April."

"What kind of appliances were on?"

"They found three heaters. Two of them had 1,650 watts and the third one 1,350. The TV, the refrigerator, a VCR and a sixty watt bulb on the porch were still on."

"Those usually burn at sixty watts to fifty watts. The fridge about ten."

"How many days were they on?"

"According to police reports they were on from December twelfth through the eighteenth 1995 to April 14, 1996, a total of a hundred and nineteen days."

"Well you know these type heaters have a kick off valve, so they are only operating at 60 percent of the time."

"Well then, just based on these rough figures can you tell when the heaters came on?"

"Pretty simple son, January, February and March they were not on. It's safe to say that the 2,734 came on around the end of March."

We were back to the "Ghosts" when Ms. Zenner heard noise in the cabin at the end of March, the same time Popcorn had escaped from Valencia County Detention Center. He had to be the one who turned on the heaters and placed the open cans of paint from the pantry and placed them into the boys' room to have the fumes catch fire from the heat. The paint from the fumes would act as delay fuse. This would have been when Popcorn went back the second time to try to burn the cabin down. Each time he tried to burn the cabin he goes back to jail for a perfect alibi. What Popcorn didn't realize was the shut off switch on the heaters would go off.

I felt after Popcorn came back from Pecos the first time he returned to the cabin and everything was in order and everyone was dead. He started one of the fires to destroy the evidence and left the cabin thinking it would burn.

I talked to the officer who arrested him on the 25th of December after he tried to run. Popcorn had a large screwdriver trying to break into a car wash coin machine. The officer told me, "Popcorn just gave up."

I couldn't believe a twenty-year-old kid who loves the adrenaline rush could not have outrun the officer. He wanted to get arrested and have an iron clad alibi. When he was arrested his property was tagged in. Evidence was never collected or analyzed

Among Popcorn's property at the detention center was a pager belonging to Ben Anaya Jr. It stayed in custody at Valencia County until we had the property moved to State Police. I got the serial number of the pager and traced it back to Christian, a friend of Ben Jr. She had bought the pager for Ben. This was another item Popcorn failed to disclose to his friend in law enforcement. Popcorn never told them about the keys in his possession and one would have thought they would have gotten his clothing out of custody and examined them for forensic value but DPS did not.

By the middle of March of 1996 Popcorn had been talking to Airie. "Have you heard or seen Ben or Cassandra?"

The answer was "No." There had been no news on TV or radio of the cabin burning down. The bodies were still at the cabin. Popcorn had to try again.

Popcorn realized that the cabin was still intact and if they found the cabin and the bodies they were coming after him. Popcorn escaped on the 24th of March 1996 from Valencia County Detention Center and returned to the cabin with the two Danny's, trashed the cabin and tried to burn it down for the second time.

It was at this time Johnny Garcia was picked up and placed on the previous burnt spot and covered with clothes. The paint cans were opened, the heaters turned on full blast. Popcorn attempted to create a delayed fire with the fumes from the paint cans and heaters. The clothes he had covered Johnny with he had hoped would catch on fire.

What Popcorn didn't realize was that, like his brain, you need oxygen to operate and in order for a fire to burn you need oxygen.

Now I had most of my questions answered. Popcorn got ranked out the end of November and Ben took him to the ranking out. Ben did not help Popcorn, instead he stood and watched as they beat him. Ben made the mistake and took Popcorn back to the cabin. When they went back to the cabin there had to be words exchanged. I'm sure Ben and Cassandra were tired of Popcorn living with them since he was not contributing any money to their living. Bonita had told Ben Jr., "Popcorn is just a leech." I believe Ben Jr. and Cassandra, on the night of the twelfth, told Popcorn he had to leave. Popcorn was still upset Ben did not have his back at the ranking out and now he had no money and no place to go.

With Ben and Cassandra asleep in their room, noise in the cabin would not have disturbed them. I believe Popcorn and Popcorn alone had the opportunity to commit the murders since Ben and Cassandra were shot while they slept. No one else could have come in the cabin. It was too secure.

If you follow the keys, there was one set found in the bedroom door. No key was on it that fit the front door of the cabin. Ben Sr. found one pair of keys in his coat pocket. The second set was in the key ring on the Jeep. The killer was getting in and out of the cabin using that key. The front door had a dead bolt on it so it had to be locked with a key from the inside as well as outside. There was never any sign of forced entry.

We knew that Cassandra and the kids had come to town to do laundry just prior to their deaths. Some of the clothes were still in the back of the Jeep in the laundry basket. Some of the boys' clothing were left at Cassandra's mother's house.

On the fifteenth of December Cassandra's mother Porfie finds her VCR missing and a bag of the boys clothes in a black garbage plastic bag. Inside were the bags and the boys' winter jackets that Cassandra would have never left behind. Someone from the cabin or from the Jeep had to leave the bag at her house and remove her VCR. Popcorn must have forgotten to tell his buddies Juan, Frank, and Mike about this.

13

Time Line From November, 1995 to May, 1996

I STARTED MY TIME LINE WITH THE POLICE REPORT FOR Armed Robbery/Car Jacking on August 9, 1995 based on the police reports found. They—Shaun Wilkins, Ben Anaya Jr., Joseph Espinosa and Shawn Popeleski (aka "Popcorn")—had carjacked a car in Albuquerque and driven it to Winslow, Arizona.

August 12, 1995: Arizona State Police stopped them on Interstate 40 and arrested all the boys. Without the knowledge of the others, Popeleski gave his name as Frank Gomez, a name Joseph Espinosa had used as his alias.

September 15, 1995: Shawn Popeleski was found asleep in a stolen vehicle. Popeleski gave the officers the name of Frank Gomez. Popeleski told the police, "I didn't steal the car. Dominic was the one who stole the car." Officer arrested Dominic for auto theft and Popeleski was set free.

November 15, 1995: Arrest warrants for Frank Gomez were issued out of Arizona for the auto theft charge stemming from the arrest of September 15, 1995. Joseph Espinosa, who had used the name Frank Gomez when stopped, was arrested.

November 30, 1995: 18th Street Gang was upset with Popeleski. Bonita who was living at 1201 Maderia SE had a party for the 18th Street gang. Ben Jr. had brought Popcorn to the party where 18th Streeters ranked Popcorn out of the gang for their three-strike rule.

December 1, 1995: Ben and Cassandra went to the store and used Cassandra's EBT Card at 11:44 pm for $140.00.

December 3, 1995: Torrance County Sheriff Deputy stopped Ben Jr.'s vehicle with Ben Jr. driving. Cassandra, Popcorn and Airie were in the vehicle. The stop was at 1900 hours. They tell the deputy they are on their way to the cabin. (No mention of the babies being in the car.)

December 4, 1995: Roy Buchner was arrested at 1100 Coors SW in Albuquerque by APD.

December 5, 1995: Roy is released from jail. Cassandra's EBT Card is used in Albuquerque at 111 Coors SW. Airie is dropped off at her house in the mountains.

December 6-12, 1995: Shaun Wilkins is arrested as a suspect for burglary and he is placed into custody at Bernalillo County Jail.

December 8, 1995: Cassandra's EBT card is used in Albuquerque at 5900 Fortuna NW.

December 10, 1995: Ben Sr. drives up to the cabin in Sherwood Forrest and takes with him pizza and drinks for the kids. Takes with him a new dead bolt lock to replace the one at the cabin. Popcorn installs the lock. This is the last time Ben Sr. will see his son.

December 11, 1995: Roy Buchner is at MVD with his grandfather.

December 12-17, 1995: Woody leaves with the girls to Juarez, Mexico.

December 15, 1995: Ben Sr. leaves for Las Vegas, Nevada. Popcorn is with Richard "Little Dreamer" at the John Adams Recreation Center. Ben Sr.'s step-daughter sees Ben Jr.'s Jeep parked in front of the house. She also see's Popcorn at the front of Ben Sr.'s house.

December 16, 1995: Popcorn, Little Dreamer, Jeremy Sedillo are selling guns to "Green Eyes." Popcorn stays with Little Dreamer until the 22nd of December.

December 17, 1995: Popcorn and Little Dreamer leave for Pecos, Texas. They spend the night at a rest area.

December 20, 1995: Popcorn and Little Dreamer spend the night in Pecos, Texas at the Holiday Inn. The Jeep breaks down and is left in the parking lot.

December 21, 1995: Popcorn and Little Dreamer take the bus back to Albuquerque.

December 22, 1995: Popcorn spends the night at Little Dreamer's house.

December 25, 1995: Popcorn is arrested breaking into a car wash coin machine and booked into Jail in Belen, New Mexico.

February 22, 1996: Popcorn is still in custody in the Valencia County Jail and is visited by Steve. (Jail records from Popcorn's file.)

March 23, 1996: Popcorn escapes from the Valencia County Jail with the two Danny's.

March 23, 1996: Ms. Zenner who have the cabin above the Anaya's cabin hear what they feel is a party at the cabin.

March 24, 1996: Popcorn is arrested in Albuquerque for possession of a stolen vehicle.

April 8, 1996: Porfie Sedillo reports to the Albuquerque Police that her daughter Cassandra and her grandsons are missing.

April 14, 1996: Ben Sr. finds the bodies at his cabin. State Police are called in. Officer DeReyes is assigned to assist.

April 15, 1996: Officer DeReyes and Agent Jacoby interview Frank Gomez in jail.

April 16, 1996: Airie, Popcorn's girlfriend is interviewed along with Cassandra's grandmother Porfie and her brother Jeremy.

April 17, 1996: Officer DeReyes and Agent Jacoby interview Frank Gomez in jail for the second time. Woody Nieto is also interviewed for the first time. Other gang members are interviewed and tell the officer Popcorn is trying to sell a .22 caliber rifle.

April 19, 1996: Officer DeReyes and Agent Jacoby interview Frank Gomez in jail for the third time. Agent Fenner is now involved in the interviews.

April 20, 1996: Pecos police recover Ben's Jeep in the parking lot and Jacoby is notified.

April 23, 1996: Officer DeReyes and Agent Jacoby interview Frank Gomez in jail for the fourth interview and find that they have now found out Frank Gomez is Shawn Popeleski.

April 24, 1996: Shaun Wilkins is arrested for a stabbing.

April 25, 1996: Shaun Wilkins is interviewed.

April 26, 1996: officers interview Salina, girlfriend to Shaun Wilkins.

April 30, 1996: Ben Sr. is taken back the cabin and interviewed.

May 4, 1996: Woody is interviewed according to the reports for the second time.

May 10, 1996: Popcorn is interviewed for the fifth time. April 23rd, according to the police reports, was the last time Popcorn was interviewed. It was hard to believe nothing was happening on the case.

May 12, 1996: Officer DeReyes and Agent Jacoby interview Popcorn in jail for the sixth time.

May 13, 1996: Officer DeReyes and Agent Jacoby interview Popcorn in jail for the seventh time. Woody is also interviewed for the third time. Roy Buchner is arrested.

May 14, 1996: Officers interview Woody for the fourth time.

May 15, 1996: Officers interview Woody for the fifth time. Popcorn is interviewed for the eighth time. We were only given one interview for the fifteenth. Popcorn, for the first time, identifies Roy Buchner as being at the cabin.

14

Truth or Consequences, New Mexico

WE HAD NEVER BEEN MORE READY FOR A TRIAL THAN THIS ONE. We knew all the facts and all the evidence. The DA had listed twenty-nine witnesses and we listed over fifty-five. Twenty-seven would be police officers, two ex-District attorneys and four defense attorneys, along with all of our experts—Tony Anaya (not the Governor), Ron Metzger, and Dr. Watts.

There had already been two trials in the Torreon murders. The confession trial of Woody was in Estancia. That was an easy win for the DA. After all, how do you lose a self-confession trial? The media and the DA were proud of this conviction. Woody got over four hundred years in prison.

Shaun Wilkin's case was next and it was to be held in Socorro County about seventy miles south of Albuquerque. Socorro had a deep history. In 1598 Juan de Onate led a group of Spanish settlers through the Jornada del Muerto, an inhospitable patch of desert. Socorro means help in Spanish. In our case that is what it gave us.

Steve Aarons and Kari Converse were able to use our experts in his case and I had testified along with Dr. Watts, Tony Anaya and Ron Metzger. The trial resulted in a hung jury. Shaun was crushed and could not believe the jury had hung. Nonetheless, Steve Aarons, Kari Converse and their investigator Troy Garrity had slowed down the train. The media was now reporting that there was some doubt in the state's case. Steve, Kari and Troy had stood in front of the train and slowed it down.

Based on Shaun's trial we now knew all of the DA's theories were not a threat to us. We were ready to go to trial. I was expecting to see the District Attorney himself try the case. Instead they sent a young DA with no help. I felt in my heart the DA did not want the embarrassment of losing the case to us. It would fall on a younger DA and not the elected DA.

When we arrived for trial we had a total of 18 boxes with us. Every day for the entire trial 12 of the boxes we used went out with us and 12 came back in with us. I looked over at the DA's files. They had three, three-inch notebooks with the trial transcript of Woody's trial. They were going to follow the same format. They had no witness files. No documents to support witness testimony. The same evidence they introduced in Woody's and Shaun's trial had been remarked and was ready for the third time.

Our plan was different. With every witness there were documents to be made into exhibits. We were bringing into court every piece of evidence, with the exception of the Jeep, into the courthouse. By the end of our trial our lettering system was eight Zs. The courtroom floor was so crowded with evidence that Ray had to watch where he was stepping.

In the middle of September the jury selection process started. Ray and Eda Gordon, a jury specialist who had worked with us in the past, spent close to two weeks selecting a jury for Roy's death penalty case. Selecting a jury for a death penalty case is very time consuming. Very often it requires individual questions of a juror.

Finally fifteen jurors were selected. We had three alternates in our case. The judge wanted to make sure if something happened we would have a jury of twelve. We knew it was going to be at least a three-week trial. One of the three alternates was a dispatcher for the Sierra County Sheriff's office. We would not want someone from law enforcement on the jury as we felt they could not be fair and impartial. The dispatcher was an alternate juror so the decision was to accept her.

Our case was being tried in Truth or Consequences, Sierra County. The city is often called T or C. The original name was Hot Springs but the name was changed in 1950 when a popular radio show "Truth or Consequences" hosted by Ralph Edwards had a contest. Hot Springs won the contest and changed its name to Truth or Consequences. For the next fifty years Ralph Edwards would return for the Fiesta of T or C. It is a community of retired people who enjoy the warm winter and the largest lake in New Mexico.

"We need to get Regina up here, Maurice, we've got too much to do. We're going to be buried in paper work, dealing with trial and the witnesses. Regina can do all of this while we're in court."

Regina was brought up to help us with our files, get hold of the witnesses, do jury instructions, keep the files organized, and get the folders for the witnesses ready for the next trial day.

She was not prepared for Ray's four AM wake up call. She came into our room at 4:10 in pajamas and a toothbrush in her mouth. She went to work, keeping our files in order and organizing all the witnesses, including their transportation. We could not have done it all without her.

On November 3rd we started trial. I got up at three that morning and the weather was fantastic. There was a full moon that morning as if there was a giant light bulb in the sky. There was not a cloud in the sky and the stars were the brightest I had seen. As I walked the path behind my room I didn't need a flashlight. I could see the jagged mountains to the east. Walking in moonlight, I could see the soft rays of the moon on the sand dunes of the dessert.

The yucca plants were standing tall in the moonlight. The yucca is a tough plant with sword-shape leaves. It is also known as the "Ghosts in the Graveyard." The yucca sticks it flower straight up as it holds its floating crown of flowers in the soft moonlight. I felt as if I was in an Ansel Adams photograph. It was a very good sign. Now when the full moon comes out it brings back the memories.

I met Ray in our war room that we had set aside for all our boxes.

"You know the DA is calling Popeleski and Woody today?"

"I have their boxes ready for them just in case they testify." Out of out 18 boxes of legal documents, four of them were Popcorn and Woody. We were ready with all of their statements.

We had planned to introduce all the evidence into the trial. Our concern was the photos of the kids taken at the cabin. In most cases all the dead photos do is create sympathy for the DA. But we were not going to hold back anything from the jury. We wanted them to get used to seeing the ugly photos of death, especially the two boys. We wanted to overcome their emotions so that by the end of the trial they would make their decision based on common sense and not the emotion of death.

We were going to play all the tapes and read all the transcripts from the preliminary hearing to the jury. We wanted to show the jury how Mike, Juan and Frank danced with the devil. If we could have had all the tapes of the interviews of Popcorn and Woody it would have been better.

15

The Trial Begins

THE JUDGE SAID, "LADIES AND GENTLEMEN, THIS IS THE BEGIN-
ning of the case, which as you know is not the beginning, because we've seen
you on at least two separate occasions before, but I still have to go over some
of the points, and some of them will be the ones covered before. This is a
criminal case commenced by the State against the Defendant, Roy Buchner.

"The Defendant has been charged with four counts of murder, burglary,
robbery, three counts of tampering with evidence, and conspiracy. To each
charge, the defendant has pled not guilty and is presumed to be innocent. The
State has the burden of proving the guilt of the defendant beyond a reasonable doubt.

"First, you should not discuss the case or anything connected with it
amongst yourselves or with anyone else during the trial. To avoid even the
appearance of improper conduct, don't talk with any of the witnesses or the
lawyers or the defendant until after the case is over, even if it concerns innocent matters or those having nothing to do with the case. Don't permit anyone
else to talk to you about the case. Please notify one of the court personnel if
someone tries to do so. The lawyers have been given the same admonition, so
don't think they're being unfriendly to you. Please wear your juror badge at all
times so that everyone will know that you are a juror and that it is improper
to say anything about the case within your hearing. Second, this case will be
reported in the news media, and I caution you, do not read, listen or observe
any newspaper, radio or television account of the trial while you are serving
as a juror. If you should inadvertently read, hear or see something about this
case in the news media, bring it to my attention promptly."

The state then gave its opening argument. "Good morning. My name is
Chuck Bonet. I'm the Deputy District Attorney prosecuting this matter. Most
of you if not all of you have seen me in the last couple of weeks here when
we went through voir dire, so you've had the opportunity to know a little bit
about me. I'm here and here for one reason only, that's to prosecute that man
right there, Roy Buchner.

"The reason I'm doing that is because he's guilty of murder, four counts.
This happened back almost two years ago, December of 1995, in which Mr.
Buchner joins with other individuals of the 18th Street gang and kills Ben

Anaya, Jr., Cassandra Sedillo, Johnny Garcia and Matthew Garcia. Now, as the Court told you, opening is not evidence, but it is to let you know what evidence will be presented. I will make my opening and defense and they will make theirs. We're diametrically opposed, and remember that throughout the trial.

"There's no middle ground between us. We think their client's guilty, they think he isn't. Back in December of 1995 when this occurred, you're going to hear testimony through video from Lawrence Nieto, a codefendant in this matter, a man who's already been convicted. Some of you have mentioned that in your voir dire. He will tell as what took place. And what took place was he was approached in a vehicle by Shaun Wilkins and the defendant, Mr. Buchner.

"They picked him up on that December day, persuaded him to accompany them up to the cabin. The cabin is a cabin in Torreon, Torrance County. It's within the 7th Judicial District, the same district that you are in. Your brethren are northeast. Living in that cabin at the time was Ben Anaya, Jr., his girlfriend, Cassandra Sedillo, and her two small boys. Johnny Ray was four years old at the time and Matthew was three years old at the time.

"Also residing with them was a fellow gang member by the name of Shawn Popeleski, gang name is Popcorn. Ben Anaya, Jr.'s gang name was Deuce. The defendant's gang name is Eazy. These are names that you will hear throughout the trial, and you'll want to keep note of that because often they refer to themselves in their gang names and not as their given names. Mr. Nieto, who's known as Woody, accompanies Mr. Wilkins, who's known as Sager, and the defendant, Mr. Buchner, up to the cabin. And while they're proceeding up there on that December, Mr. Wilkins is telling Mr. Nieto that he wants to kill Mr.—blast Popcorn. So they head up there with the intent already in mind to commit murder. Mr. Buchner is there with him. Mr. Buchner is sitting in the right passenger seat in agreement with all that is going on. They get up to the cabin, and they don't commit these murders right off the bat. There's a sense of lulling the victims into security. So they go into the cabin and they have a party. There's some drinking going on, some drug usage, some talking back and forth. Mr. Nieto plays with the kids.

"The defendant and Mr. Wilkins go look at the guns that Ben Anaya, Jr. has in his cabin. All this to make them feel relaxed, to make them calm. Mr. Wilkins gives a signal, which is taken by Mr. Nieto, and then him and Mr. Nieto and Mr. Buchner accompany them outside, and which at that time the plan begins to take form. When they decide that they're going to rob the inhabitants of the cabin, they go back inside. They decide once again to play like nothing's going to happen. And this is the tragedy in a sense of all this, because people get killed, get killed by people they thought were their friends. All this time, they had no realization what was about to befall them. The defendant and his cohorts then say goodbye. They leave and they go down the hill. And down the hill, the defendant puts on a mask, puts on gloves, and he arms himself with a 3006.

"Mr. Wilkins puts on gloves and a mask, changes clothing, as well as does the defendant, and arms himself with a .22 which he had shown earlier to Mr. Nieto. Mr. Nieto arms himself with a shotgun, and they wait. They wait a certain amount of time, because once again, they want to catch their victims unaware, sleeping at night. And then they sneak back up to the cabin. And as they get there, Popcorn is waiting outside. He is standing there.

"Now, according to the tape, he will testify that he's taking a leak at the time this occurs. But the front door's open. Nieto puts a shotgun on Mr. Popcorn there, holds him down, Mr. Shawn Popeleski. The defendant and Mr. Wilkins enter the cabin, and this is interesting when this takes place, because it is before they enter that cabin that their plans are to murder everyone inside, rob them of their guns and drugs and leave no witnesses, and they almost got away with it. The fact that he's here before you now means that he did not. But the whole idea was to get away with it, to commit murder and to get away with murder.

"They go into the cabin, and the reason we know that the plan is to kill, is because Nieto in his videotape that you will hear tells you that he's telling Popcorn at the time, 'I'm going to wait until I hear the shots and then I'll shoot in the air.' The shots he's waiting to hear are the shots that kill Ben Anaya, Jr., and Cassandra Sedillo. That's what he's waiting for. So, the plan all along is murder as well as robbery and burglary. They enter into the cabin, and within a short time, you hear a succession of bullets. They rob, they ransack the place, and in the meanwhile, bear in mind, we have two small children, four and three, who are in their bedroom.

"Ben Anaya, Jr. dies first. He dies from a single gunshot wound to the back of the left ear execution style by a .22. Cassandra Sedillo dies second. And the reason we know she dies second is because she suffers two wounds. She gets one into the left shoulder, which we assert to you propels her off the bed onto the ground, which exposes her right side and she is shot once again behind the right ear and killed. The two boys are in their bedroom. And Popcorn will tell you in his audio how he hears ransacking of the cabin, he hears furniture being moved. And you will see pictures of the condition of that cabin and the mess it's in.

"The defendant and Mr. Wilkins leave the cabin, taking with them the drugs and guns, put them in the car, and the three of them leave. And as they leave, they burn the gloves, they burn the masks, clothing, and the guns remain with the defendant and Mr. Wilkins and we never see them again. Now, the defense will make a big deal out of that, the physical evidence will be their song throughout this trial. They will say no physical evidence to put the individual there. We have eyewitness accounts that put the individual there. That defendant was there. He was there to commit murder and to get away with murder, and they almost did. The bodies are not discovered for four months.

"This occurs in December. And as they leave to make sure that everybody is dead, the defendant locks the front door, sealing those children within. They can't get out. You'll hear testimony from Ben Anaya, Sr. He owns the cabin. It was his son at the cabin. There's a double dead bolt lock, and the reason I say double, I might be using an incorrect term for it, if you'll look at that door over there, you'll notice that there's a key that needs to be inserted, pointing to the jury room door. Imagine on the other side the same thing. In other words, that dead bolt lock cannot be flipped. There has to be a key on both sides.

"There is no key on the inside one and the defendant makes sure that nobody can get out, because he locks the outside with the key and then throws the key away as they're going down the highway. He seals the fate of those two little boys. That's who you have sitting before you right now. You see him in the daytime. We're going to give you evidence of what he's like at night. They leave.

"As I said, they destroy evidence, physical evidence that would put them there, and they are laughing about what they have done. The defendant himself is laughing. We have nothing to worry about, we have killed all the witnesses, they're not going to get us. The plan is to get away with murder, and that will be their argument throughout this trial, but the whole purpose is to get away with murder. Time goes on. Nobody of these four individuals, especially the defendant, mentions anything about those children up there. And the defendant would have known they were alive when he left that cabin, because he was in the cabin with Mr. Wilkins and they knew they didn't shoot those kids. No phone calls, no anonymous calls to police, no nothing.

"And Johnny Ray and Matthew Garcia starve to death. Now you can imagine how you feel when you haven't had breakfast and lunch. You're going to hear testimony from Dr. McFeeley that the adults died sometime around the middle of December. Those children could have lived as long as to the first week of January.

"You will hear testimony of how they are discovered in April, and they're discovered in April by Mr. Ben Anaya, Sr. You see, the mountain cabin is hard to get to. It becomes very inaccessible for anybody but those having a four-wheel drive vehicle. It's a remote cabin. It's isolated. It's about eight miles from the town of Torreon and it's up a rocky grade. And since Mr. Ben Anaya, Sr. assumed that either his son was there, and then after the murders, he not knowing that the murders had occurred, that basically there was nobody up there, he never goes to the cabin.

"And so for four months, nobody goes up there to check to see what's happening to their kids because nobody thinks they're there, except who? The defendant. He knows they're up there. And he says nothing this whole time. We have different things happening with these four defendants. Mr. Buchner leaves, Mr. Wilkins. Mr. Nieto is dropped off by them. Mr. Popeleski gets himself off the ground, grabs the one vehicle, the four-wheel drive, that's the Jeep up there belonging to Ben Anaya, Sr., and he leaves. Not one of these guys says anything.

"Mr. Popeleski then heads down to Ben Anaya, Sr.'s house, leaves keys there, and Ben Anaya, Sr. is not there, but once again, never mentioned this, what occurred up at the cabin. So, Ben Anaya, Sr. is under the idea that the keys are left, that nobody's up at the cabin all this time, so he never goes up to check. And prior to that, he would go up to check, because he had seen his son on December 10th, he had seen him on December 3rd. He had known that he was up there, so they would bring them food. They would come to visit them. But during that week of December 12th to December 18th when these murders occurred is when the keys are returned to him, so he no longer goes up there because he thinks they left. Nobody's there.

"He doesn't know that there are two young boys up there starving to death with their dead mother in the next bedroom. Now, you can think about that and think about what little boys do when they're hungry and their mother is laying in the next room and that's how the defendant leaves them. Time goes on and in April of '96, we have Ben Anaya, Sr. going back up to the cabin at this time because the roads are more accessible now.

"It's too rocky and so forth, too snowy in the winter. And as it becomes spring, the roads are muddied, but then they dry up, so he's able to go back up. So, he and his girlfriend decide to go visit the cabin. Now, he's been burglarized before, so he wants to check and see if there's any damage done to it because they use the cabin. So they go up there. And the first thing he noticed is that the front gate is open, and you will see that in the evidence we present to you. And that's kind of unusual for him, because he had been security-minded and his young son was security-minded.

"And the truth is the defendant committed murder four times. Now, the defense may take you on whatever trip they want to take you. May take you on whatever thing they want to go with. Fires, things happening in March, because Mr. Popeleski escapes from jail in March for five hours.

"And they're going to claim he went up and started a fire there. But they won't be able to get past the part that Mr. Nieto and Mr. Popeleski both tell us the defendant is there in December committing these murders, and they can't because it's the truth. He is. When the defendant is confronted with the deaths of the children and all by Agent Jacoby, he says, 'Fuck the kids. I didn't know them.' That's the language he uses, and I'm not going to soften it for you now.

"And you will hear Agent Jacoby telling you that. That's the nature of the young man you have seated before you. We will bring you the evidence. We will show you what we have. We don't need to be cunning, we don't need to be crafty, and we won't. We will leave it in your hands. We will tell you now and we have every reason to assert that at the end of this trial, you will see the same beyond a reasonable doubt that this defendant murdered those four people for no other reason but that they wanted to. Thank you."

"Mr. Twohig, do you care to make an opening statement?"

"I do, indeed, Your Honor. May it please the Court, Mr. Bonet, Mr. Buchner, members of the jury, it's my pleasure today to represent Roy Buchner in this case.

"There are some people in the courtroom you haven't seen before. Let me introduce Maurice Moya at counsel table with me. Mr. Moya is the investigator who's worked with me throughout this case and who will be with me in the courtroom. You haven't seen him before because he hasn't been here during jury selection, and there are also a couple of witnesses who are in the courtroom who I will mention later on.

"Let me first address the prosecutor's opening statements. What you've just heard from Mr. Bonet is a summary of the foundation of the prosecution case. It is filled with emotion because of the terrible deaths which occurred here and because of the revulsion we must all feel at not only the scene in that cabin when Ben Anaya, Sr. went in there, but at the heartlessness of the actions that took place here. It is also based to a certain extent on some facts and on a good bit of finger pointing at my client. The tragedy of these deaths can't be overstated. Mr. Bonet has well pointed out the terrible results of the actions of the perpetrators here. It was unforgivable, not only that the killings took place, but that nobody did anything to notify anyone about the children being in the cabin, an easy thing that could have been done by the perpetrators of these murders in a million different ways.

"We have to go back a few years to set the stage in this situation, and we will actually see that the true perpetrator of these murders did do something to notify someone that the kids were present. This case depends, members of the jury, as I mentioned during voir dire, on physical evidence. It is a case in which statements will be made by those who committed these crimes, not from the witness stand here, but over tape recorders and over videotape machines.

"We won't have an opportunity to confront those people and cross-examine them here in this courtroom. You will see videotapes and you will hear audio tapes, but you will not hear a witness and I will not be able to cross examine the witness so that you can size up the truth of what that witness says. So we have to look at this case in a different way than we would think of looking at a murder case most of the time.

"We have to look at it from the standpoint of the statements that are made by these witnesses and the contradictions in those statements and the impossibility of the events taking place the way they said they took place. But most importantly, we have to look at the things we fundamentally look at when we attempt to solve a crime. We have to look at motive. We have to look at opportunity and we have to look at physical evidence.

"Roy was ranked into the Eighteenth Street gang, he became a member of that gang, the Westside clique of that gang in Albuquerque. Roy's father, Roy Jaramillo, his natural father, tried to show Roy the wrong direction he was going, and Roy went over to his dad's house, Roy Buchner went over to his dad's house and stayed for a good while and lived there, and Ben came over all the time. Ben was around constantly. And Ben was very, very close to Roy.

"Dan Burrola ultimately became a powerful, powerful influence on Roy. Dan is Roy's grandfather. Some of you have seen him here during jury selection. He'll be testifying, as well. He's the gentleman on the front row in the audience. Dan went to Roy Jaramillo's home and got Roy, Jr. and brought him to live with him and his wife, Syria, who is also in the courtroom, at their ranch, their small ranch in Corrales. Dan took Roy under his wing, and he said,

Roy, you have to get a job. Roy, you have to be responsible. Roy, you have to get a GED.

"Roy, you have to do these things and here's why. He explained these things to Roy and he helped Roy begin to turn his life around. Roy got a job. He went to work at Orly's Hydraulics. Probably very few of you are familiar with low-riders and low-rider magazines. I'm sure we've all seen low-riders, but Orly is the one who puts out the low-rider magazine that everyone who is involved in that field reads, and Orly also has a business in Corrales in which he makes hydraulic equipment for low-rider cars. And Roy, Jr. went to work for Orly.

"Thanksgiving time in 1995, Roy went on a little vacation, and when he came back, Orly was upset. Orly felt he didn't give him notice that he was going to leave on vacation and didn't tell him about it, he told Roy if you're late one time, if you miss work one day, I don't care what your excuse is, you're fired. And throughout the month of December of 1995, Roy worked at Orly's and he was there every morning. He clocked in at ten minutes to seven in the morning and he clocked out at 4:30 in the afternoon each weekday. You're going to hear the people he worked with come in and testify to confirm that fact.

"Thereafter, Roy went to work at Albertson's, a grocery store in Albuquerque. And after he worked there for a while, he got a better job at Jewel Osco, the new Jewel Osco store that was opening in Rio Rancho and was working there. And in mid April of 1996, Roy got a call saying that Ben Anaya, Jr. had been killed and it's all on TV. Roy and his girlfriend, Margaret, whom you'll hear testify, Margaret Espinosa, watched it on television. Roy was so upset he could hardly watch it. He went to Ben's funeral. He went to the rosary. He wore the T-shirt, 'In Loving Memory of Ben,' because Ben had been one of his closest friends.

"Ben had gone in a little bit different direction than Roy. Ben had gotten into more violence, had gotten into burglaries and had gotten sent off to Springer when he was a juvenile. While in Springer, he became close with Popeleski, aka 'Popcorn' with Shaun Wilkins, Lawrence Nieto, and began to hang out with them more. Roy didn't hang out with them quite as much. And after Ben got back from Springer, Roy didn't have much contact with Ben.

"Roy was amazed, distressed, shocked to be brought in and accused of committing these murders, dumb-founded. And when asked about how do you feel, Roy, about the girl that—about Cassandra and the two kids, aren't you upset about that. He said no, I'm not upset, I'm upset about Ben, I didn't even know them. Ben is the one that upsets me, Ben is my close homeboy, my partner. And that's what he was upset about.

"Now, while Roy was working and spending most of his weekday evenings with his girlfriend and while he was at his grandfather's, some things happened. And I want to go through some of these things that are additional background that are important to know in understanding this case and the motives behind this case. We have to go back to August 9th of 1995.

"At that time, Popcorn, we call him Popcorn, Popeleski, held a knife to a girl's throat and took her car, hijacked her car, carjacking. And along with Ben Anaya and Shaun Wilkins, and Frank Gomez (aka Joseph Espinosa) drove that car to Arizona, where they were arrested in Winslow on August 12th. The one who identified himself as Frank Gomez actually is not Frank Gomez. He's a man named, a young man named Joseph Espinosa. From then on, though, Popeleski used that alias, and that really upset Espinosa. These are all Eighteenth Streeters. Popeleski remained in Arizona while the others came back to Albuquerque, and it was believed by Espinosa that Popeleski was claiming that Espinosa and others actually had stolen this car, when it was Popeleski who put the knife to the girl's throat and took the car.

"That's one little tidbit that fits in, as you'll see soon. Later that same month, on August thirty-first, nineteen ninety-five, 1995, Ben Anaya, Jr. and two others committed a burglary of the home of Mr. Vandenburg in Albuquerque. And in that burglary, in addition to money and jewelry and things of that sort, stole nine firearms. The very next day, Ben Jr. was shot accidentally by one of his crime partners in that little burglary. And the police came. They were called to Ben Jr.'s home where the shooting had taken place, and at that time recovered four of the firearms that were taken in that burglary. The remaining firearms were not recovered at that time, but do show up later in this case. Please keep that in mind.

"On September fifteenth, nineteen ninety-five, only a half a month later, Shawn Popeleski, Popcorn, using the name Frank Gomez, was found sleeping in another car he had stolen. As you'll see, he's been a car thief and a burglar a good bit. He stole it from the eighty-eight hundred block of Candelaria, and when he was found sleeping in this car a few blocks away by the man from whom he had stolen it, who called the police, he lied and claimed that Dominic Molina had stolen the car. Molina was an 18th Street gang member. Molina got very upset that he was charged with stealing the car based on Popcorn's word, when in fact it was Popcorn who had stolen the car. You'll see how all this fits together in just a minute.

"On November five, ninety-five, Ben Anaya, Jr. was arrested for battery on a police officer. He bonded out of jail.

"On November fourteenth, Ben and Shaun Wilkins were arrested. Ben had warrants out for the burglary in which the firearms were stolen. Shaun Wilkins had warrants out on other matters. Ben got out of jail on that one. And during this time back in November now that we're dealing with, some other things were taking place. Popeleski was back in Albuquerque from his Arizona sojourn, he had been released, because he, you see, was going to be testifying as a witness against his fellow Eighteenth Street gang members, and was living at Nieto's home part of the time, at Ben Anaya, Jr.'s part of the time.

"Popcorn was kind of bouncing back and forth between the two. When Shaun Wilkins got out of jail at that time in November, he and Molina and Espinosa began to talk about Popcorn and what Popcorn had been doing to them, and they decided that he should no longer be an Eighteenth Streeter, he shouldn't be in their gang anymore. What they did was called ranking out, they wanted to rank him out, they wanted to get him out of the gang. Ranking out takes place much the same way as ranking in does. Ranking in occurs when the gang members beat you up, put you through an ordeal, running the gauntlet sort. Ranking out is the same way, but much less friendly.

"In November, as I say, Popeleski and Nieto were roommates. They were living together part of the time. Ben Anaya, Jr. also had Popeleski living with him part of the time. And they set up this party that was going to take place on November thirtieth. As you can see, now we're getting up closer to the date of these murders and these dates become pretty important.

"These Eighteenth Streeters talked to Ben Anaya, Jr. and they told Ben that they were going to rank out Popcorn, and they said we're going to be at this party and that's where we're going to do it. And Ben brought him to the party so they could rank him out, and that's exactly what happened. They beat him up, they worked him over with a baseball bat, and they ranked him out of the Westside Eighteenth Street. He was ostracized.

"That evening he went on back to the cabin with Ben and Cassandra and soon was ostracized by them, as well. That was too much to take for Popeleski. Here was Ben who had the guns he had stolen in this earlier burglary that was living a pretty carefree life out in the cabin. Popcorn was ostracized and he learned that Ben knew and had agreed with the ranking out. He knew that he had taken him and set him up to be ranked out.

"So on the night of December eleventh, nineteen ninety-five, Ben Anaya and Cassandra Sedillo were killed by Shawn Popeleski. They were killed with not a .22 pistol, but with a .22 rifle, a very important detail in this case. Ben was shot first, Cassandra woke up, was shot once, as Mr. Bonet has said, and then shot at closer range and killed. And you'll hear about these three .22 bullets that were used to kill her. These are .22 long rifle ammunition that were shot from a rifle, not from a pistol, as claimed later by the two prosecution witnesses. Let's go back a moment to the day before the killing.

"December tenth, nineteen ninety-five. That's an important date, too, because that's the day that Ben Anaya, Sr. comes up to the cabin to see his son and Cassandra, to bring them some food, to see how they're getting along. And another thing that he brings with him in addition to food is a brand new dead bolt lock. And the reason he does that is because the dead bolt lock on the front door is broken, not working anymore, and the front door was held closed by tape. And they were conscious, as Mr. Bonet has said, and so Ben brought up this dead bolt lock. The dead bolt lock, just as Mr. Bonet has explained it, has to have a key to open it, whether on the inside or on the outside, and this dead bolt lock had two keys. Two keys. Leave these keys in mind. He left the dead bolt lock with Popeleski to install and Popeleski did install.

"Now, the killing takes place. You're going to hear the version the prosecution is offering. You're going to hear Popcorn's version. You're going to hear Nieto's version of how this occurred. And one thing you're going to find is that the keys tell the tale of this case in its most simple form and the physical evidence really tells the story in fine detail.

"When Popcorn left after committing these murders, he took the two keys with him to the dead bolt. He took some other things, as well. He took Ben Anaya's beeper, his pager. He took some tools from the cabin. He took a number of other things, including the Jeep. He took some of the firearms that Ben had stolen in the earlier burglary. These are all things, which we're going to prove to you by showing you exactly where these items were recovered. This is not guesswork. This is fact.

"He took the two dead bolt keys, and what he did was he went and did another break-in the next day, the twelfth of December. That break-in, believe it or not, was at Ben Anaya, Sr.'s home. He drove the Jeep in broad daylight about ten o'clock in the morning right into the driveway, thinking nobody would be home. He got out, he used one of the keys to Ben Anaya, Sr.'s house that had been on the key ring. He didn't have to break in. He opened the front door himself. He went into the house. He helped himself to money, to jewelry, to whatever he wanted to in the house, basically committing a run-of-the-mill Popcorn burglary, but he did one other thing. He sort of kind of maybe slightly left a little message there that maybe Ben should go look for the keys.

"And here's how he did it. In Ben's closet was a jacket that Ben wore a lot. And later after the twelfth, Ben found in that jacket pocket a set of keys to the cabin, including a key to the dead bolt. On the twelfth when Popeleski came to the cabin, he had put that set of keys in Ben Anaya, Sr.'s jacket. That's one key to the dead bolt. That's one key to the dead bolt. Ben Anaya didn't get the message. It was a little too obscure for him. He didn't realize that this was a message to go to the cabin and he didn't go to the cabin.

"I should mention one other thing. In the Jeep that Popcorn took were clothes that Cassandra had just washed, the kids' clothes were in the Jeep. They had just been to Ben Sr.'s house on the day of the eleventh and those clothes were washed at Ben's house on the eleventh. So the day before this break-in on the twelfth, that laundry had been done and it remained in the Jeep unloaded. It wasn't unloaded and taken into the house yet that evening.

"You will also hear from Ms. Sedillo, the mother to Cassandra and grandmother to Matthew and Johnny Garcia. Ms. Sedillo found a garbage bag at her back door in January of nineteen ninety-six. The bag contained the boys' clothes and their winter jackets so how did the clothes get out of the Jeep and onto her back door? The only one who had the Jeep was Popcorn. So he must have dropped off the clothes.

"On the eleventh also, along about four o'clock that afternoon, four-thirty, when Roy Buchner got off work, his granddad, Dan Burrola, came and picked him up. Same day, the eleventh, that this killing took place. Dan Burrola came and picked Roy up after work, went out to the Department of Motor Vehicles in Rio Rancho and changed the title on his car from Dan to Roy. Dan gave Roy his car, his Lincoln, and so then it became Roy's car on the eleventh. So, this story about how the murders occurred, they went and partied all afternoon, could not have taken place on the eleventh if Roy Buchner was involved.

"Let's go back to Popeleski, though. What did Popeleski do after he broke in and went into Ben Anaya's house and committed this burglary? He then left and he attempted to sell some guns. And paradoxical as it is, one of the people that he tried to sell some of these guns to is Jeremy Sedillo, Cassandra Sedillo's little brother. Jeremy was at Green Eyes' house. Jeremy was a little kind of a wanna-be gangbanger kid, and he was over at his friend Green Eyes' house, and there was Popcorn trying to sell some of the guns to Jeremy Sedillo. Didn't say anything about his sister. Didn't say anything about the kids. Didn't say a word. The police never talked to Green Eyes who bought guns from Popcorn. Is it possible that Popcorn could have sold him the .22 rifle that was used to commit the murders.

"On the fifteenth of December, Popeleski runs into a young fellow named Richard Munoz, a kid who wanted to go see his relatives down near Dallas, Texas. Popeleski said, oh, I'll give you a ride. And so off they went. And when they left on the eighteenth, Popeleski went down to Pecos, Texas. That's how far he got. He drove through El Paso, drove down I-25, right past here through El Paso, made a turn and headed over and went as far as Pecos, Texas.

"In Pecos, Texas, the Jeep broke down, and so Popeleski and Munoz had to come back to Albuquerque. They had to get back on the bus. And when they came back on the bus, they couldn't bring the rifles on the bus that were in the Jeep, so they left them there. So, Popeleski left one of the rifles that he had taken from Ben Anaya, Jr. in the cabin that Ben Anaya had stolen in this burglary back in August.

"Popeleski came back to Albuquerque and was arrested on December twenty-fifth, nineteen ninety-five in Belen in a commercial burglary of a car wash. When he was arrested, he had certain things on him, which we have recovered. Those things included a beeper, a beeper belonging to Ben Anaya, Jr. We will show you the connection between that beeper and Ben Anaya, Jr. and show you that it was his beeper number by bringing in a witness who had his number, who called it and who knew the BIN number and it exactly matches the beeper.

"In addition, another thing that was discovered when he was arrested were some tools, tools that appeared to have come from the cabin. They remained with Popeleski and that he kept and that he used in that burglary in Belen. Well, you say, did he bring them back on the bus from Pecos, Texas, did he bring this sort of handmade hammer, did he bring these screwdrivers, did he bring this knife back on the bus? No.

"Here's what happened. Popeleski hadn't heard anything about Ben and Cassandra's bodies being discovered. Popeleski needed to do something to find out what had happened. He hadn't read anything about it in the paper. He hadn't heard about it from anybody, he hadn't seen it on TV, so he went back up to the cabin and he let himself in the cabin with his key that he had, that he had hidden somewhere.

"He had the other key of the two dead bolt keys. Popeleski took that and went back to the cabin. And when he got there, he saw that the children were dead, that Ben and Cassandra were dead, which he knew, since he did it, and he decided he had to do something about what had happened. It was obvious he was going to be linked to this whole thing. After all, he lived there, so he decided to torch the place. The ultimate solution for a crime where physical evidence could present a problem, burn the evidence.

"And he set fires. You'll hear from arson investigator Tony Anaya, who will explain to you how these fires were set and that the fires in this cabin were by no means accidental, were not set by the children looking for their mother or looking for food in their desperation. They were set to burn the evidence. He tried to torch the place, but despite his talents as a burglar, he's not much of an arsonist.

"He tried in several different ways to set fires. He set one in the couch. You could see the matches right on the couch where he tried to set it. He used accelerants. We hear about accelerants and we know that there are such things as accelerants, but some people can use them better than others. He punched holes in paint cans. He punched holes in all kinds of other cans and bottles and jars that would emit fumes that would help to torch the place, to blow the place. And he was unsuccessful because there's one little principle of fire that Mr. Popeleski wasn't aware of, and that is fire needs oxygen to burn, and if you close all the doors and you close all the windows, the fire burns for a little while, but when it uses up all the oxygen, it burns out, so he failed.

"Then on December twenty-fifth, as I said, Mr. Popeleski got arrested again, and he was locked in the Valencia County jail, and there he was watching the TV every evening, catching the news all the time and not seeing anything about any fire, about anybody being discovered, about any murders, about any deaths, about any children dying or anything of that sort, and he couldn't stand it.

"March the twenty-third, nineteen ninety-six, Mr. Popeleski and two of his friends escaped from the Valencia County jail, and it just so happens we have their escape on videotape. And they escaped on the twenty-third, as I say, of March. And Danny Saiz and Danny Silva were the other two people who escaped with him. Mr. Silva will come in and testify. Mr. Popeleski won't, Mr. Silva will. And what they did after they escaped included going back to the cabin. Mr. Popeleski tried yet again to burn the cabin and was yet again unsuccessful. He left the heaters on full blast. He used more accelerants. He moved one of the children from the bed down onto the top of an area he had tried to burn before and in the area of debris and fire.

"This is the same day Ms. Zenner is out watching the comet when she heard the noise from Ben's cabin and thought there was a party going on. She too will come in and testify.

"And one other thing that an accomplished criminal burglar will do. He wiped the place for prints. Mr. Bonet is correct that no prints were discovered. If you had little children running around in there, if you had adults living in there, at least a single fingerprint would emerge. There was not a single fingerprint on anything. The absence of prints demonstrates the place was wiped and was wiped by Popeleski when he went back up there and attempted to torch the place. The physical evidence confirms it.

"And it confirms, among other things, that the way everything was thrown around in that cabin, the way everything was torn up in that cabin, children couldn't have done it. Things that were too heavy that had to be moved were moved. Three and four-year-old children can't do that. We'll prove that to you. Popeleski tried to torch the place yet again on the twenty-third, and as was his fate throughout all of his efforts, he was unsuccessful, yet again, in torching the place.

"Let's look at March the twenty-fourth. March the twenty-fourth, Mr. Popeleski gets caught in a stolen car, a surprise. He steals a car. And in the car are discovered after a high-speed chase trying to elude police, he's caught in Albuquerque, and fortunately, the officers had photographs taken. So, a criminalist came out, a field investigator, I should say, from the Albuquerque Police Department came out and took pictures of the car, and there in the car are screwdrivers, screwdrivers from the cabin.

"Now, when Ben Anaya, Sr. went to the cabin on April the fourteenth or fifteenth, I forget which day in mid April, what he found was the front gate was wide open. That's right. He put his keys in the front gate and opened it. Then he went in and he put his key into the dead bolt lock on the front door, which was locked. When the police searched the cabin, they did not find another key to that dead bolt lock. What they did find was a key to the interior dead bolt lock, the lock to the master bedroom, and that key was there when Ben Anaya, Sr. came in. And he turned that key in the lock and opened that door and let himself into the bedroom.

"The killer can use the second key to the dead bolt lock and had let himself in and out, in and out of that cabin and tried to torch it at least twice, maybe three times. Popeleski was arrested on the twenty-fourth of March, as I say. And in order to encourage Popeleski to give him a little—give them some information when the police discovered these bodies in April, they provided him with a little help. First, Popeleski contended that one person might have done this, then another person might have done this, then that he didn't know anything about it, then that maybe he did know a little about it. And the story emerged that Popeleski maybe knew a little bit about it but didn't want to talk about it, and then finally, yeah, he was there.

"And one of the officers in this case, Juan DeReyes, is a separate completely different interesting and very related and important part of this case. He'll be here to testify. Juan DeReyes is with the gang unit of the Albuquerque Police Department. Mr. DeReyes was assigned to investigate this case because it's his role in the Albuquerque Police Department to investigate the 18th Street gang members and attempt to prosecute them. Unfortunately for Mr. DeReyes, something happened to him personally a while back that really bothered him, and that something was that there was a drive-by shooting at his home and he believed that Shaun Wilkins did it. And his family had to move, had to relocate because of this drive-by shooting, and he was very upset about that. It was, as he said during his interrogation of Nieto, personal. Mr. DeReyes is the officer that cracked this case in the prosecution approach.

"And what he did is he brought up Wilkins and he brought up Wilkins and he brought up Wilkins and he brought up Wilkins in his interrogations of Nieto and Popeleski. And pretty soon, pretty soon, like a rat on a sinking ship, Shawn Popeleski grabbed at the life raft and said, yeah, Wilkins was there. And then the story emerged and emerged and emerged that Wilkins was there and Wilkins was there. And Nieto and Popeleski, who had been roommates, came up with this whole story about Wilkins being there. Roy Buchner was an afterthought. He wasn't brought up until much later. Nobody mentioned Buchner. Popeleski, when asked about Buchner to begin with, said, no, he wasn't there.

"So, the story emerges through interrogation, through motivated interrogation that makes Shaun Wilkins the killer, that makes Roy Buchner his accomplice, and the physical evidence, the physical evidence simply disproves that, the physical evidence and the incredible contradictions of these witnesses.

"Popeleski was highly motivated. He wanted to avoid the death penalty. He wanted to avoid his own conviction for murder. He wanted to blame it on someone else, as he almost always did in the past.

"The prosecution version depends on no physical evidence whatsoever. It's not because they wore gloves. According to the prosecution version, they didn't wear gloves all during this afternoon-long party that occurred on the day of the alleged killings. So, that would mean that they would have left fingerprints on cans, on glasses, on potato chip bags, on all kinds of other things in there, but there were no fingerprints. There were no fingerprints of Roy Buchner and Shaun Wilkins. There were no fingerprints at all because Popeleski wiped the place.

"Certain physical evidence is the key to unmasking what occurred here. It proves that these prosecution non-witnesses who won't be here to testify are liars. When he leaves the cabin after the killing, Popeleski takes certain things with him, a beeper, a knife, firearms Ben stole, his own clothes, keys to the Jeep, keys to the cabin, the Jeep itself. The keys were left in Ben Anaya's pocket in the burglary of Ben's home on the twelfth. It's one set. Their set was needed to get back in the cabin. When he was with Richard Munoz, Popeleski had plenty of money.

"When he's caught at the burglary on December twenty-fifth, things directly from the cabin were seized from him. Examination of the crime scene proves that he went back and tried to start fires. It proves that and you'll see expert witnesses come in here and break this apart for you item-by-item, photograph-by-photograph. It proves that he went back and tried to start fires and that the kids did not knock these things over and did not start these fires.

"The weapon that was used is specifically inconsistent with the prosecution theory of a twenty-two pistol. It could not have been a twenty-two pistol. The cabin is in an isolated area and the evidence will demonstrate that Ben Jr. was extraordinarily security-conscious. It would not have been unlocked and opened with the keys in the Jeep the way Popeleski claims.

"Popeleski was never allowed to drive the Jeep by Ben Jr. Ben Sr. will establish that. He never did so until the day after the killings, when on the twelfth, he was seen getting out of the vehicle, on the driver's seat of the vehicle in the driveway of Ben Anaya, Sr.'s home. The details at the crime scene in great detail will prove that Popcorn did it.

"Most importantly probably of all is that we must have defendants with an opportunity to commit a crime in order for the crime to have occurred and must have a motive. The motive claimed by the prosecution plainly and simply is robbery in this case, robbery committed by Roy Buchner of his closest friend, one of his two closet friends, probably, and murder of that closest friend in order to obtain apparently it's believed some guns and drugs. But the details prove that that motive is not it.

"The motive, Shawn Popeleski's motive, he's the one with the motive; he's the one that was taken to the ranking out. He's the one who left the note at the murder scene, Joe is cool, mess around, or fuck around, I believe it said, and you'll get messed up. Now, the second thing you must have is opportunity.

In order for this story concocted by Popeleski and his roommate Nieto to have occurred the way in anything like they said it did, certain things have to have happened.

"First of all, all four people had to be there, Nieto, Popeleski, Wilkins and Buchner. So, if we take a look at where Buchner was and where Wilkins was and where Nieto was, that would help us to determine whether the opportunity actually existed for it to occur that way.

"Shaun Wilkins was in jail from December sixth until the late evening of December eleventh. He got out the late evening of December eleventh. He was with friends of his on December twelfth. Roy Buchner went to change the title to his car the afternoon of the eleventh. Roy Buchner then went home. Roy Buchner was at work the next day. He was at work every day that week. He was at work every day the next week.

"The version of the prosecution is that there was a party that started in the afternoon well before Roy Buchner could ever have gotten out of work and gotten out to this cabin. Nieto went to Juarez. He left on December the twelfth with three girls and another boy and they went to Juarez, and they went down there because they were under age and they could drink in Juarez. So they all got together and went down there, and Nieto and these three girls and the other fellow came back on the seventeenth of December to Albuquerque.

"Popeleski left Albuquerque on the eighteenth with Richard Munoz and went down to Pecos, Texas and was down there until the twenty-second of December. They stayed in a Holiday Inn, the records are clear about that, and he came back on the bus. The burglary of Ben Anaya, Sr.'s home took place on the twelfth, the twelfth of December. So, the killing took place before the twelfth. Otherwise, Popeleski would not have been in the Jeep by himself driving the Jeep and would not have left the keys in Ben Anaya, Sr.'s jacket. It had to take place on the eleventh.

"And at that time, Buchner was at work all day and then at DMV and Shaun Wilkins was locked up in jail. Members of the jury, when you finish listening to the details of this case, and I told you during voir dire there are a lot of details, you will find not only that the prosecution has not proven the case, but also that the prosecution's star witness, Shawn Popeleski, is the killer.

"And you'll find that without any hesitation, without any doubt, and that the stories that he concocted with the aid and duress, and that Nieto went along, blaming Shaun Wilkins and Roy Buchner, are simply false and unbelievable and the flakiest thing you can ever imagine to base a criminal prosecution on. I ask you to find Roy Buchner not guilty. Thank you."

This was the start we gave them the time line from the beginning. We did it during the trial, I did it in my testimony and Ray did it again at closing. We believed if the jury hears the information three times and then they get to see it on the "Time Line" they would understand the events by the end of the trial.

"The Cops Forced Me To Say What I was Saying"

Popcorn was their first witness but he was not transported from jail. His attorney got up and advised the court he would not testify. Popcorn would take the Fifth Amendment.

The DA announced they would be calling Woody next but Mr. Mitchell (Woody's Attorney) was not there yet. The attorney for Popcorn stood back up. "Your honor I talked with Mr. Mitchell and he has other matters this morning but he has spoken to his client."

The DA got back up. "Your honor we have been advised Woody is going to take the Fifth as well."

The judge was Judge Fitz and we could not have asked for a wiser and more equal judge. "Okay, thank you."

Popcorn came in, in a prison jump suit and shackles. After giving his name they asked him to identify Roy. "He's right there on the left." After that Popcorn took the Fifth on the rest of the questions.

Ray however knew the Fifth better than anyone in the courthouse. "Mr. Popeleski did you plead guilty to a felony on...."

His attorney went to bench to argue we had the documents on Popcorn and we could introduce them. The judge agreed with Ray. "You can ask those questions."

"You were arrested and then released from custody. Placed on probation to Levi Lovato (Investigator) from the DA's office and Michael Fenner from the State Police."

"Yea."

"Did you ever report to them?"

"I plead the Fifth."

Popcorn was excused and we never got our chance to talk to him. So much for the right of confrontation for the accused. Mady Malka's plan was working. Only the tapes of Popcorn and Woody would be the testimony.

"The State calls Woodrow Nieto."

Woody took the stand and stated immediately, "I plead the Fifth sir."

"Is your attorney going to be here today?"

"No, sir Your Honor."

"Is it your intention to take the Fifth to every questions asked of you?"

"Yeah."

"Do you understand you no longer have the right to the Fifth since you testified in your own trial?"

"I take the Fifth."

The DA asked Woody, "Could you point out Roy Buchner?"

"He's right there."

"Is he in same gang?"

"I don't have anything to say."

"Do you recall being with him at the cabin?"

"Huh-huh."

"I can't hear you?"

"I don't have anything to say."

"No further questions."

Ray got up. "Mr. Nieto, you've said that you're not going to answer questions, right?"

"Yes, sir."

"That's because you have already been convicted of murder?"

"True."

"You said you already have enough time."

"Yea. They convicted me. I don't have to say anything."

"And if I start asking you questions about what you were doing in December and where Mr. Popeleski was and when you two got together, are you going to answer my questions?"

My hands went from my face to my best friend, laptop.

"I wasn't with them in December."

"At all?"

"At all."

"When were you in Juarez? The date you left and came back?"

"I left on the twelfth of December and got back on the eighteenth."

"Who were you with?"

"Laura, Janessa, and Polita and Justin."

"Did you get stuck in Ruidoso?"

"Yes sir at Laura's aunt's house."

Ray was unbelievable and he had Woody eating out of the palm of his hand. Woody had a chance to tell the truth and he knew, we knew the truth.

"Then did Laura's mom go pick you up?"

"Yes sir. She brought us back to Albuquerque."

"Were you in Albuquerque from the twelfth to the eighteenth?"

"No, sir."

"In November did Popcorn live with you?"

"Only for a week, my mom kicked him out."

"If I ask you questions about what happened at the cabin that led to your conviction are you going to answer?"

Ray was going nice and slow with Woody and calling him Mr. Nieto.

"I don't know. I wasn't there. That's all I'm going to say."

The DA felt compelled to ask some question, and that was his worst mistake. He felt he could lead Woody. "You left on the twelfth?"

"Yeah."

"Now was that after the murders happened? After Mr. Wilkins and Buchner murdered Ben Anaya Jr.?"

"They didn't murder them, man."

"They didn't murder them?"

"No."

"Do you recall your testimony on tape that they murdered?"

"The cops forced me to say what I was saying."

"I see."

"They don't have nothing to do with it. I don't have nothing to do with it. I don't know."

"Do you recall in your own trial that Shaun Wilkins and Roy Buchner went into the cabin and Wilkins shot Ben Anaya?"

"I didn't say that."

"You don't recall?"

"He wasn't there man."

"He wasn't there?"

"No, nor Wilkins or me. Everything I said on tape was the cops were pushing me and ever thing because of what Popeleski had said."

"Are you concerned about gang retaliation for your testimony?"

"I'm not concerned at all."

"You're just not worried?"

"We weren't there, man. I mean I messed up and shit. You know but, I mean, we weren't there, man. He wasn't there. Buchner wasn't there. Wilkins wasn't there. I wasn't there."

"I see."

"It's just that when the cops were harassing me and stuff, I was leading with you, what Popeleski said."

"So when they came and picked you up in a vehicle and took you to the cabin..."

"They didn't pick me up."

"When you say you guys partied, you drank beer and all that stuff."

"It didn't take place."

"You're changing your story now?"

"I'm not changing. That's just the truth that I'm trying to come out with. I never said I killed them."

"Didn't you say you were at the cabin and heard shots?"

"No."

"We're going to play your video. The video is going to show all of that."

"I don't have nothing to say."

"Where are you now?"

"In prison in Grants."

"No further questions."

Ray saw all kinds of openings. "You said the police put pressure on you?"

"Yeah."

"And there is a video of your statement?"

"The early ones were the ones that really, the first ones that were."

"Who put pressure on you?"

"Gang unit and that guy right there."

"Who?"

"The gang unit and that Agent Jacoby."

"You mean Officer DeReyes?"

"Yeah."

We couldn't have asked for a better beginning. Agent Jacoby was at counsel table with his hand on his forehead his thumbs digging in. It was going to be a long three weeks for him.

On the third day the DA brought in the ATF agent who fought the subpoena because he had been reassigned to DC. He now had an important job. He was too busy to return to New Mexico. He was asked if he would like to have the US Marshal bring him to court. The agent agreed to honor the out of state subpoena.

After the ATF agent got our report from our expert Tony Anaya he revisited the cabin and found a series of fires and was now walking to the beat of our drum.

He had to stay with his theory "The space heater caused the fire." Then he changed it to the radiant heat from the heater that caused the fire.

With the help of Tony Anaya, Ray trashed the preliminary report of the agent. The agent had changed his mind several times as to which furnace was on at the time of entry. Ray got him to agree the boy's body had been moved to the burnt spot on the rug after the fire on the carpet was started.

The agent had no excuse for missing the sofa chair and how there was no soot on the bottom of the chair and how there was no soot behind the picture frame in the living room.

Ray went over with him how the blinds in the living room had melted but did not fall below and the window but instead were found in the kitchen. He had no notes on the blinds.

They went over all the protected areas on the wall and in the pantry. He had no notes on these subjects. Ray covered the smoke on the ceiling. He had no explanation for any of Ray's cross exam.

Most of his excuses were, "It was getting dark. It was around seven pm." This must have been the reason he didn't see all the matches on the floor. After his cross exam the agent left the stand, high stepping it out the door, with his head lowered, never looking at anyone.

The investigator for the DA's office was Levi Lovato. He was called by the defense to testify.

"Call Levi Lovato."

"Would you give your name, please, sir?"

"Levi Lovato."

"Mr. Lovato, what's your occupation?"

"I'm an investigator with the DA's office, Seventh Judicial District."

"What area does the Seventh Judicial District cover?"

"Catron, Sierra and Torrance Counties."

"And where is your office located?"

"In Estancia."

"And that's Torrance County?"

"Yes."

"Were you involved in doing some work in connection with the homicides that led to this case?"

"Interviewing defense witnesses."

"Did you also deal with locating some exhibits at the cabin?"

"In June of this year."

"All right. Let me show you something. I want to show you Defendant's Exhibit VVV and ask if you recognize it."

"Yes, I do."

"What is that?"

"It's an electric heater."

"Did you have anything to do with removing that from the cabin?"

"Yes, I did."

"When did you do that?"

"I don't remember the specific date, but it was in June of this year."

"June of nineteen ninety-seven?"

"Yes."

"So this would be more than a year, year and several months, I guess, after the bodies were recovered?"

"Yes."

"And after the crime scene was cleared?"

"Yes."

"Where did you locate that heater, Exhibit VVV?"

"This particular heater was inside the cabin and close or in proximity to the door where the kids were found."

"And when you went to the cabin to recover this heater, was the scene still essentially intact as it had been when the bodies were recovered and over the first few days after that?"

"Yes."

"Mr. Lovato, had you been to the cabin before this date in June?"

"Yes."

"On how many occasions?"

"Three times altogether."

"And did you find another heater?"

"Yes, I did."

"Where did you find it?"

"This was outside on the north, I'd say northeast side of the cabin."

"What type of heater was it?"

"It appeared that it was an electric heater."

"All right. Now, did you ever try to plug either of the heaters in?"

"Yes, I did."

"Which one?"

"This one right here."

"Exhibit VVV?"

"VVV."

"Did it work?"

"Yes, it did."

"This other heater here, we've got marked as Exhibit Six F's, that's six different F's in a row. Let me ask you if you can look at that and ask you if you can identify it. Can you?"

"Yes."

"Is that the other heater you found?"

"Yes."

"Did you ever determine whether it worked or not?"

"I never tried it."

"Did you ever find a large upright heater anywhere around there?"

"That was a, I think it was a brown one, a brown heater that was outside the front door to the cabin."

"It was tall and round?"

"I'm not sure if it was round. I don't think it was totally round. It was square. I remember that it was propane."

"Where were the heaters kept from then until now?"

"For a short while they were kept with me until the Shaun Wilkins trial began, and from that point on, they stayed with Deputy District Attorney Bonet."

"Sir, I want to show you a couple of documents here, Defendant's Exhibits A and B. I want to ask if you recognize those."

"I have seen them."

"What are they?"

"A is a plea and disposition agreement on State of New Mexico versus Shawn Popeleski. And the next is State of New Mexico, Plaintiff, versus Shawn Popeleski. This is B, document B, and says this is a judgment and sentence and order suspending sentence."

"A couple of questions I wanted to ask you, sir, and maybe I can put these, one of these under the scanner here so we can see it. Sir, as we look at Exhibit A, plea agreement from Mr. Popeleski, it appears to say that it takes place in the Thirteenth Judicial District, County of Valencia, you see that?"

"Yes."

"What area is the Thirteenth Judicial District?"

"I think it encompasses a few counties but I'm not sure. I know Valencia is one, maybe Cibola County. I'm not sure."

"So, Mr. Lopez is the district attorney whom you work for?"

"Yes."

"And you don't work for the DA who was handling this case right here?"

"No, I do not."

"Sir, in this exhibit, Exhibit A, which is the plea agreement from Mr. Popeleski, there is a reference that I wanted to show you. There's a reference to an agreement entered into concerning the disposition of the charges. Have you had a chance to look at that and read it?"

"Not here recently."

"Well, sir, I wonder if we could go over a couple of things in here, please. First of all, one of the terms of the plea agreement is that Mr. Popeleski will be placed on probation for a period of five years. You see that?"

"I can't."

"Do you remember that, 'Defendant will serve probation for a period of five years at a location out of state'?"

"Okay."

"You remember reading that?"

"Yes."

"And there are a couple of other terms there, but then D says, 'Defendant will contact either Levi Lovato or Mike Fenner on a weekly basis.' You see that?"

"Yes."

"And is that you, Levi Lovato?"

"Yes."

"So then back when Mr. Popeleski went on probation on November twelfth, 1996, he was to contact you every week, right?"

"I was as a secondary contact at that time as it was explained to me by Mike Fenner."

"Mr. Fenner is the primary contact?"

"He was to be the primary contact."

"Well, who is Mr. Fenner?"

"New Mexico State Police officer or agent in that period of time."

"Mr. Fenner is one of the agents that had been investigating this case, isn't he?"

"Yes."

"Very much involved in investigating these homicides that led to this case, correct?"

"Yes."

"And you were involved in investigating this case, too, for the District Attorney's office?"

"Doing witness interviews from defense witnesses."

"Well, sir, how is it that this arrangement was made in Mr. Popeleski's agreement where he was to contact you or Mr. Fenner on a weekly basis and be put on probation?"

"I was never told why that plea agreement was made like that. All I know is that I received a phone call from Mike Fenner asking me if it would be okay for me to—for him to put my name on that witness list primarily to keep in contact with a witness at that point in time."

"Mr. Popeleski was a witness?"

"Yes."

"Mr. Popeleski had not been charged with these murders at that time, had he?"

"No, he had not."

"When were those charges filed?"

"Specific dates I don't remember."

"But it was in 1997, wasn't it?"

"That's correct."

"So then Mr. Popeleski was placed on probation in November of '96 and then charged with these murders in the summertime of 1997, right?"

"That's correct."

"Did he ever call you or report to you on a weekly basis like he was supposed to?"

"Not that I recall, he never called me."

"Sir, this is the court order that follows that plea agreement, is that right?"

"Yes."

"And like the plea agreement itself, it's from the Thirteenth Judicial District, right?"

"That's correct."

"And it is the judgment which implements or carries out the plea agreement, correct?"

"That's correct."

"And it is the order of the judge, isn't it?"

"That's correct."

"And this order as a result of that plea agreement did put Mr. Popeleski on probation, didn't it?"

"That's correct."

"Now, sir, when it says that a sentence is imposed and then a sentence is suspended, I realize it's a little hard for everyone to read, sir, and I'm sure that it can be read up close better, but just so that we can go over this, it says, 'The sentence is suspended and the Defendant is placed on supervised probation for a period of five years.' You see that?"

"Yes."

"So that's the way it was going to be as far as the plea agreement was concerned, right?"

"I have no idea what the plea agreement was. I saw these documents after the fact during the Shaun Wilkins trial, which was about a month or two ago."

"But that is what I just showed you, the plea agreement?"

"Yes."

"So that's what the plea agreement calls for is this probation, correct?"

"Yes."

"And just like the plea agreement calls for, Mr. Popeleski was supposed to, as it said, contact either you or Michael Fenner on a weekly basis, right?"

"That's what it says, yes, sir."

"And that's the court order that says he's supposed to do that?"

"That's correct."

"And he never did it, did he?"

"Not to my knowledge, he never contacted me."

"No further questions."

Then there was the cross examination by Mr. Bonet:

"Now, also why don't you explain to the jury how it is that you ended up getting your name listed on that?" Ray asked.

"I got—close to this timeframe I received a call from Agent Mike Fenner from the New Mexico State Police Department. He asked if it would be okay for me to be placed on this witness list, I mean on this plea agreement to keep in contact with Shawn Popeleski for witness purposes. It is my duty to keep track—I felt at that time that it would be a good idea to do that because he was a witness in this particular case. This would give me a better chance of locating a witness than not having anything and starting from scratch."

"Was there ever any deal made with us and the Thirteenth Judicial District, when I mean us, I mean the attorneys for the Seventh Judicial District and the Thirteenth Judicial District, was there any deal made concerning Mr. Popeleski?"

"If there was, I was never privileged to that information."

"To your knowledge, do you ever know of any deal?"

"Not at all."

"Okay. Was that document that's before you now, Exhibit A, was that supposed to be some sort of deal that we made with the Thirteenth Judicial District concerning Mr. Popeleski?"

"Not that I know of."

"Okay. And also when we go to the judgment and sentence and order suspending sentence, now, you stated you first saw this a month ago?"

"During the Shaun Wilkins trial."

"So that's Defendant's Exhibit B and also Defendant's Exhibit A?"

"Yes."

"So you had never seen these documents up until a month ago?"

"That's right."

"So you had no knowledge of this condition that was being placed on this document on Exhibit B?"

"I was aware of the condition, but I was not aware of what was—what further conditions he had. I just knew that Mike asked me to be on this list just as a contact person."

"So a State Police agent contacts you and says, 'Levi, will you just be the secondary contact on this thing,' and the next thing you know, your name is on that document?"

"Yes."

"Is there any signature there belonging to any attorney or any investigator out of the Seventh Judicial District?"

"No, sir."

"Thank you, Mr. Lovato."

Then Twohig began the redirect examination.

"Sir, I believe you've told us that the Seventh Judicial District Attorney's office had nothing to do with this agreement, this plea agreement, is that what you said?" Twohig asked.

"That I know of, there wasn't."

"In other words, if they did, they didn't tell you?"

"That's correct."

"Sir, let's go through some of the facts here, now. Mr. Popeleski was a primary witness, if not the primary witness for the prosecution in connection with these homicides, wasn't he?"

"Yes."

"You were aware that Mr. Popeleski was one of the State's primary witnesses against Mr. Wilkins and Mr. Buchner, weren't you?"

"Yes."

"And you were aware that he had serious felony charges pending in the Thirteenth Judicial District, weren't you, prior to this plea agreement?"

"Yes."

"Prior to the plea agreement?"

"Yes, sir."

"You didn't know he had a burglary charge pending and an escape charge pending?"

"The escape charge, yes, but I wasn't sure why he was in jail to begin with at that point in time."

"At the time that you spoke with Mr. Fenner, did Mr. Fenner discuss how the agreement was being made down in the Thirteenth Judicial District?"

"No, he did not."

"It appears that you've said that the Seventh Judicial District Attorney's office had nothing whatsoever to do with any details of this plea agreement?"

"Nothing that I was privileged with any information."

"All right. Then isn't it correct that your answer really is you just don't know?"

"I was not privileged with the information."

"Thank you, sir. No further questions."

Agent Fenner did not want to testify. The prosecution had not called him and we put Agent Fenner on our list. Court was delayed and a recess had to be called because Agent Fenner refused to testify. General Council for the State Police was claiming there was improper service. Ray talked to counsel for the Department of Public Safety and we got an agreement that he would voluntarily appear. The following day Agent Fenner took the stand.

Mr. Twohig asked, "Sir, would you give your name, please?"

"My name is Michael Fenner."

"Mr. Fenner, what's your occupation?"

"I'm a patrol sergeant with the New Mexico State Police, stationed in Taos, New Mexico."

"How long have you been with the New Mexico State Police?"

"I've been with the New Mexico State Police approximately eleven years. I was an investigator."

"During what time period?"

"I believe it was October of ninety-one until July of ninety-seven."

"During the time period beginning with the discovery of the bodies at Torreon in the cabin, the case out there, did you get involved in working on that case as an investigator?"

"I did."

"And in that capacity, did you go to the scene itself of the cabin?"

"I went to the area of the cabin, but I never entered the cabin area, the cabin itself."

"All right, sir. And when were you first assigned to work on this matter?"

"It would have been the day after the bodies were discovered."

"That would be April fifteenth?"

"Yes."

"Have you had a chance to review your report on this matter recently? I noticed in your report, sir, the date listed, let me show you, was beginning March fifteenth of '96?"

"Yes. In two places in the report, it is, it says March fifteenth, but it should have read April fifteenth."

"Did you have occasion at any point to interview Shawn Popeleski?"

"I interviewed Shawn Popeleski on several occasions."

"Can you tell us the dates, the date when you first did so?"

"April nineteenth would have been the first occasion I had to speak with Shawn Popeleski."

"Do you know whether this was the first interview conducted with Mr. Popeleski?"

"I do not know. It was the first occasion I had with him. I believe he was interviewed earlier."

"And when you interviewed him at the State Police, was he in custody?"

"Yes, he was."

"Did he advise you as to when he met Ben Anaya?"

"Yes."

"Did he tell you that he was in jail at the time of your interview for an offense?"

"He was in, I believe in the Bernalillo County Detention Center."

"Did he tell you the charge?"

"Yes."

"What was that charge?"

"I believe it was auto theft."

"And did you discuss with him the feeling that he had in that type of situation, the situation where he stole the car?"

"I believe he referred to it as an adrenaline rush."

"Now, did he tell you about using the name Frank Gomez?"

"I don't recall whether it was during that interview or a later one, but he did mention that Frank Gomez was a name that several of the gang members would use when they got in trouble, they would change their name to Frank Gomez."

"Well, sir, let me hand you a document and ask if you recognize this as something I have provided to you earlier today."

"Yeah, I saw this about maybe five minutes ago out in the hall."

"All right. Let me call your attention to page eleven of that document, if you could turn to that page. Actually, the bottom of page ten and the beginning of page eleven."

"Yes."

"Does that help to refresh your memory about this situation?"

"Yeah, it's first changing the name to Frank Gomez."

"Yes, sir. Did he explain to you how that occurred?"

"It was a friend's fake name."

"And did he explain why?"

"He said, 'I didn't want to get busted.'"

"And did he talk about the time that he was with Ben Anaya up at the cabin? To refresh your memory, sir, it's been a while, let me call your attention to page fifteen, beginning on page fifteen."

"Yes."

"Did he indicate to you when he first went to the cabin?"

"Last year is what he referred to."

"And did he give you some months?"

"The end of November, the beginning of December."

"And did he explain to you why he went up there?"

"He said to cool down, they were in too much trouble in Albuquerque."

"Did he tell you who went up there with him?"

"Yes, he did."

"Who did he tell you he went up there with?"

"Deuce, Cassandra, Matthew and Johnny Ray."

"Did he tell you what vehicle they had for transportation?"

"He referred it to as Deuce's truck."

"Did you ask him when he last saw Deuce?"

"Yes."

"Probably last August."

"Did he tell you the circumstances?"

"He said they came to Albuquerque—yes, he did."

"And did he tell you what they were doing while he was in town in August?" Twohig asked.

"Yes."

"What?"

"It says—he says here, 'We screwed up. We stayed together for a little while selling guns and stuff like that. And we kept it on the lowdown and then we would have some movidas and split over here.' So they would come to town and then go back."

"So then you asked him about going up in December to the cabin, correct?"

"Right."

"And did he tell you when they went up to the cabin, approximately when?"

"Yes."

"And what did he indicate?"

"The end of November, the first part of December."

"And did you clarify with him whether that was the first time he went up to the cabin?"

"Yes."

"What did he tell you?"

"It was the first time."

"Did you inquire as to whether they had guns at the cabin?"

"I did."

"Did you inquire as to whether they were their guns or whether they were hot?"

"Yes."

"The middle of page twenty, do you recall whether you did make that inquiry?"

"Yes, I did."

"And what did he answer?"

"He advised they were hot."

"Did you ask him if he had a lot of guns and he gave you some specific descriptions?"

"He advised they had a nine millimeter, four .22s, a 30-06 and a gauge."

"Did he give you—did you inquire further what he meant?"

"I inquired of him if he had any .22 pistols."

"And what did he tell you?"

"He said that he got caught with a .22 pistol on the westside."

"Did you attempt to inquire about the last time that he saw Deuce and Cassandra?"

"Yes."

"And what did he tell you?"

"He said his girlfriend tried to get ahold of them."

"That was the end of that."

"Did you then ask him, 'Who do you think did it?'"

"Yes."

"Did you specifically say, 'Let me ask you this, Popcorn. Who do you think did it? You know what, from what you've been telling me, you were like best buds. Do you suspect anybody of doing it? What do you think?' Or, 'Who do you think,' is that what you said?"

"Yes."

"And what was his answer?"

"I don't want to say."

"And what was the first part of your next question?"

"Do you think Sager did it?"

"And did you then go on and say, 'Do you think—who do you think did it? Sager?'"

"Yes."

"So you're the one who brought up the subject of Sager in that interview, correct?"

"Yes."

"Now, let me call your attention to a period later in the interview, and for your information, it begins on about page twenty-five. Do you recall saying, 'I'm going to ask you a question regarding the death of Ben Anaya. Do you suspect anyone in particular of killing him?' Did you ask him that?"

"Yes."

"And what was his answer?"

"'Yes, I do.'"

"And did you then say, 'Okay. Let me write them down here so I can exclude them from the list?' And then did you say, 'Who do you think killed him? Who do you suspect? When I ask you suspect, I am saying you just suspect. You think—well, let's see. You and I know that you hung out with Ben, you guys were like brothers, and so if you guys ripped somebody off and you screwed somebody over or you walked on dope or whatever you guys did, you sold them a bad gun, if you sold, if you ripped them off, you sold them something, whatever you guys did, you did together, you were like this together all the time.

'So what I say to myself is okay, we got Popcorn and we got Ben, they do the same thing to the same people, so Popcorn should know or have an idea in his mind who killed Ben. I mean, you may not because you didn't see it and you weren't there or whatever, but you probably suspect somebody, don't you?' Did you ask him the question I've just indicated?"

"Yes."

"What was his answer when you asked him who he suspected in that fashion?"

"Cosby and Sager."

"Mr. Fenner—I'm sorry, Sergeant Fenner, did he explain to you the reasons why he thought Cosby may have been the killer?"

"Yes."

"And can you summarize the explanation, please?"

"It was over a bad gun deal."

"So did you ask him, 'And you walked on and sold him some coke. Okay. So you think Cosby did it. Okay. So you suspect Cosby and you said Sager. Why do you suspect Sager?' Did you ask him that?"

"Yes, I'm sure."

"What was his answer?"

"I—I don't recall."

"You don't recall. Well, how about looking right down below where you were looking before, page twenty-eight, see if that helps to refresh your memory."

"That's what the detective like made me think."

"Was that his answer?"

"Yes."

"And did you ask him which detective?"

"I asked him which detective."

"And what did he answer?"

"The one from APD and Jacoby."

"He said, 'Those two guys,' didn't he?"

"Yes."

"And then you said, 'The one from APD and Jacoby,' and what did he say?"

"Oh, I'm sorry. He said, 'Yeah, they made me think.'"

"So then did you ask him, 'What made you think of Sager? Why would Sager go and kill Ben?'"

(NO RESPONSE)

"'He must have wanted him pretty bad, to kill Cassandra and the kids.' Did you ask him that?"

"Yes, I did."

"What was his answer?"

"He said, 'I don't think it was like Sager doesn't like,' and he goes on to say he thought they were cool."

"Did he explain to you then that he got jumped for that and got beat up pretty bad?"

"Yes."

"Where did he tell you it happened?"

"At Bonita's house."

"And did he tell you about Bonita?"

"Yes."

"And did you then ask him if Ben helped him out when they beat his ass?"

"Apparently, they had—Ben had gone over to Bonita's house with him and really didn't participate in the beating was my understanding, but he was there."

"Did he tell you that he knew what he was getting into when he went to the party?"

"Yes."

"Did he tell you he knew they were going to jump him?"

"Yes."

"But he said let's go, anyhow?"

"Yes."

"And did he say as soon as they walked into the party, that he got jumped?"

"I believe it was shortly right after they arrived, yes."

"Did he tell you who did it?"

"Yes. I believe he named several people who were there."

"Well, did he tell you specifically how it started?"

"I don't recall."

"Would you like to refresh your memory there on page twenty-nine?"

"He started it, said, 'Let's get it over with.'"

"He said, 'Sager looked at me and he popped me in the eye right here, and then I went out the door and they started hitting me and throwing rocks at me,' and went on and described it, right?"

"Yes."

"He described getting his head smashed with boots, right?"

"Yes."

"He said Woody thinks Tiny killed Deuce, right?"

"That's what he said."

"And then did you ask him who told him that?"

"Yes."

"What did he say?"

"The detective."

"Now, sir, when he answered, 'What I found out is Woody thinks Tiny killed Deuce,' did you ask him who told you that?" Twohig asked.

"I did."

"What was his answer?"

"A detective."

"Did he go on with that answer?"

"He said, 'The detectives. They said that Sager.'"

"What did you ask him?"

"I asked him, 'And so since Sager is putting the finger on you, that maybe Sager did it and he's trying to put the heat—get the heat off of him and put it on you?'"

"How did he answer?"

"I figured that, because Woody and Tiny came up to party."

"Did you ask him who knew where the cabin was?"

"I did."

"And who did he tell you who knew where the cabin was?"

"'Sager, Woody, Deuce's dad, me and my girlfriend.'"

"So did you discuss with him if he thought that the killer was somebody that knew where the cabin was?"

"I don't know. I think so."

"And what did he tell you?"

"'That is what I assume, but I don't know for sure. I don't think it's Woody because he's one of the vatos, but what the detectives were saying, anybody could be a suspect, and I was like maybe Shaun.'"

"So did you pursue that, did you say, 'Do you think Woody could have done it?'"

"I did."

"And what did he tell you?"

"No."

"And did he explain?"

"Yes, he did."

"How did he explain?"

'He says, 'I don't know. It's like making me think. The detectives like make me think and it's like hard to say.'"

"Did you have other contacts up to that date with Mr. Popeleski?"

"Yes, I did."

"What was your next contact with him if you recall?"

"It would have been a day or two later. I don't recall exactly."

"So we'll put it on the calendar up here to help you keep track of these dates and things if it would help. Does that help you determine or remember the next date when you interviewed Mr. Popeleski?"

"Yes, it does."

"And what date was that?"

"It would have been on April twenty-third."

"Yes."

"And did you then do another one on the twenty-ninth?"

"Yes."

"Did you tape the one on the twenty-ninth?"

"No, I did not."

'Did you also interview Mr. Popeleski on the tenth of May?'

"I believe so."

"Do you remember the next date after that when you interviewed Popeleski?"

"This report ended on the twenty-ninth."

"All right. Do you have any additional reports that refresh your memory on when you interviewed him?"

"There should be another report, yes."

"You don't have that with you?"

"No."

"Let me hand you another item and ask if you can review that."

He handed him a copy of his own report.

"On May the tenth, he was interviewed again."

"All right. And is there then another date after that that you interviewed him?"

"Yes."

"What was that?"

"May the fifteenth."

"Well, didn't you interview him—"

"May the thirteenth and May the fifteenth."

"And what about May the twelfth?"

"I don't show an interview on May the twelfth."

"Do you have any notation in your report as to the first time Mr. Popeleski identified Roy Buchner as being a participant or possible participant in these crimes?"

"It would have been on May fifteen."

"May the fifteenth. And this was after how many interviews you had conducted of him?"

"At least five."

"And this was about nine days then before his preliminary hearing testimony, correct? In the preliminary hearing of Mr. Buchner?"

"Yes."

"Agent Fenner, did you continue to have meetings and discussions and interviews with Mr. Popeleski after the Buchner preliminary hearing on May the twenty-fourth?"

"Yes."

"How frequently did you have those meetings?"

"I recall picking him up for court a couple of times, transporting him."

"Where was he being housed at that time?"

"He was being housed in Quay County in Tucumcari."

"In Tucumcari. So you would go down there and get him and bring him to court appearances?"

"Yes. I believe I relayed him out one time, I took him from the court-house out or from Albuquerque out and then I brought him in one time."

"Did you visit with him at the detention center in Quay County?"

"Yes, I believe I did."

"And he had these grand theft auto charges pending in Albuquerque, right?"

"Yes."

"Initially. Did there come a time when that changed, when he no longer had those charges pending?"

"I don't know."

"Well, let me call your attention to the time period in November of 1996. Now, we're going on forward a few months. And let me first show you an exhibit. Excuse me, Your Honor. I'm sorry it took me a moment to retrieve that. I'd like to show you defendant's Exhibits A and B. Take a moment and look at those and tell us whether you're familiar with them."

"I've never seen them before."

"Well, you know the type of document those are? You've seen that type of document before?"

"Yes, I've seen these types of documents, but I've never seen this particular."

"And you realize that that is two documents, a plea and disposition agreement and a judgment and sentence, correct?"

"Yes."

"And you recognize the name of the defendant in them?"

"Yes."

"Shawn Popeleski?"

"Yes."

"Detective, let me focus your attention on a couple of details on this. First, let me focus your attention on the plea and disposition agreement itself, the bottom of page one where the agreed disposition is set forth. There is a sentence D down there which I'd like to call your attention to, give you a chance to look at it. Do you see that?"

"Yes."

"And then let me just show you a related sentence here. It's on the bottom of page two of Exhibit B, the judgment and sentence, and it's paragraph six where the conditions of probation are set forth."

"Yes."

"You see your name in both of those sentences, right?"

"Yes."

"Michael Fenner, that's you, isn't it?"

"Yes."

"And it appears as though if you read these documents, and you're welcome to take your time to do so, that there was an agreement to place Mr. Popeleski on probation on a number of felony charges and a couple of misdemeanors and to make as a condition of his probation weekly contact with you. You see that?"

"I see that."

"Yes, sir. And did you have any information about that happening?"

"This is the first I see of it."

According to Levi Agent Fenner had called him and advised him that he was also on the list for Popcorn to contact.

"And you didn't talk to anyone about that before it happened?"

"I don't recall talking to anybody about it at all."

"You notice in that same sentence is the name Levi Lovato, you see that?"

"Yes."

"You know who he is?"

"Yes. He would be the investigator for the District Attorney's office in Torrance."

"And you see that he—that Mr. Popeleski's condition of probation is that he report to either you or Mr. Lovato on a weekly basis, you see that?"

"Yes."

"You didn't know anything about that, either, his reporting to Mr. Lovato?"

"Again, I don't recall any—why, no."

"Well, did you know that Mr. Popeleski was entering into a plea agreement on those charges?"

"I had been told that he was, yeah, but I didn't know this had been effective until after—a long time after it happened, I guess."

"Oh, you did learn about it afterwards?"

"Yeah. Not that he was supposed to report to me, but that he had been placed on probation."

"I see. So you didn't know anything about this condition of his probation where he was supposed to report to you?"

"I don't recall it, no."

"So, you couldn't really determine whether he was complying with his probation or not if you didn't know anything about it?"

"No."

"Well, after he got out on probation, did he call you, do you know?"

"I don't—I don't recall him ever calling me, no. I don't—I can't remember the last time I've had contact with him. It's been quite some time."

"Well, prior to the time he got placed on probation, he was a prosecution witness in connection with these Torreon homicides, wasn't he?"

"Yes."

"And your conversation with him involved not only statements, but his role as a prosecution witness, too, didn't it?"

"I'm sure, yes."

"And were you working with someone from the DA's office about Mr. Popeleski's role as a witness?"

"Yes. I would have been working with Madeline Malka, the District or Assistant District Attorney."

"She was the one actually primarily handling the case back at that time, correct?"

"Yes."

"And did you communicate regularly with her?"

"Fairly regularly, as well as working on the case, sure."

"Is she the one who told you that Mr. Popeleski was entering into this agreement, being placed on probation?"

Agent Fenner brought up the Engineer Malka once again.

"I'm sure, yeah."

"Well, I notice that the plea agreement and the judgment are in the Thirteenth Judicial District. You see that?"

"Yes."

"You know where that is?"

"That would be Valencia, Bernalillo and Cibola Counties."

"And Sandoval County, too, right?"

"Yes."

"And did you have any involvement directly with either the burglary case or the escape case on which Mr. Popeleski was being prosecuted in that county?"

"No."

"You were not an investigator on those cases?"

"No."

"Did you ever discuss with Ms. Malka any concern about those pending cases and how they might affect Mr. Popeleski?"

"I'm sure we did. I don't understand exactly what you're asking."

"Well, what I'm inquiring about is whether or not this probation agreement had something to do with Mr. Popeleski being a State's witness at that time?"

"I'm sure it did. I don't—that would have been worked out between Ms. Malka and the District Attorney from the thirteenth."

"All right. And since you were one of the people working with Mr. Popeleski, did you realize it was important to be able to be in contact with him if he was going to be out on probation so that he could be available as a witness?"

"Yes. I would suspect that's why we're in these plea and disposition agreements."

"Well, do you see that one of the conditions of his probation is that he leave New Mexico?"

"I see that it says, 'The State does not oppose the Defendant's probation being transferred to another state.'"

"Do you know whether he was planning on leaving New Mexico, did you discuss that with him?"

"You know, I had discussed with the ADA Malka that I tried to get ahold of his dad and see if we could get him with his dad in Mississippi."

"His father lived in Mississippi?"

"Yes."

"And though he had connections in Rio Rancho, you were going to call his father. Did you do so?"

"You know, I never did because I didn't know that this had come up."

"So if I understand your testimony, then, he was released on probation apparently in November of 1996 without such arrangements having been made before?"

"Yes, as far as I know, without me making those arrangements."

"All right. Without you making. Someone else may have, but you didn't?"

"Right."

"Sir, are you aware that Mr. Popeleski was subsequently apprehended and placed back in custody?"

"Yes."

"And did you have contact with him after that?"

"I don't recall any contact with him after that at all. I've seen him in court."

"Involving court proceedings in connection with these cases?"

"Yes."

"During the time prior to his probation, would you say you were the primary contact with Mr. Popeleski for the prosecution team?"

"Probably. I had a lot of contact with him."

"Were you on a first-name basis with him, did he call you Mike?"

"No."

"No?"

"No."

"Well, the reason I'm asking, sir, is that one of the things that we noticed is that when he was testifying in the preliminary hearing, which is an exhibit in this case which the jury has heard, he referred to two law enforcement officers named Mike and Juan, Mike and Juan, whom he had talked to. And that testimony was on May twenty-fourth. Do you know of any other Mike that he talked to?"

"No. He could be referring to me."

"Now, when you investigated the case, did you look into obtaining Mr. Popeleski's property from the burglary arrest at the Valencia County Detention Center?"

"Yes. I believe it was on May thirteenth that we went to— Sergeant Branch and I took him to Valencia County and got his belongings from the burglary arrest to send with him. I believe he was going to Quay County at that time, and we sent it out with him."

"Well, sir, did you think possibly the property that he had at that time, at the time of his arrest on December twenty-fifth, 1995, the things that he had with him might possibly be evidence relevant to this case?"

"I believe that Agent Jacoby did take some of the items as evidence."

"Did you look into other items and into taking them as evidence?"

"I didn't take any of the items into evidence."

"Sir, I'd like to show you a document and ask you if you recognize it."

"Yeah, I recognize it as a criminal complaint."

"All right. Your Honor, this is Exhibit Six W's and I move its admission at this time."

"No objection, Your Honor."

"It will be admitted."

"Sir, what type of a criminal complaint is that? That is, where is it filed?"

"It shows here the Magistrate Court, County of Torrance, State of New Mexico."

"And who's the defendant in the case?"

"Shawn Popeleski, a/k/a Popcorn."

"What's the date that criminal complaint was filed?"

"June the sixth, nineteen ninety-seven."

"And can you list the charges for us in that complaint?"

"It says here, Count One would be an open count of murder with a firearm enhancement. Count Two would be an open current of murder with a firearm enhancement. Count Three, open count of murder. Count Four, open count of murder. Count Five would be aggravated burglary with a firearm enhancement. Count Six, armed robbery with a firearm enhancement. Count Seven, tampering with evidence. Count Eight, tampering with evidence. Count Nine, tampering with evidence. Count Ten, unlawful taking of a motor vehicle. And Count Eleven would be conspiracy."

"Sir, what are the dates of the offenses as shown in that criminal complaint?"

"It says here that on or between December twelfth, 1995 and December nineteenth, 1995."

"Now, in Count One, who is the alleged victim of the murder?"

"Cassandra Sedillo."

"Count Two, who's the alleged victim of the murder?"

"Ben Anaya, Jr."

"Count Three, who's the alleged victim of the murder?"

"Matthew Garcia."

"Count Four, who's the alleged victim?"

"Johnny Ray Garcia."

"Sir that was filed on what date?"

"June the sixth, 1997."

"Who signed it?"

"It looks like Levi Lovato and Madeline Malka."

"Mr. Lovato you've told us is the investigator for the District Attorney's office?"

"Correct."

"And Ms. Malka was the Deputy District Attorney in Torrance County at that time, correct?"

"Yes."

"Thank you, sir. No further questions."

Mr. Bonet then asked, "Agent Fenner, I'd like to ask you a few questions based on what counsel questioned you on."

"Sure."

"Did you know what the relationship between Popcorn and Ben Anaya, Jr. was?"

"Yes. Popeleski related it to me, yes."

"Did he relate to you that they were—it was a close relationship?"

"Related to me that they were close, like he indicated to being brothers."

"Now, when you interviewed Popcorn, and you notice your reports are there that counsel questioned you on, didn't Popcorn identify Shaun Wilkins as one of the individuals who killed Ben Anaya, Jr. and Cassandra Sedillo and the boys?"

"Yes."

"Didn't he also identify the second individual as the same size as Mr. Wilkins and being Hispanic?"

"Yes, he did."

"Didn't he also tell you that he heard two sets of footsteps removing items from the cabin?"

"Yes, he did."

"Very well," the judge said.

"You have your reports there?" Bonet asked.

"Yes."

"You recall what Popcorn told you about hearing keys?"

"He heard some rattling of the keys in the door being locked."

"You also recall if he told you anything about whether or not he had returned to the cabin after this incident in December?"

"He said he had never returned back to the cabin."

"You interviewed Lawrence Nieto?" Bonet asked.

"Yes. I recall that he asked me regarding what Mr. Popeleski asked me about Mr. Nieto, whether he thought he had done it or not."

"What was the conversation about with Mr. Popeleski concerning Nieto?"

"Whether Mr. Popeleski thought that Lawrence Nieto was involved in the murders."

"And did you have an opportunity then to interview Mr. Nieto?"

"Yes."

"Now, did Mr. Nieto tell you concerning his involvement in this matter?"

"Yes, he did."

"Would you please tell the jury what Mr. Nieto told you happened up at the cabin?"

"Mr. Nieto told me that he rode up to the cabin with Roy Buchner and Shaun Wilkins and they partied there for a short period of time. They left the cabin. They, Roy Buchner, Shaun Wilkins and Lawrence Nieto left the cabin. Cassandra, Deuce and the two younger boys were left at the cabin. They returned a short time later. He held Popeleski on the ground with a shotgun. Wilkins and Roy Buchner entered the cabin. He heard some gunshots. They left the area. They removed several items from the cabin. And then—they being Shaun Wilkins, Roy Buchner and Lawrence Nieto."

"Was there anything further he told you about that occurred then?"

"He told me that Roy Buchner had locked the door."

"Did you have reason to believe that Popcorn was in danger?"

"Yes."

"Now, is the term 'marked man' a term that's used?"

"It could be, yes."

"Okay. And what would that term be used for?"

"That would mean that somebody is after you."

"Now, you interviewed Mr. Popeleski several times?"

"Yes, sir."

"Did he ever mention to you any concerns that he had?"

"Sure. He felt unsafe at Bernalillo County Detention Center. He felt un-safe at Torrance County Detention Center, and that's why he was eventually moved to Quay County Detention Center because it was far enough away."

"Did he ever mention to you why he was reluctant to talk to you or whether he was reluctant to talk to you?"

"Sure. He said that at one point in time he had gotten beat up pretty good for mentioning Rascal's name, and therefore he felt that any time that he gave up information to the police, he could be killed or beat up."

"Now, didn't you also pick up a set of Jeep keys and stuff from the Belen Police Department?"

"There were some keys, a pager. I'm not sure what all."

"Okay. Did you turn those over to Agent Jacoby?"

"Yes, that had all been turned over, yeah."

"Now, you testified to the criminal complaint in this matter. Handing you what's been marked as State's Exhibit 105. Can you identify that?"

"Yes."

"And what is that?"

"It's an amended criminal complaint."

"And what is the name that appears on that?"

"Shawn Popeleski."

"Are those the formal charges of Mr. Popeleski?"

"These are charges that were amended from the first complaint to this complaint."

"Now, in the complaint that you point to, in defendant's Exhibit Six W's, that's a complaint that's done in the Magistrate Court, isn't it?"

"Yes."

"Okay. Now, what are the counts that are there against Mr. Popeleski?"

"Count One would be murder, open count on Cassandra Sedillo. Count Two would be murder, open count on Ben Anaya, Jr. Count Three would be murder, open count on Matthew Garcia. Count Four murder, open count on Johnny Ray Garcia. Count Five, aggravated burglary, firearm enhancement. Count Six would be armed robbery, firearm enhancement. Count Seven, aggravated burglary with a firearm enhancement. Count Eight would be a conspiracy. And Count Nine would be unlawful taking of a motor vehicle."

"Now, the first four counts being murder, are those not the same charges that are facing the defendant in this matter, Mr. Roy Buchner?"

"Yes."

"Thank you, sir. No further questions," Bonet said.

Mr. Twohig started the redirect examination.

"Sir, during your cross examination, you referred to interviews with Popeleski in which he told you certain things other than or different than the things I brought out on direct examination of your interview which I asked you about?" Twohig asked.

"Correct."

"Were those later interviews?"

"Yeah, that would have been a subsequent discussion with him, sure."

"So then is what you're telling us is that he changed his story later on from what he told you to begin with?"

"I guess you could characterize it like that if that's the way you choose."

"Well, he didn't tell you the same things about the last time he had seen Ben and Cassandra, did he?"

"No."

"In fact, he told you he was present at the cabin at the time the killings took place, right?"

"Yes, he did."

"You were also asked about your interview with Mr. Nieto where he made some statements to you?"

"Yes."

"What was the date of that interview?"

"That would have been the thirteenth."

"And were you the only one interviewing him then?"

"No."

"Who else was present during that interview?"

"Juan DeReyes with the Albuquerque Police Department actually conducted a large portion of that interview."

"And what other officers were present?"

"I don't recall any other officers being present in the interview."

"All right. And you have set forth the basic outline of Mr. Nieto's statement to you at that time, correct?"

"Yes."

"And was that his first interview?"

"No, I'm sure it was not."

"He had been interviewed before several times?"

"I'm sure, at least two or three times."

"Had you participated in any of his earlier interviews?"

"Yes."

"You know the dates of the earlier interviews with Nieto?"

"If I might look at the report, I could tell you the dates that I was involved."

"Yes, sir, please, do."

"Well, the only dates that I showed I was with an interview with Lawrence Nieto would have been May eleventh, May thirteenth and May fifteenth."

"So the one you have just described to us where he gave you the summary of facts that you've recounted to the jury is May thirteenth?"

Agent Fenner never told the court there was more than one interview on the 13th.

"Yes."

"Then let's focus on that interview, all right? Have you had a chance to review records of that interview lately?"

"All I've reviewed is just the report."

"But it was a tape recorded interview, wasn't it?"

"I believe it was, yes."

"And do you recall specific details about the interview and what Mr. Nieto said?"

"I don't remember very many specifics."

"Do you remember what Mr. Nieto said about the type of vehicle that they were riding in?"

"I remember he—I believe he said it was a stolen car. I believe he said it was a, like a Camaro or a Firebird."

"Well, sir, let me show you something and ask if it would refresh your memory. Sir, on page five, what I've shown you, does this help to refresh your memory about what type of vehicle he described?"

"He said a black Camaro or Trans Am."

"And during that interview with Mr. Nieto, did he say who was at the cabin when he arrived?"

"Yes, I'm sure he did."

"Who did he tell you was there?"

"I recall him saying that Ben Anaya, Cassandra, the two boys and Popeleski."

"Well, sir, didn't he say Popcorn was not there?"

"I may be confusing it with another interview."

"Well, let me see if this refreshes your recollection." He is shown a copy of the interview.

"That's correct. He said that Cassandra, Ben and the two children. He said no, Popeleski wasn't there."

"And did he say that they, they partied there at the cabin?"

"Yes."

"Do you recall asking him with respect to Popcorn not being there, isn't that kind of weird, because didn't Popcorn live there?"

"Yes, I do recall asking him something similar to that."

"And do you remember him saying, 'Yeah, but he wasn't there unless he seen Sager and he like ran or something, you know'?"

"Yeah, I recall."

"You recall talking about what kind of drugs were up there at the cabin with him that day?"

"I don't recall discussing drugs with him."

"Let me see if this refreshes your recollection." He is shown a copy of the interview again.

"Yes, we did discuss the different drugs that the different people were using."

"Did he tell you that marijuana was at the house, but not cocaine?"

"I asked him about crack, he said no, all he recalled seeing was molta. Molta would be a street term for marijuana."

"Did he then tell you about going outside to urinate?"

"Yes."

"And did he tell you about when that was after they got there?"

"It had been a while after they had gotten there. They had been partying for a while."

"And you asked him how long it was after they got there, and he told you right about three or four hours, right?"

"Could be."

"All right. Let me show you." He shows him the interview again.

"Yes. It was about three or four hours."

"All right, sir. And did Mr. Nieto tell you that right about three or four hours later, were these words, 'I just went outside, took a piss and that's when I heard all the gunshots,' is that what he said?"

"That's what he said."

"He then said, 'I went in and I said What the fuck's going on, you know. They just put the gun to my head and said, Sure, bro, don't say nothing. And I just—like tears came out,' is that what he told you?"

"I'm sure."

"Would you like to check it? That's what he said?"

"That's what he said."

"And did you follow-up on that or the other investigator who was present follow-up on that?"

"I don't recall."

"Would you like to refresh your memory on that?"

"Yes."

"And did he provide some details such as the exact direction he went and where he was located, etcetera?"

"Follow-up questions were, 'Did you go straight out the door, did you go straight to the left, straight to the right,' and he gave some details to where he went."

"And he amplified it a little bit, he said he heard the shots and he just went in and said, according to him, 'What the fuck's going on,' didn't he?"

"Yes."

"Yes. And did he tell you that he went in and he said, 'What the fuck's going on,' and then said, 'And he just put the gun to my head and said don't say nothing"?

"Yes."

"And did you ask—was he asked who put the gun to his head?"

"He said Sager."

"He said Sager did. Did he then describe what happened next?"

"Yes. They loaded some items up and they left."

"He said they just went down the hill, were carrying stuff down there, just went back, that's what he said?"

"Yeah."

"Did you ask him if he carried anything?"

"I did. And as I recall, he carried some guns down the hill. I'm sorry. I'm mistaken."

"Yes?"

"He didn't carry anything. He said the guns and marijuana were removed from the house."

"But he denied carrying anything at all, didn't he, himself?"

"Personally."

"Sir, in this interview, he didn't tell you anything whatsoever about holding a shotgun on Popeleski up there, did he?"

"No."

"In fact, he denied completely Popeleski even being there, didn't he?"

"Yes, he did."

"Did he tell you about people having gloves?"

"I don't recall."

"Did he tell you about stopping at a rest stop?"

"I don't recall."

"Sir, in the earlier interview you were involved in, that was May eleventh, a couple days before this May thirteenth interview we just went through?"

"Yes."

"And did you speak with Mr. Nieto then?"

"Yes."

"And do you recall the details of that interview?"

"Not specific details, no, sir."

"Who else was present at that interview?"

"I believe Officer DeReyes was present at that one, as well."

"Was that a videotaped interview?"

"I don't recall."

"Do you recall that prior to the beginning of the interview, Mr. Nieto asked to speak to a lawyer?"

"I recall an interview where that happened, yes."

"Let me show you a document and ask if that helps you to refresh your recollection. You're welcome to look at the cover." He shows him the interview.

"Yes, he did."

"Does looking at the beginning of that interview help you to remember the situation?"

"I—I remember the situation. This was, by looking at it, though, it wasn't me that—I was present in and out of this interview, but I was not there for the whole interview."

"All right. And who was actually conducting it?"

"Juan DeReyes."

"And he was the one primarily asking the questions?"

"Yes."

"So do you now recall that Mr. Nieto asked for an attorney?"

"I recall seeing that on the video, yeah."

"And do you recall Mr. DeReyes saying, 'Why do you want a lawyer?'"

"Yes."

"And he started to answer, 'Because I'm not—' and then he said, 'If you haven't been charged.'"

"Yes."

"Mr. Nieto said, 'Because you guys are blaming me.'"

"Yes."

"So then he says, 'I'm not blaming you, bro.' And Mr. DeReyes—and Mr. Nieto says, 'Well, I'm telling you the straightup truth.'"

"Yes."

"And he says, 'I'm telling you the straight-up truth, but you don't believe me,' didn't he?"

"Yes."

"So then was he asked, 'How can you request a lawyer if you haven't been charged?'"

"Yes."

"Objection, Your Honor. Once again, narrative," Bonet said.

"Overruled."

"Did Mr. Nieto say, 'I'm not, but I'm just telling you the truth, sir. You guys don't even believe me. I'm telling you the straight-up truth.' You recall that?"

"Yes."

"And then he was asked, 'Have you?' and Nieto says, 'Yeah, right.'?"

"Yes."

"The next question he was asked in that interrogation, 'And you're going to give up Sager, bro. Give him up, bro'?"

"Yes, he was asked that."

"He said, 'I'm telling you, sir, I didn't go to no fucking cabin, man.'?"

"Yes."

Ray continued reading from the transcript.

"That's what he said, wasn't it?"

All Fenner could do was nod his head.

"Well, and then Officer DeReyes pursued a little further and he's asked who did go to the cabin, and he says, 'I'm telling you I don't know,' and then he's asked, 'You told us before that Sager did, right?'"

"Yes."

"And he said, 'Well, I didn't say he did it, but he came over and said.' And he said he was there, didn't he? He said, 'Yeah. I'm telling you guys the truth, man,' right?"

"Right."

"So he's claiming he learned about Sager being there by Sager coming over and telling him that he was there, right?"

"Yes."

"And later on he was asked some additional questions about Sager as the interrogation focused on him, correct?"

"Yes."

"And wasn't he told, 'You're the one that's going to place Sager up there, aren't you?'"

"Yes. I remember reading that."

"Yes, sir. You remember seeing it on the videotape?"

"Yeah."

"And didn't he say, 'You're the one that's going to place him there, aren't you? Aren't you?' And then Nieto said, 'Whatever,' and then he said, 'Yes or no,' and Nieto said, 'Yes, sir.'?"

"Yes."

"Now, as they got further into the interrogation, they were asked about the vehicle and he was asked about the vehicle and what time Eazy and Sager came to his house, you remember that?"

"Yes."

"You remember him saying 'Around nine o'clock.'?"

"I remember him saying it was early. And it was a black or something, blue."

"Let me provide you this, sir, to help refresh your memory." He shows him a copy of the interview.

"He said around nine o'clock at night."

"Nine at night. Did he say that he had not gone in the car with them?"

"Yes."

"And then do you remember the interrogation proceeding further where Mr. DeReyes says, 'And you think something went down and you suspect one of your home boys. Who was that home boy that you suspect? Tell me.' You remember that?"

"Yes."

"And do you remember him saying, 'Who?' Sager. Sager. Why, bro? Why Sager of all the homeys? Why him? Convince me, bro." Remember that?"

Fenner responded, "I don't really recall the video in depth, but I recall that he was telling him Sager, yeah."

"Let me show you this. Isn't that what was said?"

"Yeah."

"And then didn't he say, 'They came over to my pad saying they went over there, and then but two weeks later they say they found him dead,' right?"

"Yeah."

"He was asked, 'Who told you they found him dead?' and he said, 'The news.' Right?"

"That's what he said."

"And so the interrogation then focused on the time. 'Two weeks from the time they all went to your house in a stolen car,' he was asked at page twelve, 'him and Eazy, all of a sudden the next thing you know in the news, Ben is dead, and you snap. You snapped and you said, Something's wrong here.' Was that the question?"

Bonet said, "Objection, Your Honor. May we approach?"

"You may."

After a discussion at the bench the judge allowed Agent Fenner to answer.

"Yes, he said, 'Never talked to him, sir.'"

"Do you recall the interrogation focusing further with Mr. Nieto, saying 'If you knew who killed Ben Anaya, why didn't you say Sager did it? I thought Ben was your homey,' isn't that what he was asked?"

"Yes."

"And then the interrogator pursues it, 'So why didn't you drop the dime on him, bro? Why have you kept this in? What do you owe Sager? You see that?' Is that what he was asked?"

"That is what he asked."

"And he said, 'Nothing. Scared.' So then the interrogator says, 'Did he ever tell you he would kill you,' right?"

Fenner just nodded, and Ray continued.

"So, he said, 'No, but I know he's loco.' And then he's asked, 'That he's loco, huh? And the only thing that's kept you from just saying anything, right? That's what's kept you alive up to this point till now. If you act like nothing's happening and you don't act like you know or suspect him, he's not going to bother you, is he, you see that?'"

Once again Ray hammered Fenner with the transcript.

"Uhhuh," he finally replied.

"And there's no response to that. So then he's asked further, pressed, 'You want to put him away, Woodrow, for killing your homey,' isn't he, right?"

"Yes, he's asked that."

"And he says, 'I'm telling you, man.' And he says, 'Do you want to see him go away, bro?' And he says, 'Sure,' doesn't he?"

"Yes."

"And then the question is, 'Because you know he killed your homey, didn't you. You know it. You know it in your heart that that jerk right there wasted your homeboy and those kids. You know that,' right?

"Yes."

"And he starts to answer and he says, 'Let it out, bro.' He says, 'I'm telling you. Let it out, bro. Tell me,' isn't that right?"

"Yes."

"And then he says, 'I'm telling you I'm scared even of them killing me, you know,' doesn't he?"

"Yes."

"So, even up to that point, he hasn't said he was there, has he, Mr. Nieto?"

"I don't see where he's used the word 'Sager,' but—"

"No. I'm talking about Nieto, Nieto never acknowledged himself being up there to that point?"

"Oh, I'm sorry, I thought you were asking—"

"No, excuse me. I may have misstated my question."

"No, Nieto has not said that he's been up there."

"All right. So, now, after some questioning about whether he's going to be in danger and what he might do to protect himself, he's then asked, 'Where would you go,' and he says, 'Probably like Taos or something,' right?"

"Yes."

"And then he said, 'Yeah, that would be good,' he's asked this by the detective, 'Yeah, that would be good. Do you think Eazy did it with him,' right?"

"Yes."

"He says, 'I don't know, sir.' And then the questioner says, 'Do you think that Eazy would be there, maybe not pull the trigger, but he'd be there, you see that?' And Mr. Nieto says, 'Yeah,' doesn't he?"

"Yes."

"And he says, 'Why would he not kill him?' And he says, 'They're close homeys, you know, right?' And then he's asked, 'They're very close?' And he answers, 'Him and Sager, no.' And then the interrogator says, 'Did Eazy liked Popcorn. If Popcorn was there at the place when he did the shooting or something, do you think he would kill Popcorn, too, both of them?' And the interrogator says, 'No witnesses, huh? What did you guys used to use, bro, what did you guys used to use when you were carjacking cars,' and he started to go into that about Sager, doesn't he?"

"Yes."

"Do you remember Mr. Nieto then being questioned about a drive-by?" Twohig asked.

"Yes."

"And I'd like to go through the questioning process with you. You recall the agent saying, 'We want to help you, bro.' And this begins at the bottom of page eighteen, sir. 'We want to help you bro. We'll help you. You'll get a new life. You'll get out of town, because I'll tell you right now, Woodrow, I got three felonies on you right now, homey.' He says, 'Where?' Nieto said, 'Where?' And then DeReyes says, 'A drive-by, a drive-by, bro. Tampering with evidence. Is that right?"

"Yes."

"And Nieto answers, 'Never been in no drive-by,' didn't he?"

"Yes."

"And then Officer DeReyes says, 'You did a drive-by,' and Nieto says, 'No, I didn't, man,' correct?"

"Yes."

"And he says, 'Who did, then?' And the answer is, 'I don't know who did it, but I'm—' and then the question is, 'Then why are you bragging about it, homey?' And he answers, 'I never did it.' And then he's questioned, 'Why are you bragging about it?' And he says, 'I ain't bragging about it, sir.' Isn't that right?"

"Yes."

"And the question then goes, 'and you did. You were telling stories with your homey and you said you did a drive-by. Now, who the hell did that drive-by?' Isn't that right?"

"Yes."

"He said, 'I didn't, no.' and so then Mr. DeReyes says, 'Who did it, bro? Who did it? You tell me who did it. But as it stands right now, homey, you were the man. Who did it? Who did it, Woody?' Isn't that the way he's questioned?"

"Yes."

"And he says, 'I didn't see it, sir.' That's what Nieto says, isn't it?"

"Yes."

"And then he says, 'Who did the drive-by?' He says, 'I didn't see it, sir. I didn't do it.' So he said, 'All right. If you didn't do it, then who did?' And at that point, he says, 'Sager and'— He says, 'Sager and who?' And then he says, 'Shorty and Weasel,' right?"

"Yes."

"He asked him, 'Weasel?' And he goes into where Shorty is and where Springer is, and then he says, 'They told me they shot at the gang in the paddy.' He says, 'Why?' And he says, 'Because they were in Westgate.' And then the officer says, 'And instead they shot at the gang unit's car, or house, bro. What did they use? And Nieto says, To tell you the truth, I don't know. They didn't tell me nothing.' Right?"

"Yes."

"And then he says, 'Sager, huh? Was he the shooter? Otra vez, no?' Correct? And what's that mean?"

"I'm sorry?"

"What does that mean when he asked him that?"

"What's that?"

"Otra vez."

"I don't speak Spanish."

"All right. And he says, 'Yes, sir.' And then Mr. DeReyes says, 'Do you know whose house that was,' sir, doesn't he?"

"He asked, 'Do you know whose house that was, bro?'"

"And Nieto says, 'Whose,' didn't he?"

"Yes."

"And DeReyes says, 'It was my house. That was my crib, bro. That was my house, my familia. That's personal, bro. I don't go to your pad, I don't go to anybody else's pad unless it's business.' And Nieto says, 'Yes, sir. And DeReyes says, 'And I will fuck with anybody, and the child's dead.' And Nieto said, 'Yes, sir.' Isn't that the way it went?"

"Yes, sir."

"And he says "respect" in Spanish, doesn't he?"

"Yes, sir."

"That's what DeReyes says. And Nieto says, 'I know. That's what I'm say-ing. I didn't,' and then Nieto says—I'm sorry, DeReyes says, 'You call that re-spect, bro? You broke that respect right now when you went to my house and did that shit. And I always knew they'd get you, bro, and I suspected someone. And I've been looking, bro, and I found out who it was and I wanted you to tell me who that person was. I tell you about it and you're going to pin this dude up, bro. You're going to pin him up, not only on a homicide on the homey, but you're going to pin him up on the drive-by, him, Shorty and Weasel. Where is weasel now?' Isn't that the question?"

"Objection Your Honor. May we approach?" Bonet says.

"You may."

"Once again, Your Honor," Benet begins, "we're going way, way out of field here concerning this, the use of these documents. If the court is going to allow this and obviously I'm going to go right back into all of that, too. I mean I don't see the relevance being done on these things."

Twohig says, "This is exactly how they got Nieto blaming Wilkins for these murders. This is exactly when it happened and Nieto has already come in here and testified that he was coerced, that he wasn't really there at the scene and that these detectives coerced him. That was his testimony before this jury in this case. This shows exactly how it happened."

Bonet says, "If Your Honor is going to allow it, then I'm going to probably take as long as this afternoon and I'll have to use those documents that counsel has."

"You may have to," the judge replies.

"Yes," Bonet says.

"I'll permit you to proceed," the judge says.

Twohig turned back to Fenner to continue his questioning.

"And then he begins to ask, to talk about respect with Mr. Nieto, doesn't he?"

"Yes sir, he does."

"Now, sir, they begin to talk about respect after that, correct? On down page twenty-one?"

"Yeah."

"And Officer DeReyes said, 'You ain't going to get killed, bro, because I have respect for you, no?' And he says, 'My family, you know,' Nieto expressing concerning about his family, right?"

"Yes."

"And Officer DeReyes says, 'That's right, and you better think about your family, bro, because right now, homeboy doesn't give a shit about your family. He don't care about you. He doesn't care about anybody. All he cares about is Wilkins. He's implicated you, bro. He said you were up at the cabin. Now, what kind of homeboy is going to tell on another homeboy like that, especially to you, Woodrow?' And there's an inaudible response at that point, right?"

"Yes."

And DeReyes says, 'Then why is he going to say it? Why is he going to fuck with your family, bro? Why are you going to let him do that, Woodrow? He's a bad seed, bro. He needs to be put away, no? He brought down Eighteenth Street hard, hasn't he? He's not what Eighteenth Street should have been, no?' That's what he's saying to him, isn't it?"

"Yes."

"And he's saying, 'When you do—when he does beef with somebody, you take care of it, and that gang banger is a gang banger, no? But when you mess with other people and you mess with the fiveoh, bro, it ain't going to go away,' correct?"

"That's what he says."

"And then he specifically said to Nieto, 'And it's not going to go away with me, and I'll tell you right now, Woodrow, that if you're telling me the truth, when I get Weasel, Shorty and this asshole right here, they tell me you're involved, I'm going to take you down,' doesn't he?"

"Yes."

"And then he says, 'But right now, bro, I'm going to give you,' something which is inaudible, and he says, 'You're going to owe me big time, Woodrow, because I'm going to keep your ass alive,' doesn't he?"

"Yes."

"And Mr. Nieto says, 'I don't care about me, I just care about my family,' doesn't he?"

"Yes."

"And DeReyes says, 'You better start worrying, bro, because Parrot and everybody are in,' something inaudible, 'right now on the news, you better start worrying, homey, and that's why you need to tell me now what that son-of-a-bitch has done, everything he's done that he's told you, you need to tell me now.' And he says, 'Tell me, bro. Start talking, bro,' doesn't he?"

"Yes."

"Sir, focusing your attention now at the page that I've provided you, was there further interrogation of Mr. Nieto?"

"Yes."

"And looking at that page, did Officer DeReyes in that interview say, 'I don't think you want to go down, bro. I think you know what's thewhat the thing is, no,' to Mr. Nieto?"

"Yes."

"And Mr. Nieto said, 'I'm telling you guys the truth, you know.' And then the detective says, this is DeReyes, 'Well, I'm going to see how straight up you are, bro. I'm going to see, because I want to pick up Sager and I need something on him. I need some good scandal. What you've told me now, the fact that you suspect him as being the killer in the homicide and also doing the drive-by, at least I have something now, but it ain't going to end there, Woody, because you're going to have to live, man, and you're going have to go to court and you're going to have to pin him and you're going to have to pin him hard, and you're never going to have to worry about what he thinks of you because he ain't going to touch you because he's going to be locked up for a long time when I get—before I get finished with him. And you're going to be done, bro, you're going to disappear. Isn't that right, Woody?' And he says, 'Yes, sir.' That was the question and answer there, wasn't it, sir?"

"Yes."

"And then DeReyes said, 'And I'm going to give you that chance, bro. Weasel, Shorty and Sager are going to go down on something. I had to sell my house, bro, because of that. I had to move my family because of that. How does it make you feel, bro?' Isn't that what he said?"

"Yes."

"What he said, 'They did it to my family,' and then he talks about a drive-by at his house by Westgate, correct?"

"Yes."

"And then he says on down at page twenty-nine, DeReyes says, 'What I'm going to get, bro, I'm going to get a piece of paper called a statement and you're going to give me a statement, bro, on your word that Sager, Weasel and Shorty did the drive-by, just like you told me.' And Nieto says, 'All right.' Correct?"

"Yes."

"And then he says, 'And you're going to also say in that statement about the other stuff, that you know that Sager and Eazy went up to the cabin in a stolen car the day that this happened, and that's how you're going to clear yourself, bro, because when I go to court on this to present that, they're going to ask you for that and they're not going to ask for my word, your word. They're going to want to see it on paper, because if they're going to help Woodrow, they're going—because if they're going to help Woody.' Sorry. 'If they're going to help Woodrow, they're going to know Woodrow is telling the truth and Woodrow is willing to put his butt on the line and pin that dude, because that's the only way it's going to happen and that's the only way it's going to keep you alive. Do you understand that?' That's what he said to Mr. Nieto, right?"

"Yes."

"And Mr. Nieto said, 'Yes, sir. And then after that, what, sir?' And Mr. DeReyes says, 'After that, Woodrow, you're going to go, you're going to make yourself very available to us, and if we need to talk to you, we want to know where we can find you, bro. We aren't going to want to go looking for you.' Right?"

"Yes."

"And Nieto says, 'You might find me every time in my pad.' And DeReyes says, 'That's right. And that's where we want to find you. That's where we want to find you.' And Nieto says, 'All right, sir,' at that point, doesn't he? And then a little later in the interview, he says, 'Whether it be on the drive-by,' we're looking now at page thirty, 'Whether it be on the driveby or on the homicide, this is your time right now, bro, to tell me, to come clean, to say the truth. You reach into your heart and like you tell me that you fear for your life and your family's life and that's what's making you do this, bro. I'm not twisting your arm,' he said it to him, 'I'm not threatening you, I'm only telling you where I'm coming from. And if you ask around, bro, I'm very fair, and I'm sure you've heard my name out in the street with the guys. I don't mess with anybody, bro, unless they break the law and they need to go down. And that was bullshit, bro, and you know it.' Correct?"

"Yes."

"And then he says, 'Let me get a form,' and he asked him if he'd like a Coke or a Sprite, right? Right?"

"Yes."

"And then Mr. Nieto's statement was taken, wasn't it, sir?"

"Yes."

"Okay. And then they go down a little bit further and Mr. DeReyes says, 'Okay. Start like sometime in March, all right?' That's what he tells him along about page thirty-four, right? Doesn't he? You see that?"

"Yes."

"And he says, 'And then who came to your house and what they said and if you know that to mean something, because I know sometimes you guys talk in gang talk. Try to put it in English, bro, so everybody knows what you're talking about,' right?"

"Yes."

"So then he starts out, Mr. Nieto says, 'Shaun, how do you spell Shaun,' and he helps him spell it, right? And as you go down through there, he helps him out with the statement, right?"

"Yes."

"As we go on down in this discussion, as they're preparing this statement together, the question arises as to whether Mr. Nieto went up to the cabin, right, on down along about page thirty-nine? You see that? You see that area, sir, along about the bottom of page thirty-nine?"

"Talking about drive-by's on the bottom of page thirty-nine?"

"Yes, sir. When he begins to talk about Mr. Nieto as they're preparing this statement that he says, 'You like to party with the bros and you like to do rock or whatever, you like to party down, but you don't have the stomach for drive-by's and for beatings and for the f'ing beating they gave Popcorn and you don't have the stomach for that, bro?' And he goes, 'No, sir,' right?"

"Yes."

"And he says, 'I mean, you take a couple of shots if you have to just to be in it.' And he says, 'I didn't even beat up Popcorn that day,' right?"

"Yes."

"And he says, he basically establishes from Mr. Nieto a statement that Mr. Nieto doesn't get off on shooting people and things like that and then goes to, 'Shaun does, huh,' right?"

"Yes."

"'He gets off on it bad, no?' He says, 'Yes, sir.' And then Officer DeReyes says, 'I can tell that by looking into his eyes, and the fact is I want you to think very, very carefully because I don't want you to get fucked over by him, okay, bro?' Isn't that what he says?"

"That's what it says, yes, sir."

"And he says, 'I'm telling you we're going to bring him in here and we're going to sweat his ass. And you know him better than I do, probably. What I know of him, he's a fucking little weasel, right? You know when Shaun gets mad, when you confront Shaun, he's going to blow up and then he's going to sit there and he's going to listen for a minute. And when he finds out we've got him on this murder, he's going to tell everything he knows, right? He's the cut-the-losses kind of guy and move on, don't you think? He knows when he's been had. He fesses and he plays the system to get out or whatever, right?' That's what he says, right?"

"That's what it says."

"And then he says to Mr. Nieto, 'I'm telling you to think very, very carefully. Remember back, bro, and I'm not just saying the last month or the last couple of months. Maybe November, maybe December, ever since Ben started hanging out up there, because when was that, like November, October, something like that he started going up there,' correct?"

"Yes."

"That's what he asked? So then he focuses on Mr. Nieto and whether he's been up there, correct?"

"Yes."

"And do you see on down where Officer DeReyes says, 'You know, if we bring Wilkins in here, I'm concerned that he might say you were up there. You were never up there, were you?' And Mr. Nieto says he was never up there, correct, as we go on down, page forty-two and forty-three?"

"Yes."

"So then when they try to focus on this time period when all of these things that they're working on happened, they get down to a time, a month, correct, along about page forty-seven?"

"Yes, sir."

"And then he's asking him about the statement, and he says, 'Did you finish with all this Woodrow?' And he says, 'Yes, sir.' He said, 'Everything in here might, it might be to add something or you might have left something out. Sign this one, bro. This is the one on Buchner. Same place.' And he goes, 'Which number is he?' He says, 'He's number one. He said, 'Yeah, that's right. The one that dates the vampire,' right, that's what DeReyes says?"

"I think they're going through a photo array or something at that point."

"Were you there at that time?"

"Again, I was in and out. I don't recall."

"All right. And then the questioner says, 'And this all went down in March, huh, bro?' And Nieto says, 'Sometime in March that I know.' Correct?"

"Yes."

"And then he says, 'Do you think Deuce was killed in March or do you think he was killed before that and they just went up there and ripped him off some more or what? What do you think, bro?' Nieto says, 'To tell you the truth, I don't know,' didn't he?"

"Yes."

"And then DeReyes says, 'I know you don't know. You know, I'm not saying you know. I'm just saying what do you think. Woodrow, let's say that you're the cops and you have to investigate this. Okay? Now you know they did it. When did he do it, bro?' And Nieto says, 'I don't know when he did it, sir.' He said, 'Well, when do you think?' He says, 'Maybe before that, maybe. You know, I don't know.' So he says, 'Okay.' DeReyes says, 'Okay. I think we've clarified everything. There's a couple of things here, but I think we've got it clarified. Do you want me to get a little statement on that shooting? We'll just use the same form and I'll have him write that one out.' He says, 'You're doing the right thing, Woodrow, clearing your mind, boy, clearing your soul, especially for your homey. It's dangerous to be here, bro, because I know you guys from Eighteenth Street a long time, man. You guys do some stupid shit, but when you do it, you guys take the rap on it and do your time,' right? So that's what he's telling Nieto, isn't he?"

"Yes."

"Now, sir, later on in the discussion, he goes back to the specifics of the alleged homicide, right? And he brings up the subject like of the Trans Am, along about fifty-five, correct?"

"Yes, he brings up the Trans Am."

"Does he say, 'Who drives the black Trans Am, bro?' He says, 'A black Trans Am?' And then he's describing it and Mr. Nieto says, 'The Camaro?' He says, 'Well, it might be a Camaro or it might be—' and then he talks about who drives that. Correct?"

"Yes."

"He gives him a couple of ideas of who drives that, two or three different names?"

"He talked to him about a black Trans Am with rims."

"Sir, Mr. Bonet showed you an exhibit, the amended criminal information. Do you have that up there? Let me show you the State's exhibit that Mr. Bonet showed you and the defendant's exhibit I showed you. The State Exhibit is one hundred five and the Defendant's Exhibit is six W's. To clarify this, the criminal complaint is dated what?"

"The original criminal complaint?"

"Yes, sir, the file date on that?"

"Is dated June the sixth, nineteen ninety-seven."

"And that's the one charging Mr. Popeleski initially, correct?"

"Correct."

"And then the amended criminal information filed in District Court has a date of September on it of this year?"

"Thank you, sir. No further questions."

"Mr. Bonet, you may proceed."

Mr. Bonet: "Thank you, Your Honor. "Mr. Fenner, you might recall Mr. Twohig was questioning you on the May eleventh and May thirteenth and May fifteenth interviews that you had with Lawrence Woody Nieto?"

"Yes."

"Did Mr. Nieto advise you concerning his safety?"

"He was concerned for his safety and he mentioned several times the safety of his family."

"Okay. Now, counsel was going into inconsistencies, but there are some consistencies in Mr. Nieto's statements on May eleventh, May thirteenth and the May fifteenth video?"

"Yes, there are."

"Now, do you recall if Mr. Nieto also mentioned about Roy Buchner in the May eleventh interview?"

"Yes, he did."

"And do you remember what he mentioned about that?"

"I recall that he mentioned that Roy Buchner did go up there. I do recall him saying that they came by his house, they meaning Roy Buchner and Shaun Wilkins."

"Would looking at the transcript of that particular interview help you clarify?"

"Sure."

"Showing you on page five, is there a mention of Mr. Buchner in that document or concerning that interview of May eleventh?"

"Yes. The question is, 'Who else has gone up there to meet with Sager,' and he said, 'Roy that I know of that day.' And that was Roy Buchner?"

"Yes."

"The defendant in this case?"

"Yes."

"And does he mention Roy Buchner in the interview of May eleventh?"

"Yes."

"Was that name mentioned by Mr. Nieto?"

"Yes."

"Was there any mention of how Sager and Eazy, Shaun Wilkins and Roy Buchner, got to his house?"

"They came to his house in a—a stolen car."

"And Mr. Nieto mentioned that?"

"Yes."

"And that is in the May eleventh interview?"

"Yes."

"Did Mr. Nieto express in the May eleventh interview his concerns about Sager and/or whether or not Sager would be able to contact others to go after him?"

"Yes. He—he mentioned at one time, the question was if Sager was put away, who he would contact or contract on you, and he mentioned Eazy."

"And Eazy is known as Roy Buchner?"

"Yes."

"And counsel brought up to you—in fact, he read on the record this question here, 'Do you think that Eazy would be there, maybe not pull the trigger, but he'd be there,' you recall that in the interview?"

"Yes."

"And you recall Mr. Nieto answering, 'Yeah'?"

"Yes."

"And this is all in the May eleventh interview that took place May eleventh, nineteen ninety-six?"

"Yes."

"Did Mr. Nieto express to you that he didn't want to be killed?"

"Yes."

"And that's also on May eleventh?"

"Yes."

"Did Mr. Nieto express to you that Sager and Eazy had come down and said to him that they had done some, quote, shit at the cabin?"

"Yes."

"Okay. And this was also at the May eleventh interview?"

"Yes."

"Did he mention a time in the interview when he said that Mr. Wilkins and Mr. Buchner had said that they did some shit at the cabin, did he mention a month?"

"Yes. I believe he said it was March or—I believe it was March he said that."

"Now, when we look at the May thirteenth interview, which is the next interview that occurs between you and Mr. Nieto?"

"Yes."

"Does he also mention Mr. Buchner in that interview?"

"Yes, he does."

"And he also identifies him as Eazy?"

"Yes."

"And is it in that interview that he states that Eazy and Sager came and picked him up at his house in a stolen car?"

"Yes."

"And that it's then that they proceeded to the cabin?"

"Yes."

"Now, what else did he tell you about that incident on May thirteenth?"

"He said that at that time that they that the three of them had gone to the cabin to party."

"And is that the same thing that he had mentioned on the May fifteenth interview?"

"Yes, it is."

"Did he mention anything about whether or not he had to be talked into going into the cabin or whether he went voluntarily?"

"He mentioned that they kind of talked him into this at the house. He was—he was with his family, his mom, I believe, and the others and they talked him into it."

"And the others we're talking about is the defendant Roy Buchner and Mr. Wilkins?"

"Yes."

"Did he mention anything about a gun in the possession of Mr. Wilkins?"

"Yes, he did."

"And what did he mention then?"

"He mentioned that there was a small, and I don't recall if it was a .22, I believe it was a .22 caliber chrome pistol which Mr. Wilkins or Sager had said that he wanted to kill Popcorn with."

"Also, does he mention anything else concerning about gloves on the May thirteenth, nineteen ninety-six interview?"

"Yes, he does."

"Okay. And what did he mention about the gloves?"

"I believe he mentioned that they wore gloves when they went back up to the house."

"Did he mention anything about the destruction of those gloves? Would you need the document to refresh your memory?"

"If I could look at that because I may have confused that with another interview."

"The May thirteenth, nineteen ninety-six interview, did he mention anything at that time?"

"Okay. On May thirteenth, he mentioned that they did stop at a rest area on the way back and burned the gloves."

"Is that the same thing that he also said on May fifteenth?"

"Yes."

"Did he mention about whether or not the cabin door was closed when they left?"

"Yes, he did."

"And what did he mention about that?"

"He mentioned that Roy Buchner locked it."

"Locked the cabin door?"

"Yes."

"Is that the same thing that he also mentioned on the May fifteenth video?"

"Yes, it is."

"And that was—the May fifteenth was also an interview that you were present for?"

"Yes."

"Did he mention anything about Eighteenth Street wanting to blame Popcorn for the murders?"

"Yes. He was specifically asked why he thought Popcorn was being blamed on the street foror who he thought was blaming Popcorn on the street for it, and he mentioned that and he was asked again if it was Sager. He said, 'Probably, yes.'"

"Thank you, Mr. Fenner."

16

Was Abraham Lincoln Shot by a Gang Member?

DETECTIVE JUAN DEREYES WAS THE FIRST OF THE TRIO TO testify. Ray had already limited his testimony to keep out any hearsay or any of DeReyes' opinions. Although I thought the jury needed a good laugh and DeReyes would have provide one for them.

From watching the videos we knew Officer DeReyes loved to talk in what we called the bullshit method—just throw as much shit on the wall and see what sticks.

The night before Detective DeReyes took the stand we had a chance to voir dire the detective. The DA was trying to qualify DeReyes as an expert in "gang style executions."

Officer DeReyes took the stand. "Officer on what do you base your ability to testify as an expert in the field of 'Gang Style Executions'? asked Bonet.

"Based on my experience that I have, cases that I've investigated, along with the—assisting the APD, the homicide unit and their gang-related homicide unit, it is consistent. Most of the cases that have been investigated by the APD homicide unit over the past couple of years, I would say around thirty or so, through expertise, we were able to solve those homicides based on the identification of the gang members and also on what mode of, as you would call, mode of operation that the gang members use on their victims," DeReyes answered.

"What modus operandi that you speak of."

"Basic information that you obtain. It's common knowledge in the gang world, when you're going to perform a hit on somebody, you want to make it as quick as possible, hitting someone behind the ear is one of those indicators and it is the preferred method."

"What type of firearm has been consistent in the use of those executions?"

"Again common knowledge, if you're going to blast somebody you use a small caliber, a .25 or .22 caliber based on the fact that it is small and travels fast."

I kept thinking all bullets travel fast.

"So based on your experience into homicides you would argue that the single gunshot behind the back of the head by a .22 is consistent with gang-style execution that you had seen?"

I hated that word consistent. They must teach that in DA school. Just say the word "consistent" and it becomes the truth.

"Yes. It's quick, it's easy and it prevents the victim from doing any type of retaliation back."

I could see it coming—that look on Ray's face and the fact he didn't even have to take his notes to the podium. It was going to be fun.

"Detective which murders in Albuquerque occurred that manner and were gang related?"

"There were several that were highly publicized."

"Can you give us the names of any of the defendants or victims in those cases?"

"Not off hand. There was too many."

"Not even one?"

"No."

Ray was great at making a person say it twice for the judge.

"Not even a single one?"

"Like I said, there was over thirty homicides last year that were gang-related and that's the basic choice that these individual use. One thing is the Cubans, which is an ongoing investigation now, that's their preferred method."

"So, who have the Cubans killed in that fashion?"

"They've killed themselves, they killed other members for other groups. It's common knowledge, I mean it's nothing secret. I mean everybody knows. They watch TV, their ideas are passed down from gang members."

Officer DeReyes kept saying it's common knowledge and I mean over and over again.

"The Cuban gangs do it exactly the same way as the Hispanic gangs?"

"Oh yeah. They're mostly—the Cubans are paramilitary trained, so they train in those tactics. Most of the Cubans that we're dealing with now are all military trained. You can pick up books in the library on assassination. You can write to—I can even give you a specific company you can write to."

"So you have been told they shoot them behind the ear with a small caliber?"

"That's just one of the techniques. I mean, there's hundreds and hundreds of ways to kill a human being. But the preferred method is what's been exploited from television. It is going up behind the head and behind the ear and shooting them."

"Is it only gang members that do that?"

"Some of them. Some of them have used that method and they haven't been successful. Some of their victims have lived because the bullet exited and didn't go all the way through."

"Isn't it true that other people do that, even though they're not in gangs?"

"You don't have to be a gang member. It's common knowledge. I mean you pick up a magazine called *Soldier of Fortune* and they'll tell you. go to the library, look under assassins, they'll tell you. Abraham Lincoln, I mean that's a prime example."

I couldn't believe it, Ray was nicer than I am. I would have followed up with, "Abe was involved with gangs? Or Abe was a Eighteenth Streeter?"

"So it's not a gang signature, it's just the way people sometimes kill other people? But the gangs have taken that. It might not be their signature, as you call it, but they've taken that particular M.O. and used it because it's effective. No further questions."

Our judge was a civil attorney before he became a criminal judge and did not accept the DA or law enforcement answers as gold.

The judge asked, "Officer DeReyes, how many murders to your knowledge have been committed by Eighteenth Street gang members?"

"To my knowledge, judge, there's been several, not in the name of the gang, but this is probably the only one that has been directly related to the gang."

The judge looked at DeReyes over his reading glasses, "This is the only one?"

"Yes sir."

"So you can't say that this is the way Eighteenth gang executes people?"

"No. I would say this is the preferred method of the individual."

"Well, is it your opinion because of the method, the murder was done that it was done by the Eighteenth Street gang?"

"Well, allegedly, I don't know how I can go into that. During the course of this investigation, that's what appeared to us and it was a gang hit based on the information we got."

"On the fifteenth the bodies were found and they were autopsied. The cause of death was known at that time. The type of bullet was known. At that point, did you form an opinion this was gang killing based on the form of the killing?"

"Yes."

The judge took a surprised look on his face. "You did?"

"I felt strongly at that time it was."

"Despite the fact that you know of no other Eighteenth Street gang killings in which this form of execution was used?"

"Yes. I mean similar individuals that committed a homicide for whatever reason." *Officer DeReyes went on rambling.* "I mean, this is why it caught us by surprise that they would use this type of method. We thought at first it was professional hit by other subjects."

The judge was very familiar with all the facts. "How do you explain the killing of Cassandra Sedillo, which was not done in the method you say?"

DeReyes went back to his M.O. and recounted on and on about how Cassandra woke up and tried to get away. On how he read the OMI report, the path of the bullet.

The judge finally had to cut him off. "Tell me again your opinion that this is a gang-style killing and is based on what?"

DeReyes was now getting very nervous and he started looking at the DA for help but all he could see was the DA chewing on his pen.

"I would say based on the M.O. used. Like I said, it's common knowledge." Officer DeReyes continued talking hoping something would stick. "I think this whole thing was planned."

It was getting late and the judge was not happy. "When you form your opinion what do you base it on? You read a book, you have any textbooks any... I know you mention one magazine."

"I didn't want to get into that. I mean what I'm saying is based on what we investigated, the position of the body. I have read a lot of books on assassination techniques, other information I can't disclose because that's part of my military records. It's classified. But like I said you can go to the library or watch TV."

The DA tried to rehabilitate Officer DeReyes but he couldn't get past the fact there have been no other homicides this style. Even out of the thirty gang related cases there was none. DeReyes tried to back fill by saying, "They've been similar, but the victims were shot or stabbed, but it's consistent with the same type, execution style, I think."

After arguments Ray got up. "Your honor it is simply impossible to imagine how this could be possible helpful to the jury. It's too confusing. It's based on unnamed examples. And to tie it to Eighteenth Street gang requires some uniqueness. He says everybody does it that way, but he can't name even one except the person who killed Abraham Lincoln, and that's been a few years."

The DA was lost. "I don't know a witty comeback for that Abraham

Lincoln statement. I don't believe I do. But I would ask the court to allow the testimony that it is consistent."

"Consistent with what style?" The judge was not finding it humorous any longer.

"I think he mentioned a few others besides Abraham Lincoln, although he is the most famous, he just couldn't mention any other cases."

"I do not understand how this could be helpful to the trial of fact? How is it helpful in deciding who is guilty of murder?"

The DA got up and used the word "consistent" with gang style executions.

The judge was also getting tired of the word. "I don't think using the phrase 'consistent with' makes it relevant, I asked him this specifically, any basis for the opinion all he could say was 'It's common knowledge' and if it is common knowledge the jury already knows it, I am not going to permit this type of testimony."

So much for the rambler testifying as an expert in gang homicides. It was not going to happen.

17

The Darren White Letter

"STATE YOUR NAME PLEASE."

"Jose Beltran, B, as in boy, ELTRAN."

"What is your occupation, sir?"

"I am a latent fingerprint examiner for the New Mexico Department of Public Safety in Santa Fe."

"And how long have you been with them?"

"I've been with the department for a period of just over twenty-two and a half years, sir."

"And what are your duties with them?"

"My duties mainly consist of receiving items, items of possible evidence for the development of possible fingerprints on items and/or surfaces that one might come in contact with."

"Mr. Beltran, I'm showing you what's been marked as State's Exhibit One Hundred Two, please, sir. Could you identify that particular letter?"

"Yes, I can. It is a letter from the Department of Public Safety, Mr. Darren White, Public Safety Director."

"And would he be classified as your boss?"

"He would be classified as the head boss over the entire Department of Public Safety, yes, sir."

"Read that letter to the jury, please."

"Yes, sir. Dated May fifteenth of ninety-five. It says, 'To all law enforcement agencies,' it reads as follows: 'The crime laboratory bureau of the Department of Public Safety has been responding to calls for assistance in handling the processing of local crime scenes since 1972. Through the years, this effort has placed an everincreasing burden on our limited resources... In recent years, everincreasing requests for analysis of evidence combined with a continued response to process crime scenes have contributed significantly to the growing backlog of cases requiring laboratory analysis. Currently, we are faced with a backlog of between 750 to 1000 cases awaiting analysis in our northern laboratory and southern labs combined... In order to support your operations in the most responsible, efficient and timely manner, changes must be made in our operations. We believe we will best serve your needs by concentrating our limited resources on laboratory analysis of submitted evidence.

As a result, we are phasing out responding to crime scenes, and as of July 1, 1995, we will only provide technical support and guidance in this area... Crime scene processing will be the responsibility of the agency, agencies having jurisdiction over the resulting investigation. In anticipation of this decision, the Department of Public Safety Law Enforcement Academy Advanced Training Bureau has hired Robert Urista, crime scene expert, and recently trained 59 officers in crime scene processing with two additional classes scheduled after July 1 of 1995 Additional training courses of crime scene processing are also offered periodically by the FBI... If I can answer any questions or concerns regarding this or any other matter, please do not hesitate to call. Best regards, Darren White, Cabinet Secretary.'"

"So pursuant to your boss' letter to law enforcement agencies, you are not going out to crime scenes any more after July first, nineteen ninety-five? Were you going out to crime scenes after July first, nineteen ninety-five pursuant to that?"

"No, sir, we were not."

"Okay. So, the homicides occurred in December of ninety-five in Torreon. The bodies were discovered in April of nineteen ninety-six. Is it pursuant to that letter there and pursuant to your boss' instructions why it is you did not go out to the crime scene?"

"Yes, sir. We were not responding anymore."

"So that's why you didn't respond to the Torreon homicide case?"

"Yes."

"Why didn't you respond to the Torreon homicide case?"

"As of the—this letter, the directions from the Cabinet Secretary, which is the boss of the entire Department of Public Safety, we would no longer be processing crime scenes."

"Thank you very much."

18

Gummy Bears

WE WERE AT THE LAST TWO POSSIBLE WITNESSES, ROY AND ME. We had always agreed Roy would be the last one to testify. I was the second to last witness for the defense. After sitting at counsel table all this time, I was to take the stand that afternoon. Like the Shaun Wilkins trial, there was a fight over my testimony.

The DA in this case chose not to do a pre-trial interview of me thereby not allowing me to testify since the DA did not have my interview.

"Your honor, Mr. Moya had not made himself available to our office for his interview. Therefore we request Mr. Moya not be allowed to testify."

The judge would not hear it. "Mr. Moya has been on the witness list for over a year and he has been at counsel table for three weeks. I'm not going to hear it. You can have the lunch hour to interview Mr. Moya and then he may take the stand this afternoon. Court is adjourned until one-thirty."

Ray looked over at me, "Maurice I'm going to get some lunch across the street. Any questions before you go talk to the DA?" He had a grin on his face when he asked me.

"No, I'll be fine."

Ray had known me long enough that we knew how to play the game. He knew he could trust me in front of the DA to answer in three sentences or less. Sometimes it would be only one word.

I did my talking on the stand in three sentences and then paused and waited for Ray to say 'and then' and Ray knew what was going to come next. Ray was like my handball partner. We knew one another.

I went into the conference room and sat down. The DA looked over at me trying to stare me down. "Why do you hate Agent Jacoby so much?"

I couldn't believe it. This was an interview about my testimony not my feelings. "I don't hate him. I think he's a fine officer."

The DA opened up a bag of gummy worms and started munching them down. Not even offering me any. "So tell me about yourself Maurice."

After a three sentence response, he asked, "So what are you going to testify to?"

It was going to be a very long lunch hour. "I have no idea until Ray or you ask me questions."

"You ever testified as an expert before?"

"Yes, I have."

"In what areas?"

"Crime Scene reconstruction, Expert in Collection and Preservation of Evidence, Interview and Interrogation and in my early days Accident Reconstruction."

"Where at?"

"In District Courts in New Mexico and Federal Courts in New Mexico."

"By who? Who qualified you as an expert?"

"You mean the first thirty to forty times?"

"Yeah."

"Those would have been DAs."

"Did you prepare a report in this case?"

"You've seen my time line and the three by four exhibits we've had in the courtroom for the last three weeks."

Before I knew it the lunch hour was up and people were coming back into court. Ray came over and asked me, "Did you get lunch?" I told him no and he gave me one of his power bars from his bag.

"Did the DA eat lunch?"

"No, not really. All he had was gummy bears to eat."

The bailiff came back into the courtroom, "All rice." He had his own English term for 'rise.'

The judge looked at Ray, "You may call your next witness Mr. Twohig."

I started to get up moving my chair to the side. Ray looked over at me with a big grin knowing I was going to be all right. Ray was relaxed with his chair back and his usual grin on his face.

"I call Roy Buchner to the stand."

The DA was sitting back in his chair and almost jumped out of it. He was scrambling to find his legal pad. Roy's grin had quickly faded from his face and was in shock. We were going to go over his testimony tonight and he was supposed to be the last one to testify.

It felt like hours before the DA, Roy, and myself could believe what Ray just said, "I call Roy Buchner to the stand."

The DA was not ready for Roy and he had no script to follow. Roy had never testified before and the DA was not prepared. The DA was ready for me from my last testimony in Shaun Wilkens case.

Ray looked at me and said, "Maurice can you get me a cup of coffee from the judge's office. We're going to be a while."

Ray did not want Roy to be prepared for his testimony. Roy already knew the truth he wasn't at the cabin. After direct exam Ray the DA stood up lost for words. "Show us a gang sign."

Ray jumped up and started to object but the judge was already ahead of Ray. "Approach the bench." The judge was not going to have any of this.

It was one of the finest moments I had ever seen is a courtroom. After trial that day Ray and I laughed all through our supper and any time we need a laugh all we have to mention is 'gummy bears.' Ray told me later on that he thought the DA would be wound up on all that sugar and would have a terrible afternoon.

That evening in between laughter Ray and I got ready for my testimony.

During my testimony the DA would get up in front of the jury, "Your Honor. Mr. Moya is giving closing arguments."

The DA would interrupt other times my testimony. "Your Honor, this has gone too long. Why don't we put Frank Agent Jacoby up here and beat him with a stick. I mean that's, that's happening here. That's all that's continually been happening here. I mean, if he wants to speak of expertise, fine, but to say, this was done here and then to beat on him as why to do this, I've never had that happen."

Ray just looked at him and told the judge, "Your Honor I do my own closing."

The DA continued ranting to the judge about my testimony on the stand.

Ray just smiled and said, "Your Honor, I don't know if this is an objection or a speech."

In a loud whisper the DA said, "It's an objection, Counsel you can count on that."

"The witness will be allowed to comment."

Reluctantly the DA went back to his table but after three more questions the DA stood up again.

"Objection Your Honor. Can we approach? Your honor, Mr. Twohig is doing the same thing only asking a different question. What he is asking for is hearsay. All it's being done for is to bash the state. It's clearly all it's being done for. Mr. Moya was brought in as an expert on Investigative Techniques. He can say the investigative techniques he would have followed in such a case but that's not what he's doing now."

"The objection is overruled."

Again the DA would get up.

"Objection you Honor, may we approach. Your honor once again closing argument through Mr. Moya. He makes a statement, arson, which has not yet been established. He's making statements that the body has been moved. Once again he's arguing their case before the jury is through questioning. Now he's going into a third thing. He's arguing the case to the jury. I told the court that all the way through."

Ray argued to the judge, "Your honor, what Mr. Moya is doing is very simple and straight forward and this is what the court said he could do."

The judge agreed with Ray. But once again the DA was standing up.

"Objection your Honor may we approach? Your Honor, Mr. Moya was brought in as in an expert concerning investigations. It's now turned into the prosecution of Popeleski by Mr. Moya and Mr. Twohig in which they're offering things that are not in evidence. It's gone way too far. And again it's closing arguments."

"Mr. Twohig, you are going where?"

"It's exactly what I told the court and what the court said I could do in the sense that we're looking at the gathering of information. I am going to link up the investigative avenues and the linkup between the pager and the address book and the method of obtaining the book."

"I'll permit it."

After my direct exam was done with Ray, the DA was going to have their shot at me. I poured a full glass of water as I thought this was going to be long cross.

The DA asked me two questions. And ended his exam of me. I thought my direct exam had lasted over four hours and the DA only had two questions for me.

After my testimony the DA brought back Agent Jacoby for rebuttal. I felt sorry for Frank. Later on I told Ray, "It looks like Agent Jacoby was trying to throw himself onto a stake, but it was a square stake and he couldn't stab himself. He just kept bouncing off the stake. It was a slow death for him on the stand."

During the trial one of the jury members had a death in the family. It was the schoolteacher who was one of the jurists. He had to leave the court. Now we had the dispatcher from the sheriff's office moving up from alternate to jurist. We were getting concerned.

At approximately 9:15 am the court received a note from the jury. The note read as follows: "Your Honor, we, the jury members, are hopelessly deadlocked on all counts as charged against the Defendant Roy Buchner." Signed by the foreman.

Ray asked if they could go back and try some more. One more day passed. The jury returned, "Your honor we are dead locked."

Despite the all facts that had been presented to the jury. There were alibis for all three defendants who were not present at the cabin ever especially between December 10th to the 12th. The only possible suspect who was at the cabin was Popcorn, the difference in the false confession of Woody and the false statement of Popcorn.

The fact that there were only two sets of keys and Popcorn had them both. The fact the killer returned to the cabin twice after death. Despite the fact Ben Sr. had seen his son, Cassandra, and the kids alive on the 10th of December and Popcorn having the Jeep and breaking into Ben's Sr. house on the eleventh and leaving the keys in Mr. Anaya's jacket. Despite the fact the only one selling guns that week was Popcorn and never once told Porfie Sedillo or called 911 to tell them there was two small boys alive in the cabin.

The fact that Popcorn lied to the investigators telling them he had dropped Ben and Cassandra off at their homes. Never telling them about the Jeep and where it was. The fact Popcorn had escaped on the same day the Ms. Zenner heard noise coming from the cabin. The fact the fires were set after the death of the boys. Despite the fact that Roy Buchner was not identified in the first five statements of Popcorn. Roy was not mentioned until nine days before the preliminary hearing in Estancia. The jury was hung.

Not once during the entire direct, cross, and redirect did Agent Jacoby, Agent Fenner or Officer DeReyes ever testify that Woody was ever interviewed two to three times on May 15th. They had plenty of opportunity to place in their reports all of the interviews conducted they did not do so. ADA Malka who was present during the bulk of the interviews also had that knowledge.

The jury was dismissed. The vote was ten not guilty to two for guilty, a hung jury. The dispatcher had convinced an eighteen year old that Roy was guilty. They would not budge.

Roy was crushed as he did not want to go back to solitary confinement. "I can't go back to the yelling and screaming at me, no more showers, eating off the floor. It's not right I didn't do anything."

Ray felt the Judge knew the facts and asked the judge to release Roy to my custody. This had never been done before in the state's history to allow a person who is facing the death penalty to be released to a third party.

The judge knew the facts like the back of hand and agreed. The DA and the media went crazy. I called home and told my wife, "Guess who's coming home for dinner?"

Roy would stay at my house during the week and then could go to his parents or grandparents on the weekend. We had to retry the case all over again.

I could not believe the verdict. Roy, Shaun, and Woody were not present during the time Ben and Cassandra were murdered and the boys were locked in the cabin. We showed that to the jury.

19

The Golden Nugget

THE BATTLE IN COURT CONTINUED AND I KEPT PUSHING RAY that they were still hiding tapes and Ray kept bringing it up. We had our usual pre trial hearing in Socorro. I asked Ray to bring it up that they were hiding tapes.

Ray who was getting tired of me asking said, "This is the last time Maurice I am going to ask the judge as he is getting tired of me asking."

Ray got up and asked again about the discovery of tapes. The DA knew it was I pushing Ray.

"Your honor if Mr. Moya thinks we're hiding evidence we have an open file policy at our office. He can come and look at our discover any time he wants." Ray looked at me as they were calling our bluff.

Five months went past and I was in Socorro, the city of "help," on another murder case. I had finished up by mid-morning and saw the DA's office and thought I'll take up the DA's offer and go look at their boxes.

I walked in and was easily recognized, "What can we do for you Maurice?"

"I came to look at the discovery."

"Who told you, you could look at it?"

"Ron, the District Attorney, told the Judge in open court any time I wanted to look at the evidence he had an open file policy at his office and here I am."

"Just a minute. Ron's not here, let me call him." She got on the phone with Ron and then looked back up at me.

"Okay, Maurice, you can see the discovery but there is no one here to show it to you."

"I'll wait."

After staring down the secretary for over an hour, one of the DA's investigators came in and she was not happy to see me.

"You've seen all the discovery, we gave you all the discovery, what more do you want?

"I want to see your discovery."

"Fine."

We walked into the library and for the first time I saw their discovery in order. I was interested in the video and audiotapes more than the paper documents. I knew the tapes by heart.

Then I saw two tapes on the 13th of May. Woody's interview, but the times were different. One was marked 1239 the other 1242 pm. "Why the two different tapes with two different times?" I asked. I knew we had the 1242 tape but not the 1239.

"They are the same tapes. Someone just put down different times but they are the same tapes. We have given you all the tapes."

I could see we were going to bump heads and I was not going to lose and I was not going to argue. "I want copies of both tapes with the same markings."

"I told you we gave them to you."

It was getting heated and I was not going to back down.

"I want copies of both tapes."

"We don't have any blanks."

"I'll go buy some."

I walked out walked over to the drug store thinking, what are you doing wasting your day at the DA's office. It's going to take some time to copy them.

I took the blanks back, "I want the same marking on those two tapes onto my tapes."

All she could do was glare at me. "It's going to take some time. You can come back or I will call you when they're ready."

"No, I'll wait."

After a couple of hours the tapes were done and I headed home. I put the tapes away and went on with my other cases.

A month had passed after returning from Socorro. Ray had called me, "We have a pre trial coming up on Roy's case Maurice. You have anything new?"

I remember the tapes, "I don't know. I got more copies of the May thirteenth interview, the one we call the slump block video. Let me look at them."

I put the video into the VCR then the other one. I had seen them so many times. I was sick of Officer DeReyes and Agent Fenner's voice. They looked the same but something was different and they kept showing up in a different office.

Then I remember Agent Jacoby had said in the tape, "We've been talking for about an hour and a half now and were in a different office."

I put the first tape back in and it was the first interview of Woody on the 13th of May. They were hammering Woody giving him the facts that would be in the second interview.

I rushed over to Ray's. I felt like I was having a heart attack.

"You're not going to believe this." We put the tape in and watched the hammering being done to Woody.

"We need to get it transcribed and copies made for the judge." One of the missing tapes was now in our possession. We could prove Woody was coerced during his interview and they kept it from us.

We gave copies to the judge along with the transcribing of the tape before the hearing. The DA (Ron Lopez) did not want to argue this against Ray. He again sent another DA to argue at the hearing. Ms. Romo from the DA's office had not bothered to view the tape or the transcript we had done.

The judge entered with a red face. "Has the DA reviewed this tape?"

"We have Your Honor and we have brought State police officer Eric Lucero in to testify."

"I asked if you have reviewed the tape?"

"We have Your Honor and it is the same tape. They are both identical."

"You are not familiar with this tape. I am."

The judge ruled that coercion had been used in the confession of Woody Nieto and dismissed Roy's case. I didn't find all the missing tapes of Popcorn and Woody, but this tape turned out to be our golden nugget.

Two months later Shaun's case would be dismissed. Seven years later the tape would resurface and Woody's sentence was reduced from 440 years to 17 years. Woody was to be released, as of 2012, but the legal system changed Woody's time.

On June the 6th, 1997, Popcorn was charged with Count 1 would be an open count of murder on Cassandra Sedillo with a firearm enhancement. Count 2 would be an open count of murder Ben Anaya Jr. with a firearm enhancement. Count 3, open count of murder Johnny Ray Garcia. Count 4, open count of murder Matthew Garcia. Count 5 would be aggravated burglary with a firearm enhancement. Count 6, armed robbery with a firearm enhancement. Count 7, tampering with evidence. Count 8, tampering with evidence. Count 9, tampering with evidence. Count 10, unlawful taking of a motor vehicle. Count 11 would be conspiracy.

Popcorn was convicted of two counts of child abuse resulting in death and was sentenced to 18 years on both. The judge ran the sentences together and Popcorn got 18 years. Under the old rule Popcorn had to serve only half of the 18. He got what was called Day for Day and was out in nine years.

He moved out of state and was soon arrested in Las Vegas, Nevada for attempted murder. He is still in custody awaiting trial, as of 2012.

Mady left the DA's office due to some mistakes with the courts. As of 2012, she is teaching at a law enforcement academy.

She returned for the civil rights trial of Roy and Shaun. Mady testified it was she and the DA's office that had the tape. DAs are given immunity for their actions.

The jury found in favor of the officers and ruled against Shaun and Roy on their civil rights case.

Agent Jacoby never got a chance to put up another sign in his office and the sign stayed stuck, "One down Two to go."

I ran into Frank Jacoby in Federal Court during our civil rights trial. We were both talking the same elevator down. Frank looked at me and said, "Take another elevator."

I walked into the elevator and Frank walked out. Roy Buchner and Shaun Wilkins never got any mental health for what they went through. Roy became isolated, never coming out of his apartment, wanting to stay out of the limelight.

The one time Roy did go out the bartender charged him for three drinks instead of one. When Roy refused, the police were called and several officers came to arrest Roy. When he was taken into the jail the arresting officers announced, "Make way for the baby killer."

Shaun turned to drugs to self medicate himself. Got into domestic violence with a gun, got arrested and plead to the charges. Shaun has never injured anyone. Shaun is still a very close friend of mine, but his new nickname is "Tommy Boy."

It is difficult for the boys to start a life with Google. When they meet people their names are "Googled" and they show up as the killers in the Torreon Cabin Murders.

Ray and I are still working together. And we're still dealing with false confessions and false statements. Regina is still our wonderful secretary.

We continue to work cases where false confessions and false statements are made, and false prosecutions continue. Real killers go free, cases go unsolved and families have to live with the unknown.

BIBLIOGRAPHY

Doyle, Sir Arthur Conan. *A Study in Scarlet*. Philadelphia: J.B. Lippincott &
    Co., 1890.
Doyle, Sir Arthur Conan. *The Sign of Four*. London: Hurst & Blackett, 1890.
The King James Study Bible. Nashville: Thomas Nelson Publishers, 1988.

APPENDIX

Text of
AFFIDAVIT OF LAWRENCE NIETO
April 26, 2004

I, LAWRENCE NIETO, under penalty of perjury state that the following statements are the truth:

1. I was the Defendant in a criminal case in Torrance County, New Mexico in which I was convicted of four counts of Murder, conspiracy to commit murder, tampering with evidence and armed robbery. The conviction was upheld on appeal by the New Mexico Supreme Court, reported at 2000 NMSC 31, 129 NM 688, 12P.3d 442. I presently have a state habeas corpus petition pending challenging my conviction.

2. I have reviewed the two videotapes of my statements to police on May 13, 1996 as well as the transcript of the testimony I gave in the trial of Roy Buchner, and the transcript of the testimony I gave in my own trial.

3. I am executing this affidavit at the request of Ray Twohig, the attorney for Shaun Wilkins and Roy Buchner. I am doing so of my own free will.

4. I went to school until 9th grade. I was in Special Education classes. I was diagnosed with ADD. I was in YDC and the New Mexico Boy's School at Springer on and off from age 14 through 18. I have had a hard time learning things in school. I haven't done very well with reading and understanding what I read.

5. I was questioned by police in April, and then again on May 11. Both times, I denied knowledge of the killings of Ben Anaya, his girlfriend and her two children. I was being truthful in denying my participation and my presence at the time Ben Anaya and his girlfriend were killed at the cabin where their bodies were later found.

6. On May 13, 1996, I was in police custody, and was interrogated for many hours. I had been picked up early that morning after being out partying all night. I was very tired, and was yawning and distressed during the interviews. That is obvious on the first videotape of May 13.

7. Some of my interrogation was videotaped. Once I reviewed the two May 13 videotapes, which were provided by the State to Mr. Twohig, it was obvious to me that a lot more interrogation took, place outside of that which was videotaped.

8. Detective DeReyes pushed very hard for me to claim Shaun Wilkins was involved. He said that my brother and my family would be in danger. He said Wilkins "is an animal." And said Wilkins would kill me. They also said that if I didn't tell them what they wanted, I would be in the same cell or next cell with Wilkins, and he would kill me.

9. DeReyes said Wilkins had done a drive by shooting on his (DeReyes') house, and that it was personal and his family was threatened by that and had to move.

10. He also said he knew what had happened at the cabin, and then he and Agent Fenner told me a story which they claimed that Mr. Popeleski had told them. He showed me a report, which he said had a story, which he and the other officer said Popeleski had told them. I read and heard that story and I saw that Popeleski had claimed that I was at the cabin and that Wilkins and Buchner were involved in the murders.

11. I was told by DeReyes and the State Police officer that the word would be let out that my brother was a snitch, and that he and my family would be killed if I did not go along with this story. I was also told that the police would talk to the DA about helping me.

12. DeReyes and Fenner did most of the questioning and most of the threatening. They made me afraid for the safety of my family. I believed their threats that they would make it look like my brother was a snitch in another case so that gang members would come after my family. I didn't think I had any choice except to go along with the story they said they knew and said Popeleski had told. They went over it in detail, then talked to me on the videotape, then went over it again, then talked to me again on the videotape. They put words in my mouth. They supplied the details of the story, then when I told them something, they pressured me to change it.

13. After the first May 13-videotaped part, I was taken to another room. At their request, I drew them a diagram in which I showed where the bodies were. But, I was just guessing. I later learned that the bodies were in the bedroom and I had drawn them near the door. The diagram has apparently disappeared.

14. I had already asked for a lawyer, and they told me that I didn't need one, so I was sure I had no way to get any help at all.

15. I could see that it was obvious that DeReyes and Fenner were forcing me to make the same statement Popcorn had made if I wanted my family to stay alive. I also got assurances that if I did so, nothing would happen to my family or to me. They talked about moving us away to protect us, and even mentioned helping us to go to live in Taos.

16. As I started to do what they wanted and tell them details that I made up from the ones they gave me, they corrected me on the details and got me to change them. The second May 13 videotape shows me telling a story about how the murders took place, which didn't have Popeleski being present. I described stopping at a rest stop to burn things. I didn't know if there was a rest stop or not. I later learned that there is no rest stop on the highway. I described Ben Anaya as being fully dressed when he was shot, and seeing him on the floor in the bedroom. I later learned he was found in bed, obviously being shot in his sleep. I said this because I was trying to make up things which would keep them from putting out the word that my brother was a snitch.

17. My brother was going the right way, has never been to prison, but was suspected of being involved in a gang related murder in Westgate. He was not charged with it. Another person was charged with it, and police were threatening to make it look like my brother had informed on him. This would definitely have put my brother in a very dangerous position.

19. It was not the story they wanted. They then came up with a different story of Popeleski's saying he was there and that I held him at gunpoint. On May 15, before State Police Detective Eric Lucero videotaped me for that statement, DeReyes and the other officers, including Jacoby, had come to the jail and gotten me, and took me to the State Police office in Santa Fe. They then coached me to change the story by showing me a report showing what they said Popeleski told them. I went along with that because they pressured me to do so. They went over the story many times with me so it was the way that they wanted it. A lot of it changed from the second May 13 interview to the videotaped May 15 interview.

19. I was not at or near the cabin when Ben Anaya was killed. I did not ride to the cabin with Wilkins and Buchner. I did not see either of them with guns. I was not held at gunpoint and did not hold Popeleski at gunpoint while Wilkins and Buchner went into the cabin. I did not see Wilkins and Buchner go into

the cabin. At the time the police claim that these murders took place, I was in Juarez with friends or on the way back from Juarez, possibly in Ruidoso.. I did not make up this story myself. It was given to me because it was what Popeleski said. I was forced to tell this story to save the lives of my family, especially my brother.

20. Because I was threatened the way I was, I could see that I had no choice other than to go along with the story which DeReyes and the State Police gave me. And I changed it like they wanted it for the same reason. If they had not threatened and coerced me, I would not have said that I was at the cabin, or that Buchner and Wilkins were there, or that I knew anything about the killings.

Further affiant sayeth not.

CPSIA information can be obtained at www.ICGtesting.com
Printed in the USA
LVOW11s0501220914

405041LV00005B/5/P